THE GARDEN PLANNER

Editor
Piers Dudgeon

Assistant Editor
Tim Shackleton
Editorial assistance
Victoria Huxley

Consultant in charge of
nomenclature
Robert Legge

Plant index
Dorothy Frame

Production Consultant
D. Cheyne

Designer
Mike Ricketts

Design Assistant
Safu-Maria Gilbert

Illustrators
Rob Shone
Vana Haggerty
Harry Titcombe

Photographer
Neil Holmes

First published by Fontana Paperbacks, 1981

Conceived and produced by Pilot Productions Ltd, London

Copyright © Pilot Productions Ltd, 1981

This edition published 1981 by
William Collins Sons & Co Ltd
London · Glasgow · Sydney · Auckland ·
Johannesburg

Production by B P S Ltd, London

Typesetting by V & M Graphics Ltd, Aylesbury

Origination by NG Graphics Ltd, London

Made and printed by Henri Proost et Cie, Turnhout, Belgium

ISBN: 0 00 411662 3

THE GARDEN PLANNER

Consultant Editor

Ashley Stephenson
The Gardener Royal

Collins

Contents

PART IV   PLANT PLANNING

PART V   PUTTING THE GARDEN TO USE

Contributors

Robert Adams qualified as a horticulturist at Reading University and later as a landscape artist in London. He is an associate of the Landscape Institute. He has specialized in Mediterranean and Middle East landscape projects, having worked abroad for a number of years. In England he is a consultant to the Department of the Environment and various local authorities, and also works in the private sector. He has written articles and reviews on landscape architecture and dry land horticultural technology and is co-author of *Dry Lands: Man and Plants*.

Alan Bloom set up his nurseries at Bressingham, near Diss in Norfolk, in 1931. His retail and wholesale business, specializing in hardy perennials, alpines, ferns, bamboos, dwarf shrubs, conifers and heathers, is combined with gardens, which are on show to the public, and the popular Bressingham Steam Museum. Since 1944 he has published eighteen books on a variety of topics, as well as writing in the gardening press and making television and radio appearances. A comprehensive catalogue is available from Bressingham Gardens, Diss, Norfolk.

Beth Chatto has combined her childhood enthusiasm for plants with her husband's life-long study of the ecology of garden plants to produce her celebrated four-acre garden near Colchester in Essex. Divided into three sections – dry, shade and bog gardens – it is the home of over a thousand different kinds of plant. She made good use of her experience here in writing the very well received *The Dry Garden* and then turned her attention to *The Damp Garden*. Beth Chatto has won five gold medals – four of them at the Royal Horticultural Society's Chelsea Show – and since 1967 has run a highly successful nursery for unusual plants (White Barn House, Elmstead Market, Colchester). She writes for *The Garden*, *Popular Gardening* and *Green Fingers* and is a frequent broadcaster and lecturer.

William Davidson has spent over thirty years at the famous houseplant nurseries of Thomas Rochford and Sons at Broxbourne, Hertfordshire. He writes a weekly column for *Garden News*, is a regular on radio phone-ins and is the author of seven gardening books, principally on indoor plants.

Leslie Godfrey regards himself as essentially an amateur gardener who has, since his retirement, applied the problem - solving methods of the industrial and business world to the production of fruit and vegetables in the domestic garden. He outlines his practical methodical approach in *The Planned Vegetable Garden*.

Richard Gorer, a Fellow of the Royal Horticultural Society, is a journalist and author. He has written over a dozen gardening books on such topics as trees, shrubs and propagation.

Jack Harkness, rose breeder and author, is a director of R. Harkness and Co. (Hitchin, Herts, SG4 0JT), the Hertfordshire nursery whose roses have won nearly two hundred awards. He himself has been awarded the gold medal of the Rose Nord (Denmark) and the Royal National Rose Society's Dean Hole Medal. He is Vice-President of the latter society and Secretary of the British Association of Rose Breeders, as well as being the author of four books on roses and how to grow them.

Roy Hay is the son of the famous gardener, Thomas Hay, CVO, VMH, who was superintendent of the Central Royal Parks in London. In 1937, after spending ten years with a large wholesale seed firm, Roy joined the staff of *Gardener's Chronicle*, becoming editor in 1955. In 1939 he became associate editor of the Royal Horticultural Society's journal *The Garden* and the Society's other publications, and during the war was closely involved with the Ministry of Agriculture's food production schemes. For many years he conducted a radio gardening programme for the BBC and has made many television appearances in Britain and France. A prolific author, he is now the gardening correspondent of *The Times* and contributes regular articles to the *News of the World* and *L'Ami des Jardins*. Roy Hay is a Member of the Order of the British Empire, Officer de l'Ordre du Merite Agricole of France and Belgium, and holds the Victoria Medal of the Royal Horticultural Society. He has made a special study of labour-saving techniques and the needs of handicapped and elderly people in the garden.

Frank Hope has worked in the Parks Departments at Heywood and Eccles in Lancashire and studied at the Royal Horticultural Society garden at Wisley. After four years as a lecturer at the Cheshire College of Agriculture he moved to become general manager of E. W. Hurn and Sons of Thorney, near Cambridge, where 430 acres of commercial crops are grown. He is the author of *Turfculture*, a complete manual for the groundsman, and *Recognition of Pests and Diseases of Farm Crops*.

Anthony Huxley spent many years on the staff of *Amateur Gardening*, finally as editor. In 1971 he relinquished his position to devote more time to writing: he contibutes to *Country Life* and *The Garden* and to date has written or edited some twenty-nine books. He is a member of the Council of the Royal Horticultural Society and has been awarded their Veitch Memorial Medal and Victoria Medal of Honour. Chairman of the International Dendrology Society and President of both the Horticultural Club and the Saintpaulia and Houseplant Society, he has a special interest in wild flowers and has travelled extensively to find and photograph them, often escorting botanical tours and treks.

W. E. Th. Ingwersen is a life-long collector and grower of alpine plants, and as a plant hunter he has travelled widely in mountainous regions of the world. The results of his interest can be found in his nursery and in a number of books on alpines. President of the Alpine Garden Society, a vice-president of the Royal Horticultural Society and a past president of the Horticultural Trades Association, he regularly contributes to gardening magazines and lectures in Britain and the USA. He holds the Victoria Medal of Honour from the Royal Horticultural Society. Birch Farm Nursery is at Gravetye, East Grinstead, W. Sussex.

Roy Lancaster began compiling information on local fauna as a Lancashire schoolboy. This interest led to him joining his local Parks Department, where he first gained a love for foreign plants. Serving with the army in Malaya, he collected over a thousand specimens for various international institutions. Since then his horizons have expanded ever wider, and he has visited Spain, Turkey, Greece, Nepal, Kashmir, Iran, China and Russia in search of plants. After studying at the University of Cambridge Botanic Garden he joined the Hillier Nurseries as a horticultural botanist. Many years work culminated in the publication of the now-famous *Hillier's Manual of Trees and Shrubs*. In 1970 he became the first curator of the Hillier Arboretum – one of the largest collections of hardy woody plants in Europe – a position which he relinquished after ten years to concentrate on writing, lecturing and, of course, plant hunting. The author of a number of books and many more articles in horticultural journals, Roy Lancaster is a Committee Member of the RHS (becoming the youngest person to win the Veitch Memorial Medal) and a Fellow of the Linnean Society. The Hilliers catalogue is available from Hilliers Nurseries, Ampfield, Romsey.

Sheila Macqueen is a familiar name to flower arrangers throughout the world. She is a constant traveller, lecturing and demonstrating in Britain and Europe, and regularly makes lecture tours of the United States, as well as Australia, Canada and South Africa. She is the author of three books on flower arranging, writes regularly in *Amateur Gardening* and *Flora*, and appears on the BBC's *Gardener's World*. She holds the Katharine Thomas Carey Medal of the Garden Club of America – the first person outside the United States to receive this honour – and the Royal Horticultural Society's Victoria Medal of Honour.

Frederick McGourty, who edited this book for American readers, is a graduate of Pennsylvania and New York Universities. He joined the staff of the Brooklyn Botanic Garden in 1966 as Associate Taxonomist, and since 1969 has been editor of *Plants and Gardens*, the BBG handbook series to which he himself has made many contributions. He has also written for the *New York Times* and the Royal Horticultural Society's journal *The Garden*. President of the New York Hortus Club, he was awarded the Gunlogson Medal by the American Horticultural Society in 1978.

Alan Mitchell is probably the world's leading expert on trees. In his position as Dendrologist with the Forestry Commission ('the only one they have ever had, or will, I suspect, ever have') he is responsible for the National Tree Register, a compendium of data which he has amassed on some 68,000 trees of 1350 species throughout the British Isles. He is the author of, among other books, the comprehensive *Field Guide to the Trees of Britain and Northern Europe* which has appeared in no less than six languages, and is now working on a similarly definitive study of trees in North America. He is a holder of the Royal Horticultural Society's Veitch Memorial Medal and Victoria Medal of Honour and the Gold Medal of the Royal Forestry Society.

Allen Paterson has been Curator of the Chelsea Physic Garden in London since 1973. He trained in horticulture at the Botanic Garden of Cambridge University and the Royal Botanic Garden at Kew and then, having qualified as a teacher, taught rural and environmental studies for some fourteen years. A Fellow of the Linnean Society and Chairman of the Garden Historical Society, he lectures widely at home and abroad, leads botanical tours and writes for *The Garden, Country Life*, and *Amateur Gardening*. He is the author of eight gardening books, three of which have been for younger readers.

Frances Perry was trained in horticulture at Swanley Horticultural College and started her

professional life at one of Britain's best known nurseries, Perry's Hardy Plant Farm at Enfield in Middlesex. Later she became horticultural adviser and in due course senior administrator for Middlesex County Council, finally becoming Principal of Norwood Hall College of Horticultural and Agricultural Education. A prolific writer and regular broadcaster, she is gardening editor of the *Observer* and the author of some fifteen books including *Water Gardens*, the standard work on the subject. She has lectured in Britain, Australia, New Zealand, the United States, Canada and South America. The first woman elected to the Council of the Royal Horticultural Society, she has lately become its first and only lady Vice-President and holds the Society's Victoria Medal of Honour. She has also been awarded the Veitch Memorial Medal and the Sarah Francis Chapman Medal and is a Member of the Order of the British Empire. She is married to Roy Hay.

Takashi Sawano is one of a new class of university trained landscape gardeners and designers to emerge from Japan. He was awarded a B.A. degree in Ornamental Horticulture at the University of Minamikyushu and holds a Master's degree in Japanese Flower arranging from the Sogetsu School of Ikebana. Seven years ago he travelled to England and more recently instigated The Ikebana Centre (24 Holborn Viaduct, London, EC1), whose purpose is to develop interest in and explain the oriental arts as they relate to horticulture and flower arrangement. Mr Sawano has designed and made many Japanese gardens in the United Kingdom and is the author of *Ikebana*, published in 1981 by Ward Lock Ltd, London.

Alan Toogood is editor of *Greenhouse* magazine and a specialist in plant propagation and greenhouse plants. A qualified teacher, he holds a Diploma in Horticulture from the RHS's garden at Wisley in Surrey and lectured for some years at the Merrist Wood Agricultural College at Worplesdon. He is the author of seven books on gardening topics.

Ashley Stephenson pictured with Queen Elizabeth, The Queen Mother, at the opening of the new rose garden in St. James's Park, London.

Ashley Stephenson is Bailiff of the Royal Parks – a job which puts him in overall charge of the running of some 7,000 acres which includes Buckingham Palace Gardens, Hyde Park, Kensington Gardens, St James's Park, Green Park, Lancaster House, Clarence House, St James's Palace, Downing Street, the Houses of Parliament, the Tate Gallery, the National Gallery, Ham House, Osterley Park, Richmond Park, Regent's Park, Primrose Hill, Greenwich Park, Hampton Court, Bushey Park, and Osborne on the Isle of Wight. The son of a colliery pay clerk, his interest in gardening began in the family allotment at Heddon-on-the-Wall in Northumberland. His uncle, who was Parks Superintendent at Whitley Bay, found him a job in the Newcastle-on-Tyne Parks Department, from which he went to private work at Lower Gosforth House in Newcastle. For two years he immersed himself in learning how to grow plants for show and then moved to work for a commercial landscape gardener and nurseryman. His horizons were further extended by a diploma course at the Royal Horticultural Society's Garden at Wisley, following which, in 1954, he became Gardener Grade 1 in the central nursery of the Royal Parks. His particular speciality has always been trees and shrubs, but he also has a wide knowledge of plants used for bedding and other decorative purposes. This vast experience of all aspects of horticulture is now combined with the planning and administration of all matters which concern the Royal Parks. In the 1979 Birthday Honours list Ashley Stephenson was made a Member of the Royal Victorian Order, an award for services to the sovereign which comes from Buckingham Palace rather than from the Prime Minister's office.

Introduction by Ashley Stephenson, M.V.O.

There are very few people completely unskilled in gardening technique. Many garden owners may not use gardening tools regularly, but most have some experience and there is certainly no shortage of books which cover the technical aspects of gardening for the complete newcomer.

A book of ideas

The Garden Planner is a book of ideas about making the most of any garden – ideas which have been suggested by some of today's most experienced and inspired horticulturalists and gardeners to satisfy a wide range of needs and tastes – and we encourage you, the reader, to formulate your own. It does not set out to teach the basic skills of gardening.

Preparation
These ideas have been deliberately arranged in a sequence that recognizes one of the two most important principles of garden planning: **timing**; there is an optimum order in which planning ideas should be put into practice. A high percentage of failures is due to the absence or poor quality of preparation. Local environment should be taken into account; have a good look round the neighbourhood and see what does well. Then observe how features in your garden (including boundaries, 'interior' structures, trees and large shrubs) affect planting limits apparently imposed by local, climatic conditions. See also how such features contribute to or detract from the garden's appearance (for example, by making it seem larger or smaller, narrower or wider, darker or lighter, or by masking or effectively incorporating buildings or landscape features outside the garden).

Designing a layout
Once you have made sense of the *status quo*, you will be ready to design a basic layout. It is very helpful, and quite easy, to put your layout ideas on paper. Then, it becomes a question of clothing this skeleton with plants in a way which suits individual taste.

Plant planning
Clothing a garden involves more personal decisions than does its layout. For although garden structures and 'backbone' plantings of trees and large shrubs will to some extent reflect your own needs (e.g. you have little gardening time, so you choose hard surfaces rather than a lawn), such decisions are more usually the result of environmental *data* and climate, and have a practical purpose. Of course environment is also a factor when choosing plants – soil, in particular, though this need not be a limiting factor – but many plants are adaptable and when planning a decorative garden, the second of the two most important principles comes to the fore: there are no hard and fast rules; gardening is something to try and, being personal to you, it should reflect *your* taste.

Choosing plants for your garden
To the beginner there will appear to be an inordinate number of plants with unpronounceable and instantly forgettable names. This, I am sure, has a frightening effect upon many new gardeners. Unfortunately, there is no way round the name game; it is only by knowing the correct name that one can be sure of identifying a particular plant. Common names are of limited value as not all plants have them, and some have more than one.

But lack of botanical knowledge should not deter you (it will come with experience and be useful later on). What we have tried to do is to point out how plant characteristics can be used to fulfil different purposes and create pleasing associations and groupings. When giving examples of plants we describe their vital characteristics and suggest attractive combinations, or tell you why they are well suited to the type of garden under discussion.

The point is to think of plants in terms of their shape, form, height, growth rate, colour, texture and scent as well as their preferred growing conditions. Paint the picture of your desired garden in your mind's eye (even on paper) and look for plants which display appropriate qualities when visiting other gardens, nurseries and garden centres, or when reading a catalogue. The strategy is to decide what plant characteristics will achieve your purpose, observe which plants display them, and use plant names as they were meant to be used – to facilitate reference.

Garden planning is something which can be done by anyone so long as he or she understands the principles discussed here. There are no secrets known only to the professional gardener. Provided you avoid taking short cuts and follow these common sense guidelines, the results will, I promise you, be very gratifying. The book fills a gap between the many purely practical books about gardening and the more sophisticated books on landscape design. It is the work of professionals but aimed directly at the amateur who has decided to put his dreams into practice.

Recognition and preparation

I

In this section, we look at your garden mainly from the plants' point of view. Whether you have firm ideas or few preconceptions about what to do with your garden, the first step must be to analyze the environment. This applies equally to a new uncultivated plot and a garden which expresses a previous owner's ideas or yours which you have decided to change. When and for how long it gets the sun, its location in town or country, the character of the soil, regional climate and how it is distorted by garden or neighbourhood structures, trees and vigorous shrubs – all these must be considered because they will determine how best to proceed.

Using a simple soil testing kit is about as technical as you will need to be. *Observation* is the keynote. One of the main aims of the contributors is to open our eyes and make practical sense of what we see.

In order to survive, a plant requires light, goodness from the sun, water, air and food. But plant needs vary quantitatively; a plant's diet is decided by its genetic make-up which has evolved over many years in its natural habitat. It is, therefore, frequently useful to know where a plant comes from, though many plants are marvellously adaptable. (Such plants as the hybrid tea rose, the azalea, the chrysanthemum, the primula and many more have been successfully introduced from foreign climates by adventurous plant hunters, and this process continues today.) Every garden provides at least a measure of what all plants need. Here, besides showing you how to analyze garden environment, we look at ways to improve conditions and alter some of them entirely to suit apparently difficult specimens. We also display many attractive plants which actually prefer what at first appear to be restrictive conditions.

Garden environment

By observing plants already growing in a garden, the experienced plantsman can acquire a number of useful clues about garden environment. The presence of rhododendrons and azaleas will tell him that the soil is acidic. A delicately blooming garden of alpine plants suggests a light, airy soil which enjoys a good deal of sun. Primulas and trilliums indicate that there is fairly constant moisture in the garden. And so on.

Although it is rare for a gardener to take over an area of land that is as nature intended, if he did the wild plants or weeds would also tell him a great deal. Kidney vetch is known to grow naturally in lime soil a little on the sandy side. Sea holly (*Eryngium spp*) enjoys a sandy soil too, and as its name suggests it succeeds where other plants fail when exposed to a salty breeze. *Drosera rotundifolia*, the sundew, grows in a wet, peaty bed. The maiden pink, *Dianthus deltoides*, prefers a dry, alkaline position and, given the chance, parsley piert (*Aphanes arvensis*) will take over bare dry ground.

But whatever you manage to deduce from wild or cultivated plants in the neighbourhood, there is no substitute for analyzing the particular environmental conditions that exist in your garden – not least because they can vary considerably from plot to plot. Having done so, you are in a position to consider improving or modifying that environment to suit the plants *you* want to grow.

What plants need to survive
All plants need water and sunlight in order to manufacture food.

How plants feed
Photosynthesis is a food-making process peculiar to plants. They absorb light through the green pigment of their leaves, stems and flowers. This pigment is known as chlorophyll. Plants also need air, and during the daylight hours when photosynthesis takes places, they breathe in oxygen and carbon dioxide through tiny leaf pores called stomata.

Through photosynthesis, carbon dioxide and water (which is drawn up through the plant roots) combine in the presence of sunlight to produce sugars, starches and fats. The process produces 95% of the food plants use for growth.

The rest of their food is absorbed in solution from the soil or from fertilizers. This travels through the root hairs towards the inside of the root by osmosis and suffuses the plant by a process of rapid evaporation at the leaf surface called transpiration.

Observe prevailing conditions and which plants tolerate them.

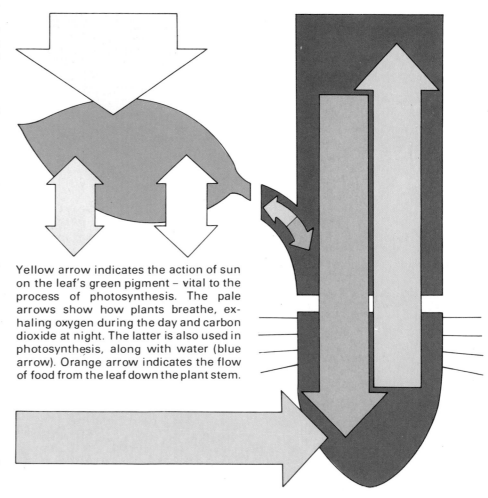

Yellow arrow indicates the action of sun on the leaf's green pigment – vital to the process of photosynthesis. The pale arrows show how plants breathe, exhaling oxygen during the day and carbon dioxide at night. The latter is also used in photosynthesis, along with water (blue arrow). Orange arrow indicates the flow of food from the leaf down the plant stem.

There is, therefore, an upwards and downwards motion of food-carrying sap. The products of photosynthesis move down the stem; dissolved mineral salts, which supplement the plant's diet, move up the stem from the earth via the roots.

How much sun does your garden get?
Notice where the sun travels across the garden, the types of obstruction to it, and at what times of day the sun's rays are masked or filtered.

Note the seasonal shift of the sun's arc

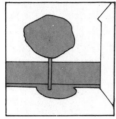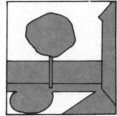

Aspect and other localized conditions
In the northern hemisphere, gardens open to the south and west are warmer and can be planted earlier than those facing north and east. The reverse is true in the southern hemisphere. If a

Topography, another factor to consider when observing how much sun the garden gets. Slopes can intensify positive and destructive effects of the sun.

northern hemisphere garden slopes towards the south, it is of particular value since a greater surface area of soil receives direct sunlight. By and large, south or west facing gardens are those with the greatest potential in the northern hemisphere.

There is of course a great deal of difference between shade cast by trees or loosely growing climbers on a trellis and that cast by a building. Plants often merely filter the light, and during their dormant months deciduous trees and shrubs allow a great deal of sun to reach subjects planted beneath them. An area in permanent shade from a wall will support only the likes of ferns, ivies, etc. See also **Planning ideas for shade.**

The part of the day when an area is shaded from the sun will vary from season to season. It is worth being aware of those areas, if any, which catch the early morning sun. In times of frost, early morning sun can scorch plants. Similarly, note those areas which bear the brunt of the high-in-the-sky, middle-of-the-day summer sun.

How wet or dry is your garden?
Rainfall cannot usefully be calculated in isolation from the effects of sun, wind and soil, though it can be measured, daily, with a simple water gauge. Annual rainfall and the height of the water table can be checked at a meteorological office. The former can often be found in a local paper.

Evaporation by sun and wind
Water loss caused by evaporation from the leaves of plants varies from day to day and depends upon the amount of sunshine in your garden and the degree of exposure to a drying wind. So, while rainfall is a significant factor it cannot, alone, answer the question of how much water your plants can actually call upon in the process of growth.

How soil deals with moisture
How the soil in your garden copes with rainfall is another major consideration. There are loose, free-draining soils through which water drains past plant roots as if through a colander. At the other end of the scale there are heavy soils composed of tiny particles of earth, each encircled by an absorbant material known as a colloid, which literally soaks up water like a sponge, swelling as it does so. These clay soils retain vast quantities of water in which some plants will drown.

You can roughly establish the character of your soil by picking up a handful when it is fairly wet. Squeeze it; if it coagulates and forms a sticky, firm ball then you have a heavy, water-retentive clay. If it refuses to coalesce, then you have a light, sandy soil. These are extremes in a wide range of soil textures. Recognizing soil types is dealt with in detail on pages 16 to 17.

Even if you have a light, airy soil it may not be free-draining. If the ground has been consistently cultivated to a single spade's depth or by a mechanical cultivator over a long period, a hard 'pan' or consolidated layer of subsoil can form below the cultivated depth. This will trap water so that, eventually, it builds up in the top spit of soil.

Sometimes, particularly in a new garden after excavation works, the soil surface may become compacted. Heavy snow and even heavy rain can cause this, but more usually it is due to the constant tramping of feet. Then, rain is not given the opportunity to find its way into the soil to plant roots, and a characteristically water-retentive soil will remain dry.

Another effective method of establishing how your ground copes with moisture is to dig a hole, say 76 cm (2½ ft) deep, and fill it with water. If the ground is free-draining, the water will disappear within twenty-four hours. If you dig the hole deeper, to about 1.2 m (4 ft), and water seeps in from the sides, you can be sure that the water table is fairly high in your neighbourhood.

Distribution of rain around the garden
Rain rarely falls vertically; it is diverted by wind. On the leeward side of a wall, the soil will receive far less rain than in an exposed area.

Thirsty, full-leaved trees extract enormous amounts of moisture from the ground and create *dry shade*, a most serious planting problem. Areas generously planted with evergreen shrubs will diminish the amount of moisture in the soil and limit the growth of plants nearby, sometimes quite severely.

Check the height of the water table

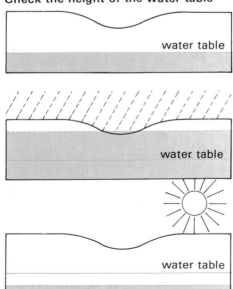

There is underground water everywhere, even in deserts. The level at which soil and rocks are fully saturated is known as the water table and its height varies from area to area. Even a free-draining, sandy soil will not remain dry if the water table is high and the rainfall is especially heavy in the area.

Garden environment

Is your garden exposed to wind and frost?

Except in the early stages of life, most plants will tolerate some wind. More delicate specimens will need some form of protection (see pages 40 to 45). The important point is to look at your garden's boundaries and notice how solid they are. The most effective barriers allow some wind through; very solid ones cause turbulence over, under, or around them.

Most people think about wind in terms of the direct damage it can cause – flattening plants or snapping branches. But it has other, more subtle effects.

A prevailing wind can dehydrate buds on the windward side of trees and tall shrubs so that they refuse to develop. Lopsided growth is as much a tell-tale sign of a strong prevailing wind as plants bent in its path.

But wind has positive roles too. It stirs up the garden environment, encouraging pollination in one season, preventing frost from settling in frozen blankets of water vapour in another. In sloping gardens, the wind will ease frost downhill to drain away through a suitably placed gap in a boundary structure at the bottom of the garden. Although pests and diseases are also carried by the wind, poor air circulation will actually encourage them to become established more virulently.

Town or country garden?

They may be a matter of a few miles apart, yet a town garden and one in the country can provide completely different environments for plant growth.

There is pollution, of course. Air pollutants, soot, lead poisoning and the like will asphyxiate much plant life. As for most other environments, however, here in the harsh environment of the city there are plants which have successfully adapted themselves. The plane tree is possibly the best example, being tolerant of pollution to a high degree. The common holly is also a good survivor. The periwinkle (*Vinca spp*) withstands soot polluted air and the *Fatsia japonica* has foliage which accepts being covered with soot for most of the year.

But pollution is not the only difference between town and country. Actual climatic changes occur. An area such as New York, with its huge expanse of paving stones and other light-reflecting materials, will be much warmer than a country area further south. Nowadays modern buildings have more glass. They tend to be straight-sided, too, and made from materials of a reflective nature. All these factors conspire to

Pollution tests the adaptability of most plants, but built-up areas tend to be warmer than nearby country districts.

make surrounding areas much warmer – as any city worker will acknowledge during periods of hot weather. Furthermore, buildings are heated and, no matter what the fuel, have to have flues to release unwanted gases. Where there are gases there is heat which raises the temperature. And the more heat there is being released into the air, the

less likely it is for the temperature to react suddenly to climatic changes.

In the country, the situation is obviously different. Air movement is different too. Air travelling across exposed areas is more likely to pick up cold and bring the temperature down. Town gardens tend to be more frost-free and their soils will warm up quickly in spring. They will thus react more favourably to early planting than will their country neighbours.

How topography alters climate

Geographical position (how far north or south you live) can give a misleading impression of garden potential. On the same latitude, warm, wet air coming in off the

sea cools and forms rain clouds when reaching a hilly region. On the lee-side, it will have a quite different effect. Climate might be distorted by garden barriers and screens.

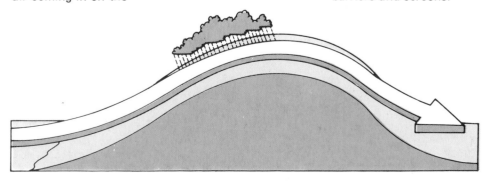

The mini-climate of a private garden
Recognizing and understanding the implications of garden environment is the first step in garden planning. It may differ from that of a neighbour's garden in significant ways.

Densely planted shrubs and trees make poor windbreaks. The wind is directed over and around them to cause turbulence that will damage plants. Wind also has positive roles. It can keep frost on the move, ushering it through a strategically placed boundary gap, encourage pollination and help prevent pests and diseases settling.

How much sun and when it reaches parts of the garden will affect your positioning of plants.

Before establishing a plan, note both the high summer and low winter arcs of the sun's path.

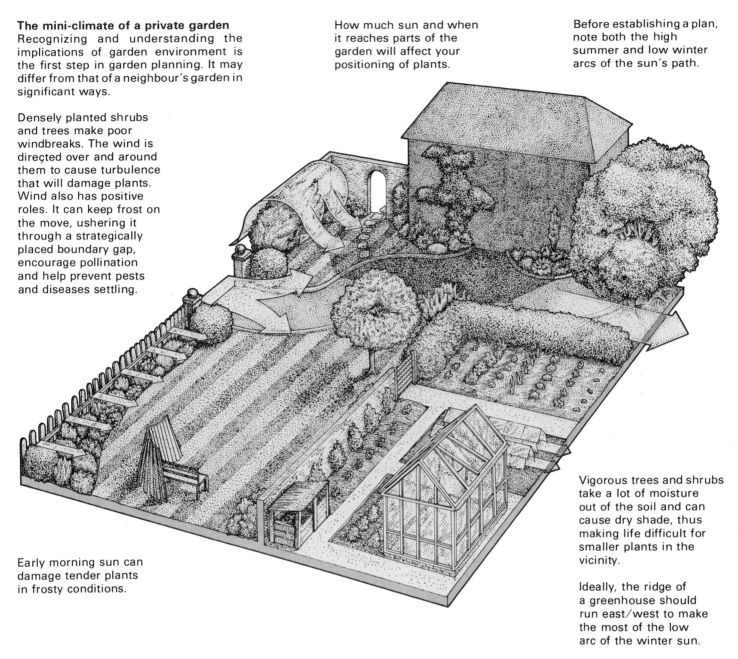

Early morning sun can damage tender plants in frosty conditions.

Vigorous trees and shrubs take a lot of moisture out of the soil and can cause dry shade, thus making life difficult for smaller plants in the vicinity.

Ideally, the ridge of a greenhouse should run east/west to make the most of the low arc of the winter sun.

Local climate
By now it should be clear that while regional climate shouldn't be ignored (climatic zones offer a broad idea of the types of plants which can be grown), the environment of your particular garden is what really matters.

A sheltered garden with a sunny aspect in the north of England can actually produce a wider range of plants than many in the south.

On a global scale, of course, natural quirks can similarly create climatic conditions at odds with what might be expected from geographical position alone. For example, many countries on the same latitude as Britain are far less mild, due to the Gulf Stream which has its source in the warm waters of the Gulf of Mexico and sweeps across the Atlantic towards the coast of Europe, acting as a natural water heating system. Large bodies of water frequently have this effect. In America land to the east of the Great Lakes is milder than that to the west because the prevailing wind is from the west.

So it is not surprising that geographical position can give a misleading notion of a garden's potential, too. How much use you make of the fact that it is a contrived and artificially demarcated section of the landscape, is up to you.

It is a small step from recognizing how soil, land form, structural and plant boundaries, etc. materially affect what you can plant to considering ways in which you can actually manipulate these factors to create a new environment sympathetic to a quite idiosyncratic choice of plants. Some methods are obvious – irrigation for a dry area, drainage for boggy ground.

Creative planning
However, while every committed gardener wants to make the most of his garden environment, it is not necessarily a good idea to jump in and alter conditions which appear to limit plant choice. Suppose drought is a regional problem. Shade from the sun, shelter from the wind, improved soil texture, an irrigation system – all these can widen your choice of plants. But before you decide to alter garden environment, be aware of the many plants, and some outstanding specimens, which do grow in so-called difficult conditions.

You may well find that the choice is wider than you thought; that by attempting to create ideal growing conditions for the widest possible range of plants, you have forsaken the chance to produce a fine garden that is in tune with its original environment.

Soil analysis

Recognizing soil types

Soil is the most significant factor in determining the success of your garden plan. It can of course be changed completely. Alternatively, pockets or raised beds of different soils can be introduced; the composition of existing soil may be altered to suit special requirements; or, if the soil is poor nutritionally, it can be improved. But whatever you plan to do with it, the essential first step is to recognize what type of soil you have.

Terminology

There are a few terms which should be explained at an early stage. They are frequently used, less frequently understood:

Topsoil

This is the layer of fertile, living soil which contains nearly all of the humus present in the soil and is, generally, darker in colour than the subsoil. As its name suggests it is normally to be found at the top of the soil, and may be as shallow as 50 mm (2 in) or as deep as several feet in well-worked gardens. Make sure there is a topsoil if you have moved to a newly built house. It fetches a good market price, and it is not unknown for it to be removed or, where there has been a good deal of digging during building works, for it to have been buried beneath the subsoil. To examine the profile of your soil, either dig a ditch or use a soil auger, which acts like a hollow corkscrew as it retrieves a soil profile.

At all costs avoid mixing this active layer with the subsoil. When excavating, stack topsoil on one side, keep it covered and don't make the piles so deep that they destroy the small crumbs of soil particles that form the essential structure of good topsoil.

Subsoil

In normal circumstances lying beneath the topsoil, the subsoil is in a transition stage between the bedrock from whence it came and the living, active topsoil. Generally useless for growth, subsoil is often lighter in colour and may contain hard subsurface layers (pans) which should, at cultivation time, be broken up to allow the soil to breathe and any excess moisture to drain away.

Humus

Humus is the jelly-like substance which coats minute particles of soil and turns them into loam. It has a miraculous effect. It helps the soil hold a larger amount of nutrients; it encourages a good 'crumb structure' which will retain moisture yet aid the drainage of excess water; it encourages root growth to produce better plants; it helps make a good seed bed; and it darkens light soils to aid heat retention. In short, humus is the wonder substance in the soil which makes the difference between a good crumbly loam and particles of finely ground infertile particles of rock. You cannot add humus as such to the soil, but you can add well-rotted organic matter – compost or manure which nature then turns into humus. This process is called humification.

pH of soil

This is the measure of alkalinity or acidity in soil. Chalk and lime make a soil alkaline, while the constant addition of manure, compost or peat tends to make it more acid. It is, however, more difficult to make chalky soils more acid, than acid soils more alkaline.

Literally, the term pH means 'the negative decimal logarithm of hydrogen ion concentration expressed as moles per litre'! You could be forgiven for ignoring that definition. Regard the pH scale as an expression of how acid or alkaline the soil is, and plant or treat the soil accordingly. See page 28.

Throughout the book, where pertinent, attention is drawn as to when you should be aware of your soil's pH.

Most large garden suppliers provide testing kits, which, provided their instructions are followed, are simple to use. Readings less than pH7 indicate an increasing presence of acid in the soil, while readings higher than pH7 indicate the measure of alkalinity.

There is no ideal pH level for all plants, but most will accept a reading of 6 or 6.5 – just on the acid side of the neutral pH reading 7. So, unless you have good reason to suspect that you are dealing with extreme conditions, or want to grow plants which will be seen to demand a particular pH balance, a kit is probably unnecessary.

Soil types

Soils do not come neatly parcelled into the following groups; they come in mixes. But once you know the basic types, it is a relatively simple matter to ascertain the advantages and disadvantages of your soil, and make use of the information on pages 28 to 39 about making the most of or changing what you have.

Sandy soils

As their name indicates, these soils are made up of more sand than anything else. All but the finest sand particles have relatively large air spaces between them, and are loose to the touch. This does make them one of the easiest soils to work. Being so loose

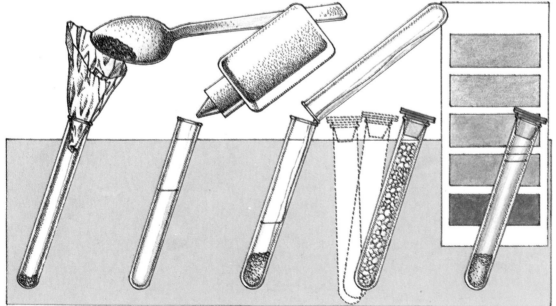

1. Spoon a soil sample into the test tube using a paper funnel.
2. Measure the correct amount of soil solution.
3. Add the solution to the soil sample.
4. Cork the tube and shake vigorously. Allow 5 to 10 minutes.
5. Read off the colour of the solution against the test card.

Difficult soils
Of the two possible ways to garden on 'difficult' soils, choosing plants to suit the soil is, generally, more satisfactory than modifying the soil to suit particular plants (but see page 28). Nor is it an impossible task to select decorative plants for extreme pH levels (pages 18 to 21). In Roy Lancaster's chalk garden, this approach was preferred to that of making an alkaline soil more acid. The photographs were taken just two years apart.

they have a poor water holding capacity but warm up quickly in springtime.

Being 'early' soils, they are suitable for crops such as soft fruits and those crops which need to work themselves into the soil, such as carrots, which may become distorted in stony soils.

However, because they find it difficult to hold moisture, they need frequent watering in summer, and nutrients vital to the growth of plants are too readily washed out (or leached) from them. They are, therefore, hungry soils and require liberal doses of humus-making material and fertilizers.

Silty soils
Silts are very similar to sands, but have smaller pore spaces and so retain larger quantities of water.

Clay soils
These are characterized by having very tiny air spaces between the particles. Retaining a high proportion of water, they swell and become compact and sticky to the touch, rather than loose, gritty and rough. When wet, they may even stain the hand.

Clay soils are, therefore, more difficult to work, indeed unworkable in periods of heavy rainfall, tending to stick to spade or boots. It is a good idea to dig them thoroughly in the autumn to give the elements a chance to break them down. Very probably, a drainage system will also be necessary. See page 34. During prolonged dry spells, they will dry out and may crack.

Their advantage is that they are usually rich in plant nutrients, and although they do not warm up quickly in the spring, a wide range of crops is possible. It really is a question of improving their texture to get the best out of them.

Stony soils
These may be sandy or clay, but are, typically, rich to work. Don't go to a lot of trouble removing all the stones as they assist in keeping the soil open. The odd larger stone can of course be removed without detrimental effect.

Alkaline (chalky) soils
These contain large quantities of calcium, have a naturally high pH level, low nutrient holding capacity, and a tendency to become sticky when wet (though they are not as difficult to

work as clay soils – indeed, when dry, they are far easier).

The problem with chalky soils is that they rarely have much depth to them, and being free-draining as well, plants can be starved into suffering from what is known as lime-induced chlorosis. This stunts growth and turns leaves yellow, but can be treated. Replenish the soil with large doses of well-rotted compost and add a compound such as Sequestrene.

Peaty soils
Peaty soils look dark and rich in nutrients, which indeed they are. They are generally easy to work and prepare for a wide range of plants provided the pH level is not too far below 7. Some such soils will need to be drained; he governed by actual conditions. See page 13.

Loam
Used regularly, there is no wholly satisfactory definition of the term, although it generally describes normal good soils which favour growing most plants. It is the ultimate fertile mix of sand, silt and clay, with a percentage of humus.

17

The acid soil garden

Plant planning in an acid garden

The success or failure of your plant planning will depend in the first instance on recognizing the pH level of your garden soil.

If tests show an extreme pH reading – either very alkaline or very acid – do not be put off. It may even be that your soil varies in respect of pH in different parts of the garden. Whatever the tests show, rest assured that there is a fine range of plants to suit both sides of the neutral reading, pH7.

So attractive are the many lime-hating plants (which prosper below pH7) that suitable conditions are now commonly created to support their growth in otherwise alien situations. Raised bed features isolated from the rest of the garden soil are filled with peat or a mixture of soil and peat. Peat blocks are increasingly (though less usually in America) utilized as 'bricks' in low retaining walls which make terraces of gently sloping ground. These blocks are ideal for interplanting lime-hating plants and their structural purpose (see illustration) are an additional boon.

There are provisos, however. It is unlikely that lime-hating plants will be supported for long in alkaline gardens that have merely been interspersed with plant pockets filled with acid peat. Peat blocks themselves contract when dry and unless kept moist will deteriorate both as structural and life-support features for lime haters. It is of course important to irrigate peat blocks with lime free water if the constructions are to remain fruitful.

Creating a peat garden

Starting at the lower end of the pH scale the most important genus is the rhododendron. It prefers a pH of 5.5 or below, although the hardy hybrids which tolerate a higher level make this a plant which could be included in all but chalky soils.

Rhododendrons are shallow rooted by nature, though good soil cultivation will encourage them to send out fairly deep roots. In general, therefore, avoid placing them near especially hungry plants that will deprive the upper reaches of soil of nutrients and moisture vital to their survival. Also because of this growing habit, they respond very favourably to mulching (see page 32).

Some of the rhododendrons are almost tree-size whilst others are quite small and fit very nicely into a tiny niche on a rock garden. *Rhododendron fictolacteum* can reach 9 m (30 ft plus) and it has large leaves with pale pink

or white spotted flowers. It will grow in almost any slightly sheltered site. *R. calophytum* is also a big plant but the foliage is not as attractive. However, it does flower profusely with large trusses of pale pink blooms. Still on the large side is *R. macabeanum*. This has large trusses of creamy flowers but it is its large leathery leaves which make it so distinctive.

In the medium-size range, there is a wider selection. *R. augustinii* has almost blue flowers and when in flower the bush is a mass of leaves a lot smaller than those on the plants

Peat blocks used as retaining walls in a terraced acid soil bed. They can also be useful to contain an imported bed of acid soil in an otherwise alkaline garden.

mentioned above. *R. campylocarpum* introduces a yellow flower into the range and makes a nicely shaped bush with quite attractive leaves. *R. griersonianum* also has much to commend it; its scarlet flowers are very bright, and as the trusses are quite big it stands out well provided the sun is not too strong in that part of the garden. *R. wardii* has more rounded leaves than others so far mentioned; its flowers are a strong yellow.

For smaller gardens the many small and dwarf rhododendrons are ideal. *R. yakusimanum* is thoroughly recommended. It is dwarf and dense and becomes dome shaped with age. (It is sometimes regarded as a hybrid because seedlings do not come true to form.) Flowers are in compact trusses which are pink in the bud, but as the flower opens it becomes much paler; its leaves are long and narrow in relation to the bush's overall size. *R. pemakoense* is smaller still, reaching no more than 30 cm (12 in) high. When in good heart, the bush is covered with

lavender flowers. *R. mucronulatum* is a deciduous plant but as it flowers early in the year (as soon as the weather allows) it is well worth consideration. Its rosy lilac flowers make a bright splash when there is little other colour in the garden.

There are many hundreds of varieties of hardy hybrids. Look particularly at 'Cynthia', rosy carmine; 'Doncaster', scarlet; 'Gomer Waterer', pale pink; 'Pink Pearl', fleshy pink; 'Purple Splendour', purple; 'Faetuosum Flore Pleno', mauve; and 'Sappho', white. These, as has been said, will accept a higher pH level than the species. If your garden approaches pH7 try the common wild *R. ponticum*, a big plant certainly but much more at home than any other on nearly neutral soils.

Planning the rhododendron bed

Colour and height are clearly important considerations. And because of the wealth of colour tones available – crimsons, scarlets, claret reds, true pinks, salmon pinks, white, cool clear purples, blue (to name some) – it might be an idea to select one or two areas of the colour spectrum. Which areas will of course depend on which colours you like (and quite possibly which are most freely available). Having selected say a colour range of crimson to true pink, it is a question of arranging for the most attractive tonal development of colour within the range.

While the bushes are still young and relatively small, you might consider filling some of the spaces between them with hardy heaths which are certainly compatible. There are other alternatives perhaps more suitable when one remembers that the rhododendron clumps will soon look tightly packed. *Cistus laurifolius* is one. It grows a good deal faster than the rhododendron and is relatively short-lived. By the time it has exhausted its life-span, the rhododendrons will be ready to fill the space. Part of the rock rose family, *C. laurifolius* is a white flowering evergreen shrub often neglected precisely for its short life and vulnerability to frost. *Lilium auratum* is another imaginative choice, for not only does this so-called Queen of the Lilies enjoy acid soil conditions but it flowers through late summer and autumn as the rhododendrons complete their flowering time.

Brilliant colour in the peat garden

Azaleas are more reliant upon an acidic soil than many of the rhododendrons, but have the advantage that they are generally more brightly coloured. Moreover the deciduous varieties exhibit particularly brilliant colouring before their leaves fall. All the flower colours of azaleas harmonize well, though you may prefer to group them so that the lighter colours – white, pale yellow and pinks – lead up to the stronger orange, copper and scarlet-crimson varieties. It might seem odd that although azalea and rhododendron are botanically related, in form and colour of flower many are not obviously compatible. In a limited space you may find it is worth choosing one or the other.

Heaths and heathers

Another large family which prefers an acid soil is the *Erica* or heath genus. Some forms will tolerate a measure of lime, but the majority do best in soil that is very much on the acid side. The callunas (heathers) insist upon lime-free soil and are sometimes known as Scottish heather or Ling. *Calluna vulgaris* is a synonym for *Erica vulgaris* and is the name for heathers commonly seen growing on the English moorlands.

E.v. 'Beoley Gold' has golden foliage and white flowers, the foliage colour remaining long after the flowers have gone. *E.v.* 'County Wicklow' has shell-pink double flowers. *E.v.* 'Gold Haze' has golden foliage which persists all the year round; its white flowers are perhaps not so eye-catching. *E.v.* 'H.E. Beale' has been with us a long time and is still one of the best; it has long arching sprays of double pink flowers throughout the summer and autumn. This is one of the varieties which can be cut for indoor decoration. Said by some to be an improved 'H.E. Beale' is 'Peter Sparkes' which has deeper pink flowers. *E.v.* 'Robert Chapman' has foliage colour that blends well with its soft purple flowers; it begins as gold in the spring and changes to orangy red as the season progresses.

If space allows, consider planting a heather garden that makes use of colour contrasts, perhaps even contriving colour patterns from monochromatic groups of plants. This approach can be especially effective upon a rolling bank which might otherwise pose a grass maintenance problem.

Beauty of leaf and flower

Camellias used to be regarded as luxury plants but they are well capable of holding their own in both semi-shade and full sun. An evergreen shrub or small tree, the camellia flowers from late winter to mid-spring, so avoid spring frosts by protecting them from cold winds. It is attractive even without its blooms, for it carries glossy deep green leaves which rarely suffer from disorders that can affect other species.

A variety called 'Donation' has large semi-double deep pink flowers which can sometimes look like waterlilies. 'Inspiration' is similar to 'Donation', but the flowers are a deeper pink. 'J.C. Williams' has single flowers but is floriferous and one of its distinctive features is the mass of stamens which effectively offset its blush pink bloom. 'Adolph Audusson' is a vigorous plant which carries masses of deep blood-red flowers. 'Grand Slam' has scarlet flowers but is not as good as 'Adolph Audusson'. Its habit is more open and although it also produces semi-double flowers the effect is less dramatic. If white is required try 'Mathotiana Alba' the flowers of which are fully double and extremely attractive. It is not a compact grower but still makes an excellent bush for a sheltered position. (The whites are more easily hit by frost than the other colours.)

A plant known as the calico bush (*Kalmia latifolia*) is another evergreen to use. It has rosy pink flowers grouped in large terminal clusters, and thick, leathery, shiny green leaves. Although similar in outline to the rhododendron, there the similarity ends. They are only happy in soils which are definitely acidic.

Winter colour in a peaty soil

Hamamelis spp, the witch hazel, is very much at home. *H. mollis* has sweetly scented yellow strap-shaped flowers with a scent that is readily perceptible from many yards away. *H.m.* 'Pallida' is a lovely plant with sulphur yellow flowers, and leaves which unlike the species have a shiny upper surface. *H.m.* 'Jelena' has flowers with an orangy hue formed by the florets being bi-coloured. Really, all this family can be recommended for colour in the dullest months.

Recommended for milder areas

Where more than a little protection can be given, it is well worth trying

Both heathers and azaleas enjoy an acid soil, the latter being among the brightest of all flowering shrubs.

Embothrium coccineum var *lanceolatum* 'Norquinco'. A most conspicuous evergreen shrub which in late spring becomes a mass of orangy scarlet flowers. If the climate is not right, you could try confining it to a warm wall and hope that a cold wet winter will not make it suffer too much. But really it does best in an open situation in a mild climate where it has a deep, moist acid soil bed. Its long curling tubular flowers surround the ends of branches and resemble a honeysuckle's.

Eucryphias require some protection too, if gardening in a cold area, but their white flowers, many stamens and shiny foliage are very eye-catching. *E.* x *nymansensis* will accept a soil close to a neutral pH, but the hardier *E. glutinosa* likes a somewhat lower pH.

Lime-hating lilies in all their glory

Lilium auratum is not alone among lilies in its tolerance of acid soil. *L. canadense* is one of the most beautiful summer flowering lime-hating lilies, with its candelabra type yellow flower and deep maroon spots towards its centre. Then there is *L. japonicum*, the bamboo lily, with its pink trumpet-shaped flowers. This should be positioned in a sheltered position. Again successful in warm areas (and notably western North America, Australia and New Zealand) is *L.* x *parkmanii* with its white flowers spotted with yellow or crimson and carried on stems sometimes as tall as 2 m (7 ft). *L. rubellum* is somewhat smaller and unsuitable for hot dry situations, but produces beautiful trumpet-shaped deep pink flowers. *L.* x *parkmanii* has been crossed with *L. japonicum* to produce the highly recommended 'Pink Glory' strain with delicate deep pink flowers spotted and dashed with pale crimson. There are also very fine forms of *L. speciosum*, generally white or pink with thick petals and small papillae.

19

The alkaline soil garden

Plant planning in an alkaline garden

Alkaline soils have sufficient lime in their make-up to produce a pH reading above 7. In general they are easier to plant than acid soils, but it cannot be over-stated that soils close to a neutral reading (whether slightly alkaline or slightly acidic) will support a wide range of plant life. In alkaline gardens, planting difficulties only really begin when the pH rises above 8, for most plants accept a low lime content quite happily. In fact even lime-haters need some lime, though these plants are usually adapted to take what small quantities they need from soil which has very little.

Improving an alkaline soil

Where the soil depth is adequate, limy soils can be very good because they are characteristically free-draining. However, they are often short of humus and a priority when gardening upon limy soils (particularly when the soil is shallow) is to enrich them with the very best humus-makers. Organic matter actually breaks down fast in these soils, so use heavy doses either as a mulch or, better still, at the time of cultivating dig it into the soil itself.

Take great care when gardening upon a limestone base with a shallow topsoil. Break up the base before proceeding with planting and never mix good topsoil and poor subsoil together. This is standard practice with nearly all planting but is more critical under these conditions. When planting, add good soil to the planting hole to give the plant a fair chance of success.

Trees and shrubs for an alkaline garden

One of the first trees to look at, should you have room for it, is the beech (*Fagus sylvatica*) which is found in large forests on chalk downs. Beech does not transplant well as a big tree, so select normal nursery stock and leave room for development.

Hornbeam will also tolerate very alkaline soils. Its leaf shape is much like that of the beech, but is probably a better choice for the average garden because it rarely grows as big as the beech and has a particularly attractive bole and shape.

The common horse chestnut also does well, but it spreads wide and must be given the room it needs. Unfortunately it has a habit of shedding large limbs without warning, so use it only in safe areas. Its other drawback (or bonus for children, perhaps) is its 'conkers'.

Smaller trees are of course easier to fit

Both conifers, some of which like limy soils, and barberries (centre) provide colour, texture and form for autumn.

into most garden situations. *Acer negundo* is small for a tree with attractive leaves and bark, furthermore its habit is fairly upright. The hawthorns, *Crataegus spp*, are also excellent for chalky soils. They provide colour in the spring followed by berries in the autumn, and in many cases the leaves turn, giving autumn colour as well. Some of the better ones include *C. prunifolia* (this has showy fruits and brilliant autumn colour) and *C. x lavallii* (the leaves persist on the tree longer than most and the orangy red fruits remain well through the winter).

Some conifers like limy soils and being evergreen they can be relied upon to provide interest through the winter. Although many are suitable, here are a few to start with: *Libocedrus decurrens*, the incense cedar, is sometimes known as *Calocedrus decurrens*; an upright form called 'Columnaris' is the one to select. It will make a tall tree but being column-like (or fastigiate) does not take up much room in the garden. The common yew is also worth a place – *Taxus baccata*. Once mature, and if given room to spread, it will take on a rounded form. It grows to a very old age, but has the disadvantage of being poisonous to children. One of the most planted of trees at the moment is the leyland cypress, x *Cupressocyparis leylandii*. This too likes chalk although

it will do nicely on any fertile soil. As it establishes itself it makes a nicely shaped small tree. Almost a large shrub, though best classed as a small tree, is *Cercis siliquastrum* – the Judas tree. On chalk it will make a fine flowering subject covering its branches with pea-like, deep pink flowers. As the flowers fade the typical pea pod seed heads are visible and add more interest. Flowering trees in the *Prunus* and *Malus* species do well when the pH is high, and there are many hundreds of varieties.

Flowering shrubs

The backbone of any garden is its shrubs, and on alkaline soils there is a wealth of good plants to choose as a foundation for future planting. Looking at the extremes first, plants which will do best on strong limestone should include the barberries. It is a big family and there is a wide range from which to choose. One of the best known is *B. darwinii*. This will stand comparison with any flowering shrub in any situation; its small glossy leaves are evergreen and orangy yellow flowers cover the bush in the spring. It is so dense that it makes a good hedge and an effective cat and dog

Philadelphus 'Manteau d'Hermine' likes light, alkaline soils and is smaller than most with fragrant, double flowers.

deterrent for the garden. *B.* x *stenophylla* is different in habit, having arching sprays of yellow flowers in the spring. *B. thunbergii* is more compact and the green forms turn in the autumn to give brilliant scarlet colour its berries are also bright and long lasting.

All forms of buddleia thrive under these conditions too. The well known *B. davidii* has dark purple, white or bluish purple flowers which are especially eye-catching and have the great advantage of attracting butterflies to the bush in the summer. There is a wide range of cultivars to select from: 'Black Knight' has deep violet trusses, 'Empire Blue' has rich violet flowers, 'Alba' white flowers and 'Royal Red' reddish purple flowers, to name but some.

A plant often seen in the hedgerows on chalk is the fuchsia. These are the 'wild' ones but all the forms grow quite happily even on solid limestone. It is a plant which succeeds where all else fails. *F. magellanica* has long graceful branches covered with scarlet and violet flowers; cut it hard back each year. *F. m.* 'Variegata' has coloured leaves, margined creamy yellow, and

the whole has a pink flush which highlights the scarlet and purple flowers. *F.* x 'Brilliant', one of the best of the hybrid fuchsias, has large scarlet and rosy purple flowers. It is a vigorous plant, hardy under all but severe winters. *F.* x 'Alice Hoffman' has scarlet and white flowers which are even more distinctive.

On limy soils which are not too strong, the lilacs do well, *Syringa spp*. There are many varieties to select from and all have something to offer. Lilacs make big shrubs and they need room to grow, you may find the hybrids most suitable for garden use. 'Mdm A. Buchner' has semi-double pinky mauve flowers; 'Souvenir de L'Spath', wine-coloured flowers; and 'Mdm Lemoine', white flowers; all are scented.

Other shrubs which thrive on chalky soils so long as they are not too limy are the forsythia, their bright yellow flowers heralding the spring. Hypericum (St. John's wort) brings yellow at a later time to cover banks, perhaps, or as groups in borders. *Philadelphus spp*, known as the mock orange because of its scent, is a deciduous shrub which varies in size. Some are very big (up to 4 m or 15 ft) but others, such as *P. microphyllus* are quite compact. White scented flowers envelop

the bush and make the plant a 'must' in any limestone garden plan. *Weigela spp* is less massive and its flowers are pink to red, adding to the general background of colour in mid-summer.

Climbing plants

The clematis will add another dimension to the garden, taking colour to a new level. In some cases they can be planted into the limestone base; in all cases they prefer their roots to be in shade or semi-shade, and their shoots reaching up to full sun.

The hybrids are very colourful and some, such as *C. montana*, are vigorous and cover a lot of space.

Another species, *C. flammula*, known as the fragrant virgin's bower, has masses of scented white flowers in the autumn which are followed by silvery grey seed heads. Hybrids include 'Nelly Moser', blush white with a carmine strips down each petal, 'Ville de Lyon', flowers of carmine red shading to crimson; 'Jackmanii', rich purple flowers; and 'Comtesse de Bouchard' with its cyclamen pink flowers.

Herbaceous plants for the alkaline garden

Most annuals and perennials make light work of alkaline soils, in the sense that many of them accept some lime. One which will tolerate *very* limy ground is *Paeonia spp* (the tree peonias as much as the herbaceous ones). Take care they are not planted on a cold aspect or in shade.

Lilium candidum likes lime and establishes so well; it's surprising it is not seen more often in chalky areas. *Dianthus* in its many forms prefer this type of soil to all others so long as it is reasonably fertile and well drained. These can include the pinks and carnations as well as the dianthus used on the rockery.

Fruit trees

As a rule, these do not like a soil which has free lime, and it is wise to make special preparations if it is decided to grow top (i.e. tree) fruits. Usually this means isolating them from the soil *in situ* – mounds of good soil or some form of raised bed is the best way to tackle it.

Growing grass in alkaline conditions

Lawns do not like high pH soils; the result is usually a thin cover which welcomes weeds and moss. To enable lawns to do well, they must be fed regularly with acid type fertilizers. It is also good practice to solid tine or hollow tine, i.e. spike the ground with a specially designed hollow fork, and add an organic mulch.

21

The dry garden

Here in the dry garden, the owner faces the possibility of weeks of drought, not just as the occasional hazard, but as a regular fact of life. Drought may be caused by a very shallow or light and free-draining soil, a very low average rainfall, or both.

On the credit side there will probably be more than average sunshine and a warm winter soil, both of which are great advantages to some plants.

Before considering the plants which will thrive in dry conditions it cannot be said too often that every effort should be made to improve the nutritional and water-holding capacity of the soil.

Many drought-loving plants do not need to be over-laden with humus. It can promote lush growth which is out of character and could be the cause of suffering in a bad winter.

To get drought-loving plants started, either spread a reasonable amount of compost all over a bed or, when re-planting, put a handful or bucketful – according to the size of plant – into each planting hole.

Choosing the plants - basic considerations

If lawns in your district spend much of the summer looking burnt-up and unsightly, either consider the virtue of grasses suited to arid conditions (page 77), and be prepared to install a sound system of irrigation, or reduce the grass area to a minimum, or use paving cobbles or gravel instead.

Assuming the garden is new, consider a natural framework composed of trees and shrubs with small tough leaves; avoid soft-leaved trees that adapt poorly to dry conditions.

Choose plants for their shapes and long lasting foliage. Beth Chatto recommends roughly asymmetrical, triangular groupings which could start at ground level as mats and carpeters running into cushions and clumps, which in turn lead the eye into a shrub, and finally, at the highest point, a tree (or maybe a wall or gatepost covered with a climber). Within this type of grouping allow a few slender vertical plants to pop up here and there to provide a little excitement. Tall alliums, drought-enduring lilies, or a frothy column of fennel are ideal.

What are drought-resistant plants?

You are already familiar with some. These include wallflowers, (*Cheiranthus spp*) antirrhinums (snapdragons), thymes, alyssum, aubrieta, lavender, rosemary, cistus and brooms (both genista and cytisus).

The original forms of these plants – many of which we grow and love in their natural state – have been found growing wild on sunny, crumbly, rocky slopes in warm lands that border the Mediterranean. Many more come from similar situations in the temperate world. All endure hot summers, low rainfall and winter frost. Plants which cannot survive frosts are not included although there are some such half hardy plants which can be bedded out in summer.

Nature has provided drought-resisting plants with built-in protection. Some have reduced their leaf size to the minimum and those tiny leaves are tough and leathery, often protected by aromatic oils which fill the air with perfume on still summer evenings. Others have a protective coat of wool or felted hairs over their green leaves, so

A dry garden profile

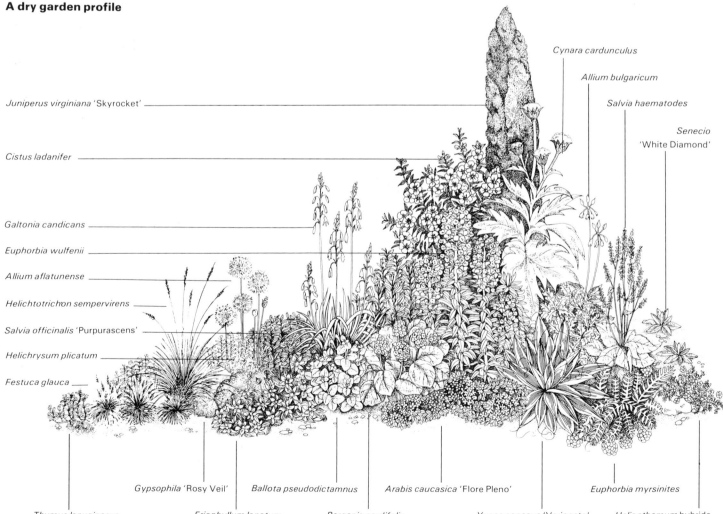

Juniperus virginiana 'Skyrocket'

Cistus ladanifer

Galtonia candicans

Euphorbia wulfenii

Allium aflatunense

Helichtotrichon sempervirens

Salvia officinalis 'Purpurascens'

Helichrysum plicatum

Festuca glauca

Cynara cardunculus

Allium bulgaricum

Salvia haematodes

Senecio 'White Diamond'

Gypsophila 'Rosy Veil'

Ballota pseudodictamnus

Arabis caucasica 'Flore Pleno'

Euphorbia myrsinites

Thymus lanuginosus

Eriophyllum lanatum

Bergenia cordifolia

Yucca concava 'Variegata'

Helianthemum hybrids

they appear grey or silvery. Among these plants are included the artemisias and santolinas. Those plants which appear pewter coloured or even blue, such as *Ruta graveolens* (Jackman's blue rue) and some of the spurges (*Euphorbia spp*), have leaves coated with fine wax which rubs off if you touch it, like the bloom of a grape. Sedums (stonecrop) and sempervivums (houseleeks), many of which grow naturally on top of rocks and survive with very little soil, have learnt to store up any available moisture in their fat juicy leaves (rather as the camel does) as insurance against bad times.

Some plants to use in dry gardens

For the backbone of dry sunny borders look first for something to provide height. Among the trees and large shrubs are upright junipers, such as *Juniperus communis* 'Hibernica', or *Juniperus viginiana* 'Skyrocket', and the lovely blue-grey cypress *Cupressus glabra* 'Pyramidalis'. The common bay tree, *Laurus nobilis*, makes vast bulk and healthy looking green at all seasons. Large, open, tree-like shrubs include the Mt Etna Broom, *Genista aetnensis*, and the silvery leafed

pineapple scented Broom, *Cytisus battandieri*. Tree heathers can also make spectacular height and bulk provided the soil is lime free and has sufficient depth. Buddleias are possibilities, but the large flowered varieties can wilt in prolonged drought. The grey-leafed *Buddleia fallowiana* is better, while *Buddleia crispa* which is so heavily coated with felt that its young leaves and clustered flower buds appear white, never shows the least sign of distress growing in a sunny aspect on a very poor gravel soil. In richer soil, and unprotected from cold prevailing winds, this beautiful buddleia can be damaged.

Next look for medium-sized shrubs to make a comfortable background. These will include many kinds of cistus which, when grown tough and leathery on poor, dry, well-drained soil will survive most winters. *Cistus ladaniferus* and *Cistus corbariensis* have survived the hardest British winters over the last twenty years, with little damage other than a bit of leaf scorch. The hardiest forms of rosemary thrive, while the common lavender is completely hardy. The *Senecio* Dunedin hybrid 'Sunshine',

long known erroneously as *Senecio greyi*, is invaluable, and not to be despised for being seen so often. It is a pity to let it degenerate into an unsightly straggling heap. Regular trimming after flowering will encourage fresh growth and keep its immaculate, rounded shape. Few shrubs have more handsome foliage which simply grows whiter through weeks of dry weather.

Among these shrubs place *Euphorbia wulfenii*, which is not a shrub but a perennial plant making a sturdy clump 1.2-1.5 m (4-5 ft) high and as much across. Its stout stems are completely clothed with whorls of narrow, strap-shaped leaves which are a strong pewter blue-grey, and a perfect foil for the huge heads of lime-green flowers.

Then look among the multitude of smaller shrubs and cushion plants, choosing predominantly those which remain evergreen or ever-grey, which most of the trees and shrubs already mentioned do. Use the shrubby sages, coloured-leafed forms of *Salvia officinalis* (common sage), ballota, santolina, ruta and helianthemum.

Around these, and on to the edges of paths and paving, would be many varieties of thyme, dwarf artemisias and other low creeping plants. Many of these provide cover for spring bulbs, such as crocus. Although beautiful in spring (and autumn), bulbs can do significant damage when their quantities of grass-like foliage flop all over the more delicate mat plants. So scatter them around shrubs where there untidy leaves are less of a problem.

There are many colourful flowering plants which can be added to this basic planting, but more important are a few spectacular plants that add drama to the grouping, making bold contrast to predominately rounded shapes and masses of small leaves.

Try the jagged soaring silvery leaves of the cardoon, *Cynara cardunculus*, or the great *Crambe maritima* with its clouds of honey-scented, cream-coloured flowers floating over 1.8 m (6 ft) high and as much across. These two are perennials. Two biennials which have architectural stature are the so-called Scotch thistle, *Onopordon acanthium*, (it is not Scottish) and a huge mullein, called *Verbascum olympicum*. This makes a rosette of white/grey felted leaves which lie on the ground like a great dahlia flower sometimes 90 cm (3 ft) across. From the centre emerges the flower stem, thick as a broom stick branching towards the top like a candelabra some 2.45 m (8 ft) tall. Bright yellow flowers dot the woolly branches for weeks.

A dry garden plan

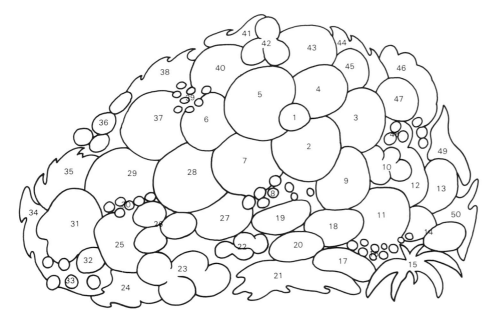

Dry garden plant list

Key to Plan:

1. *Juniperus virginiana* 'Skyrocket'
2. *Cynara cardunculus*
3. *Euphorbia wulfenii*
4. *Cistus x corbariensis*
5. *Cistus ladanifer*
6. *Senecio* Dunedin hybrid 'Sunshine'
7. *Euphorbia wulfenii*
8. *Lilium* hybrid 'Viking'
9. *Santolina incana*
10. *Salvia haematodes*
11. *Senecio* 'White Diamond'
12. *Melissa officinalis* 'Aurea'

13. *Euphorbia epithymoides*
14. *Alyssum* 'Citrinum'
15. *Euphorbia myrsinites*
16. *Allium pulchellum*
17. *Anaphalis triplinervis*
18. *Coreopsis verticillata*
19. *Sedum* 'Autumn Joy'
20. *Calamintha nepetoides*
21. *Arabis caucasica* 'Flore pleno'
22. *Euphorbia niciciana*
23. *Bergenia cordifolia*
24. *Eriophyllum lanatum*
25. *Onosma albo-roseum*
26. *Iris pallida* 'Variegata'
27. *Santolina virens*
28. *Potentilla fruticosa*
29. *Helichrysum plicatum*
30. *Allium aflatunense*
31. *Gypsophila* 'Rosy Veil'

32. *Helictotrichon sempervirens*
33. *Festuca glauca*
34. *Thymus lanuginosus*
35. *Origanum vulgare*
36. *Dianthus* 'Sops in Wine'
37. *Salvia officinalis* 'Purpurascens'
38. *Thymus* 'Doone Valley'
39. *Galtonia candicans*
40. *Ballota pseudodictamnus*
41. *Aubrieta* 'Aureo-variegata'
42. *Verbascum chaixii*
43. *Ruta graveolens*
44. *Thymus* 'Golden Carpet'
45. *Ceratostigma wilmottiana*
46. *Phlox subulata*
47. *Haplopappus coronopifolius*
48. *Asphodelus luteus*
49. *Sedum* 'Green Mantle'
50. *Cerastium tomentosum columnae*

The dry garden

Dry shade

Here, there are fewer plants to choose from, fewer that will provide colourful flowers. In fact for much of the year, you must condition yourself to see colour and variety in foliage rather than flowers.

When you have done all you can to improve the moisture holding capacity of the soil, the following list may provide a few ideas for planting in this environment:

Flowering plants

Include cyclamen but do not allow them to be smothered by ground coverers. You could also use *Alchemilla mollis* and several forms of dicentra, but not *D. spectabilis* which needs more moisture. Foxgloves (*Digitalis spp*) do very well; try the creamy-yellow and white forms in preference to the common *Digitalis purpurea*. Other flowering plants include *Helleborus foetidus*, *Polygonatum spp* (Solomon's seal), *Vinca* (Periwinkle) and *Viola labradorica*. Most of these plants have useful and attractive foliage. *Vinca minor* and its varieties are far preferable to *Vinca major*, except *Vinca major* 'Variegata' which is too good-looking to leave out.

Handsome foliage

For contrast you might include *Arum italicum* 'Pictum', acanthus and bergenia can be chosen but preferably not planted in too densely shady an area, while *Iris foetidissima* and *Euphorbia robbiae* will successfully penetrate the gloomiest places. *Brunnera macrophylla* and the spotted pulmonarias are valuable for their foliage effect, but neither will give their best in the driest of conditions. *Liriope muscari* will grow in deep shade, and flower there surprisingly well in the late autumn with multitudes of slim violet spikes.

Wet and dry gardens in close proximity

Above: dense and light foliage in dry shade.

Below left: a euphorbia in (yellow) flower and, in the foreground, a sun-loving, apricot helianthemum.

In Beth Chatto's garden the average rainfall is about 50 mm (20 in). There are all kinds of soil from sunbaked free-draining gravel to spring-fed bogs. There is no irrigation in the garden, but by

choosing plants adapted to the individual sites, and preparing these sites carefully, they look as though they are blessed all over with good soil.

Left: low-lying ground covers soften the line of the steps.

Below middle: the silver-leaved artemisia is well set off by a yellow *Coreopsis verticillata*.

Below: cytisus in background, veronica in foreground with *Polygonum affine* behind it.

The wet garden

Basic considerations

* Comparatively few plants will grow in stagnant soil. There are marginal plants, such as water-loving primulas and irises, which will grow in the swampy soil at the edge of natural ponds or artificial pools, but the rest, although needing moisture in summer, will drown if the soil is waterlogged.

* However contradictory it may seem to suggest taking the water away, there must be a free flow of water through the soil, whether your land is watered from above, or beneath from underground springs.

* The texture of heavy land can be vastly improved to ease the passage of air and water through it, but takes time and effort.

One way is to spread a thick layer of fine 5 mm (3/16 in) gravel all over the surface together with as much vegetable waste as you can find. Then rotovate, or dig it all into the top spit to produce an aerated workable soil. You may find that compost or F.Y.M., without the grit, is not enough.

Elsewhere, you may have the problem

The damp garden

'I began my damp garden with an overgrown hollow, soggy and wet, full of underground springs which fed a central drainage ditch. Over the last twenty years I have learnt what I can, and cannot do with plants in these conditions.

'Where the land is sticky and wet we have dug a set of trenches 84 cm (2 ft 9 in) deep, filled them with coarse 20 mm (¾ in) stone to within 30 cm (1 ft) of the surface, then put a layer of polythene over the stones and finally top-filled with soil. The polythene prevents the soil washing down and blocking the drainage through the stones. Where we have picked up a gushing spring we have lain plastic drainage pipes in a bed of gravel and led these into our natural pools which we have created as the focus of our water gardens. Some of my land is close textured silt, that is a black fine soil with scarcely any stones. Wet in winter (but not waterlogged now after our drainage methods) and slow to dry out in summer, although once the surface does dry, it is next to impossible to irrigate properly.'

of plasticine-like clay. Where it is possible, along the edges of borders, remove the top spit and cart it elsewhere. It may not be feasible to take it far in many gardens, so put it to the back of the border. A little extra under shrubs does not hurt, whereas you will need well-prepared soil for the smaller plants towards the front.

Next collect all the lightening material you can find. It may be sand/gravelly soil from elsewhere on your land, plus any vegetable waste, including farmyard manure. A load of muck makes an uncommon but welcome present to a dedicated gardener. All this is piled on top of the raw clay and left there. Over the years add to it, building up a new soil on top of the clay. The worms will come to your assistance and gradually the top spit will improve.

25

The wet garden

Planting

Having taken care of the soil conditions, plant groupings in a damp garden will vary according to the amount of moisture available during the growing season, and also whether the site is exposed or shaded. The choice of trees and shrubs that flourish in soils with plenty of moisture is large and bewildering. Here are some which might be considered basic for waterside planting, but which can also be grown where rainfall is adequate. For stateliness in all seasons, plant both *Taxodium distichum*, the swamp cypress (bold cypress), and *Metasequoia glytostroboides*, the dawn redwood. These are both leaf-losing conifers, narrowly conical in shape, with almost fernlike foliage, which in the swamp cypress turns to a rich foxy-red in late autumn, while the foliage of the *Metasequoia* becomes a softer pinky-copper tone.

There are willows to suit every size of garden. The well-known weeping-willow eventually makes a large tree unsuited to small ornamental pools, but easily grown almost anywhere else. The shrub-forming willows look fine massed round a large lake or shrubbery, but they can be used individually in smaller gardens, and nothing will be lost by pruning them hard about every second year. The resulting straight strong shoots will look most handsome, especially in winter, if you choose those which have polished coloured stems.

The white willow, *Salix alba*, makes an elegant tree, very tall but graceful. Smaller and better suited for the average-sized garden is the silver-leafed *Salix alba* 'Sericea', whose leaves are of a glistening silvery-whiteness which make this lovely tree stand out from everything else around it. There are also low-creeping willows which can be used tumbling over a rock, or as edging round a pool.

The dogwood genus (*Cornus spp*) could not be left out of this necessarily short list. From a large and interesting family choose forms of *Cornus alba* which include several with variegated leaves as well as brightly coloured stems in winter.

Having suggested a possible framework for a water garden, the next thing is to find plants for the water's edge, or if you have it, marshy ground. These are called marginal plants. They thrive in swampy soil, even in a few inches of water.

Iris pseudacorus 'Aureus' is the handsome form of our native water iris which has bright creamy-yellow leaves

for several weeks in spring. Good to plant around it is the Pyrennean form of the Cuckoo flower, *Cardamine latifolia*. The cool heads of strong lilac-coloured flowers make effective contrast with the pale iris leaves which become green as they mature. *Iris laevigata* provides large blue, white and old rose coloured flowers, and is at home in the pond or on the edge. Creeping Jenny (*Lysimachia nummularia*) forms a mat among these, preferably the yellow-leafed form which is not quite so vigorous.

Not all damp-loving primulas like to be waterlogged, but most of the candelabra types do well, and so too does the late summer flowering Himalayan cowslip (*Primula florindae*) with stems 1.2 m (4 ft) tall from which droop lemon-yellow bells dusted with palest green farina.

There are several kinds of marsh marigold, both single and double, white and bright yellow. The double kind makes the neatest plants while there is a single yellow one which can make great rafts of round leaves which look splendid by lakesides. It is called *Caltha polypetala*.

Several kinds of musk or monkey flower (*Mimulus spp*) are useful for masking the edges of pools, and you might enjoy the masses of pale blue froth which is made by the thousands of tiny blue flowers of the water forget-me-not (*Myosotis palustris*) reflected in the bright water.

For contrast, and to create a natural effect, consider various kinds of grasses and rush, but take care not to plant anything that may get out of control. Too many underground workers, however attractive, can become your worst enemy, and riddle their way through everything else.

Two giant plants which add considerable drama are, regrettably, only suitable for naturally damp soil and can scarcely be entertained in small gardens.

The first is *Lysichitum americanum*, the bog arum (in U.S. the Western skunk cabbage). Very early in the spring, large butter-yellow arum flowers emerge through the mud, to be followed by a rosette of leaves much the shape of spinach, but smoother. They can stand up to 1.2 m (4 ft) tall.

A damp garden plan

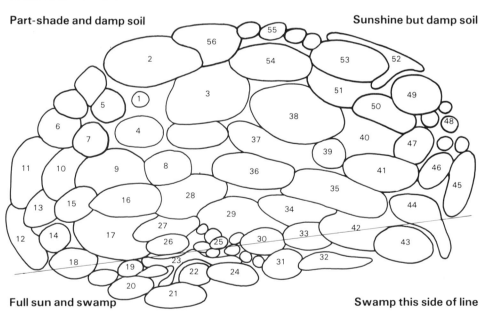

Part-shade and damp soil

Sunshine but damp soil

Full sun and swamp

Swamp this side of line

Wet garden plant list

Key to Plan:

1. *Taxodium distichum*
2. *Cornus alba* 'Spaethii'
3. *Salix alba* 'Sericea'
4. *Miscanthus sinensis* 'Silver Feather'
5. *Hosta* 'Thomas Hogg'
6. *Dicentra spectabilis*
7. *Veronica virginica* 'Alba'
8. *Phormium tenax*
9. *Rheum palmatum*
10. *Phlox paniculata* hybrids
11. *Polygonum affine*
12. *Hosta sieboldiana*
13. *Filipendula palmata* 'Elegans'
14. *Cyperus vegetus*
15. *Aruncus sylvester*
16. *Polygonum amplexicaule*
17. *Rodgersia podophylla*
18. *Cardamine pratensis* 'Flore pleno'
19. *Cardamine latifolia*
20. *Iris pseudocorus* 'Aureus'
21. *Pontaderia cordata*
22. *Iris laevigata*
23. *Lysimachia nummularia* 'Aurea'
24. *Mimulus guttatus*
25. *Primula bulleyana*
26. *Lythrum virgatum*
27. *Matteucia struthiopteris*
28. *Euphorbia palustris*
29. *Astilbe* hybrids
30. *Carex stricta* 'Bowles Golden'
31. *Caltha pratensis* 'Flore Pleno'
32. *Myosotis palustris*
33. *Iris kaempferi*
34. *Trollius europaeus*
35. *Polygonum bistorta* 'Superbum'
36. *Veratrum album*
37. *Polygonum hybridum*
38. *Salix eleagnos* (rosmarinifolia)
39. *Angelica archangelica*
40. *Miscanthus sinensis* 'Zebrinus'
41. *Ligularia* 'Greynog Gold'
42. *Ligularia clivorum*
43. *Lysichitum americanum*
44. *Houttuynia cordata*
45. *Astilbe chinensis pumila*
46. *Ranunculus speciosus plenus*
47. *Lysimachia ephemerum*
48. *Molinia coerulea* 'Variegata'
49. *Hosta lancifolia*
50. *Aster lateriflorus* 'Horizontalis'
51. *Aster frikartii* 'Mónch'
52. *Mentha rotundifolia* 'Variegata'
53. *Rudbeckia speciosa*
54. *Ligularia* 'The Rocket'
55. *Carex morrowii* 'Aureo Variegata'
56. *Brunnera macrophylla* 'Variegata'

The second is *Gunnera manicata*, usually called 'that giant rhubarb'! But it has nothing to do with rhubarb of the kitchen variety. There are handsome forms of ornamental rhubarb which, while needing deep rich soil, would rot in the moister conditions that suit gunnera. Gunnera makes the largest leaves that can be grown out of doors in temperate countries (and milder parts of America) – up to 1.5 m (5 ft) across, on thick stalks so tall you can shelter beneath the prickly parasols.

Unless the land is flat and marshy the soil will be saturated with water only a short way from the water's edge. Further away it becomes less wet, but will still be ideal for many fine herbaceous plants which must continuously find enough moisture to retain healthy foliage throughout the summer. These would include many daisy-like plants such as the ligularias, rudbeckias, and even michaelmas daisies. Both *Aster novi-belgii* and *A. novae-angliae*, the parents of the garden hybrid michaelmas daisies, are found wild in swamps and damp rough places in N.E. America. You may have been exasperated to see these lovely autumn plants reduced to ruin by

drought which also aggravates their worst enemy, mildew.

With the daisy-type flowers, and the rounded masses of border phlox, you could consider some spire-like plants, These include lythrum and lysimachia, both quite different but both confusedly called 'loosestrife'.

Compatible with the soft-pink bottle brush heads of *Polygonum bistorta* 'Superba', is *Trollius europaeus* with its pale yellow globes. These two are commonly seen growing together in damp meadows in the European Alps. There are many more useful polygonums, from giant herbs to low creeping ground covers.

Several kinds of meadowsweet (*Filipendula spp*) provide frothy heads of pink or white flowers during the summer months. By the autumn *Eupatorium purpureum* dominates damp borders, its 2.45 m (8 ft) high dark purple stems topped with flat heads of fuzzy cinnamon-pink flowers. Some of the most tantalizingly desirable plants are those which need a cool moist air as well as damp soil. Found wild on the edges of mountain or lowland woods

they are the most difficult to please but with underground springs, plenty of humus, and good shelter both from sun and wind they can be grown. Try the exquisite Himalayan blue poppy, *Meconopsis betonicifolia*. If this seeds all over your garden you can probably grow many other treasures that in less sympathetic environments will not survive. In the cool moist garden many different primulas will join them together with a host of graceful ferns. And remember hostas; the delicate golden leafed forms and the small choice blues need cool damp shade to show their best.

Among the small plants which love cool conditions (ideal to plant along the edges of borders) are some of the little wild pansies. Called violas, they have grace and delicacy, poised like tiny butterflies on tall slender stems. They are produced in great abundance over many weeks, some are in flower from spring to autumn. Among them look out for *Viola cornuta*, *V. gracilis*, and *V. cucullata*.

It has been possible to give only the briefest outline plans. See also pages 160 to 169.

A damp garden profile

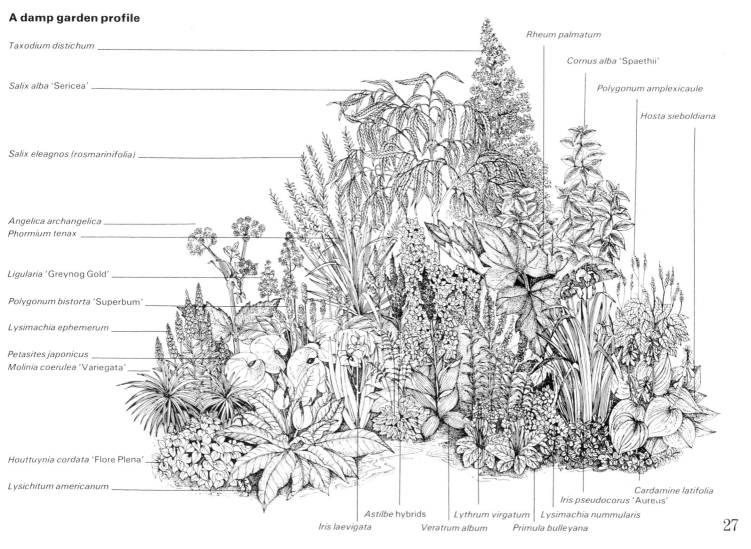

Taxodium distichum

Rheum palmatum

Cornus alba 'Spaethii'

Salix alba 'Sericea'

Polygonum amplexicaule

Hosta sieboldiana

Salix eleagnos (rosmarinifolia)

Angelica archangelica

Phormium tenax

Ligularia 'Greynog Gold'

Polygonum bistorta 'Superbum'

Lysimachia ephemerum

Petasites japonicus

Molinia coerulea 'Variegata'

Houttuynia cordata 'Flore Plena'

Lysichitum americanum

Astilbe hybrids

Iris laevigata

Lythrum virgatum

Veratrum album

Iris pseudocorus 'Aureus'

Cardamine latifolia

Lysimachia nummularia

Primula bulleyana

27

Changing the quality of soil

Improving the soil

Soil is composed of minute particles of inert rock. When organic matter (i.e. matter of animal or plant origin) falls or is placed on the soil surface, it begins to decompose and is carried into the soil by worms and insects. There, bacteria and other micro-organisms break it down to form humus. Humus is thus well-rotted organic matter with its own massive population of bacteria (some living, some dead).

By picking flowers, cutting down plants, gathering vegetables, clearing leaves, and mowing the lawn, the soil is deprived of this natural process of humification (the creation of humus). If your soil has been starved of humus, then for several years you will need to put back more organic matter than you take out.

You can use fresh or well-rotted organic material to create humus. The problem with fresh organic material, such as grass clippings or straw, is that during decomposition the activity of micro-organisms consumes quantities of nitrogen (an essential part of a plant's diet). The nitrogen will be returned once decomposition is completed, but in the meantime your plants could suffer. Stunted plants with small, insipid looking leaves are a tell-tale sign of nitrogen deficiency.

Animal manure is another organic humus maker; it also contains plant nutrients in small quantities. But allow that to rot down too, as in its raw state it contains acids harmful to plants. Keep it raised off the ground, cover it with a few inches of soil, and provide a roof of some sort to protect it from the elements. Good quality animal manure is hard to come by and varies greatly in nutritional value. You can also buy organic manures based on spent hops, peat or seaweed, but these are very expensive.

In the end, the cheapest and most natural way to add humus to your garden is to return all possible plant material to it, via the compost heap. The important thing is to ensure that your compost is well-rotted and of good quality. See below.

Humus

A list of things that humus does to the soil is given on page 16. When first presented with it, it is difficult to absorb the fact that well-rotted vegetable matter can perform one function for one type of soil and an apparently different function for another type. How does it facilitate drainage in a heavy, water-retentive clay, yet retain moisture in a free-draining, light sand?

The trouble with clay is that its very tiny particles coagulate in the presence of water. In order to improve its structure, you can dig it over in autumn and let the elements break down its mass. By then adding lime, these particles will bind together into soil crumbs. Humus stabilizes these crumbs and maintains a structure in the soil which greatly eases the passage of both air and water.

Liberal doses of humus-making compost in thirsty, open soils, will have the effect of providing a retentive layer. The humus helps the loose particles cling together so that drainage spaces are clogged up.

But the most valuable characteristic of humus is that it encourages fertility in all soils. In making humus, the active bacteria working on the compost convert complex chemicals present in the soil (or added to it in the form of fertilizer) into a form which can be assimilated by roots and turned into proteins and other food substances which a plant needs. So the trick is to give the bacteria that carry out the humification process the ideal conditions they need for efficient and speedy work. This is best begun in properly made compost heaps.

Changing the pH level

We have seen how to create acid soil gardens by introducing peat blocks or suitably filled raised beds. pH levels can be adjusted in other ways, though as stated on page 16 it is far easier to make an acid soil more alkaline than vice versa.

Raising the pH level

*Improve drainage (see page 34).

*Add lime in the right proportions. Lime hastens the break-down of humus and too much will lock up iron and manganese in the soil and cause chlorosis (page 17). Add about ½ lb of hydrated lime per square yard of soil just on the acid side of neutral; ¾ lb if more acid. Use a little less than these quantities on light soils, a little more if you have a heavy clay. Lime is best worked in after autumn digging, but leave it until early spring if manures have been applied, and until winter if a fertilizing programme has been carried out.

Lowering the pH level

*Add generous quantities of peat or well-rotted compost.

*Flowers of sulphur will help (about 1½ oz per square yard). Check on the efficiency of the application by soil testing again in five or six weeks. Repeat the treatment if necessary.

What good compost heaps need

A mixed diet. Heaps made from just one material, such as lawn mowings, will give a poor result.

Moisture. Dry material should be wetted, but not made sodden.

Air. Micro-organisms need this in order to survive and do their work. The air flow should be provided underneath the heap to rise through it.

Shelter. The bacterial activity heats up the compost heap. Should cold winds, rain or snow be allowed to penetrate the heap then the process of decomposition, which includes the killing of weed seeds and perennial roots like couch grass and dandelion, will be held up.

An activator. This is an organic source of nitrogen which replaces that consumed through bacterial activity. It is not necessary in the spring and early summer, as ample nitrogen will be supplied from lawn mowings and young weeds. But it is very useful in autumn and winter when the material consigned to the heap is tougher.

Animal manures or urine are ideal activators. Add what you can get. Otherwise sprinkle a good handful of dried blood, fishmeal or hoof and horn to every alternate layer. Assuming the heap is about 1 m (3 ft) square, each layer should be about 150–230 mm (6–9 in) deep. You can buy proprietory inorganic activators rich in nitrogen, but the organic varieties release their nitrogen slowly over a longer period.

A little lime. Bacteria that cause decay cannot live in excessively acid conditions. Peat, a kind of soil made up of dead plant remains which are *not* decayed, occurs because the ground is excessively acidic and water-logged – anathema to bacteria. So mix some lime with topsoil and for a 90 cm (3 ft) square heap add about 100 g (4 oz) to the layers which did not receive the activator. Of course, if you are about to use the compost in soil supporting rhododendrons, heathers, and other lime-hating plants, omit lime from the heap altogether.

A top blanket. This is to help contain the heat generated by bacterial activity. Make sure that it is porous so that gases can escape. Sheets of thick plastic (opened-out plastic sacks) with 25 mm (1 in) diameter holes, cut 23 cm (9 in) apart in each direction, are recommended. Add hessian (burlap) sacks during cold weather.

Materials to include in a compost heap. All vegetable and animal matter from the garden and kitchen can be used provided it will rot down quickly. Don't include anything that is woody, bony, greasy or badly diseased. Miss out, for example, rose leaves heavy with black-spot and the roots of all brassicas (the cabbage family) in case they have club-root disease. If you use their stems, pulverise them first.

Mature tree leaves that fall in the autumn are best rotted separately into leaf-mould (see page 32). You can include a few of them in the compost heap, but give most evergreens a miss. They rot down too slowly. Amongst suitable quick-rotting materials are:

All spent plants and soft prunings from the vegetable and flower gardens. Soft clippings from shrubs and hedges can also be included.

All weeds, with the proviso that if you only plan a make-shift compost heap do not include weed seeds and perennial roots.

Lawn mowings. Include these in alternate layers with other materials.

Small quantities of tree leaves, with the proviso that they do not exceed 10 per cent of the heap.

Any organic manure from poultry, pigeons, guinea-pigs or rabbits. Human urine is productive too.

Small quantities of soft papers such as newsprint can be used provided you tear it up into small pieces, soak it for twenty-four hours, and mix it well with the other materials. Again, let it be no more than 10 per cent of the heap. Glossy or coloured paper is unsuitable.

All kitchen fruit and vegetable refuse, crushed egg shells, and tea leaves (although there is not much goodness left in them).

Feathers can be used if you have plucked a bird. You could even incorporate those from old pillows and eiderdowns, but wet them well during the opening operation or they will spread everywhere. Cotton flock can be added too, but only use it in small quantites mixed in with other things, otherwise it will take too long to rot down. Don't add man-made materials or fibres.

Mixing
Good mixing of the various materials in each layer promotes an even distribution of moisture and an even spread of micro-organisms throughout. It also allows proper ventilation. The layers are illustrated above right.

Compost layers

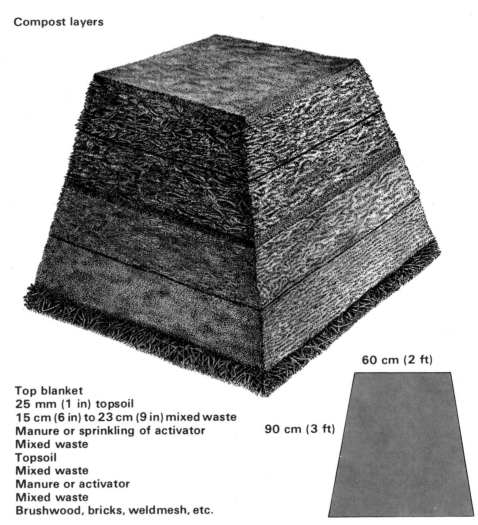

Top blanket
25 mm (1 in) topsoil
15 cm (6 in) to 23 cm (9 in) mixed waste
Manure or sprinkling of activator
Mixed waste
Topsoil
Mixed waste
Manure or activator
Mixed waste
Brushwood, bricks, weldmesh, etc.

Shredder for pulverizing
bulky organic material

60 cm (2 ft)

90 cm (3 ft)

Quality control
Compost, like our food, can range from better-than-nothing to what plants might regard as a connoisseur's diet.

Better-than-nothing compost
If you do not have the time or the inclination to make proper compost bins then a heap in the corner of the garden is better than nothing. Put some brush wood at the bottom to open up an air supply. Build the heap up in layers to a height of about 1 m (3 ft), starting with the base about 1 m (3 ft) square, sloping to a 60 cm (2 ft) square top so that the heap doesn't topple over. Cover it with a blanket of plastic sheeting with 25 mm (1 in) holes every 230 mm (9 in), and some sacking. Then start a second heap.

When the centre of the heap has rotted (up to three months later in summer, six months in winter) rearrange the heap so that the unrotted outer material goes to the centre. Cover it over and leave it to rot again.

Don't use this better-than-nothing compost as a mulch; it may well contain live weed seeds. In the autumn, dig it in and give the soil a few months to break it down further.

Changing the quality of soil

The connoisseur's compost

At the other extreme, consider the finest possible product. This is made in one operation so that the whole heap reaches a temperature of 60°C (140°F) and 'cooks' weed seeds, roots and disease spores to give a friable sweet smelling product that can be used as a mulch or 'dug in' in the normal way. Sufficient mixed materials to fill a compost box in one go should be chopped up with a shredding machine (or run over several times with a mower), and dampened right through (but not made sodden). Then, lightly fork over the soil beneath the box before loading the compost (coarser material first to keep the air supply open) to a height of 30 cm (1 ft) higher than the box top. This will allow for settlement. Next cover the heap with the holed 'blanket' of plastic sheeting, plus hessian sacks or some kind of porous matting, and, finally, build a roof to protect it from the elements.

Within seven days a peak temperature of over 60°C (140°F) will be reached and steam may be seen if the top blanket is lifted back. Two weeks later, just after cooling down has begun, fork the material into another box, the outer material to the centre, and replace the

Building the connoisseur's compost bin

Many materials are suitable for making the sides of compost boxes, among them (from **left to right**) are bricks, building blocks, railway sleepers (ties), kerb stones and bales of straw. The drawing below shows how these might be used.

blankets. If this is timed correctly (before the temperature falls too far) there will be enough energy left in the material to bring the temperature back up to 60°C (140°F) for total weed destruction. The breaking-down process is completed by worms which appear through the aerated surface of the soil beneath the box, and move in. The result – a fine crumbly product.

After another couple of weeks, the heap will have shrunk to about half its original size. In another two weeks, it can be used as mulch. If it is to be used near young plants or seedlings, it should be left to mature further for a few weeks, otherwise traces of ammonia in it may cause damage.

Compost boxes and how to make them

Compost boxes help to contain the heat generated by bacterial activity, and protect the valuable humus-making material from cold winds, rain and snow. They should allow an air supply at the base, be easy to load and unload, and allow the gases from the compost to escape at the top. Compost boxes were traditionally made from wooden frames and planking. New wood is now very expensive, as are proprietary

plastic compost bins (which do make a reasonable product if the instructions are followed). With a little ingenuity, however, good solid compost boxes can be made from a number of materials.

The make-shift box

The box should have three fixed sides and a removable front of loose boards. The heap should sit on well-spaced, loose boards, or strong weld-mesh, resting on rows of bricks on the soil. Alternatively, pile brush wood at the base and build the heap on that.

For its sides, use railway sleepers (ties), bricks, building blocks, old kerbs, corrugated iron sheets, old packing cases, or if you live in the country, bales of straw. These are excellent at retaining heat and eventually become compost themselves.

Each bin should measure 1 m (3 ft) by 1 m (3 ft) by 1 m (3 ft). If you position more than one box side-by-side they will help each other's contents keep warm and moist, and it will be easier to move compost from one to another. Make sure that you leave at least a 30 cm (1 ft) clearance between the top of the heap and the roof to make it easy to load, as shown below.

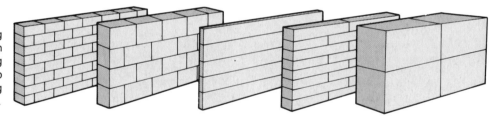

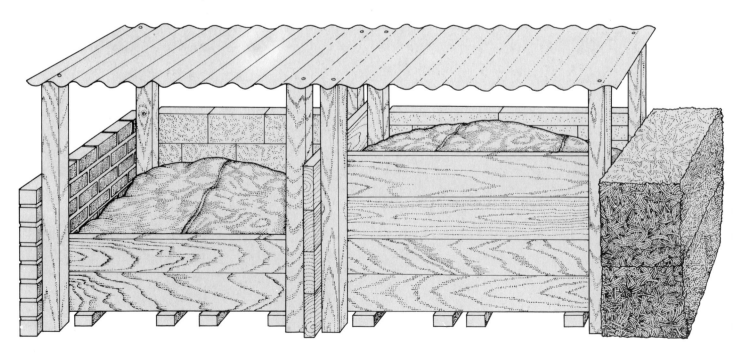

Each bin should measure 1 m (3 ft) by 1 m (3 ft) by 1 m (3 ft).

Constructing a compost bin for a top quality product

For front retaining boards use planks of wood about 70 cm (2 ft 4 in) long to drop in behind the front uprights.

Lay out 36 bricks on the ground to give a clear air space beneath the structure.

Buy 2 sheets of galvanised weldmesh, each about 70 cm (2 ft 4 in) wide by 1.22 m (4 ft) in length to lay on top of the bricks and support the compost. Measure exact sizes after you have built the bin.

Weldmesh is made in various thicknesses and mesh sizes. A 75 mm (3 in) by 25 mm (1 in) mesh of 10 gauge material does very well.

Materials	
Uprights	length
10	1.67 m (5 ft 6 in)
3	1.98 m (6 ft 6 in)
2	2.28 m (7 ft 6 in)
Back rails	
12	1.83 m (6 ft)
Side rails	
36	1.22 m (4 ft)
Roof support rails	
2	2.13 m (7 ft)

Buy corrugated sheets to build a 2.13 m (7 ft) by 1.37 m (4 ft 6 in) sloping roof.

* Treat all timber with preservative, especially the uprights which will be set 60 cm (2 ft) in the ground.

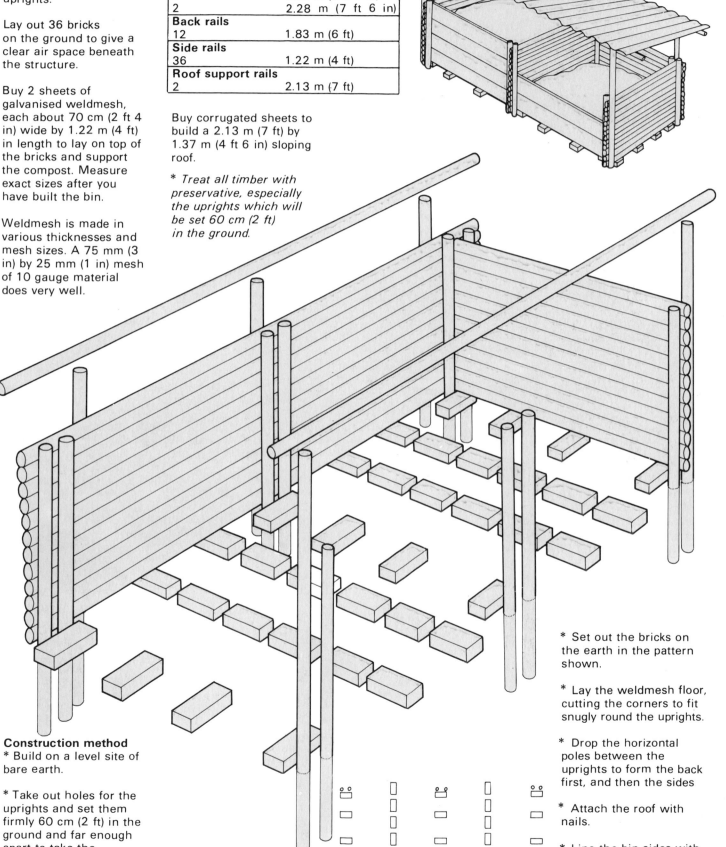

Construction method
* Build on a level site of bare earth.

* Take out holes for the uprights and set them firmly 60 cm (2 ft) in the ground and far enough apart to take the thickness of the back and side rails.

* Set out the bricks on the earth in the pattern shown.

* Lay the weldmesh floor, cutting the corners to fit snugly round the uprights.

* Drop the horizontal poles between the uprights to form the back first, and then the sides

* Attach the roof with nails.

* Line the bin sides with opened out cardboard boxes to retain the heat.

Changing the quality of soil

Mulches

A mulch is a layer of bulky organic material placed on the surface of warm damp soil. It has many advantages:

* It contains warmth and moisture in the soil by preventing evaporation.

* It prevents soil becoming a mushy mess in heavy rain.

* It prevents topsoil becoming compacted.

* It smothers seedling weeds, though no mulch will prevent the emergence of deeply-rooted perennial weeds.

* It produces humus as it decomposes and so encourages fertility in the soil and improves its all-important texture.

* It can look very attractive.

* Trees and shrubs prefer not to be disturbed by cultivation. Mulches, therefore, provide a practical alternative method for soil enrichment.

* Some mulches, like well-rotted manure and leaf-mould, are rich in chemicals which plants turn into food substances.

Many materials are suitable mulches – manure, leaf-mould, seaweed, peat, pulverised bark, straw, lawn or soft hedge clippings, spent hops or rotted wood chippings.

They should be applied in autumn after weeding, and when the soil is warm and damp. It is no good laying a mulch on a dry soil as it will act as a shield against rain. Lay a mulch after the first heavy rain has fallen but while the soil is still warm. That way you make the most out of its ability to insulate the soil.

In a wet winter take care not to place the material too close to the stems of plants which are quick-growing and soft at ground level. This is really only a problem when you use a bulky, coarse mulch. If you are concerned, put down small pockets of fine gravel around the plant stems to a depth of about 25 mm (1 in). Use limestone chippings for alkaline plants and granite for others.

Eventually, organic mulches will decompose as they lie on the soil surface and produce humus. Remember that the rapid increase in bacterial activity involved in decomposition of *fresh* organic matter consumes nitrogen (an essential plant food). In such circumstances, plant growth can suffer, so in spring add a little nitrogenous fertilizer to restore the chemical element.

Pulverised bark or dampened peat are good mulches for herbaceous plants. Lay a fine mulch of this sort in a 25–50 mm (1–2 in) layer. Bulkier varieties, such as straw, should be laid in thicker layers to allow them a chance to settle.

If the wind or your cat has disturbed the mulch surface, or if you have to disturb it to add a new plant at a late stage, rebuild it straight away to the correct depth. Never take a mulch off completely. By the time spring comes round, an organic mulch will have changed into humus. Then is the time to gently fork it into the top 50 mm (2 in) of soil and let the worms pull it down to the plant roots. (If you don't do this you will encourage plant roots to come to the surface looking for food.) The soil then has a chance to absorb the spring and summer heat before you apply the new autumn mulch.

One final point, effective as mulches are at smothering weeds and making weeding less of a chore, air-borne seeds will germinate if they fall on top of any mulch, except straw. Keep a sharp eye out for unwelcome visitors.

Fertilizing the soil

With the help of sunlight during the process of photosynthesis (see page 12), plants make a sugar called glucose out of carbon dioxide and water. From glucose they form other food substances like fats and starches. But they depend upon chemical elements in the soil itself to make the remaining important parts of their diet. From nitrogen, phosphorus and sulphur, for example, they make proteins.

Most gardeners ask a lot from their soil. It may not get much rest even in the autumn in some gardens. The more demanding you are of your soil, the more likely it is to be starved of essential food-producing chemicals. Fertilizers supplement the soil's natural food store and thus promote healthy growth.

Some fertilizers are manufactured; others are organic. There is some contention amongst experts as to the effects of the two types. Some maintain that plants cannot tell the difference between them; others that the manufactured variety interferes with the natural balance of soil. In the absence of a definite opinion, when applying inorganic fertilizers, ensure a generous supply of humus-makers to encourage bacterial activity.

Organic fertilizers work very slowly, providing plants with their requirements steadily over a long period of time. Although they do produce small quantities of humus, they should not be used in place of the humus-makers discussed elsewhere as they are spread thinly. Inorganic fertilizers are more concentrated, dissolve easily and act fast. However, no inorganic fertilizer will improve soil texture, in fact over-application will damage the soil. It is, therefore, very important to follow the manufacturer's instructions about rate of application.

Always store fertilizers in a dry safe place out of the reach of children.

Three chemical elements most important in the food-making process are nitrogen, phosphorous and potassium.

Nitrogen
Being essential to the production of healthy foliage, nitrogen plays an important role in the growth of many plants. There are many fertilizers, both organic and inorganic, which contain it. Amongst the former are dried blood, hoof and horn meal, and fish meal. Well-rotted animal manure will also help replenish a nitrogen deficiency, and will provide similar assistance in soils short of phosphorus and potassium (see below). Sodium nitrate, potassium nitrate, ammonium nitrate, ammonium sulphate, calcium nitrate and urea are amongst the inorganic fertilizers designed to provide nitrogen in the soil.

Phosphorus
Poorly developed root systems produce stunted growth, and if you are growing root vegetables it is never more important to ensure an adequate supply of phosphorus. Amongst the organic fertilizers, bone meal is the best, but make sure that it is sterilized. Leaf-mould is rich in both phosphates and potassium (see below). Super-phosphates are the inorganic fertilizers useful in this respect.

Potassium
This is the key to successful flower and fruit growth. Tasteless vegetables or bland colour tones are signs of potassium deficiency. Potassium sulphate consists of about half its make-up as potash. Amongst organic fertilizers, blood, fish and bone meal contains roughly as much potassium as it does nitrogen and phosphorus, and wood ash is a useful provider of potassium, provided that you understand that it also contains about one third lime.

There are compound fertilizers which contain both organic and inorganic fertilizers and are designed to fulfil a soil's needs for the three major elements. Some compound fertilizers have been made with specific balances suitable for particular plants, so read the packages carefully. There are also fertilizers packaged to supply one particular chemical additive.

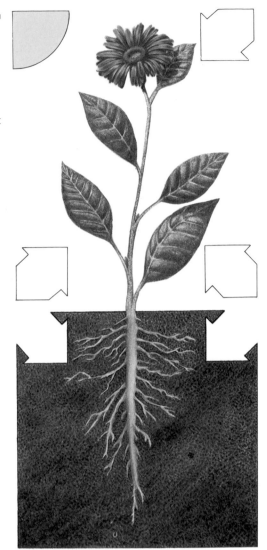

Sunlight used in the process of photosynthesis (described page 12) is absorbed by the green pigment (chlorophyll) of plant leaves. But plants also depend upon chemical elements in the soil to supplement their diet.

Potassium encourages successful flower and fruit production.

Nitrogen is essential to the production of healthy foliage.

Phosphorous encourages the development of a healthy root system.

Lime neutralizes acidity and is anathema to some plants (pages 16 to 19). But in plants which tolerate its application, moderate amounts improve leaf and root growth.

Other elements needed by plants to make food
Lime has been seen to improve the soil by neutralizing acidity and so encouraging bacterial activity. It can also discourage pests and diseases, and plays an important role in breaking a heavy clay into a potentially productive crumb structure. But another very important effect of adding lime to soil is to supplement a plant's diet with calcium. Use it if your plants have poorly developed roots and yellowing leaves, unless, of course, you plan growing lime-hating plants nearby. See also *chlorosis* page 17.

Magnesium and sulphur are, like calcium, needed in moderate amounts. A good compound fertilizer or magnesium spray should suffice. In industrial areas, sulphur is washed into the soil by rain. There, it is unlikely to be in short supply.

There is, finally, a range of further chemical elements (referred to as 'trace elements') including iron, manganese, boron, copper, zinc, chlorine and molybdenum, which plants draw upon in very small quantities. There is little need to worry about trace elements provided that you have ensured a plentiful supply of humus and have correctly supplemented the soil with the three chemical elements most important to successful growth.

Application
Food-supplying, well-rotted animal manure can be laid in a thin layer as a mulch, or dug in.

The slow-acting, organic fertilizers should be dug into the soil to a depth of around 150 mm (6 in) during autumn and winter. The quicker acting inorganic fertilizers can be used during the growing season and raked into the top 50 to 75 mm (2 to 3 in) of soil. Make sure you spread these evenly and avoid their coming into direct contact with leaves and flowers.

Liquid fertilizers are a particularly useful way of feeding soil as they travel straight down to the roots in solution, where they are immediately accessible. Do make sure that the ground is moist before application.

33

Improving soil drainage

Unless you *want* a very wet or boggy area in your garden where you can make a pond or formal pool, or grow a fine range of primulas, trollius and other plants that thrive in constantly moist conditions, there is no reason to tolerate badly drained ground that lies cold, sour and wet for many months of the year. Dips in poorly drained terrain are the only exception. There is little you can do during periods of heavy rainfall, other than pump out the water or create a pool and plant appropriately.

The extent of drainage problems depends not only on rainfall and land form but, as we have seen, upon soil type, shelter and the height of the water table. Generally, the worse the problem the more drastic the treatment will need to be.

Drainage methods
Maintaining and improving soil texture
A good soil texture will allow both water and air easy access to plant roots, and since this is vital to plant growth your first job must be to open up a dense, heavy soil and let it breathe freely. Dig it thoroughly before it dries out completely, and allow the winter elements to break it down.

If a hard subsoil pan has formed as a result of cultivating to a consistent depth over a long period, drainage will be radically improved by breaking up the consolidated layer. If you have a large garden, this can be hard work and you could decide that installing a land drain system is an easier, more long-term solution. But you must do one or the other for although surface-rooting crops may survive, the roots of deep-rooting plants will drown.

Although it is common practice when planting a tree to line the planting hole with peat, in a heavy clay soil be sure to dig over a large surrounding area. Otherwise moisture will be trapped in one place and serious water-logging could result.

When there were coke-fired gas works, bits of crushed coke breeze were plentiful and very useful in helping to open up a dense clay soil. Since their demise, coarse grit from builders' merchants has become a good ready substitute. This is essentially gravel from which the fine sand particles have been washed and then screened to produce particles up to 6 mm (¼ in) across. Every time you turn the clay over, work the grit into the top spit at the rate of a couple of pounds to the square yard. This will only bring about a gradual improvement and you must be careful not to overdo it, particularly if you intend planting root crops

Drowning roots
Dig over a wide area of soil to a sufficient depth when planting deep-rooting trees and shrubs in a heavy soil, and add plenty of humus to encourage the free passage or air and water. Inadequate cultivation can lead to a hard, sub-surface pan forming, where water is trapped around the plant's developing roots.

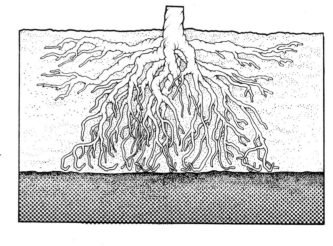

(carrots, for instance) whose growth and shape may be inhibited or distorted by the grit.

Peat or compost will greatly improve texture. Perlite, vermiculite and Hortag (small baked clay particles) are effective too, but because they are quite expensive, they are mostly used in beds and borders. One of the very best methods is to work in gypsum at the rate of about three pounds to the square yard. Seek out pure gypsum from horticultural suppliers, not from builders' merchants as it is usually mixed with lime for plastering and

may not be suitable for your garden.

Spading in straw is a time-honoured way of improving soil drainage. Lay it on the soil surface and 'split it' with a spade a few inches into the earth. Indeed any organic matter like bark fibre, sawdust and (popular in parts of America) corn cob husk, is useful. But remember that these organic mulches could produce a nitrogen deficiency in the soil, if they are not thoroughly decomposed.

Laying land drains
The installation of land drains is

The herring-bone system
A drastic measure for very difficult ground.

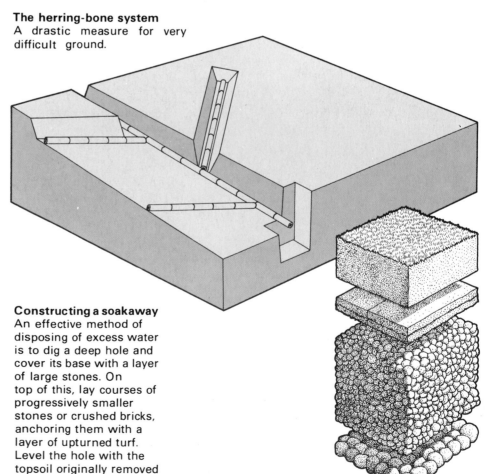

Constructing a soakaway
An effective method of disposing of excess water is to dig a deep hole and cover its base with a layer of large stones. On top of this, lay courses of progressively smaller stones or crushed bricks, anchoring them with a layer of upturned turf. Level the hole with the topsoil originally removed from the site.

particularly effective when the water table is normally between 60 cm (2 ft) and 1.2 m (4 ft) below the surface. Land drains consist of porous clay pipes laid 45 cm (18 in) deep, herring-bone fashion. Leave very small gaps between the joints and surround these with free-draining material such as coarse gravel. The herring-bone pipes connect to a central drain which conducts the water to a soakaway at the lowest point in the garden. A soakaway is a hole which lies lower than any of the pipes leading to it, and should be dug 1.2 m (4 ft) square and then left uncovered until you are satisfied that it is sufficiently deep to cope with the water.

When laying drains or soakaways always retain the topsoil on one side. When you are satisfied that the soakaway is sufficiently large, cover the base with large stones and these with progressively smaller stones. Then add two layers of upturned turf to prevent the stones wandering into the soil. Finally, replace the topsoil.

Laying land drains to one or several soakaways is an expensive operation and should only be attempted if drastic measures are necessary. Strategically placed soakaways may suffice, or trenches dug at the garden's lowest point which should also be rubble-based. Years ago soakaway drains were laid with brushwood rather than stones. The disadvantages of this design is that eventually the brush-wood will rot down.

Where the water from your garden drains to is an important consideration. Legally (as well as ethically) it is unwise to drain it off into your neighbour's garden, unless you have made prior provision for it. Again, don't direct the water into public ditches unless you have discussed the matter with local government officials.

Natural drainage

There is one other very effective method of reducing excessive moisture in the soil, and that is to plant a tree or trees that will draw it up and by transpiration drain it away into the atmosphere. The willow is the classic example of a natural 'air drainer' – a mature weeping willow will give off a ton of water a day in hot weather. In fact any full-leafed tree will have a similar effect.

The process of transpiration in plants has already been touched upon in the section on photosynthesis. It is not unlike perspiration in animals. All trees work this way, some more vigorously than others. Hard pruning can encourage vigorous growth.

How much water is drained away into the atmosphere is not wholly dependent upon size of leaf (or size and number of stomata). The evaporating effect of sunshine and wind is also a significant factor. Furthermore, it should be stressed that the great majority of trees require good drainage in order to survive, and if the site is very poorly drained no amount of trees will help solve the problem.

Planting air drainers in a small garden

You should not overlook an important point which will affect any decision to plant 'draining' trees near buildings:

It has been known for years that trees cause damage to buildings by the action of their roots. Actual structural damage can occur where a building with a shallow foundation is set in a heavy, shrinkable clay soil. The roots of poplars, willows, elms, ash, oaks and cherries can, in time of drought, extract enough moisture from the clay to cause it to shrink and upset the building. In general, conifers do not have this intensive kind of rooting, nor do many of them survive in clay. Beech will not root into wet clay and birches do not grow strongly in this soil, so they are not a difficulty.

In order to decide what size and at what distance a tree needs to be planted so as not to cause damage, remember that tree roots generally grow as long as the tree is high, and spread well beyond their crown edge and increasingly with age. Even knowing the variety of tree, crown formation, and soil shrink-ability, only crude rule-of-thumb guidelines are possible. On a stiff clay, it is safer not to plant a poplar within 45 m (150 ft) of a building that does not have deep pile foundation, or an oak within about 30 m (100 ft).

In gravelly soil and sands there is no danger from shrinkage. The only trouble here is that some trees, willows especially, will put roots into any leaky pipe and block it. So consider carefully before including 'natural drainage' in a small garden.

Beating a high water table

If the water table is high, or wherever drainage is a serious problem, it is a very good idea to consider building beds for planting raised say 30 cm (1 ft) above the surface of the soil. They will require special 'weep holes' to prevent water building up behind the bed walls. These are discussed fully on page 68 as an integral part of the construction of raised beds.

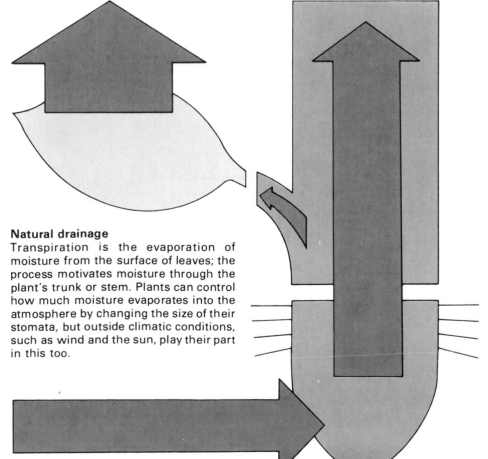

Natural drainage

Transpiration is the evaporation of moisture from the surface of leaves; the process motivates moisture through the plant's trunk or stem. Plants can control how much moisture evaporates into the atmosphere by changing the size of their stomata, but outside climatic conditions, such as wind and the sun, play their part in this too.

Making the most of what you have

Plant irrigation

In A.D. 1300 Barlanglicus, a monkish chronicler wrote, 'Water is the cause of all bread and breedeth corn and fruit and bring forth trees, herbs, and grass.' And nothing has changed since then. If plants suffer a check through want of water in their early stages of growth, they will never catch up and their yield will be far below normal.

In very hot countries, the need for an irrigation plan is obvious. In temperate climates, it is frequently underestimated. Some gardeners say that once you start, you have to go on. This attitude has been handed down for several generations and harks back to the old

days when heavy thirty or forty gallon 'water barrows' had to be pushed to the thirsty area.

On page 13 it was shown that certain parts of the garden benefit less from rainfall than others. Shaded beds under trees or very close to buildings, and beds in the vicinity of vigorously growing evergreen shrubs and trees require particular attention during the early establishment of other plants. Periodically, invasive root growth from a particularly thirsty hedge or boundary screen of trees may need to be checked by driving a space through surface roots.

How much water to apply

This depends on the character of your garden environment – rainfall, the intensity of sunshine, wind, soil conditions and other localized factors such as dry shade – as well as the plants or crops you wish to grow. A loose, free-draining soil can be made more water-retentive by adding compost or peat.

Mulches (page 32) can be very useful in retaining moisture in the soil and in many instances will cut out watering problems almost completely.

Different crops; different needs

There is a measure of common sense in

A hand-held water spray (**above left**) attached to the end of a hosepipe. It can be locked to give any setting from a full jet to a fine mist, making it a useful multi-purpose watering tool. Oscillating sprinklers (**above**) swing the spray gently from side to side over a predetermined area, thus ensuring even distribution of water. Alternatively, you can use drip irrigation directly into the soil (**below**).

discovering how much water plants need. Leafy vegetables and other surface-rooting crops such as strawberries and raspberries need moisture where their roots are – near the soil surface. Fruit trees and other deep-rooting crops don't rely upon topsoil moisture in quite the same way. As they establish, their roots penetrate deep down into the soil seeking sustenance from underground water.

Species planted after the autumn or sown in spring will require careful fostering during late spring and early summer. Bulbous plants like daffodils, and all small bulbs greatly benefit from copious watering in dry springs from the time the flowers fade until the foliage begins to die down. Whereas tulips do not mind a hot baking as they get that in their native countries.

Sowing at the best time

Everyone knows how difficult it can be to establish a lawn during the spring. There is a strong argument for sowing grass seed during early autumn so as to avoid the problems of a hot, dry spring. If the seed germinates and the tiny plants dry out, the result will be patchy or even a failure. Whenever you sow, it is not a bad idea to cover the sown ground with hessian (burlap) sacking and keep it wet. Not only does this encourage you to water adequately, it

also keeps the birds at bay. The grass will grow through the sacking which can simply be lifted off when the lawn is established.

Watering at the best time

How much water to apply partly depends upon the time of day. Water liberally applied during the hottest part of the day is not the most effective method. The water evaporates before it has a chance to filter down to the roots. Less water can be more effective during the latter part of the day, say in the cool of the evening, or preferably in the early morning so as not to encourage fungus forming on plants during the night. If you need to irrigate during cold spells, do so before conditions become freezing. Water will bring down the temperature of the plants still further.

Finally, as a rule-of-thumb, always apply at least a gallon of water to the square yard. Lesser amounts are a waste of time as they evaporate quickly and encourage roots to stay near the surface. 25 mm (1 in) of rain, incidentally, is approximately equivalent to 4½ gallons per square yard. The exception to the above 'rule' is during a dry spell immediately after small seeds have been sown. Then, use about ½ gallon per square yard.

How to apply the water

Methods of irrigation vary from the modest watering can, invaluable for watering seedlings, to 'irrigation flooding', a method that was very popular in extremely hot countries and is still used in Egypt. It involves dividing the area to be irrigated into squares of ground bounded by ridges of soil and connected by a main channel. The water, poured from the area's highest point, literally floods the soil. Effective as it is, it is wasteful where water is often at a premium. Modern technology has largely made the method redundant, although the principle is evident on a more modest scale in private gardens where shallow depressions are made around individual

A moveable overhead sprinkler system (**above**) wafts a fine spray on to the plants beneath. A perforated hose (**right**) can be used at ground level to water lawns, borders and beds. Irrigation of individual plants can be achieved by using mini-sprinklers (**below left**) or by drip-feeding from a hose leading off the main pipe at a T-junction (**below right**).

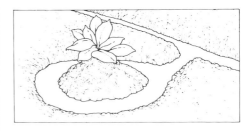

plants and connected to each other by a main channel as shown in the illustration. Although evaporation still makes it a wasteful procedure, these depressions effectively direct most of the water to plant roots.

37

Plant irrigation

Equipment

Plastics have revolutionized irrigation equipment both in large commercial nurseries and in the more humble back garden. Least sophisticated, but very labour saving, is the 'through feed' hose reel. This can be mounted on a wall or post near the main water supply. In a large garden it is worth having several take-off points, strategically sited and supplied by a permanent hose line from the main.

There are various hose head attachments available. Some can be adjusted for long or short range irrigation. Sprinkler heads may be rotating ('flip-flap') or oscillating ('to-and-fro'). The latter are useful for particularly large areas and can be adjusted to irrigate set patterns – rectangles, wide or narrow, and there are others which may be set to water any section of a rectangle or circular area. A pulsating sprinkler is available on a 1 m (3 ft) leg which permits very long range irrigation and is often used to pass over the heads of tall plants to others behind.

But range is not all, of course. How much water a sprinkler puts on will depend on its size and shape, and the manufacturer will be able to advise you on the differences. Water pressure is also an important factor. At weekends, for example, when more people are likely to be watering their gardens and washing their cars, the pressure will probably be at its lowest ebb. Measure out the area you want to irrigate, then put the sprinkler into a two gallon bucket, measuring the time it takes to fill. You will then know how long it takes to spread two gallons over the area on that particular day.

Besides rate of application, the size of the water drops is a consideration. Very large drops can damage soil structure, turning the surface into a mush which can cause erosion problems on a slope and may even leave the surface compacted so that neither water nor air can penetrate the soil. Mulches can be useful in preventing this. Finely-set spray heads, on the other hand, are very slow and tend only to dampen the surface of the soil. Unless applied for a considerable time, a spray will merely wash the dust off the plants, nothing more.

One advantage of a plastic hose is that you can puncture it along its length to produce quite an effective permanent system along the edge of borders. A more modern development of this is the 'ring main' of plastic pipe round the garden. Lay flexible plastic pipe right down one side of the garden or as appropriate. At intervals insert a plastic 'T' joint, which is also a tap. By

means of a plug inserted into each 'T' joint socket, attach short lengths of lightweight plastic hose to the middle of the garden or wherever you want to irrigate. Either an oscillating or a 'flip flap' sprinkler can then be fitted to each connecting hose.

This rids you of the weary process of coiling and uncoiling lengths of hose which may have trailed through mud.

'Pop-up' nozzles are useful for lawns. These are easily installed just below the level of the turf so that a mower can pass over them quite safely. Cut the turf and prise it up, scoop out some soil, lay the plastic pipe in the shallow trench, replace some of the soil and firm down the turf. When the water is turned on, the sprinklers pop up and return below the level of the turf when the water is turned off.

Watering equipment
1. Travelling sprinkler
2. Watering can, the best method if you have time
3. Oscillating sprinkler
4. Spray gun
5. Rose head
6. Fan spray head
7. Perforated pipe for permanent installation
8. Spinning head sprinkler

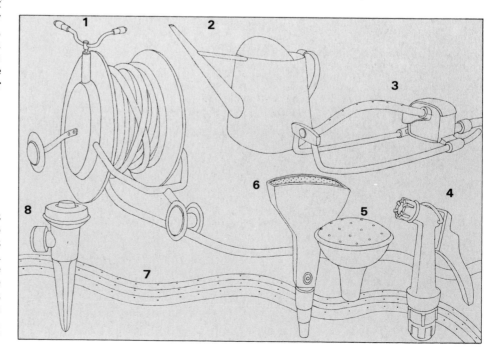

Suitable for large gardens.
Pipes could be perforated
or headed with sprinklers.

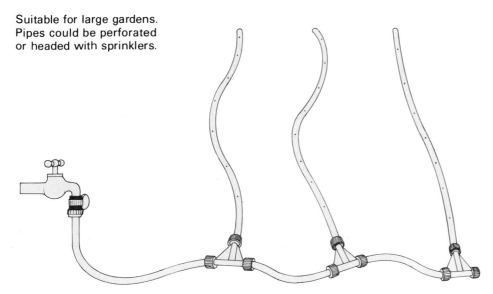

Permanent system for containers

The spaghetti system
described here has been
put to excellent effect in
tubs and hanging baskets
in Roy Hay's garden.

It reduces labour and
obviates the need for
baskets to be positioned
sufficiently low for
hand watering.

Well-placed pipes
need not impose on the
visual impact of tub
plantings, and watering
is easily controlled.

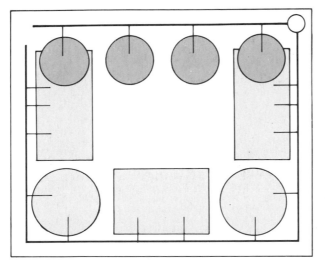

There are other more sophisticated
systems suitable for larger areas or
where moisture loss is a serious
problem. One method, recently developed in New Zealand, is not dissimilar
to fire sprinklers set in the ceilings of
public buildings. Sprinkler valves
react to moisture and dryness to
determine whether **watering** is necessary. Such a system scores if you are
going on an extended holiday or in
large areas in very hot countries where
constant supervision is a problem.

Then there are 'travelling sprinklers'
which are set to crawl along a hose pipe
laid around a garden. Again, these
need little supervision. You simply set
the revolving spray arms to move
along until they reach the end of the
pipe and turn off the water.

Irrigating pots, tubs and baskets in garden and greenhouse

Another very ingenious irrigation
system has been produced for watering
planters, window boxes and hanging
baskets. One might describe it as a
'spaghetti system'.

These planters dry out more quickly
than beds or borders. Hanging baskets
may need watering every day or even
twice a day in hot weather. They are
frequently difficult to reach with a can
or hose.

The system consists of a connector
with four outlets to which may be
affixed lengths of 10 mm (⅜ in) plastic
pipe. This pipe is taken around the
various planters, and at appropriate
points a hole is pierced in it to take a
very thin 'feeder hose'. One 'feeder
hose' might be sufficient for a basket or
tub; two may be needed for a long
window box or stone sink.

This system can also be used to water
rows of vegetables or fruit, and is
effective in watering sub-irrigation
benches or borders in a greenhouse, in
frames or under cloches.

Care of irrigation systems

Gone are the days when a plumber had
to be called in to lay galvanized iron
pipes two feet underground and make
lead joints to taps (all at vast expense).

Indeed, one of the big advantages of
plastic hose is that it does not have to
be buried deep in the soil to avoid
freezing. You can lay it on the soil or
decide, for aesthetic reasons, to bury it
an inch or two below the surface so that
it is out of sight. The water may still
freeze, of course, but the plastic will
expand and not burst. However, it
remains as important as ever that you
empty the system completely each
autumn.

Enclosures and screens

Boundary structures have a three-fold purpose – protection from the wind, rain and sun; concealing unwanted views and viewers; and providing a safe enclosure for children and pets.

Later the point is stressed that all garden structure materials should be compatible with each other and with your house. They can either harmonize with each other or serve to highlight the other materials in the homestead. There are two kinds of boundary structure – natural and artificial. These can be combined to make the most of their functional and aesthetic features. In this section, however, they are considered mainly from the functional point of view.

Artificial barriers
Walls
Boundary walls are usually free-standing and require less maintenance than fences or plant boundaries. They are, however, much more expensive.

They may be left bare, painted with light colours to brighten a sombre garden, or covered with climbing plants. There may, however, be local legal limits to the height of a wall and it is a good idea to get in touch with your local authority before building begins.

How effective walls are in protecting a garden from windy conditions depends upon **height** (the higher the wall, the greater distance leeward is the garden protected. Too high a wall will, however, cut out air circulation altogether and can encourage frost pockets), **solidity** (a solid wall causes increased wind speed around the ends, over the top, and eddies downwind, all of which may be destructive to plant life), and **position** in relation to prevailing wind direction, though its position will almost certainly be determined by the boundary limits of your garden.

Not only does an open wall structure minimize the first two of the problems described above, but if the open spaces are arranged imaginatively, they can add to the visual effect.

In cold or temperate climates, the sun is too rare a delight to be classed as a problem, but in hot climates how to create shade becomes an important consideration. Height, solidity and position of sun barriers remain the principal factors. Wherever you are, open structures or loose plant screens permit a pleasing, dappled effect of light and shade.

Fences
There are many different fence designs. The tall, tight, close-board type may be very useful for screening views and onlookers but, as with solid walls, they can cause havoc amongst plants if used as wind breaks. You can avoid this with an open pattern fence or one made out of mesh. If safety is the all-important factor, a loose structure may need to be covered with wire mesh, of which there are many different sorts – some coated with coloured plastic.

Both natural and artificial structures can of course be built within a garden to separate different areas. The essential principle when erecting a structure to screen a view is that the nearer it is to what is being screened, the higher it will have to be.

Natural barriers
Plant boundaries have the same disadvantages as solid walls when no care has been taken to choose plants loose enough to permit wind to filter through. Beware, too, of creating a dense wind break of trees whose foliage does not extend to the ground; this can result in a wind tunnel beneath the barrier. Also, a very dense plant barrier may be vulnerable to breakage by sudden, violent gusts of wind.

Sometimes gardeners steer clear of plants as barriers because they believe that they take too long to establish themselves. This of course depends on how urgent your need is. In favourable climates, larches will, in two years from kneecap height, be growing 50 cm (20 in) to 1 m (3 ft) a year as

Some of the many walling materials available
1. Building bricks laid in the 'Flemish bond' style.
2. Shaped concrete partitions make an attractive screen or barrier, and effectively disperse wind currents.
3. Reconstituted stone is light, fairly inexpensive and available cut-to-size.

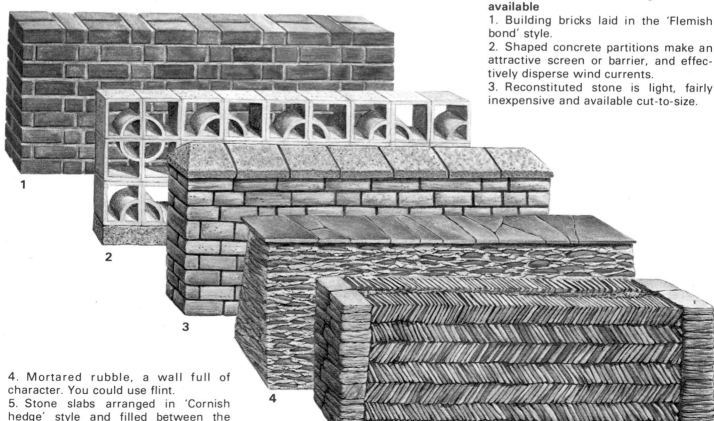

4. Mortared rubble, a wall full of character. You could use flint.
5. Stone slabs arranged in 'Cornish hedge' style and filled between the courses with soil and rubble.

sturdy, unstaked, well-branched trees. Sticks of white or crack willows pushed into the ground will, after one year cut back to a single shoot, grow at a similar rate, as will balsam poplars. Seedling birch, easily raised in quantity and planted out when 50 mm (2 in) to 10 cm (4 in) tall, will grow 1 m (3 ft) a year. The English holly, which makes an excellent boundary hedge, can be successfully planted when 1.5 m (5 ft) tall. In principle, though, for quick growth, you should not purchase well established plants. They are generally not easy to re-plant successfully and are more expensive. The quickest results are usually obtained from young plants. Finally, be wary of plants advertised as quick-growing solutions for the time-pressed gardener, plants which either continue growing at an alarming rate or burn themselves out.

If you live in an area where providing adequate shelter is a special problem – such as the Great Plains in North America – you could look to the following shelter belt trees: the box elder (*Acer negundo*) in its green-leaved type, Russian olive (*Elaeagnus angusti-folia*) with its grey-green leaves, the maple, *Acer ginnala*, and red ash, *Fraxinus pennsylvanica*. None is a very good tree in a benign climate, but they have an important place where growing conditions are wretched.

You might decide to double-plant a set of quick-growing plants together with your first choice, the former acting as protection for the latter. Indeed the trees mentioned above could all give rapid shelter, on a temporary basis, if scattered around edges and throughout in little groups. In their shelter, other plants will establish easily. Having done their job, the shelter trees can be cut down, except perhaps for a few good ones around the edge.

Alternatively, erect a structure – a fence perhaps, or screen of hessian or burlap – as a temporary windbreak until plants have had a chance to establish.

In selecting plants for a screen or as a permanent shelter, be aware of their habit, eventual growth rate and ultimate height. Plant boundaries should be set so that when fully grown they will not intrude upon your neigh-bour's property. Give a thought too to the vigorous root growth of some plants – the poplar mentioned above, for example – which will deprive nearby plants of vital sustenance. The privet (*Ligustrum ovalifolium*), too, has a greedy root system which may have something to do with its fall from popularity in England as the 'ideal' suburban boundary hedge.

A natural barrier changes constantly. Cutting back and pruning makes the difference between a formal and more liberated plant structure. For a spruce, formal effect you should look to a twiggy variety which is responsive to close clipping, like box (*Buxus sempervirens*) for example. Some plants, like privet and most hawthorns (*Crataegus spp*), respond to pruning at the appropriate times by becoming more dense and bushy. Others, like the yew (*Taxus spp*) and holly, do not. Maintenance therefore affects the growth pattern of hedges and it is up to you to choose how you want them to look, and clip or prune accordingly.

There is no one time to clip all hedges but it is generally best to wait until the new season's shoots are established, but before they become woody.

Grouping of plants to form a hedge

How close you group specimens together is another important consideration as it will affect the height of the eventual barrier. Some plants are more suitable for tall screens than others (see below). How easy it is to manipulate hedge height can be seen from a re-creation of the Elizabethian tradition of the knot garden with its low-lying hedges of the box cultivar 'Suffruticosa'. Such hedge plants would have to be planted 15 cm (6 in) apart to maintain their dwarf pro-portions – just right for weaving pat-terns out of flower beds.

Fence designs can also be idiosyncratic
1. Louvred timber.
2. Featherboard.
3. Woven.
4. Board-on-board.
All timber should be treated with preservative or painted with suitable 'outdoor' paint. Avoid anything harmful to plants.
The hedge (5.) is *Escallonia macrantha.*

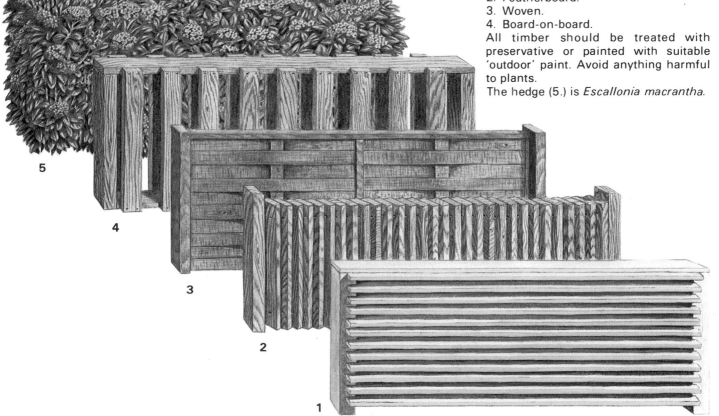

5

4

3

2

1

Enclosures and screens

Hedge plants for screens

Both evergreen and deciduous plants can be used. The former are generally more effective and should be selected when sheltering tender plants from sea winds or prevailing cold winds. However, the deciduous beech (*Fagus sylvatica*), which was suggested as a suitable plant for chalky gardens, is a joy throughout the year with its bright green spring foliage and an autumnal hue of reddish brown. Hornbeam (*Carpinus betulus*) has similar virtues and withstands hard winters better. Both are quick to grow and can provide tall screens for an overlooked garden. Another deciduous plant, hawthorn (*Crataegus monogyna*), provides an ideal nesting place for birds as its springtime, white-flower clusters give way in autumn to dark red haws.

The evergreen box (*Buxus sempervirens*) produces a tight, closely-knit hedge and makes a sound subject for topiary. The common hollies make good screens in a shady environment and have the additional advantage of being a deterrent for cats and other garden invaders. Privets grow dense foliage fast from cuttings. Particularly useful, in that it reacts well to most soils, is the yew (*Taxus baccata*). It makes a fine hedge but is slower growing than most. The cherry laurel (*Prunus laurocerasus*) produces a looser hedge with its large shiny leaves and can be raised to a height of 6 m (20 ft).

There is a variety of shrubs suitable for a more natural hedgerow; their forms do not lend themselves to close clipping, though periodical pruning without removing all their shoots will maximize their effect when flowering. Both the forsythia (*Forsythia* x *intermedia* 'Spectabilis') with its bright yellow flowers and, in mild areas, one of the thorny barberries (*Berberis* x *stenophylla*) with its arching yellow flowering stems make good informal hedgerows. They should be pruned when the flowering season has come to an end. *Berberis julianae* may be substituted in areas with moderately severe winters. The fuchsia hybrid 'Riccartonii' produces scarlet and violet blooms to make a very attractive hedge, though in areas of frost it will be impeded or killed. The evergreen *Rhododendron ponticum* is especially useful in certain problematic conditions, being shade-tolerant and preferring a bed of acid soil. It has a characteristically compact mauve flower. The plant can be raised from wild plants by seed.

Trees as screens

In most soils, the holm oak (*Quercus ilex*) is one of the most effective evergreen screen-makers, though rather dull and slow. The whole of

A bamboo hedge likes plenty of humus and the moist air of the seaside.

the splendid garden at Abbotsbury by England's Dorset coast nestles among holm oaks. On poor, sandy or rocky soils in mild climates, the Monterey cypress (*Cupressus macrocarpa*) is more bushy and dense, and is preferable when there is room for the depth of only one tree; in cold areas Japanese black pine (*Pinus thunbergii*) is a standard choice for such sites, especially along the coast. Pines need to be planted two or three deep to be as effective as the Monterey cypress.

In places with prevailing cold winds, the holm oak does well, but the Californian varieties are less reliable, and the Austrian pine (*Pinus nigra* var *nigra*) is best used on high-lying chalk or limestone soils. Inland, shelter can be given by yew (*Taxus baccata*), cherry laurel (*Prunus laurocerasus*), Lawson cypress (*Chamaecyparis lawsoniana*) or Leyland cypress (x *Cupressocyparis leylandii*). These, you will remember, can also be planted as relatively small clipped hedges. In particularly wretched climates, Lawson and Leyland cypress are frequently unsatisfactory and can be substituted with arbor-vitae (*Thuja occidentalis*), the white cedar.

In a small garden, the shelter belt may be one of the few spaces available for a large tree, so it is worth trying to include a variety of colour and form, best displayed in such evergreens as the Lawson cypress and the 'Castlewellan' and 'Robinson's Gold' varieties of Leyland cypress. In colder areas, gold-leafed junipers or colourful forms of *Chamaecyparis pisifera* (Sawara cypress) are sound choices.

Planting a tall screen

Apart from their effects on wind currents, solid walls of trees often appear too obvious as obstructions. Confronted by a blank wall – a vista abruptly curtailed – the eye may be offended, the mind questioning what exactly needs to be so well hidden. It is rare that an object is so unsightly that it cannot even be glimpsed between the trees. If you plant tall screen trees in distinct groups, not only will they grow better, but you are freer to choose a mixture of species of which some can be less resistant. Placing strong colours or forms on each side of any gap creates an eye-catcher and the filtered view of the object behind is actually distanced, the eye returning constantly to the trees. Placing trees in this way encourages a sense of space rather than one of being shut in.

For eye-catchers on a moderate scale, nothing is more effective than a mix of the bright gold and bright blue grey of a number of Lawson cypresses – 'Stewartii', 'Lutea', 'Lane's Golden' and 'Winston Churchill' among the gold forms,

'Penelope', a finely scented, vigorous hybrid musk.

and 'Triumph of Boskoop', 'Milford Blue Jacket', 'Columnaris' and the uniquely soft 'Pembury Blue' for the blues.

If something a little less dazzling is preferred, small uniform groups of narrowly upright green trees will do well - Dawyck beech, Cypress oak or Lawson 'Green Spire', or the incense cedar, *Calocedrus decurrens*.

Climbers and plants for wall and fence-work training
Some climbing plants adhere to structures by sucker pads or clinging root growths, and apart from trimming to limit their growth they need little artificial help. Others are really ramblers rather than climbers, and need to be trained to climb up a structure and must be provided with some form of support.

Support methods are various. Twining plants may be trained up a wall via vertical wires, though the most efficient method for vines and suchlike involves horizontal wires. These pass through metal 'eyes' implanted in the wall, ideally at construction stage, and are tightened at one end by a tensioning bolt. There are also ready-made fence-like trellis structures to attach to walls. Remember that the climbing plant is only as strong as the structure on which it is trained. Wire and plastic

survives better than wood. Avoid automatically covering the whole of a wall with plants unless it is an eyesore. Vines, for example, can very effectively be used as *tracings* against brick, stone or concrete. Consider planting fruit trees, fan-trained against a wall. They need a sunny aspect, but their 'silhouettes' add great interest to bare structures. See page 214, etc.

Roses
Just how evolution has shaped the habit of climbing plants is well illustrated by the rose. A climbing rose has long, fairly stiff shoots, which tend to grow upright. It learned this habit from competing in the wild with other vegetation in order to survive. Its constant objective is to lift its flowers high, upwards into the sunshine. Its shoots only needed to be fairly stiff because it used its competitors for support.

A completely different method was chosen by some other roses. These grew sideways, either along the ground or through other plants. They had no need for stiff shoots so, because their journey to the sunshine was likely to be a long one, their shoots became long and tenuous. They are usually known as ramblers, although 'trailers' is a more accurate descriptive term.

Understanding this basic difference is

a prerequisite of selecting a rose so that it will suit the function you want it to. There is one kind to look up at, and another to look down upon - one kind to lift up its arms on high, the other to tumble like a waterfall. And, nature being what she is, there are also intermediate varieties. Don't let them confuse you - look upon them as a bonus.

The obvious place for a climber is where it must lift its arms on high - probably a wall, either a tall boundary or the outside of a house. Few sights are more welcome in early summer than the first roses blooming high upon a warm wall. And they are as pleasing to a viewer inside the house as they are to the passing traveller. Of course, if you want them to be seen from far away, their flowers will need to be large. Climbing hybrid teas are ideal - not only the climbing forms of bush varieties, but other such as 'Compassion' and 'Mme Gregoire Staechelin'. There are others suitable types like 'Mermaid'. This is single, but highly effective with its amber yellow centre of stamens and stigmas amongst the characteristic wide, creamy, five-petalled blooms. For shorter walls, 'Aloha' is particularly good, and has been bred to match the large flowering variety.

Smaller flowering varieties, which grow in abundance, include 'Félicité et Perpétue' and 'Banksian Yellow', though the latter suffers from hard winters. Climbing floribundas, of which 'Clg Iceberg' is outstanding, are also candidates.

In choosing climbers, be aware that some varieties are reluctant to flower. This is where a reliable nurseryman, one's local rose society (or a national body), or friends who have solved similar problems can be of help. Never be concerned that blooms will clash with stonework since leaves tend to intervene between rose and wall, and they, not the masonry, are the foil.

Climbing roses can also make a living fence to order. But remember that they send out long and thorny shoots which can be a menace to neighbours. Tie these in carefully with durable twine, and make sure that the fence can withstand the weight of the rose.

A fence made of posts set in the ground joined by rails or wires, on which the climbers are tied as they grow, can be developed into elaborate structures such as pergolas. Whereas all climbers and trailers can be grown on a fence, trailers which tumble downwards are best selected for pergolas, arbours and arches.

Enclosures and screens

Don't be tempted to plant roses too close together or in three or four years you may find you have created a thorny jungle. Not only will your blood run cold at the thought of pruning, but wind may be a problem to the whole structure. Think of planting 3 m (10 ft) apart as a minimum (and more as a general rule) according to the vigour of the varieties.

A very effective screen can be made by erecting a series of solid posts, each planted with a trailing rose. Pruning is easy. Simply trim back the side shoots that flowered, renew the ties, and cut off anything which grows above each post beyond 60 cm (2 ft). Do not, however, cut off all the shoots which flowered. The posts could be linked into a chain by suspending ropes from one to the other and training the rose along the ropes.

Climbers can also be grown in clumps – a pleasing project for an informal garden. Plant three to five fairly close together, using short posts for support during their first few years. By then they will have formed the sort of thicket their wild ancestors knew, their shoots providing mutual support. Choose one variety only for a clump, one that makes plenty of basal growths and is fragrant. 'New Dawn' is a worthy contender. Restrict pruning so as not to reduce the plant's support.

There are also climbers which attain an enormous height whose habit is to form a loose mound and shoot up into the branches of a nearby tree. Growing through the tree, they flower in a great cascade of white petals. The best

'Climbing Korona'
Rosa longicuspis

known and most vigorous, of these is *R. filipes* 'Kiftsgate'. *R. longicuspis* and *R. helenae* are also suitable. Plant them well away from the trunk under some low lying branches. They will flower most on the sunny side and least in the shade, and may require extra watering if raised in the dry shade of a tree.

R. filipes 'Kiftsgate' and *R.* 'Félicité et Perpétue' will cover a tree.

Other plants for structures

Among the many other plants suitable for clothing screens or boundary structures is the popular genus *Clematis*. There are spring flowering, summer flowering and late summer species. *C. montana* with white flowers, 'Nelly Moser' with mauve-pink flowers, 'The President' in deep violet, and the bright carmine-red 'Ville de Lyon' provide superb displays in succession through this period, and with *C. cirrhosa* and *C. cirrhosa balearica* flowering with off-white and greenish-yellow blooms respectively, between late winter and spring, the genus virtually survives the four seasons.

Clematis

Clematis have tendrils that cling to frames. Their root systems prefer cool shade and plenty of water, their flowers, sun. It may therefore be necessary to improvise shade to cater for these needs.

Wisteria

A fast-growing twining plant which can produce magnificent blooms in late spring and early summer provided you do not buy a seedling. A plant growing from seed could take many years to flower, so buy a grafted plant, and be sure to prune correctly. During the summer cut back all laterally growing shoots to within 30 cm (1ft) in length. Then in winter cut back further to within 25 mm (1 in) of the old wood, leaving spur shoots for future flowering. *Wisteria sinensis* has a marvellous scent and, typically, is mauve in colour. If you prefer a white variety seek out *W. sinensis* 'Alba', or the Japanese variety *W. floribunda* 'Alba' whose white blossom is offset by copper-tinted foliage.

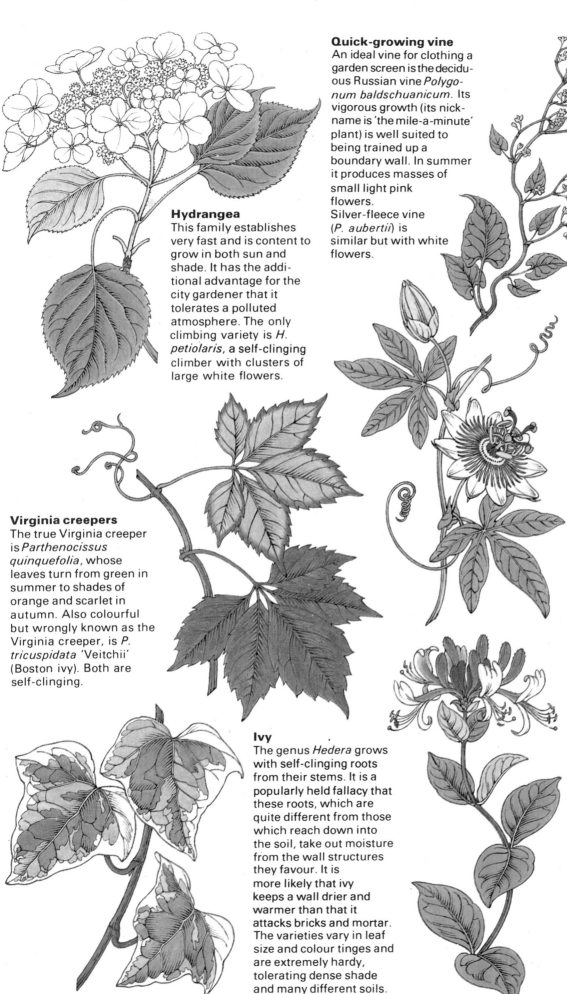

Quick-growing vine
An ideal vine for clothing a garden screen is the deciduous Russian vine *Polygonum baldschuanicum*. Its vigorous growth (its nickname is 'the mile-a-minute' plant) is well suited to being trained up a boundary wall. In summer it produces masses of small light pink flowers.
Silver-fleece vine (*P. aubertii*) is similar but with white flowers.

Hydrangea
This family establishes very fast and is content to grow in both sun and shade. It has the additional advantage for the city gardener that it tolerates a polluted atmosphere. The only climbing variety is *H. petiolaris*, a self-clinging climber with clusters of large white flowers.

The Passion flower
Blooming from early summer to autumn, its name is derived from its flowers supposed representation of the instruments used in Christ's Passion – the crown of thorns (the stamens and pistils of its central corona) and the ten apostles (the corona is surrounded by five blue-white sepals and five petals). The association between the flower and Christ's Passion was first made by Spanish priests in the flower's native Brazil. It clings by means of tendrils and thus needs a supporting structure on which to grow. It is, however, quite tender and is successful only in warmer parts.

Virginia creepers
The true Virginia creeper is *Parthenocissus quinquefolia*, whose leaves turn from green in summer to shades of orange and scarlet in autumn. Also colourful but wrongly known as the Virginia creeper, is *P. tricuspidata* 'Veitchii' (Boston ivy). Both are self-clinging.

Ivy
The genus *Hedera* grows with self-clinging roots from their stems. It is a popularly held fallacy that these roots, which are quite different from those which reach down into the soil, take out moisture from the wall structures they favour. It is more likely that ivy keeps a wall drier and warmer than that it attacks bricks and mortar. The varieties vary in leaf size and colour tinges and are extremely hardy, tolerating dense shade and many different soils.

Honeysuckle
This twines rather than clings and is often the first choice for clothing structures because of its free-flowering nature and fragrance (though not all honeysuckles are scented). The fragrant *Lonicera periclymenum* has two varieties 'Belgica', an early summer flowering bushy form often stocked by nurseries, and 'Serotina', which blooms from summer until autumn. One species, *L. japonica*, is a bad weed in the American South but is sometimes grown in cool-climate gardens and in California, where it is better behaved. Also recommended is *L. sempervirens*, though it and its hybrid 'Heckrottii' are slightly tender.

45

Structural planning

The second question to consider (after 'What sort of garden do you have?') is 'What sort of garden do you want?' It is essential to draw some sort of plan, however rough. You cannot hope to come up with all the answers while standing in your garden, and what better pastime to wile away the evening hours than developing your ideas on paper.

This section considers the skeleton of a garden's design. Wherever one sees outstanding plant displays there are structures which underlie and enhance them. Very often they perform important functions too. But though practical considerations – such as the position of a sitting area in relation to the sun – are vital, an awareness of the texture, colour and other qualities of man-made materials, including their compatibility with one another, are also essential ingredients of a successful design.

Later, in Part IV, ways of clothing this skeleton are discussed. In practice these two elements of garden planning are not so distinctly separate because trees and shrubs can be used as backbone elements as much as walls, raised beds, trellises, pools, decks, etc. But here we are only concerned with the *shape* of a plan – a tree might be suggested as a means to mask a view, for example, but it is left until Part IV to suggest which tree will perform the function most effectively.

From basic layout to making landscape changes, considering ideas for containing space to best advantage, creating visual illusions in difficult situations, selecting materials for structures, and more technical information about how to build walls and erect fences, Part II introduces the reader to the principles of garden design and how, in structural terms, to put those principles into practice.

Planning strategy

Starting points

There is no reason why you should be limited by the mistakes of the garden's previous owner. Equally, before discarding even the worst-laid plans, consider what it is that you don't like and why. Doing so may suggest ways in which some aspect of the existing plan can be turned to your advantage, and could save you a great deal of unnecessary work.

Visibility

Are there trees which seriously affect visibility hide an attractive skyline, perhaps, which could become part of the garden view if they were taken down, merely trimmed or pruned? Is there a tree which has been planted too near the house for its size? How much more acceptable would these and other eye-catchers be if they were part of a different surrounding plan?

Boundaries

You may be faced with rigid, sombre hedges around the garden, or parts of it, that darken the atmosphere. Quite apart from their maintenance, clipping and pruning – an important consideration – are you really happy with them? Would they better suit your ideas if they were allowed to grow into a looser form? Or should they be taken out altogether and replaced with others that would relieve the gloom?

Use of space

How well has your predecessor made use of the space available? Is there a simple visual image, or one that is confused by too many elements in one place? How does his layout improve or emphasize the worst aspects of the garden's dimensions? Has he attempted to deceive the eye with successful visual illusions, or has his plan compounded existing environmental problems? Has he devalued the central focal point by drawing attention away from it? Are you happy with structures such as paths and steps which link one space with the next? What of the materials he has used? Are they too formal or too rustic, compatible with the house and one another, in unhappy contrast, or simply dull?

Plants

What thought has he given to the more aesthetic characteristics of plants? Later, in Part IV, these are discussed fully. Is there harmony of colour or is there violent contrast, and where is it? What seasons of the year has the garden been planned for? Can a few more well-chosen plants stretch its appeal through the bleakest times of the year? The seasons bring about a host of textural and colour transitions in plants. Textural contrast between plants, leaves in particular, provide

subtle variations which add to a garden's overall effect. Is there sufficient interplay between plant textures to hold interest without disturbing the perspective you want? Are there contrasts of light and shade in the colour tone of leaves?

Scale

Very important is the question of scale and balance. Is one area of the garden disproportionately large, out of scale with the rest, visually unsatisfactory? Is the balance of plants and beds too formal for you? Can you add a plant here or there to create a more asymmetric feel, a more informal design?

All the time you are thinking about what is there and the effects which the existing plan create, bear in mind practical considerations. Make a detailed list of special requirements. What will the garden path be used for, for example? Does it need to be wide enough to take a pram? Perhaps you need to be more aware than the previous owner of the safety hazards of a flight of steps.

If you can identify what you dislike or what does not satisfy the special requirements of local climate and your needs, it is straightforward. If you cannot put your finger on what seems out of balance, then time will tell.

Drawing a rough plan

It will be of enormous help if you can prepare a rough plan of what you think you want in your garden. Start by measuring your property. The entrance should be marked on the drawing, as should any garage doors, back doors, front doors, garden gates, french windows, even the important windows from which the garden can be seen.

If you can, take photographs of the garden from the doorway and other important viewpoints. Further photographs should be taken in the garden looking back at the house. All these will help you pinpoint any particular detail you want to preserve. Register such points of interest on your drawing.

The law

The two most basic considerations are the height of boundary walls and fences (which should be checked locally as laws vary considerably), and compensation for injury in the garden. Every home insurance policy should include a provision for this.

There are a number of other important considerations which come under three main headings.

The effect of plants
Damage to neighbouring property
Land drainage

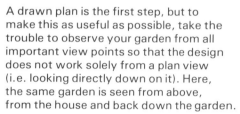

A drawn plan is the first step, but to make this as useful as possible, take the trouble to observe your garden from all important view points so that the design does not work solely from a plan view (i.e. looking directly down on it). Here, the same garden is seen from above, from the house and back down the garden.

If you want to remove or heavily prune large trees in your garden, make sure you discuss the matter first with local government officials. In Britain, within conservation areas, no trees whatever may be removed or pruned.

Neighbours are allowed to prune back to their boundary any trees which overhang their properties, provided they do not make the trees unsafe. If your neighbour cuts overhanging fruit or flowers, these must be returned to you. If you build a garage over roots from your neighbour's tree (even after cutting the original roots away) and its walls subsequently crack, your neighbour is not necessarily liable.

At no time during the construction of your garden can you damage or alter the state of your neighbour's garden without his consent. Should damage occur you will be liable. Even if a contractor is called in to do the construction work for you, you are still liable for any damage he does. It is, therefore, best to have a legal agreement with your contractor which will probably involve his being insured against such actions and those brought against you in the event of damage to service lines such as water, gas, telephone, electricity or drainage systems.

During excavation works, it is likely

In gardens with limited ground area use the vertical dimension as much as possible and keep focal points clearly visible from the house. Scented plants around seating areas are recommended.

that surplus materials will have to be carted away. Anything, including soil, which falls and is left on the public highway becomes your responsibility and you are liable. Again, make sure that it is the contractor's responsibility, and in his contract, to clear the highway when this happens.

If you are unsure whether your contractor can undertake the expenditure of your work before you pay him, ask him to arrange a bond with his bank. Keep it until he completes the work, and the guarantee period ends. This will cost you extra, but may well be worth the peace of mind. Additionally, never be afraid to ask to see your contractor's insurance policy covering him for damage caused.

Guarantees can also be given when plants are supplied and planted by a contractor. The usual periods are twelve months for shrubs and other plants, as well as standard nursery stock trees. If you plant advanced nursery stock trees the guarantee period can extend to twenty-four months, but there may be a proviso for the contractor to maintain the plants during this period and this will cost extra.

Water from your land may not drain on to the public highway or on to your neighbour's property, unless provisions have been made. All your works should drain on to your land or into the drains on your property.

Finally, when you sell your property, the question often arises as to whether you can take some of your plants with you. Because by doing so you are effectively changing the property you are selling, private agreements should first be reached.

Planning strategy

Drawing your plan on graph paper

Having done the basic recording, you can either proceed directly to planning, using your rough sketch as your base, or you can prepare a drawing to scale. This is a drawing which is representative of a unit of measurement on the ground. In imperial terms, the representative scale could be 1 in = 4 ft on the ground, and in metric this would become a scale of 1 cm = 50 cm on the ground. Using the scale does give you the opportunity of planning very accurately, and is much more useful than a rough plan. If you decide to do it, use squared paper that suits the scale you are working in.

The changes in level can be worked out too, fairly simply. In Britain the standard difference between the floor of the house and the outside pavings is 150 mm (6 in). Each step in the garden usually has the same height, so one measurement only is needed there. Heights of brick walls can be calculated by counting the number of brick rows, usually laid 75 mm (3 in) deep. But remember that the top row will be 115 mm (4½ in) if the coping on the top of the wall is brick-on-edge. Falls across pavings to help surface drainage are usually between 1 in 100 and 1 in 50, in simple terms.

Once you have these dimensions and your rough scale drawing, you can start preparing your ideas on tracing paper. All this work should be done in pencil, H or HB, for easy erasing. If you have the time, it is a good idea to allow a whole month for this, so that you can re-examine your ideas weekly. You will be surprised how your ideas will change. But after a while you will settle on those that are particularly suitable. This is the moment to start preparing your final drawing.

It is possible to design your garden directly from photographs, but there is one important drawback. Photographs are only really suitable for vertical elements, unless you can take photographs from high up. Otherwise, you cannot get a real feel for the space between you and, say, the end of the garden. You can, by following the rules of perspective drawing, get an approximate estimate of its length, but generally this is very difficult.

Equally, drawing curved paths on paper distorts reality. A drawn plan portrays a path as if viewed from a point high above the garden. In reality you see it only from eye level.

Adding colour to the final drawing you have made helps distinguish one surface from another – even subtle

At the ideas stage, go at least as far as a roughly drawn plan. Initially, you may produce sketches that don't please you; retain them, they could be useful later. If you draw to scale, the next stage – transferring your ideas to the garden – is made much easier.

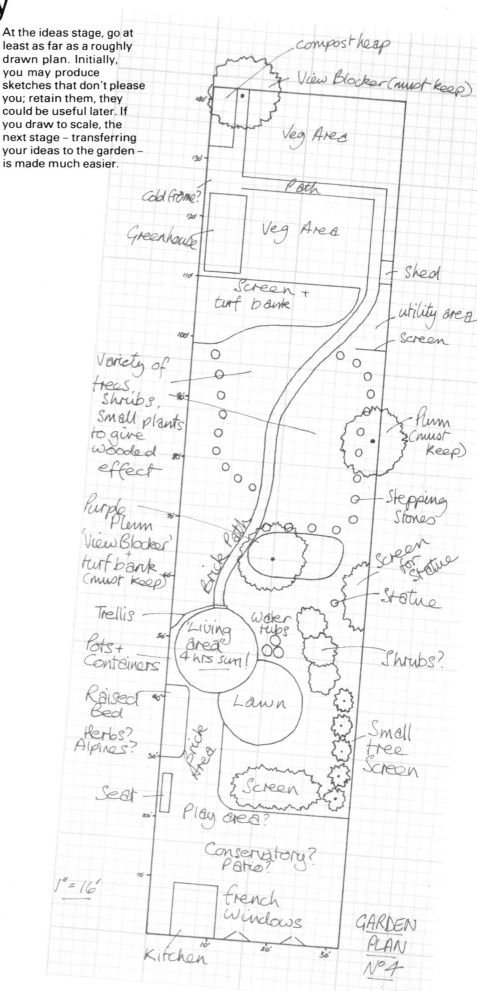

changes will help you establish variations in height. This can be one of the most pleasant of all the design exercises – trying to make your plan stand out in the third dimension.

Budgeting
Having arrived at a scale plan which satisfies you, make up a detailed budget. Calculate what capital expenditure the plan involves and also what its ramifications are in terms of running costs.

Preparatory works
Preparatory works should be carried out in the following order:

Creating an effective garden enclosure.

Deciding which elements of value should be preserved in the garden.

Clearing all those elements (including plants, surfaces and structures) that have no place in your plan.

Removing and stacking topsoil from areas due for excavation.

Once you have enclosed your garden (pages 40 to 45) the next step is to see what can be retained, and what you want to move. Trees, provided they are not too close to the house, or in need of extensive surgery, should always be saved if at all possible. If plants are to be kept they should only be moved in the autumn, in England. In America, depending on climate, they may be moved in spring or autumn, though in the coldest areas replanting in spring is desirable.

Clearance of the garden, if this is your intention, should come next, whether a small area of paving is to be taken up or the whole garden is to be cleared. All vegetable matter that can be composted should be. Burn what you can of what is left and spread the ashes over the planting beds and dig in. To save money, as little material as possible should be carted away.

The demolition of structures and pavings may leave you with lots of surplus material. In a big garden you can dispose of this either under banks you are about to construct, or for use under new footpaths or under new terraces. Break it down into small pieces – say 100 mm (4 in) × 150 mm (6 in) and compact it into position. Bricks and stones are particularly useful (if they cannot be used again) as they compact well and break down further only slowly with time.

Should clearance of the garden involve the lowering of ground levels, and a resultant surplus of topsoil and subsoil, preserve the topsoil. The subsoil could

be used in new banks, under new structures that can withstand settlement, or, provided nutrients are added, it could be included in the compost heap. As an example of the amount of soil you will need to shift in order to lower levels by 150 mm (6 in) over a 6 m × 6 m (20 ft × 20 ft) area, you first have to remove say 100 mm (4 in) topsoil or 3.6 cu m (132 cu ft) and then 150 mm (6 in) subsoil or 5.4 cu m (200 cu ft). Finally, you will have to replace the 3.6 cu m (132 cu ft) of topsoil. You will then have moved 12.6 cu m (464 cu ft) of soil. To do this will take you a minimum of thirteen hours! Obviously, the key to this is to move no more soil than is necessary or use a contractor.

If your budget is limited (and whose isn't?) you may have to be prepared to phase your work over more than one season, especially the construction work.

Specialized works
Specialized works should be staged as follows:

Alteration of land form.

Excavation to foundation levels for walls, paths, steps, etc., excavation for drains, irrigation lines, lighting cables, etc.

Construction of actual structures. Walls are usually built before pavings so that surfaces can be tightly butted up against them.

Once the garden levels have been completed, prepare the ground for planting. This will involve breaking up soil which has been compacted during heavy construction works, spreading the topsoil over areas for grass seeding or planting, feeding the soil, and finally setting out the plants.

Planning strategy

Action hints for preparatory and specialized works

Preparatory works

* The preservation of elements of value, such as pavings, should be decided by their appearance and physical quality as well as their suitability. If a surface is very badly damaged it may be simpler to replace it altogether. On the other hand it may be cheaper to cut out only the damaged areas and replace them with new materials. You could stop and ask yourself whether introducing planting pockets might be better than replacing the paving. If a brick wall is no longer upright, it may be unstable and have to be replaced. But if the bows and bends are not too serious, consider adding an extra buttress – it may save you a lot of money. Do check though that the foundations are sound. If they are not, adding a buttress could be a false economy.

* Painted boundary surfaces will have to be regularly maintained. Never use poor quality paint, for when it ages, the surface may be difficult to clean and repaint. Always repaint before there is too much deterioration.

* If you wish to preserve any trees, check whether there is any damage, holes or depressions in the crown or in the branch crutches. Has the bark been damaged in any way? If it has, cut away all the damaged material and, if you wish, paint with a tree wound paint, like Arbrex 805. Do not in any circumstances use an oil-based paint for this will cause further damage.

* The only general guideline about retaining shrubs is to see whether the specimen is still growing actively – whether you can see any growth from the previous year, or whether it looks old and has a lot of dead wood.

* During land clearance, the secret is to take away as little as possible and, if you can, use what you clear in your garden. Topsoil should be carefully stored in heaps not higher than 90 cm (3 ft) and if left for twelve months should be turned over once every three months to help preserve its structure. If left for a long time, fertilizers should be added once a year and turned in. Composts and manures should be added when the topsoil is spread.

If you have to clear pavings and walls, can the stone be used elsewhere? If you want to have a new path leading down to an orchard, say, these materials are ideal for providing a firm base. A heavy garden roller should suffice to get a good flat surface. The decision whether to keep or store subsoil will depend on its qual-

ity. If your garden is on clay or chalk and the quantities are considerable, then you would be best advised to get rid of the surplus amounts.

Specialized construction works

* When soil is excavated for irrigation lines etc., it increases in volume. Put it all back and leave a slight mound over the excavation, for over the years this will settle. If you have to take up turf and intend replacing it, do compact the soil and fill carefully as you return it into the trench. Also, cut neat sods, for these will mend more speedily than ragged-edged ones.

* Trenches opened for foundations need care. If the sides are not naturally strong they will need strutting with boards to prevent a cave-in. Water can accumulate in the bottom of trenches and if a concrete foundation is to be laid the water will have to be pumped out. To minimize this problem, protect trenches from rain with covers.

* Trenches that cut across tree roots cause great damage to tree growth and affect stability. If possible direct the trench along the line of the canopy of the trees (the outer line of the spread of its branches) or burrow under the tree roots. At no time should the feeder or main roots of the tree be severed.

* Before excavating, check with your local authority where water, gas, electricity, foul drainage or telephone lines come into your property. Should they be cut, it could cost you a great deal to put them right. If using a contractor, make sure he has insured himself against this happening.

* Where ground modelling or mounding is proposed, watch out for drainage problems and make sure water does not flow off a mound into your neighbour's garden. Rain falling on to a mound will flow downwards to find the lowest level. If you have a hollow in your garden the water can collect there. If this is a lawn, a pond could develop during the winter. Any water lying about for a long time will eventually kill or damage the lawn. To reduce the chance of this happening, consider excavating a french drain at a point where the mound slope meets the flat lawn. A french drain is no more than a small ditch, up to 90 cm (3 ft) deep and 30 cm–38 cm (12 in–15 in) wide at the top. All the subsoil and topsoil is removed, and coarse gravel of 50 mm (2 in) diameter is placed in the ditch to the full depth. Turf can be placed over 150 mm (6 in) of topsoil above the drain though this will impede the rapid dispersal of water, but this may not matter if heavy rains are not expected.

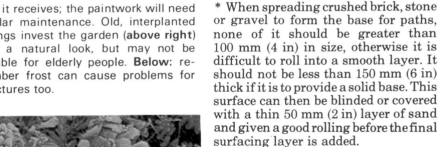

The planning of the garden pictured on page 52 and above left is described in detail on page 122. Here, 'before' and 'after' pictures show the care with which plants and structures were planned. **Top right:** a basement, courtyard garden has been painted white to reflect what little light it receives; the paintwork will need regular maintenance. Old, interplanted pavings invest the garden (**above right**) with a natural look, but may not be suitable for elderly people. **Below:** remember frost can cause problems for structures too.

* When spreading crushed brick, stone or gravel to form the base for paths, none of it should be greater than 100 mm (4 in) in size, otherwise it is difficult to roll into a smooth layer. It should not be less than 150 mm (6 in) thick if it is to provide a solid base. This surface can then be blinded or covered with a thin 50 mm (2 in) layer of sand and given a good rolling before the final surfacing layer is added.

* Always consider the effect of weather on any feature you build. It is a help to know from which direction the prevailing winds blow, as they can affect the comfort of a sitting area, for instance. By following the sun's movement during the day, you can identify where the hottest points in the garden are, and the coolest, where perhaps the sun never penetrates. As we have seen, frost pockets can develop at low points on sloping land if no gap has been left for it to drain away. Consequently, avoid siting any special features that will impede the flow of air.

* The quality of the soil can sometimes affect the choice of building products. Cement for mortar for walls is usually a standard product, but for foundations where the soil has sulphates in it, a sulphate-resistant cement should be selected.

Changing the landscape

Your garden is not an isolated unit, but part of a wider landscape, and when considering altering land form it is important to remember that. If your house is situated at the bottom of a slope, or worse still from a drainage point of view, in a dip, there are strong arguments for levelling the ground as shown in the illustrations. This will prevent rain water running off higher levels and accumulating in the house foundations. If your house is situated on the bank of a slope, as is more usually the case, and the garden runs away from the house and down the slope, levelling is probably only necessary behind the house. You may

even need a fairly sophisticated drainage system that will divert water around the building. How important these considerations are, will of course depend upon the likelihood of flooding in your area and the height of the water table. If a garden slopes very steeply, then 'land creep' may become a serious additional problem. 'Land creep' refers to the fall of earth due to erosion by water. A series of retained terraced levels is an answer, which could be attractively connected by steps. All retaining walls must allow for adequate drainage of the soil that remains.

Cutting and filling for slopes and tilts

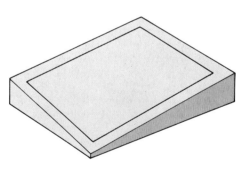

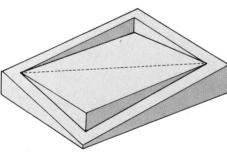

Newly terraced slope

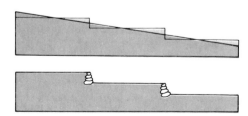

A less drastic solution on a gently sloping plant bed is to lay it with peat which gives it added stability.

'Cut and fill'
This is the usual method employed to level ground. It involves cutting into a slope, moving the topsoil to the bottom of the garden (ensuring that you do not

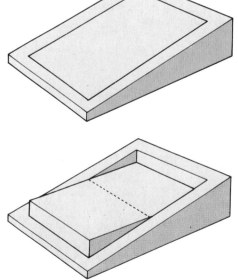

Having removed the topsoil and stacked it to one side, excavate a wedge-shaped section of soil from the upper part of the slope and use this to build up the lower section. When the subsoil has been levelled, replace the topsoil.

Use a similar technique to level sites sloping diagonally through the garden. Whatever slope is being 'corrected', some sort of retaining wall must be built to compensate for the landscape change. See page 68.

build very high piles of earth and run the risk of compacting it and destroying its valuable structure), levelling the subsoil, and replacing the topsoil on the level surface. The advantage of 'cutting and filling' is that you don't have a problem of what to do with surplus soil. Of course it is not always desirable to level the surface of a garden. If the slope is not very steep, you may well enjoy the effect of sloping or even undulating ground. The important principle is to examine land form critically and make a decision early in your garden plan.

Variety is a significant aspect of small as well as large gardens, and making changes in surface levels is one way of establishing interest at the most basic stage of a plan.

Tilts
Where a house is set at right-angles to the slope of the land there may be special problems.

Usually the tilt will be gentle. Should the garden come right up to the house and not be separated from it by a patio, cutting and filling to balance a serious tilt across the house face could weaken the house foundation. The illustration below shows an actual garden that was terraced near the house to form a patio. The gardener also wanted to correct a tilt running from west to east across the garden and he used some of the surplus earth from the terrace excavation. He then built a low retaining wall to prevent 'land creep'

into the next-door garden. The tilt is still present in the middle section and lower vegetable garden, but is not visible from the house because the raised rose bed neatly interrupts the sight line down the garden. Once in the middle section the tilt becomes an attraction in itself running away from the ornamental pond.

The owner of the garden makes a heartfelt plea to others with similar problems to consider the practicalities of doing such a job themselves. Although he is well satisfied, he doubts that he'd attempt the task again. If you choose to bring in outside contractors for any major work, shop around and cost the programme with care.

Restructuring land form in a suburban garden
A tilt running west-east across the garden has been eased by building up the lower section with soil, excavated in the course of terracing the upper garden. A retaining wall has been built at the east boundary to prevent 'land creep' into the neighbour's garden.

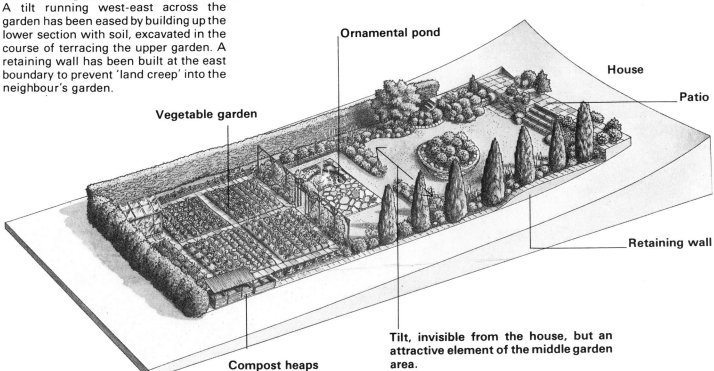

Ornamental pond

House

Patio

Vegetable garden

Retaining wall

Compost heaps

Tilt, invisible from the house, but an attractive element of the middle garden area.

Planning ideas

Any corner of your garden can accommodate one of a number of different scenes. Those illustrated on this page are mainly decorative; the scenes featured on the facing page are mainly functional. Your first priority should be to decide how your garden, or parts of it, will serve you and your family best. Once that is settled, specific ideas will begin to emerge. Limits will be set upon the very wide choice of possible features.

It is also a good idea to make a realistic assessment of the scale of activity with which you, as a gardener, want to be involved. Do you want a garden that needs year-round maintenance, or are you strictly a weekend gardener?

A preponderance of hard surfaces, container plantings and limited bed space planted with ground-hugging shrubs to keep down weeds would suit the latter, but be anathema to the gardener who is looking for a natural haven of tranquillity far removed from the pressures of modern-day life.

Making each idea a part of the whole design

Perhaps you will settle for some elements of each. How much space there is, and your ability to harmonize distinctive styles, will determine the success of that plan. A kick-about area is as much an integral part of the design as a well-stocked herbaceous border, a hard-surfaced barbecue site, a scent or rock garden, or a vegetable patch, but it is not enough to throw all or some of these together without a thought about how each will interact.

Environmental conditions

As with choosing plants, environmental conditions play a role in the decision-making process.

Already we have seen how the form of enclosures is partly determined by prevailing climatic conditions. More obviously, climate has an active role to

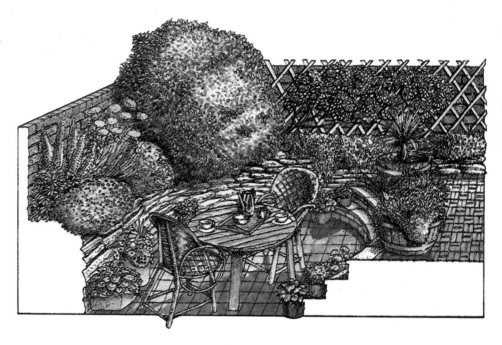

Decorative features
Top shows an ideally sheltered position for a sitting area, but how many hours of sun will it get? Note interest created by paving, wall and raised bed materials, and plant contrasts of 'spikes' and 'domes'.

Centre: Note lack of steps, more suitable for old or disabled.

Bottom: Wall bricks obscured to help natural look of rock garden.

play in the type of structure that you might select as a focal point of interest in the garden. The 'outside' room' in the illustration top left is a clear choice for a mild climate, mainly decorative garden – though in a very hot climate, in a bid for shade, a tree of suitable form could be substituted for the corner shrub.

There too, gardeners might choose an ornamental fountain, a miniature waterfall in a green-leaved grotto or cascading through a rock bed of delicate alpine plants (as illustrated bottom left). The sound of babbling water, the cool greens of many shrubs, grasses and other perennials, and cool bluish-tinged flower colours all help to create a desirable antidote to strong summer heat. Whereas bright red flowers and light-reflecting structural materials will enhance a less luminous place.

Practicalities

Think carefully about who, besides yourself, will be using the garden. For elderly, infirm or disabled people you will want to provide easily negotiable surfaces – no steps, no paths interplanted with fleshy-leaved specimens, no poorly drained surfaces which will freeze over in winter. Thorny plants offering long waving branches would also be inappropriate. Raised beds, raised planters (tubs, sinks, pots, etc.), wide paths, even height adjustable bird tables could be incorporated for the disabled.

Again, what sense is there in planting delicate flowers near a children's play area? Safety is once more a significant factor in planning a garden where children will play. Railings or balustrades will be needed for steps, for example. An imaginative plan to tuck a water garden behind an old stone wall, bedecked with flowering trailers may make an appealing surprise 'discovery', but no mother of small children would relish the responsibility.

Functional features
Top: Plants serve to soften utilitarian elements.

Centre: Construction provides climbing frame, 'house', and box for outdoor toys. Rounded corners and sandpit are useful safety factors. But how easy will it be to cut the lawn to its edge?

Bottom: Accessibility essential in vegetable gardening. Are the paths sufficient?

Creating illusions

Creating a composite garden

In a fairly large garden you have the opportunity to create a number of different scenes. A barbecue, a play area, a vegetable garden, an orchard, an area where you can sit and relax – whatever you choose. In planning them, it is generally useful to start with the house as the main focal point of the garden. Once you accept this, the plan is already underway. Near the house you can heighten interest and attempt to integrate the two with climbing plants, pots and tubs set on a forecourt or patio, or a conservatory perhaps. See page 200.

Making the most of garden space

If you introduce a hard-surfaced patio area make sure that it is large enough. A common error is to design garden structures on a smaller scale than is useful or suitable for the 'open plan' nature of an outdoor garden.

Having planned this link area between house and garden, the next step is to consider how the remaining ideas you have can be allocated to other areas of the garden.

Ideas for long gardens

Beyond the patio, if that is what you have chosen, one idea is to plan a vista which gives a sense of space when looking from the house. How you proceed will depend upon the shape and space of the garden. If you are fortunate in owning a very long garden, its length can be effectively

Start with a 'link' between house and garden.

split into two or three significant areas, though care is needed to ensure that each area arises naturally from the next. You could, for example, plan two large areas at either end of the garden with a small contrasting secret garden in between. This would have an additional advantage of retaining a spacious area in front of the house.

One very successful solution for a long town garden is illustrated here. The far end is used for a vegetable garden; the area near the house provides a children's play area and 'outside living room'; and the central area is a garden of flowers, plants and

trees in which great thought has been given to colour harmony, interest through the year, and the effective arrangement of all the plants in terms of their varying characteristics. The areas are connected by a winding path which complements the curved shape of all the plant beds. The 'living' area is separated from the middle area by the intrusive contour of a plant bed and a purple-leaved decorative plum tree set to tease the eye into exploring the delights which lie beyond. The vegetable garden is more definitely divided from the rest of the garden, though trellis and climbing plants leave no doubt that something lies beyond.

The principle of blocking views in a long town garden

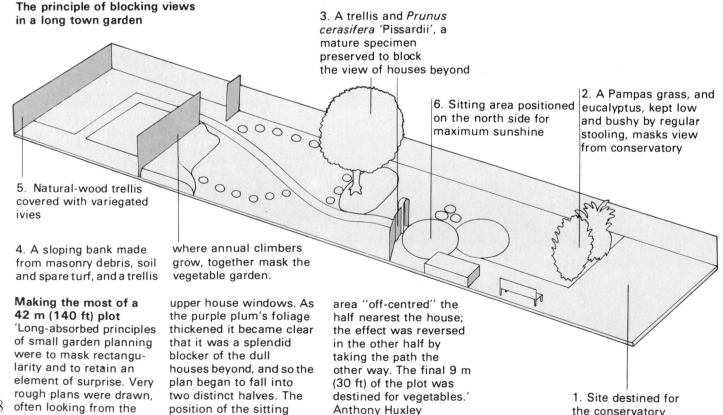

3. A trellis and *Prunus cerasifera* 'Pissardii', a mature specimen preserved to block the view of houses beyond

6. Sitting area positioned on the north side for maximum sunshine

2. A Pampas grass, and eucalyptus, kept low and bushy by regular stooling, masks view from conservatory

5. Natural-wood trellis covered with variegated ivies

4. A sloping bank made from masonry debris, soil and spare turf, and a trellis where annual climbers grow, together mask the vegetable garden.

1. Site destined for the conservatory

Making the most of a 42 m (140 ft) plot

'Long-absorbed principles of small garden planning were to mask rectangularity and to retain an element of surprise. Very rough plans were drawn, often looking from the upper house windows. As the purple plum's foliage thickened it became clear that it was a splendid blocker of the dull houses beyond, and so the plan began to fall into two distinct halves. The position of the sitting area "off-centred" the half nearest the house; the effect was reversed in the other half by taking the path the other way. The final 9 m (30 ft) of the plot was destined for vegetables.'
Anthony Huxley

Ideas for narrow gardens

Very narrow gardens belonging to town houses are generally best with one central garden area only. Indeed the narrower the garden, the more control is needed over the number of effects to be included. Overfilling a narrow space with features or objects can produce a closed, claustrophobic effect. Also, avoid splitting such a garden down its length into two equal halves. It will only emphasize its narrow limits. If you want to lay the garden surface with a hard floor, consider using bricks arranged in a

series of adjoining circular patterns. They will appear to increase its width, particularly if adjacent plant beds reflect the shape round the side areas of the circles' circumferences as shown in the illustration. Whatever you decide about its surface, curved beds intruding towards the centre of the garden help avoid a tunnel effect. Another way to relieve the tunnel image of a long narrow garden is to plant a tree say half way down one side so that it spreads over the sight line down the garden and catches the eye before reaching the far boundary.

Long, narrow gardens

A long, narrow site can seem like a tunnel if very formally arranged – the eye is pulled through it to the far boundary, passing any cold, narrow side beds with little interest. To avoid this, use curving, irregular shapes to disturb the eye's path and suggest that there are some surprises in store.
Top: a tree interrupts the sight line; a winding path suggests 'discovery'.
Middle: Assymetrically intrusive beds appear to broaden the site and interrupt the eye. **Bottom:** a circular theme adds width, but fails to overcome the tunnel effect.

Ideas for small gardens

Common problems in a small garden include the overbearing impact of the house (the feeling that it is always staring down at you), walls which cast dark shade and inhibit plant growth, soil which is too poor to sustain plant life, and overcrowding. Most of these problems are analyzed later. In terms of garden construction, three points could be considered:

1. Make the ground surface as useful as possible. In a restricted space the constant passage of feet can destroy a lawn. Choose a suitably hard wearing type of grass (see **The Lawn**) or a hard surface. If you choose to lay a hard surface be sure to select a practical and fairly unobtrusive material. Over-decorative effects can look very self-conscious in a small space.

2. Consider creating one focal point to lure the eye away from the garden's claustrophobic dimensions. It may be a garden table and seating area, a grotto bedecked with climbing plants, or a small fountain with burbling water flow. Above all, simplicity and a sense of scale is important. If possible, site the focal point so that it enhances the view from inside the house as well as in the garden itself.

3. Experiment with outside lighting, mirrors, paint, in fact anything which will serve to brighten the surroundings. Basement wells can benefit from old mirrors fastened to walls and a bright colour-wash of boundary buildings. Extra lighting is quite expensive, but mercury discharge lamps – the kind often used for street lighting – are especially efficient.

Creating features

Planning focal points

In many countries climate determines that gardens are mostly viewed from inside the house, and in planning a layout it is important to consider this. You may find it useful to take photographs of views from windows and elsewhere and notice how these views are framed and how different they appear from various positions. Are there unsightly buildings or a pleasant landscape in the distance? Do you want to preserve the views and focal points which already exist, mask them or create a subsidiary interest which leads the eye away from them? Of do you wish to erect or plant something which will become the main point of interest in the whole garden or one particular section of it?

If you decide to create a new focal point, it may be difficult to decide just what it should be. It doesn't necessarily have to be a statue, tree or fountain. Even a lawn, provided it is imaginatively contained, can be an effective point of interest in its own right. If you do decide to plant or erect a natural or man-made object, its size in relation to its surroundings is the first important consideration. Be aware of the eventual height of trees when planting – a very large tree would be overpowering in a small garden.

Decorative features
Left: an effective grouping which makes much of a variety of foliage forms is given unity by a decorative vase. **Above:** the iron pergola makes a main feature for a large garden, and is well set off by the silver shrub, *Rhamnus alaternus* 'Argenteovariagata'. **Right:** a statue lures the onlooker into a cool, shaded 'secret grotto'.

Right: a well-contained lawn in a large garden makes a fine focal point. **Far right:** the partly hidden seat and 'house' glimpsed through climbing plants are perfectly compatible with the wild garden.

Should the chosen focal point be looked at closely, then its texture – surface interest – should also influence you in making your choice.

In a wider sense, too, a garden plan can reflect a similar intention. Simplicity remains the key note. A successful plan creates a readily accessible overall impression, but contains a variety of focal points which on close examination further stimulate the senses.

Making the most of a large garden

The garden illustrated here is an artist's re-creation of Frances Perry's garden. It is not intended to be a strict likeness, but serves its purpose in showing a number of small areas (some ornamental, others utilitarian) which have been successfully integrated into the whole plan. Walking round it, one can appreciate the care with which each focal point has been planned for constant surprise and continuous interest. Television crews like it because they can readily capture a variety of different scenes which, on their own, could make entire, smaller gardens. Approaching the house from the base of the picture, on the right can be seen an attractive *Gleditschia triacanthos* 'Sunburst' and an evergreen cypress which immediately pulls the eye beyond it. Walking a few paces left of the entrance is a hard path leading to a statue clothed with variegated pelargonimums and backed with fastigiate evergreens. Passing through the arch (enhanced with trailing plants and the upright phormium plant) the eye is caught by a tall evergreen cypress at the far end of the garden and appreciates the sheer expanse of space between. At the rear, there's a real *gardener's* leisure spot bounded on one side by frames and a greenhouse. Continuing round is Roy Hay's garden (pictured page 39) and then an old-fashioned seat wreathed in petunias, nasturtiums and *Schizostylis coccinea*. Finally one comes back to the evergreen cypress.

Choosing materials

Planning structures

Having decided to include structures in your garden, be they raised beds, trellises, plant or man-made barriers, pools, rock gardens, retaining walls, roofs, decks (see page 66), railings or paths, it is important to consider how they will relate to one another. Successful garden design is the difference between an integrated series of structures which complement one another and an unrelated clutter of functional elements.

Compatibility of house and garden

Just as the visual character of your house is an integral part of the overall character of your neighbourhood, so it is a good first step to look to your house as a design base for materials.

Some specialists firmly believe that it is wrong to import soil into an area to grow plants which would not naturally flourish there. For them it's a matter of professional integrity not to grow lime-haters in a garden situated on the chalk downs. But when it comes to structures, compatibility with existing forms and materials is not so much a matter of integrity as sound design sense.

Of course visual contrast can be as effective as harmony. One type of constructional material can be employed to highlight the colour or texture of quite different, though compatible, ones.

Again, a boundary structure can be clothed to produce quite different effects on either face, so enclosing or accommodating different styles of layout inside and outside the enclosure. Then the question arises as to whether the eye can sustain and appreciate the sudden transition between different styles.

Choosing materials for a large garden

As the garden retreats from the house, so the dominance of the latter recedes. But it remains inadvisable to plan anything which bears no physical or visual relationship to it.

In Part IV we see how an extended bed of diverse plant colours can become very effective by arranging the colours in a gradual tonal development. The bed might include bright, shocking colours and quiet, sombre shades, yet be organized so that its overall effect is a subtle progression from one extreme to the other.

As in choosing effective plant combinations, materials used in garden structures should be selected for their visual compatibility. Use the house as a design base.

As with variegated colour, so in arranging structural elements, thought can effectively be given to a subtle progression of building materials. Near the house, materials should complement those used in its construction. As the garden scene develops away from the house, you can change the visual character of materials between one area and the next, so permitting quite different effects within the garden.

Laying floors

Flooring materials

Materials for decks, patios, terraces, and paths will need to be functional – durable and safe in all weathers – as well as attractive and 'in tune' with those used in constructions nearby.

Loose materials

Mulches, such as bark or woodchips, serve to protect the gardener from mud as he walks from one place to the next. They may also be a solution for a children's play area where hard materials can cause injury. To help prevent loose materials being scattered over surrounding areas, dig out the ground which they will cover. If there is likely to be a lot of rain, it is wise to set loose flooring materials on a bed of gravel to aid drainage. Mulches can, of course, be set within raised enclosures of brick or wood.

For a town house, you may consider that gravel, pulverized brick or stone are more apt. The latter should be wetted and compacted with a roller in two layers to produce the most stable of loose stone surfacing. Gravel is the first choice of budget-conscious gardeners and many enjoy its natural appearance and the unique sound it makes when walked upon. Do not lay gravel in deep layers or it will be difficult to walk on.

Weeds are a problem with loose paving materials. The problem can be reduced by placing beneath them a plastic or durable felt sheet, peppered with holes to permit the passage of air and water. The use of a non-selective herbicide is also advisable.

Brick floors are very popular and may be either permanently or loosely fixed into position. There is a wide choice of colour, texture and general appearance. Included among the many varieties of brick available is one specially designed for paving. It is thinner than usual and clean surfaced.

Bricks may be loosely laid directly on to subsoil, provided it is well drained and compact. Otherwise it is advisable to lay them on a flat sanded surface.

There are practical advantages of laying bricks loosely, rather than permanently in concrete. You can lay them in any pattern and easily replace them when damaged; you can remove a section and introduce plant beds. They do not have to be expensive – very often they can be obtained from demolition sites at low cost. You may well find exterior bricks, suitably weathered in appearance, ideal for your particular needs.

Always remove the topsoil before laying

Loose floors are of course easier and less expensive to lay than permanent paths. Thorough preparation of the base is, however, very important.

Besides offering flexibility (materials can easily be replaced when need be), inorganic materials. When preparing a sand base for bricks it is a good idea to wet the sand and level the surface by drawing the edge of a board towards you. Having tapped the bricks into place, sprinkle them with sand and brush the sand into the gaps to aid stability. Ash can be used in place of sand. Probably the most successful foundation for loosely laid bricks is one prepared on levelled subsoil and com-

loose floors look natural and will enhance a similarly relaxed plant plan.

prising a 75 mm (3 in) layer of compacted hardcore beneath say a 50 mm (2 in) layer of ash or sand.

Other inorganic materials, such as concrete slabs and stone, can be similarly laid. Clearly local stone is worth considering since it is more likely to blend with surrounding structures and may be readily available and less expensive.

Laying floors

Materials laid loosely on top of a prepared base of subsoil, sand or ash – **Left:** brick; **above:** stone blocks; **below:** gravel. Each has its own distinctive character.

Firmly fixed floors

These tend to *look* very permanent and spruce, which is fine if that is what you want. Obviously it is less easy to change them should you ever alter your plans. The most permanent flooring structure will be founded on a concrete base and have mortared joints between brick or stone work. You will have to design the surfaces so that water can run away along a predetermined course.

Portland cement, a bonding agent, mixes with proportions of water, lime, sand or gravel to make concrete or mortar. Whether you are constructing paths, patios or steps, concrete should be poured into shapes moulded by wooden frames. It will save you much heartache if you divide large areas into manageable framed sections.

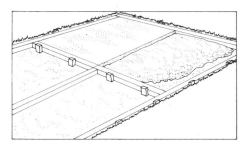

You might choose paving surfaces set permanently in position on a concrete or mortar base, as are illustrated on this page and the foot of page 64. With all paths, some provision for drainage is advised. Loose brick paths should be slightly 'mounded'. Some 'tilt' can be useful for permanent paths with no gaps between joints to allow water to drain away. The point is to avoid any area for water to settle and frost to form.

Very small areas are best laid with a ready mixed cement. Add precisely the amount of water specified by the manufacturer. Otherwise a mixture of 1 part cement to 2 parts sand, 3 parts gravel, and 1 part water is advised (the water should be added slowly as the best consistency may be achieved with less than 1 part). It is essential to the success of permanent floor structures that the concrete be well mixed. Never pour in freezing conditions. Furthermore, as concrete sets by a process of hydration, which is dependent on warmth and moisture, cover the area after it is sufficiently hard with wet sacking or straw for a week, keeping the covering wet at all times.

Concrete does not have to be dull. It can be mixed before it sets with some interesting stone ingredient or, say six hours after laying, drawn into a ripple effect with a stiff brush. But in areas susceptible to frost, guard against providing gulleys for freezing water to gather and become a menace.

There is such a wide range of possible paving materials from tinted or textured concrete. slabs to reconstructed stone that it is often a good idea to obtain samples before making a final decision.

Sculpting the landscape with wood

Decks

Long popular in Australasia and America, decks are fast becoming the choice of European gardeners too. In constructing them, care is needed to select both the colour of the timber you use and its finish.

The difference between a terrace and a deck is that the latter does away with the need to level land and, in sloping terrain, rids you of the task of building retaining walls and elaborate drainage systems. How far a deck should be raised from the ground will depend upon its surroundings. It should blend effortlessly with the landscape, sculpt it rather than ride on top of it. Trees and plant beds can be incorporated into its structure.

Choose wood suitable for outside use and prepare it appropriately with preservative. You must also observe building regulations. They may demand concrete foundations, heavy-duty posts, etc., and construction may be best left to a professional contractor.

Which deck suits your requirements?
Low-level: suits damp or uneven location; **hillside:** sculpts a slope to create terraced levels; **roof:** makes a vantage point and could harbour a garage beneath. First check local planning and building laws.

The same environmental and practical considerations hold good for decks. Examine position in terms of aspect, wind, etc.; choose materials with an eye for harmony and durability.

A low-level deck, as illustrated below, is supported directly on wood posts or concrete piers. It is simple and makes an inexpensive and practical alternative to a paved patio.

Good planning is the secret of success

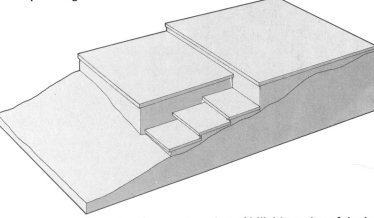

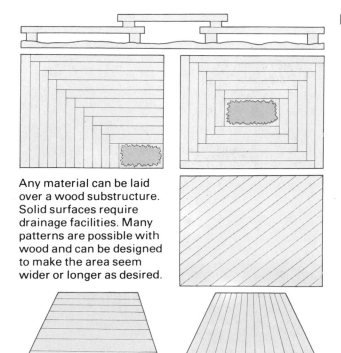

Any material can be laid over a wood substructure. Solid surfaces require drainage facilities. Many patterns are possible with wood and can be designed to make the area seem wider or longer as desired.

Planning the construction of hillside and roof decks

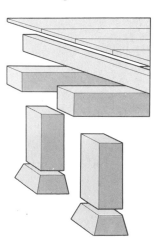

There are 5 main elements in a deck structure: the surface (see left), keep it light; the sub-structure – joists across the underside or surface boards and main beams must support 50 pounds per square foot; posts to support the sub-structure; concrete piers with a top surface larger than is needed to take post attachments; a concrete footing. Certain terrain conditions will require professional help; cost this carefully.

67

Walls, steps and fences

Walls

Walls as boundaries are usually free-standing. The other type of wall is called a retaining wall for which there are three main uses: raised plant beds, terraces and level changes on sloping ground. These are always in contact with soil, which is usually wet. Moisture in walling material is especially problematic when frost is a characteristic of the garden climate. Adequate drainage of the soil behind the wall must be provided.

The type of drainage required will depend upon climate, soil characteristics and the amount of ground being retained. For raised beds, 'weep holes' are generally adequate. These consist of small diameter pipes made of clay, asbestos, concrete or heavy plastic, 50 mm (2 in) to 75 mm (3 in) in diameter placed at 1 m (3 ft) intervals and

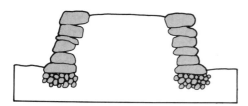

usually within the lower third of the wall height. The pipe should extend the full depth of the wall and about 30 cm (1 ft) into the soil behind. The pipe is generally set into some free-draining material. When installing weep holes, remember that the drained water will fall on to the surface below the exposed end of the pipes. If the surface is paved, or indeed has a path of any kind, it is a good idea to allow for a gulley, slight slope, or some means to direct the water elsewhere. Besides being dangerously slippery, freezing water collecting on paving in winter can rapidly break up the surface material.

An accumulation of water behind a sloping tract of land can be especially treacherous. A very effective method of drainage is the installation of a

Terraced raised beds provide planting space up when there is little other space.

perforated drainpipe encased in free-drainage material such as coarse gravel at the base of the back of the wall. Direct the pipe towards a soakaway.

To give the illusion of two levels on a gently sloping lawn, build a low wall across it leaving room for a short flight of steps connecting 'upper' and 'lower' lawns; fill the space between wall and 'upper' lawn with earth and plant it.

A decorative solution
Cross-section of a dry stone retaining wall with pockets of trailing plants and one 'weep hole' visible on the near side, set into free-draining stones.

Building walls

Usually, boundary or screen walls and retaining walls are made from brick, concrete or stone. We know that there is a wide choice of brick, there is also a choice of mortar which can radically alter the overall appearance. Mortar joints can be finished in various ways, too. Flush joints are suitable for a wall in which bricks and mortar blend well together. But if you are faced with a lighter mortar, which may stand out as more important than the brickwork, then you might consider sanding the mortar so that it recedes into the brickwork.

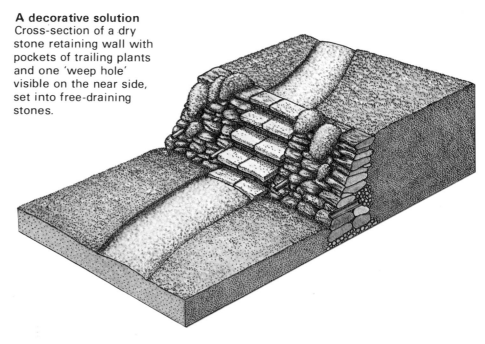

Retaining walls made with bricks and mortar cannot, of course, be interplanted, but flowers can adorn them from beds or boxes atop and beneath. Note too the variety of patterns that can be achieved.

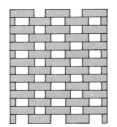

Consider too how the bricks will be laid. The common way is side-on, possibly with bricks set end-on at the top of the wall. But you can use the end-on idea more frequently through the structure or intersperse end-on and side-facing bricks, provided that the wall structure maintains 'overlap' stability as shown in the illustration.

From the start, decide whether the wall in question is to be left bare, painted, or clothed with plants. Choice of materials is clearly most important if the wall itself is to be the main point of interest. If paint is to be added, it may be that the wall's texture needs most careful thought. Concrete does not have to be plain: blocks can be bought with all sorts of different rough or lined finishes. Should you decide to cover the wall completely with plants, the aesthetics of wall materials is irrelevant. However, if you plan to grow twining plants, such as vines or any species which needs training and does not naturally cling to structures, fix the eyes at construction stage.

Boundary walls differ from walls inside, in that both sides are open to the elements. Select materials known to be frost resistant; if necessary take professional advice.

Foundations should be twice as thick as the wall itself, made of concrete mixed with 1 part cement, 2 parts sand and 6 parts gravel, and poured between wood frames on to firm subsoil below the frost line. The depth at which

soil is not affected by frost varies from one climatic region to another, and will be lower in heavy soils. Seek advice from your meteorological authority.

If building a particularly high wall, or a retaining wall over 90 cm (3 ft), sink vertically positioned steel reinforcement rods into the concrete foundation. If building a brick wall, either thread the rods through holed bricks and mortar round the rods, or if dealing with solid bricks, build a pier. If using standard 22.5 cm × 10 cm (9 in × 4 in) bricks, the pier will be 32.5 cm (13 in) square. Be sure to cement the rods inside the pier.

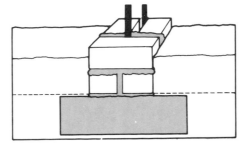

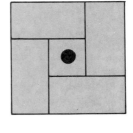

How thick a wall should be depends on its intended height, and in the case of a retaining wall on the mass of retained material. Brick walls over 60 cm (2 ft) tall and all retaining walls should be two or three bricks thick. Walls made out of pre-cast concrete blocks up to 1.2 m (4 ft) high can be only one block thick. Always make the mortar in brick walls less strong than the brick (say 1 to 6 mix of cement and sand) so that when frost makes any water present in the bricks expand, the give will be in the mortar and not the bricks.

All bricks take in water, which is why some local authorities insist upon including damp courses in free-standing walls. These are generally built into the wall just above the ground to take care of rising moisture and just below the coping or cap of the wall. A coping can consist of concrete or stone pre-cast into a roof-like shape, or simply a line of bricks laid edge-on above two layers of building tiles. Water can damage both bricks and mortar and in freezing conditions resultant cracking can lead to serious structural weakness.

Walls, steps and fences

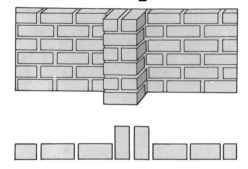

Further stability can be given to long runs of wall by building buttresses at regular intervals along its length, though this is unnecessary in the case of a wall which weaves its way serpent-like through a garden. Long runs of wall also need expansion joints, whose function is to take up the movement that occurs when the wall is heated or cooled. Expansion joints are vertical gaps which break the solid barrier from top to bottom. With heat, a wall expands in all directions but most on the side facing the sun. With a drop in temperature the stones or bricks contract. If the wall is wet in freezing conditions, the water expands, so swelling can occur in winter too. If you need an expansion joint, consider making it wider than is strictly necessary, say 22.5 cm (9 in), provided neither security nor privacy are impaired, so that you can look out at the surrounding environment.

Wall building
Action hints
* Before beginning to lay foundations, lay out a guide line for the wall with stakes and string.

* Having laid the foundation, let the concrete stand for at least twenty-four hours before laying bricks. Pay great attention to making the foundation level and before laying the first course of bricks make a dry run.

* Lay the corner bricks first and work towards the centre, paying special attention to how straight and level each course is. Again, guide lines can be indispensable.

* Lay only a little mortar at a time.

Dry stone walls
Dry stone walls may be either free-standing or retaining types. They may be laid upon sand, hardcore or concrete foundations. The width of the base of the wall must be equal to half its height.

A well-built free-standing dry stone wall is very stable. It is also very attractive in compatible surroundings. Its stability depends upon how success-

fully you foil gravity in constructing it. Well built, it will taper from base to cap. Set it upon two large stones and build upon them so that each stone leans slightly downwards and the whole structure inwards. Fill the middle section with smaller stones.

Dry stone retaining walls should be built reclining back towards the retained ground, the stones tilting slightly upwards at the front. Both dry stone and low brick retaining walls can be interplanted, the latter by leaving out a brick here and there.

A free-standing dry stone wall
A natural-looking, very stable construction with excellent planting possibilities.

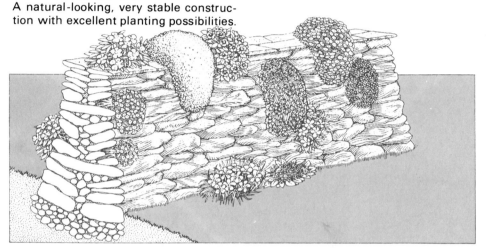

Steps
Step design will depend in part upon who will be using them. Elderly people and children need safety precautions. Rails or balustrades should be considered for flights of stairs, but once again the most important safety element concerns the effect of water settling on their surfaces. Frost will turn it to ice, accidents can easily result and legal claims could be made against you. To minimize the risk, give each step a slight slope, sufficient to allow water to run off it. Rough surfaces, even on ramps, will deter water from flowing away. So, if you choose a rough material, consider cutting drainage grooves at the design stage.

The height of risers should relate to the length of treads. A simple standard is 15 cm (6 in) risers to 30 cm (12 in) treads. If you want a shallower riser, make the tread longer. Remember to keep the riser measurement constant throughout a flight of steps. Variations in height will not look very effective and could well be dangerous. Stone and brick flights should have their bottom step founded in a 45 to 60 cm (18 to 24 in) deep concrete base.

Once again, materials for steps, rails and balustrades should in their design contribute to the whole visual image of that part of the garden.

The naturalness of a dry stone wall is particularly well complemented by informal plantings of delicate flowing forms. If you plan to interplant a dry stone retaining wall, pack soil between the stones like mortar and lay it along the top of each course. It is important with any dry stone retaining wall to ram the stones into the retained earth as you build. Every so often along the exposed wall face insert pockets of topsoil and sand for planting. You could use the topsoil you removed to build the foundation. Use an equal amount of sand for a durable consistency.

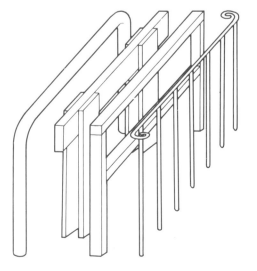

There is a variety of materials suitable for all kinds of garden steps. Logs with sand, gravel or compacted earth as treads can be a very good answer to long sweeping slopes in a rural or informal garden design. Sculpted stone or even concrete can very effectively split up a steep bank of ground cover, particularly if the steps weave amongst the cover in a geometric fashion. The important point is that the material should be in tune with the overall design image you have in mind.

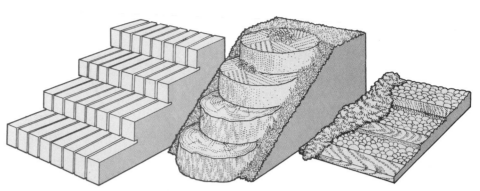

Choosing a fence

The point has previously been made that the criteria for selecting a fence should depend on its intended use. But, as in choosing materials for other garden structures, design continuity is also important. Hurdle fencing, for example, is well suited to an open country setting, whereas the more formal post and rail fence could be an attractive solution for a suburban front garden. There is a whole range of picket or palisade fence designs to choose from. Once the general category of fence has been decided on, finer points become the objects of choice. Do you want all the boards in the post and rail fence to be the same width? What of the detailed decorative nature of the picket fence?

Just how creative one can be is shown by the fence illustrated right. It was designed as an attempt to break away from the rigid appearance of most barriers and tries to create the natural feel of a hedgerow. Even the dowels were left proud, and the band saw marks left to complete its rustic appearance.

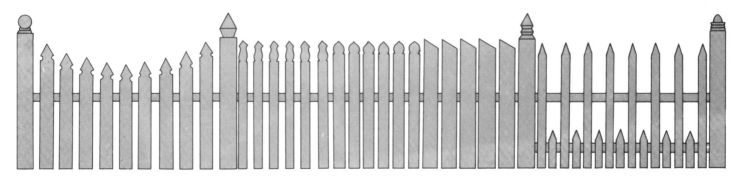

Erecting a fence

All wooden structures should be treated for rot and insect attack before assembly. The first step in construction is to stake out the fence line and run string between the stakes. Then mark the positions of the fence posts. It is tempting to make use of an interposing tree as a fence post. But remember that trees grow and change in the process. Eventually it could ruin the fence line. Simply leave a breathing space and allow the tree to maintain its position in the garden.

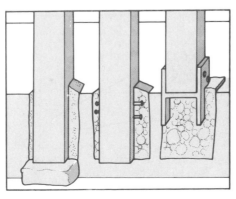

Fence posts can rot below the surface too, of course, and particular care should be taken in treating those parts with preservative. It is possible to overcome this by affixing a metal 'anchor' to the base of a wooden post, sinking the metal into a concrete foundation.

Foundation bases do not have to be concrete for wooden posts, though for greater stability they should be. If you set posts directly into the soil, place a large stone at the bottom of each hole to help drainage.

The Lawn

'Nothing is more pleasing to the eye than green grass kept finely shorn.' Francis Bacon

For centuries the lawn has been an important part of garden design. Well-contained, it can be the single most significant feature or focal point in the garden, investing the site with a sense of peace and equilibrium. Well-maintained, it provides a foil for all the other features, a neutral area which at once separates and connects them. Well-designed, it can add depth and perspective to a site in need of them. In short, the lawn makes its own special contribution to the visual impact of a garden, an impact which can be sustained the whole year round. So simple is its contribution, however, that there is too often a temptation to embellish it unnecessarily with trees, shrubs and other features that interrupt the eye in the appreciation of its unique qualities.

The smaller the garden, the more true is the principle: no features on a lawn. Any trees which do encroach should do so from the sides to promote a glade effect, or as an eye-catcher at the end of a sweeping vista.

Good lawn design facilitates maintenance, so avoid small fussy curves and narrow dead-end strips, and leave generous verges at the base of walls and fences.

As with all plants, it is important to recognize the conditions in which grasses grow and to understand how to improve them to suit the type of grass which you have selected as being suitable for your purposes. The various grasses illustrated here are suitable for a variety of conditions and uses, but their aesthetic qualities should be appreciated too. Colour and texture play their part in the decision-making process.

Recognition

Creating an ideal lawn

Creating the 'bowling green' look of a truly first-rate lawn may not be every gardener's aim. In fact, the production of a fine-leaved ornamental lawn is not only expensive, but time-consuming to care for, and poorly resistant to the constant tramping of feet. There are, however, certain basic characteristics that most of us look for in a lawn. Later we look at ways to ensure them.

* A uniform green colour and even texture throughout the year. This is dependent upon good site preparation and lawn care, but in the first place requires you to choose grass varieties which grow in such a way as to form a closely knit even sward of the same colour.

* Freedom from weeds. How important this is to you may depend upon what you intend using the lawn for. Sports areas must be weed-free, whereas occasional weed species may be acceptable on an ornamental lawn. Wind carries weed seeds from neighbouring sites and although shelter can be provided, no enclosure should cut out air circulation altogether. In any case, the presence of weeds is likely to be more your fault than nature's and a sign of poor site preparation, choice of turf or lawn care.

* A lawn that is capable of use throughout the year. In many modern, smallish gardens, lawns are used as thoroughfares. If a lawn is poorly drained and provides regular access to specific areas (e.g. the greenhouse or vegetable patch at the bottom of the garden) it will become messy and difficult in winter. Failure to improve the soil texture, or install a suitable drainage system, is probably at the root of the problem.

* Freedom from brown patches. These can be caused by a range of different factors, from disease, buried debris inhibiting growth, soil compaction possibly due to heavy rolling, over-fertilization, to drought. The problems are assailable both in the preparation stage and later.

* Freedom from pests and diseases. Turf suffers from all sorts of pest and disease-related problems, including infestation by soil-inhabiting insects and mammals, and leaf-attacking fungal diseases. There are cures. Frequently gardeners do not look upon the worm as a pest; worms are associated with rich soils and their presence in flower beds is welcomed because of their ability to aerate soil and pull down rotting organic matter into it. However, cast-forming worms produce a water-resistant lining for their tunnels which impairs drainage, and the casts they make are unsightly. When trodden on, the casts will damage the grasses they bury, leaving patches of soil vulnerable to the establishment of weeds.

*A reasonable ability to rejuvenate. Areas sown with slow-growing grasses find it difficult to revive following heavy wear or bad weather. The fine-leaved bents and fescues are poor in this respect.

* An absence of bumps and hollows. Level, gently sloping or undulating lawns are preferable. Not only are they more attractive, but easier to maintain and less liable to be 'scalped' or missed during mowing.

* Easy mowing. Avoid awkward corners, fussy shapes or any shape which will interrupt the mowing process. Nothing looks more unsightly than areas of turf left uncut when mowing is finished. Keep lawns away from structures and allow generous verges so that the mower can cut the lawn edge. Also avoid paths which lead directly onto the lawn; they make it much more difficult to preserve the lawn edge. If you insist upon beds within a lawn, and in some cases they can be effective, be aware of the problems of dry shade caused by overhanging trees, in addition to their possible interference with sight lines down the garden. Select simple shapes for beds with an eye to ease of lawn maintenance, and in planting them try to preserve a sense of proportion with the lawn itself.

Planning a lawn in a small garden

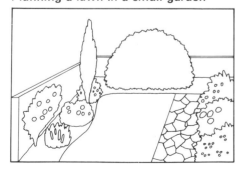

Simplicity
Above: neat, clean verges and the absence of fussy curves all help facilitate maintenance. The lawn is the main focal point of this garden and could act as a foil for a wide variety of plants on flanking beds. Too strict a formality of design is to some extent allayed by a gentle curve along its left-hand side.

Confusion
Above: overhanging plants and a number of other obstacles to mowing do not recommend themselves to the labour-conscious gardener. In fact, here, the lawn takes second place to every other feature. Remember the principle that the smaller the garden, the less effective is an interplanted lawn.

* Freedom from moss. Some of the cultural practices which encourage moss are:
Mowing too closely
Insufficient topsoil
Growing under dense shade
Poor drainage
Extremes of pH
Poor soil fertility
Clippings returned to the lawn during mowing

Overcoming site problems
Lawns are grown in a wide variety of climatic and soil conditions. There are types of grass suited to quite severe climatic extremes, but as with every other aspect of plant life in the garden, successful establishment depends upon recognizing, improving or making allowance for the specific environmental conditions that exist.

The landscape

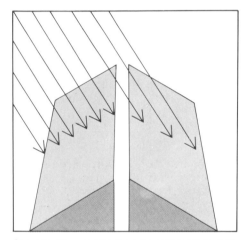

Sloping lawns can be very attractive, but the effect of the sun and rain can add to your seeding problems.

Steep sloping sites pose general problems for the gardener. In selecting grass for a slope be especially aware of how it lies in relation to the sun. Its aspect may intensify the effect of the sun's rays, for example. Soil erosion by rain can be alleviated by choosing a grass with a strong root development that will bind the soil together, growing grass through wire netting, or re-shaping the landscape into a series of terraces. In general, for sloping sites, laying turf is preferable to seeding, though over a large area, you might consider hydra-seeding.

Hydra-seeding consists of sowing seeds in a mixture of water, nutrients and some form of binding agent. It is usually carried out by a professional contractor with specialized equipment.

Maintaining sloping lawns is also problematic. Hover-type mowing machines can help, and on certain areas it can be beneficial to use growth

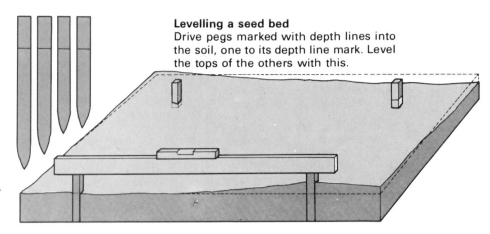

Levelling a seed bed
Drive pegs marked with depth lines into the soil, one to its depth line mark. Level the tops of the others with this.

retarding chemicals. But seek professional advice before applying these.

For the faint hearted, a ground cover such as *Vinca minor* or *Pachysandra terminalis* could prove a satisfactory substitute for grass. See also page 125.

Levelling
The process of levelling has already been covered. Build up the level lawn base in 15 cm (6 in) layers, treading each subsoil layer before laying the next. Having provided a sound foundation, ensure that the topsoil layer is free of bumps that will make mowing a misery. To this end, divide the lawn area into easily manageable sections (say 1.8 m (6 ft) squares). Buy or make a sufficient number of pegs to be driven into position at the corners of these squares, but first mark each peg to a consistent depth. Lay a flat board across the top of each pair of pegs and check that they are level with a spirit level. Finally, adjust the soil within the squares until it is levelled to the marks on the pegs.

Whether you are laying turf or seed, the principle of caring for topsoil during excavation works remains true.

Soil
Though grasses grow in a variety of soil types, a rich, easily worked, free-draining loam is the best medium.

Anything that you can do to improve your soil's structure and texture should be done whatever method of lawn laying is intended (i.e. seeding, turfing or vegetative propagation). No work should be done on sites which are very wet – heavy treading can seriously damage the structure of wet soil.

The best pH level for grass is around the 5.5 to 6.5 mark. Failure to maintain this can discourage fine-leaved grasses, and, in some circumstances, encourage the appearance of broad-leaved species in fine lawns. First analyze the soil and, if necessary, take steps to change the measure of acidity present.

Poor drainage not only restricts the use of a lawn to dry periods, but leads to the drowning of large areas of turf. Severe drought is also a problem, and it is essential to be fully aware of how to cope with these two problems at site preparation stage. See pages 34 to 39, and note that any technique which encourages healthy root development also makes the most of infrequent rainfall. Techniques include aerating the soil in autumn with a fork, mowing high rather than low (but not so high that a finer grass is asphyxiated by a coarser subject – say 30 mm (1 ¼ in)), applying top dressings which will improve a soil's water-retentiveness, and ensuring a proper diet of the root-making chemical, phosphorus. Finally, in arid or semi-arid conditions it is essential that the correct drought-resistant species are chosen.

Shade
Grasses are no different from other plants in their need for light to produce food by the process of photosynthesis. Although certain species survive the dry shade beneath trees better than others, permanent shade is a severe problem. It is, of course, especially important to give dry-shaded areas more water than those exposed to rain and away from thirsty tree roots.

Salt-laden atmosphere
Conditions in coastal regions can adversely affect the growth of many plants. Damage is mainly due to the salt carried in moist sea breezes. There are grasses that are capable of growing in these conditions. In fact some highly prized turf is produced on sea-washed marshes. Unfortunately it is expensive and tends to deteriorate when removed from its natural environment.

Polluted atmosphere
The smoke and grime-filled air of cities can seriously impair a lawn in a roadside garden. Well constructed boundaries can help prevent unwanted exhaust fumes, dirt, etc. from reaching the lawn, but there is little else that can be done.

Principal grasses for all conditions

All grasses belong to the family *Gramineae*, a large, diverse group whose members exhibit a wide range of growth characteristics. Not all grasses are capable of producing high quality swards, so it is essential to select suitable types for specific areas.

It cannot be stressed too highly that the correct choice of grass is an essential precursor to the formation of a high quality lawn. All the pre-sowing preparation will be to no avail if you procure the wrong species or use seeds of a low quality.

In recent years, plant breeders and seed houses have selected and bred varieties of the commoner turf grass species. The new types cope well with modern day requirements, and you can rest assured that, sown under the correct conditions, they will produce excellent turf.

Some of the features looked for during the selection process are good colour, drought and disease resistance, hard-wearing qualities, tolerance of shade and close mowing, and the ability to blend with other grasses.

Grass mixes

The actual range of grass mixes can be awe-inspiring, and it may be advisable to get in touch with a seed house or horticultural merchant. The problems are more serious than matching colour, for example; some tougher species, such as rye grass, actually steal moisture and fertilizer from more valued grasses in a mix. However, a well-chosen mix can be the answer to those parts of a lawn vulnerable to shade dryness or excessive moisture, or parts which you intend to use for some form of activity. A single grass, selected primarily for its attractive appearance, could fail in such conditions, whereas the seedlings of a mix will, by the process of natural selection, take over those areas to which they are naturally suited.

Classification by climate

As lawns are grown through much of the world and under varying climatic conditions, the chief grasses suitable for lawn production have been placed under two categories – cool and warm season grasses. The former group prefers temperatures commonly associated with Britain, Europe, and parts of America, namely 20°C (60°–70°F). The latter group prefers warmer climates, say 30°C (80° to 95°F). But just as global climatic zones are inadequate guides to which flowers will flourish in a particular garden, so cool season grasses may well succeed in warmer climates if the direct rays of the sun are filtered by leaves of trees.

Cool season grasses

The Bents
Agrostis spp

The bent grasses are diverse in habit, ranging from closely tufted specimens to types that spread by stolons or runners. All are fine leaved and produce extremely high quality lawns. Though found in a range of soils, they prefer slightly acid conditions. They demand great care – regular watering and disease control. Fine and soft, this group is often associated with the traditional English lawn, and is well suited to that climate. In America, they will thrive in humid areas of the N.E. and Pacific N.W. Often used on golf courses, they are tolerant of close mowing, 20 mm (¼ in.), and light shade, but benefit from frequent doses of fertilizer (say every other month) and daily watering in hot weather.

The Fescues
Festuca spp

The genus *Festuca*, large and very adaptable, is capable of producing top quality lawns, though not quite as velvety as the bents. Fescues are commonly divided into two groups – the sheep fescues and red fescues. They are sturdy, tolerant of both sun and shade, provided the latter is not too deep. They survive the less fertile, sandy soils. They establish well in Britain and Europe. In America they thrive in the N.E., Pacific N.W., and, with irrigation, in some of the more arid areas. Fertilize in the summer; mow to a height of about 50 mm (2 in), 75 mm (3 in) in hot weather.

Browntop bent
Agrostis tenuis

This species, known as colonial brown-top in America, is one of the most widely used species for fine lawns. A tufted perennial with fine flattened leaves, it has the ability to spread by the production of short rhizomes or stolons. Examples of commercial varieties are: 'Highland', 'Boral', 'Tracenta', 'Astoria', and 'Exeter'.

Chewings fescue
Festuca rubra var *commutata*

This species, also known under *Festuca rubra* var *fallax*, is used extensively in the production of fine lawns. Quick to establish, it is a densely tufted perennial which blends well with other species, especially Browntop bent. Cultivars include 'Highlight', 'Flora', 'Waldorf', and 'Boreal'.

Creeping bent
Agrostis palustris
A. stolonifera

Creeping bent is a vigorously tufted perennial which spreads by the production of large stolons. It is variable in habit and can produce either fine or coarse knitted lawns, depending upon the strain purchased. Used in America to produce lawns by vegetative means (see page 81). Examples of commercial varieties are 'Colansey', 'C52', 'Penncross', 'Penneagle', and 'Toronto'.

Velvet bent
Agrostis canina

Velvet bent is a long lived, fine leaved grass which forms excellent turf. It spreads by the production of creeping stolons and can be used to produce lawns by vegetative means. Commercial varieties are 'Noro-bent', 'Kingston', 'Acme', and 'Raritan'.

Sheeps fescue
Festuca ovina

A species with a dwarf tufted habit, sheeps fescue grows well in arid conditions, but will survive in most soils. The best strain for lawns is the fine leaved sheep fescue *F.O. tenuifolia*, but another available variety is 'Novina'. It is probably best known for a clump-forming ornamental grass, *F.O. glauca*.

True creeping red fescue
Festuca genuina

This is a vigorous species, quick to establish. It has a rather loose growing habit, but good colour and is drought resistant. It is often used in high quality mixtures, one of the best available strains being S59 originating from Aberystwyth (unavailable in America).

Meadow or Blue Grasses
Poa spp

Three main species of the genus *Poa* are used in turf production, namely *P. pratensis*, *P. trivialis*, and *P. nemoralis*. A fourth member, *P. annua*, frequently invades lawns and is generally classed as a weed. 'Blue' is a reference to the colour cast by meadow plants growing in this grass in the wild. It is both a sturdy and attractive group, some types being excellent choices for playing fields.

Rough stalked meadow grass
P. trivialis

A quick establishing, tufted, creeping perennial, this spreads by means of stolons or short runners. It grows best in moist, rich soils, its vigour being markedly reduced in poor, dry conditions. It is not recommended for very fine lawns, but is suitable for utility areas and sites which are slightly damp. Mowing and fertilization programmes should be similar to those advised for Kentucky blue grass.

The Rye Grasses
Lolium spp

Rye grasses are free tillering, broad leaved, and establish very easily in any soil. They are also tolerant of partial shade and salt air. In America, they are popular in the Deep South. Mow to a height of 50 mm (2 in), and apply fertilizer if the leaves turn yellow, a sign of nitrogen deficiency.

Miscellaneous Species

Crested dogstail, *Cynosurus cristatus*, and Timothy, *Phleum pratense bertolonii*, are occasionally used for lawns. Both types withstand hard wear, but are unsuitable for fine lawns.

Smooth stalked meadow grass
(Kentucky blue grass)
P. pratensis

Slow to establish, but tolerant of light, dry soils, it has a rhizomatous habit. Not used for very fine lawns, it can be incorporated in lower grade mixtures. It is popular in America (in the N.E., the Pacific N.W. and irrigated sections of the West) and Europe. Commercially available cultivars include 'Merion', 'Newport', 'Nugget', 'Fylking', 'Prato', 'Baron', 'Modena' and many others. Spring, summer and early autumn fertilization programmes are advised. Mow to 50 mm (2 in), 75 mm (3 in) in hot weather.

Wood meadow grass
P. nemoralis

Occasionally used under shady conditions, this is a long lived perennial, but tends to grow rather slowly. It should not be used on its own and is unsuitable for use in fine seeded mixtures. In North America, rough stalked meadow grass is preferred to wood meadow grass for shady positions.

Perennial rye grass
L. perenne

This, the most commonly used rye grass, will produce a good sward if sown alone. It is a free-tillering hard wearing species that can be used for most types of lawn except very fine ones. Flourishing quickly in winter, it will be taken over in the spring by finer grasses in a mix. Commercially available cultivars are 'Citation', 'Diplomat', 'Omega', 'S23', 'Stadion', 'Manhattan' and 'Melle'.

Warm season grasses

The Bermuda Grasses
Cynodon spp

The genus *Cynodon* includes some of the most important warm season grasses. They originated in East Africa, but have since been widely distributed throughout the warmer regions of the world. A number of species are used in turf culture, the commonest being *C. dactylon*, *C. transvaalensis*, *C. bradlevi* and *C. magennisii*. Hybridization does occur, and for this reason all improved varieties are classified under *C. dactylon*. Like most warm season grasses, they will turn brown in cool weather, though some hybrids are tolerant of light shade. They require feedings at least three times a year and a good sharp mower to cut to about 40 mm (1½ in). Hybrids are tolerant of even closer mowing.

All of the above produce aggressive swards and all except *C. dactylon* are essentially propagated vegetatively. Commercially available varieties are 'Midway', 'Texturf 10', 'Uganda'.

St. Augustine grass
Stenotaphrum secundatum

Only one of the three species of the genus *Stenotaphrum* is used in turf production. *S. secundatum* is indigenous.

The Zoysia Grasses
Zoysia spp

Z. japonica, *Z. matrella* and *Z. tenuifolia* are three closely related species suitable for turf production. They produce a dense, uniform, high quality sward. Usually established vegetatively, some cultivars show a marked resistance to drought while others tolerate heavy shade. In America they are used mainly in the warmer states or around vacation homes in the north. Commercially available varieties are 'Emerald', 'Meyer' and 'FC 13521'. Fertilize in early spring, midsummer and early autumn. Mow to about 40 mm (1½ in).

Carpet Grass
Axonopus spp

Two species of carpet grass are occasionally used for lawn production, more often in the American Deep South. Of the two, common carpet grass, *A. affinis*, is more widespread and established best by seed. Tropical carpet grass, *A. compressus*, comes better by vegetative means. *A. affinis* produces a coarse textured, light green coloured sward. No commercial variety of either species is available.

to Mexico, Australia and the West Indies, but is also widely distributed in other countries. In America, it is found in Florida, along the Gulf Coast and in the Deep South. It grows well in moist, loamy or sandy soils (indeed is a useful stabilizer for loose sands), and tolerates heavy shade. The plant has a coarse leaf and spreads by means of vigorous stolons, although it does produce an attractive turf. Varieties include 'Bitter blue'. Fertilize in early spring, summer and late autumn; mow to a height of 25 to 50 mm (1 to 2 in).

77

Preparation and production

Preparing the ground
Digging the site
On small sites, digging or rotary cultivation may be all that is necessary, but for the larger garden, ploughing, discing and harrowing may have to be considered. Before that is started, however, it is always advisable to remove all extraneous rubbish from the site. If necessary, also remove any overgrown herbage. This can be done by either mowing, scything or, if very dense, burning off with a flame gun.

The best time for digging is during dry spells in autumn or early winter. This will give the elements a chance to break down the soil. Clods left in the ground will produce an uneven lawn when the soil has had a chance to settle down. Well-rotted organic matter from the compost heap can be incorporated at this stage to improve the texture and structure of the soil.

The soil should be cultivated to a depth of about 230 mm (9 in) though it is of course important that subsoil is not mixed with topsoil. If there is less than 150 mm (6 in) of topsoil, import some to make up the deficiency.

During cultivation, look out for and break up any hard subsurface pan that exists. Doing so will allow the soil to breathe and any excess moisture to drain away to a lower level.

Weed control
Weed control at this stage is extremely important. The aim should be to eliminate all deep-rooted perennials and biennials and to reduce the number of short-lived and annual weeds. Control can be achieved in two ways – one cultural and the other chemical. The choice is yours.

Cultural methods kill weeds without the use of chemicals. On small areas a hoe is the answer; on larger sites some form of soil moving equipment is required. One of the methods of cultural control is known as fallowing.

This consists of keeping the soil free from weeds for a number of months by periodically hoeing or discing any that germinate. Be sure to tread the soil between hoeings and repeat the process regularly. Fallowing is best carried out during the summer months, so that the site is ready for its final preparation in early autumn.

If the presence of any soil borne pests or diseases is suspected, it may be worthwhile incorporating some form of insecticide and fungicide during the fallowing process.

Chemical weed control consists of applying a substance which actively destroys plant growth. It is not a system that is necessary for the small garden but on larger ones it may have to be considered. As a general rule it is best not to apply chemicals for a period of six months before the lawn is produced, as it takes about this long for any harmful residues to dissipate from the soil. The use of 2, 4-D as a weed-killer, however, enables you to sow the lawn a month after application.

A relatively new method suitable for small areas is the use of chemical sterilants. These are incorporated into the soil and sealed in for a period of time during which they kill harmful pests, diseases and weeds. Basamid is an example of this type, although it is not approved for general use in the U.S.A. Seek advice locally.

Final soil preparation
The best time for the final preparation to take place is in early autumn after fallowing has been carried out, although it can be done during mild periods through to early spring. These times have been found to be ideal for germination, but if irrigation is available, or local conditions allow it, sowing can take place at most times of the year.

The preparation consists of raking and firming the soil to form a fine, moist, well aerated seedbed. On small areas

this can be done by using hand rakes and 'treading' the soil, whereas larger sites may demand the use of more sophisticated equipment.

The number of times that the site is raked and treaded will depend upon the soil structure, the aim being to produce a firm seedbed.

During final preparation, a base dressing of fertilizer can be incorporated to encourage rapid establishment of seeding grasses. Any fertilizer that contains high percentages of phosphorus will encourage good root development, and ones with potassium will aid the over-wintering of the seedlings. However, if sowing in autumn, try to avoid fertilizers containing a high proportion of nitrogen. They produce a lush growth which is susceptible to damage during the winter months. Compound fertilizers are only suitable then if they have a high phosphorus and potassium content with a very low nitrogen content. If for one reason or another you decide not to produce the lawn during the autumn, and sowing is delayed until spring, the percentage of nitrogen in the base dressing can safely be increased.

Before sods are laid, a finer layer of ashes, grit or sand is sometimes spread on the soil surface. This fine layer provides a good base, but it is not a substitute for correct site preparation.

Irrigation
Before seeds will germinate they require the correct amounts of oxygen, heat and moisture. If the soil conditions are dry when sowing takes place, the seed will either be unable to germinate or will germinate and then perish. It is important therefore to ensure that the soil moisture content is at the correct level. Too much water will cause waterlogging and could lead to the seeds damping (rotting) off. The soil moisture for sowing or turfing should, therefore, be as close to saturation point as is practically possible.

Sowing a lawn
Sow lawn seed in September (Autumn 1) or early May (Spring 3 – when watering is especially important).

1. Remove overgrown herbage. 2. Stack topsoil, cultivate. 3. Replace topsoil, rake and firm.

Methods of lawn production

Lawns are produced by three main methods: seeding, turfing (laying sods) and vegetative propagation. Each method has advantages and drawbacks and the final choice will depend upon circumstances and, of course, personal preference.

The production of lawns from seed is a very well established practice. Although, typically, the initial site preparation involves more work than with laying sods, it will usually result in a good lawn which will be relatively easy to manage.

The advantages of using seed as opposed to other methods are fourfold:

1. The initial cost of seed is lower than that of sods or vegetative sprigs.

2. Specific species can be chosen to suit particular sites.

3. If the site preparation is good the lawn should be free from weeds.

4. Once established, the lawn has good keeping qualities.

The main disadvantage of seed is one of time, because seeded lawns take a long period to become established.

Modern techniques of turf production can give you some of the advantages of seed. Turves can be purchased which are free from weeds and are composed of selected grass species. They establish much more quickly than seed and give an 'instant lawn' effect. Their main disadvantages are the initial cost and the possibility of a number of stubborn perennial weeds if you are not prepared to shop around for a well-selected, more expensive product.

Vegetative production, more popular in warm parts of America than other countries, consists of planting sprigs or plugs of the grass species, typically zoysia and two or three mild-climate grasses. These clumps are put closely

Seed	Cheapest method Wide choice of mixes	*But*	Lengthy establishment Thorough preparation vital
Turf	Quickest method Binds slopes of soil	*But*	Expensive May harbour weeds
Vegetative production	Quicker than seed Can re-plant edge cuttings	*But*	Planting time-consuming Restricted choice

together and then covered with a top dressing. Once established, they produce runners and stolons which colonize the site and fill in any bare patches of soil.

Seeding

The practice of producing lawns by seed is universally popular. On large sites it is done by machine, using seeding units and harrows, but on the small site it is carried out by hand.

When purchasing seed, care should be taken to ensure that it is of the highest quality. Always buy from a reputable merchant and check that the seed has a high germination percentage and a low percentage of impurities. You can buy seeds as straight species or mixtures. Mixtures are the best buy for garden lawns as they can be produced for the site's particular conditions. In fact, most seedhouses are very willing to discuss problems and to give recommendations where appropriate.

The blending of grass species is a professional occupation and, though tempting, is best left to the specialist. Having said this, if straight species are to be tried, it is better to keep the individual types to a minimum. For example, it is possible to produce a very fine lawn by using 80% chewings fescue and 20% browntop bent. However, this may work out to be rather expensive, and if a lower quality sward is acceptable the inclusion of some perennial rye grass or other fescue, at the expense of some of the chewings, will considerably reduce its cost.

Where specialized features such as alpine meadows, turf walks or turf bridges are wanted you should consider the major characteristics that the constituent grasses should exhibit. For

instance, grasses for alpine meadows should be fine-leaved, low-growing and tolerant of dry situations. As they will be left unmown for long periods – such as during bulb flowering in spring – their flower heads should be attractive but should not detract from the beauty of other naturalized species. Again, where you want to produce one of these features, consult a reputable merchant who can recommend suitable mixtures.

Seeding is carried out at two main times of the year: autumn and spring. Autumn is recognised as the best time as the soil is still warm after the summer months and establishment occurs before winter sets in. Conversely, if sowing takes place in spring, the soil is still cold after the winter months and seed germination is slow.

Where sowing is done by hand, it is advisable to divide the site with string into convenient areas – one square yard or square metre per division would be ideal – and then weigh out the seed to cover each individual block in the grid. This will then ensure that the seed is evenly distributed.

If a combination containing bentgrass is used, it is important to see that the seeds are mixed correctly since small ones can very easily settle to the bottom of the bag. This could lead to poor distribution of the finer grass with the subsequent production of an inferior sward, so remix the seeds if necessary to produce a balanced blend.

The rate at which the seed should be sown will vary with the soil conditions and the type of mixture used. Fungal diseases can be encouraged if the seed is sown too thickly and establishment will be very slow if sown too thinly. As a generalization, a rate of 1½ oz per square yard (45 g per square metre) is adequate. If the soil conditions are ideal for a very fine seed mixture to be used, then the rate can be as low as ¾-1½ oz per square yard (20-30 g per square metre).

Once sown, the seed should be covered with soil, the simplest method being to rake lightly over the site. Don't cover it too deeply, otherwise germination may be seriously affected.

Under good conditions the seeds should take approximately seven to fourteen days to germinate, the time being dependant upon temperature and the

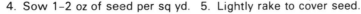

4. Sow 1–2 oz of seed per sq yd.   5. Lightly rake to cover seed.

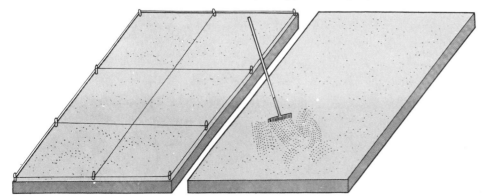

Preparation and production

moisture content of the soil. After germination the grass should be allowed to grow to a height of at least 50 mm (2 in). At this height it can be given its first mowing. The mower should be set to remove about half the growth, i.e. 25 mm or 1 in. In a hot climate, grass should never be cut as short as this because the strong sun induces scalping. Keep to a height of 50–65 mm (2–2½ in). This light cutting encourages the seedlings to produce side shoots (tillers) which help to form a dense turf. Prior to mowing, it may be beneficial to give the area a light rolling. This will firm the seedbed and prevent the seedlings from being torn out by the mower blades. Be careful, though, not to cake the surface of the soil. Once the sward is established, the height can gradually be reduced until it is cut to its final required length.

Turfing

Turf (sod) laying is an extremely useful method of establishing a lawn. It produces a sward much faster than seed, mainly because thin mats of densely rooted grass are used. Turf can be purchased from a number of sources, but the quality of each sample will vary depending on its location, management, the species present, pests and disease problems, the percentage of weeds and its cost. The major consideration should be the species of grass present in the sample, as although weeds and diseases can be controlled by chemicals, the composition of the sward itself is difficult to change.

In some areas of Britain, quantities of high quality turf may be difficult to procure, mainly because transport costs can be prohibitive. In America it is big business and more readily available at local levels. As a generalization, it is probably best to purchase sods from a local source. This will help to keep the cost to a minimum, and in normal circumstances will enable you to inspect the sample before buying.

If a small amount of turf is to be lifted from a private source the use of lifting irons, or 'floats' as they are sometimes called, will be the most · economic method, but where large quantities are required, use a specialized lifting machine.

The turf should be cut into easily manageable pieces of the same thickness, although the ultimate size will depend upon the type of soil, age of the sward and the method of lifting. The commonest sizes range from 30 cm × 45 cm (1 ft × 1½ ft) to 30 cm × 90 cm (1 ft × 3 ft) being approximately 25 mm (1 in) thick. The thickness is traditionally controlled by boxing, i.e. placing the

sod, grass downwards, in a 25 mm (1 in) deep box and removing excess soil with a sharp blade.

To obtain maximum establishment the sods should be laid as soon as possible after they have been cut. Short delays are inevitable but if prolonged, serious damage can occur. If, for any reason, they have to be stored, they can either be laid flat in a single layer or stacked with their opposite sides turf-to-turf and soil-to-soil.

Preparation of soil before laying turf should be similar to that for seeding, except that the final seedbed need not be as fine. Don't skimp on soil preparation by trying to form a level surface using ashes or sand. This may lead later to an uneven surface.

When laying sods it is advisable to stagger them as this encourages rapid, even establishment. When laying, work forwards. Lay the first row or two

and then work from a plank which can be placed over the sods. This prevents excess damage to the turf and gently firms it into position. Always lay them as tightly as possible, as this restricts shrinking around the edges and reduces the amount of top dressing required when you have finished.

Once laid, the whole area will benefit from a top dressing of peat and sand with a little fertilizer. This should be evenly spread and brushed into any cracks between the sods. Applications of this kind encourage the sods to knit together and reduce the risk of drying out. If dry weather follows laying, the site should be well watered. Otherwise shrinkage occurs and large gaps will appear.

A few days after top dressing, the lawn can be given a light rolling. The effect of this is to settle the sods into the seedbed, it is not intended to remove hillocks from beneath the turf.

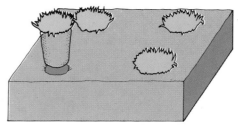

Plugging

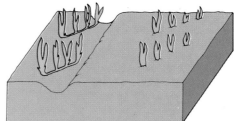

Stolonizing

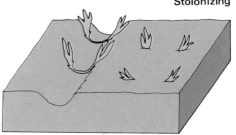

Sprigging

Centipede grass
Eremochloa ophiuroides
Moderately drought resistant and fairly easy to maintain, it is a coarse, warm-climate grass which produces a relatively dense sward and prefers soils on the acid side. Because of its slow growth, establishment is often by vegetative means though seed can be used. Fertilize in spring and autumn and mow to 50 mm (2 in). The straight species is most commonly planted but selected cultivars are available.

Chamomile
Anthemis nobilis
Seed sown in spring soon carpets the ground, frequently with white flowers.

shallow channels approximately 25–50 mm (1–2 in) deep. Soil preparation is the same as for seeding, but the finer the tilth the shallower the planting can be. The channels are usually spaced about 25–32.5 cm (10–13 in) apart and the plants spaced at 75–150 mm (3–6 in) in the row. The general cultural techniques are similar to plugging and stolonizing, although irrigation is more critical.

Special plants for lawns
In addition to the methods and species previously mentioned, it is possible to produce lawns from other plants besides grass. The most typical example of this kind is probably chamomile *(Anthemis nobilis)*, though others that have been occasionally used include *Thymus, Cotula, Antennaria* and *Sagina spp.* Note, though, that these are not as commonly successful in America.

The site preparation should be similar to seeding, taking special care to eradicate all perennial weeds. Plant spacings vary depending upon the species, size of plant, and soil conditions, although most will establish readily if planted 150 mm (6 in) apart.

The beauty of these lawns is that they produce a mass of colour during summer and many have strongly scented foliage, but unfortunately they are rather time consuming to maintain and are now rarely seen.

Once the sods have knitted together, general maintenance such as mowing can begin.

Vegetative propagation
The vegetative propagation of grasses using stolons, rhizomes and small pieces of sod is very popular in the South and West of America. Three techniques are common: plugging, stolonizing and sprigging.

Plugging involves the planting of specially produced pieces of sod. The commonest species used are zoysia grass, St Augustine grass and centipede grass *(Eremochloa ophiuroides)*. Soil preparations should be the same as for seeding and turfing, but the finer the tilth the greater will be the establishment. Planting is usually done in late spring to early summer as this allows for maximum establishment and growth during the season. On small lawns it can be done by hand, but on larger areas specialized machines may be

hired. The plugs should be 50–100 mm (2–4 in) in diameter and should be planted firmly at about 25 cm (10 in) centres. Immediately after planting, the whole area should be rolled and, if necessary, irrigated. Once growing, the area may be given a light top dressing and a few days later a light mowing can be carried out to encourage lateral stolon or rhizome formation.

Stolonizing is commonly used when producing lawns with creeping bent and Bermuda grass. It consists of spreading stolons over the site, firming them in, and lightly covering them with bulky top dressing. The initial preparation and maintenance is usually the same as for plugging, but the timing of planting can vary. For example, it is better to plant creeping bent in late summer and Bermuda grass in autumn.

Sprigging is the term used to describe the planting of stolons or rhizomes in

81

Maintenance and care

A Table of Year Round Maintenance for Lawns

Month **Work Necessary**

January
Winter 3

Very little work necessary.
Lawns are usually semi-dormant or dormant and conditions are not conducive to work.
Mowers may be serviced.
Construction work can be done during mild periods.
Keep a wary eye open for diseases.

February
W. 4

Similar to January.
A light brushing during dry weather will be beneficial.
If necessary, remove worm casts.
If mild, and worms are active, they can be controlled by chemicals.
When weather permits, preparation of seedbeds for spring sowing can take place.

March
Spring 1

A light mowing can be given in mild areas where growth has occurred.
During a dry period rolling can be carried out to firm the soil after winter frosts. The roller should not weigh more than 2 cwt. Never use a roller when the grass is wet or thin. Avoid any temptation to roll out bumps.
Carry out worm control.
Apply top dressings of fertilizers.
Trim edges.

April
Sp. 2

Control soil inhabiting insects if they pose a danger, e.g. leatherjackets.
If necessary, control diseases.
Give a light top dressing of nitrogen.
Gradually reduce height of mowing.
Repair damaged areas.

May
Sp. 3

Seed or lay new areas.
Carry out mowing (mow in different directions each time).
Give an occasional brush. This is not really necessary in warm or hot areas unless the lawn has been left a long time between mowings. There, the grass clippings will rot down more quickly than in a temperate climate where they will only serve to cloy the soil and deprive it of nitrogen.
Control weeds.

June
Summer 1

Carry out mowing.
Irrigation if necessary.
Fallow land for autumn sowing.

July
S. 2

Carry out mowing and occasional brushing (see above).
Irrigate if necessary.
During dry weather a light spiking will assist the entry of irrigation water.
Give a light top dressing of nitrogen.
Continue fallowing for autumn sowing.
Control weeds where necessary.

August
S. 3

Continue mowing, brushing and irrigation when necessary.
Prepare seedbeds and, at end of month, sowing can commence in cooler areas.
From the end of August turf repairs can be commenced.

September
Autumn 1

Seed sowing may be continued.
If necessary control worms.
Commence aeration.
Reduce frequency of mowing.
Control weeds where necessary.
Turfing may be carried out (irrigation may be necessary).
Apply autumn top dressing: low in nitrogen, high in phosphorus and potassium.
Control moss if necessary.
Scarification can be commenced.

October
A. 2

Control diseases if present.
Carry out worming.
Give the last mowing.
Remove leaves.
Continue turfing.
Forking or, in heavy soils where drainage is poor, hollow tine coring can be carried out in September and October, followed by applications of sterilized top dressings.
Control moss with lawn sand or Velvas G.

November
Winter 1

During mild weather control worms and leatherjackets.
Continue constructional work.
Continue turfing.
From November to March remove any unwanted overhanging branches from trees.

December
W. 2

This month is similar to November, remembering that work should not be carried out during frosty or very wet weather.
This is a good month to plan any new features.

Fertilizers and top dressings

It may seem odd for experts to encourage growth by the use of lawn fertilizers. After all, do we not spend a good deal of time cutting grass back? The answer is, of course, that fertilizers, consisting mainly of nitrogen (the leaf-maker, important in spring and summer) and phosphorous (the root-builder, important in autumn), and to a lesser extent potassium, are not used simply to encourage tall growth.

Ideally, a regular feeding programme is carried out when the soil is moist and the grass dry (the month-by-month calendar and specific instructions in the **Principal Grasses** section suggest fertilizing times). Mowing drains the nutritional stores held in the soil. Compound fertilizers help to restore these reserves and encourage a full, green, closely-knit turf with a good resistance to disease. As with all fertilizers (page 32) rate of application is vital, so read instructions carefully.

Top dressings don't make much of a nutritional contribution to soil, though they help stimulate new growth. A good dressing consists of sphagnum peat, loam and sand in a 1:2:4 ratio for clay soils; use more peat and less sand for a light, free-draining soil. A top dressing helps to insulate the soil against the effects of alternate freezing and thawing in winter and spring; it improves drainage in heavy soils and encourages loose soils to retain moisture; it also helps maintain a level soil base provided you brush the dressing off the grass and down to the soil following application.

82

A Table of Pests and Diseases

Common Name	Latin Name	Symptoms	Control
Pests			
Leatherjackets	*Tipula spp*	Seen after damp periods in autumn. Damage roots and underground stems. Plants wilt during sunny weather and eventually die.	Trap beneath sacking during the evening. Applications of H.C.H. (formerly B.H.C. – Benzine Hexachloride).
Wire worms	*Agroites spp*	Severe symptoms rarely occur in established turf. Main problem in new lawns. Attack roots and stems. Damage similar to leatherjackets.	Seed dressings of H.C.H. or work H.C.H. into the soil before sowing.
Chafers	*Papillia spp* *Melolontha spp* *Phyllopertha spp* *Amphimallon spp* plus others	Caused mainly by larvae feeding on turf roots. When serious, turf can be rolled up like a carpet or dead patches will occur.	Apply H.C.H. in early spring or late summer.
Cutworms	*Agrotis spp* *Noctua spp* *Euxoa spp* plus others	Feed on stems and roots at ground level. Plants wilt and eventually die.	Apply H.C.H. to seedbed.
Fever fly	*Bibio spp.* *Dilophus spp*	Larvae eat the roots of turf. Plants wilt during drought.	Apply H.C.H. where necessary.
Earth worms	Many	Certain species produce unsightly worm casts, but they require moisture to live and won't be a problem in dry areas.	Avoid application of lime unless essential. Box grass clippings. Apply chemicals when necessary e.g. Carbaryl.
Moles	*Talpa spp*	Produce molehills.	Traps or poisonous baits.
Turfgrass weevil	*Hyperodes spp*	Produce uneven patches of brown turf.	Apply Diazinon.
Japanese beetle	*Popillia spp*	Larvae eat roots. Produce brown patches.	In the USA Carbaryl is the standard treatment for adults, Diazinon for the larvae. Can apply H.C.H.

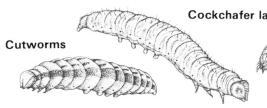

Cutworms

Cockchafer larvae

Cockchafer beetle

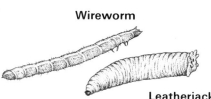

Wireworm

Leatherjacket

Common Name	Latin Name	Symptoms	Control
Diseases			
Seedling diseases	*Fusarium* *Pythium spp* *Cladochytrium spp* and others	Cause damage to seedlings.	If necessary apply Thiram to seeds before sowing or Captan to the seedbed.
Fusarium patch	*Fusarium spp*	Small, yellow, water-soaked patches which can increase to over 30 cm (12 in) diameter. Patches turn yellow; grass can be killed.	Carry out good turf management. Apply preventative sprays of Benomyl or Quintozene.
Red thread	*Corticium fuciforme*	Small patches of water-soaked turf can become bleached. Leaf tips can die; grass looks pinkish.	Control as for Fusarium.
Dollar spot	*Sclerotinia homoeocarpa*	Individual spots appear about 12 mm (½ in) in diameter. Can be larger and turn yellow.	Apply Benomyl or Thiram.
Fairy rings	*Marasmius spp* *Psalliota spp* and others	Symptoms vary, producing either staining or dead circles of grass.	In extreme cases, remove turf, saturate soil with Formaline.
Grey leaf spot	*Piricularia grisea*	Oblong grey to brown spots on leaf with purple brown margins.	Use Thiram for control.

83

Plant planning

This, the longest section of the book, reflects the contributors' brief to suggest ideas for choosing decorative plants to stimulate the senses, create pleasing moods and enhance difficult garden environments. There are also suggestions for gardeners who can spend less time in their gardens than they would like.

The aim is not to provide a comprehensive list of garden plants, rather to reduce the bewilderment which many gardeners experience when making a choice by showing how plant characteristics – shape, height, growth habit, flowering time, colour, scent and texture of leaf – can be employed to good effect. It is, of course, quite possible to compile buying lists from the many hundreds of plants mentioned to suit a wide variety of needs and tastes.

In *Solving Problems*, earlier ideas for wet and dry areas, and planting in acid and alkaline soils, are now attended by ideas for the small garden, gardening in shade, in the city, by the sea, in containers, on the roof, and for low maintenance. In *Creating a Haven of Tranquility*, the special delights of the English country cottage scheme (so easily adaptable to some of today's gardens), the natural garden, and the perfumed garden are brought within the reader's reach. We look too at ways to attract living creatures to a site. Finally, there are special features about creating water gardens, gardens on a Japanese theme, rock gardens, tropical gardens, how to plan in advance for interest throughout the year, and how to create useful and pleasing effects indoors.

The text is designed to encourage you to come up with your own ideas by developing a good flower-eye and by observing how others have failed or succeeded.

The plants in your garden

A definition of terms
Woody plants
Trees and shrubs are classed together as woody stemmed plants. They are distinguished by the fact that a tree has a distinct trunk and always grows above 4 to 5 m (12 to 15 ft).

Woody stemmed plants may be either deciduous, in which case their leaves last for one growing season only and then fall to the ground leaving their branches bare, or evergreen, in which case they never display bare branches but shed their leaves gradually through the year.

Non-woody plants
Herbaceous plants have non-woody stems and die down during their dormant period. Confusingly, you may hear the term 'herbaceous' used to refer to any plant growing in a border, be it woody or non-woody. Herbaceous plants may be annual, biennial or perennial in habit.

Annuals are plants that complete their whole life cycle within one year. The seed germinates; the plant grows; it flowers, sets seed and dies – not necessarily within a calendar year, but always within a period of twelve months.

Biennials will also perish after they have set their seed, but they take longer to pass through the various stages of their growth. Literally, the term suggests that biennials survive for two years, but in practice it is nearer eighteen months. If you think of biennials as slow-growing annuals, you will not be far from the truth.

Perennials include *all* plants which survive more than two years of growth, and that means trees, shrubs, hardy non-woody plants traditionally used for stocking herbaceous borders, their tender relatives (suitable in temperate climates for greenhouse culture), bulbs, corms, tubers and rhizomes. When discussing garden flowers in the following sections, 'perennial' is generally used to refer to hardy non-woody plants for beds and borders.

Hardy, half-hardy and tender plants
A plant is hardy if it is capable of growing in the open air throughout the year. Consequently the application of the term to a plant depends upon regional climate and how well a garden has been protected from the effects of rigorous climatic conditions.

Half-hardy plants cannot withstand the effect of frost. Other than that there is no strict definition, though half-hardy plants can be said to withstand

Plant classification

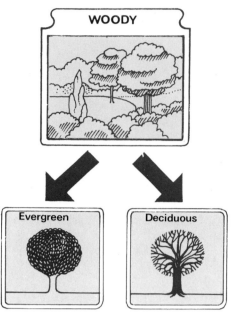

WOODY

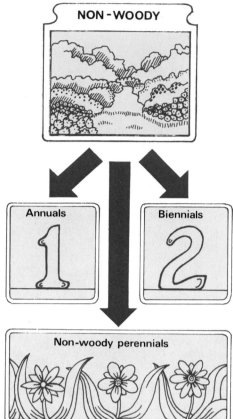

NON-WOODY

Evergreen — Deciduous — Annuals 1 — Biennials 2

Non-woody perennials

Trees and shrubs are the first concern when plant planning. Besides being useful in creating a favourable environment for other plants, they provide the basic decorative structure. Non-woody plants are the flesh and blood of the plan, providing accents of form, texture and colour.

lower temperatures than so-called tender plants.

The term 'tender' is widely used to refer to plants which are sensitive to rigorous climatic conditions and demand higher temperatures than half-hardy plants.

Because climate is the variable factor in all these definitions, sometimes the gardener and the botanist will be at odds. For example, a British gardener treats South African lobelias and the attractive *Begonia semperflorens* as half-hardy annuals, sowing their seeds in a heated greenhouse in late winter and putting the plants out when there is no risk of frost. They continue to flower until the first frosts come, when they perish. However, if they were grown in a more genial climate they would survive the winter and reveal themselves as perennials. Indeed many British gardeners lift begonias before autumn, pot them up and bring them into the house for winter decoration.

Trees – the backbone of garden design
We humans are bound more closely to trees than to any other form of life. Life in trees shaped the evolution of our arms and legs at the most critical period. Trees have created almost all

the soils upon which our lives depend. Where they cannot grow (in deserts, on high mountain tops, in polar regions) few men can live. But there is a more positive link between man and trees than this. Through history, man has brought trees, sometimes from afar, to grow wherever he has settled. The prairie lands from Saskatchewan in Canada to Texas, and the arid land through New Mexico and Arizona to southern California are far from the tree-barren tracts that some think them to be. Creeks and hollows are full of willows and poplars, and human settlements are attended by clusters of 'imported' trees. Many come from Asia and Europe; the Siberian elm, Russian olive, Swedish birch and Lombardy and pyramidal white poplars being most widespread. In the south-west the creeks have poplars and willows again, and the dusty, gravelly plains are scattered with junipers and edible-nut pine. Settlements stand out with Siberian elm, red and blue gums, tree of heaven, canary and Aleppo pines, and many more.

But there are two sides to man's relationship with trees. He may plant them where he wants to live, but he also destroys forests as he discovers them. For hundreds of years sheer monetary greed hardly allowed a significant presence of trees in cities.

Now, they are regarded as essential. When downtown areas are rebuilt, squares, plazas and courts are planted with a variety of trees. This is evident in the Barbican in London, and in Toronto, Atlanta, Oklahoma city and many other heavily populated areas.

The function of trees in our environment
Trees cannot hide huge skyscrapers nor should they be required to. Such artefacts are parts of the landscape in their own right. (In Upper Manhattan from Central Park; Calgary from across the river; Chicago from the Lake Shore parks; San Francisco from the Golden Gate; all have an astonishing beauty. They are accepted, as they should be, as a form of scenery, albeit man-made). But trees furnish the parts used by humans, beneath, on a *human* scale.

The character of trees
Trees are the ideal foil for buildings, which tend to be rectilinear, angular, hard textured and unchanging. Trees are diffuse, curved, partly permeable to light, soft, and change through the seasons. They provide shade, reduce glare, give shelter from wind, display varying textures, colours and forms, filter the views of massive blocks and form intriguing views of the tops of the more distant ones. They humanize and diversify man-made complexes, so providing a *natural* illusion of an obviously man-made environment.

Trees are inherently pleasing to man's aesthetic sense, too. They grow and evolve interesting shapes with time. They are structurally sound, and are seen to be so, growing in response to their surroundings but in the best way to express *their* form. This form is one of stability, displayed by their tapering boles, buttressed branches and flexible shoots. They are, of course, the only organisms to achieve near-permanent heights much greater than man.

The character of tree forms recommends the conservation of at least some existing specimens when planning a new garden. Character tends to increase with age and an old tree with imaginative surrounding plantings often offers more to the eye than a new 'carbon copy' specimen.

The form of trees
The first question you should ask, when choosing trees, is 'What form of tree is best for a given situation?' Consider how tree form will relate to other plants, buildings, the space available, or how best it will achieve the required practical functions (e.g. shelter, shade or screening a view).

Once this question has been answered, your choice can be narrowed down by considerations of reliability and availability, which have the most pleasing texture, shade of green, fruit, flower, autumn colour or winter form, colour of bark, growth rate and flowering time.

There are two basic forms of tree, different but aesthetically both very satisfying. Each year most conifers grow a single straight main shoot with a ring of minor, basal shoots. This trait builds a regular conic crown, sometimes very slender and always tapering to a spire, which leads the eye to the sky. Most of the big-growing broad-leafed trees, like oaks, beeches and lindens, grow in this form for only a few years. Then the main shoot will branch into sub-equal shoots, and the crown becomes diffuse and forms a great dome on high, radiating big branches. Each form is complementary to the other; they mix well. But there are particular places in many landscapes where one or the other may seem more pleasing.

Trees in gardens
Besides their practical role, trees are necessary in any garden to supply the dimension of height. Sweeping lawns and long borders are fine, but without some trees they would make a bleak and monotonous garden. Even very small gardens benefit from a tree or two, but they must be trees of suitable stature. Many trees both deciduous and evergreen add winter colour and interest. Evergreen trees can provide the immutable backbone of a garden throughout the year. All sorts of trees add an enormous variety of foliages, forms, textures, flowers, and fruit as well. The clean, columnar grey bole of a beech or an oak is a prime garden feature on its own, and a group of them is even finer.

Shrubs in the wild
A seasoned traveller could not fail to notice, time and again, the balanced associations which exist where the destructive shadow of man has not fallen. In a typical wooded valley, whether it be in North America, the Himalayas or western China, there is a rich representation of plant life to which trees, shrubs, vines and herbaceous perennials all contribute. Except where the canopy of the trees provides such dense shade that few plants can survive, the temperate woodland flora is full of change and surprises.

Let us take as an example a hillside at 8–10,000 ft altitude in East Nepal. Here the dense forests of rhododendron and fir are interspersed with areas of 87

The plants in your garden

deciduous woodland in which maples, rowans, magnolias, whitebeams and birch abound. The shrubs in this plantman's paradise are generally dispersed throughout the trees but crowd open glades and declare their presence on cliffs, steep-sided gullies and wherever else trees do not eclipse them. In late winter these open places are scented by the sweet flowers of *Daphne bholua*, a shrub which forms many-stemmed clumps and produces its white, purple stained flower clusters from the tips of each shoot. The daphne is followed by the equally fragrant flowers of two viburnums. At lower altitudes, *V. erubescens* holds sway, giving way to *V. grandiflorum* higher up. Both have white, pink-tinged flower clusters, and whilst the former is rather too tender for general cultivation in temperate regions the latter is a parent of the very popular winter-flowering and fragrant *V.* x *bodnantense* 'Dawn'.

Spring in these glades brings a rich cavalcade of flowering shrubs in which the creamy-white blooms of *Rosa sericea*, the yellow pea clusters of *Piptanthus nepalensis* and the white wreaths of *Clematis montana* predominate. The shrubby rhododendrons with pink, red, lavender or yellow flowers add a more solid permanence to the scene and their evergreen clumps and domes create interesting shapes and provide a dark background for the flowers of deciduous shrubs.

During the early summer the shrub layer provides a tapestry of subtle greens with the occasional splash of copper or bronze-red where *Pieris formosa* grows. The summer shrubs begin to flower here in June with *Cotoneaster frigidus*, *Spiraea* x *arguta*, and the sweetly scented blooms of the Himalayan musk rose, *Rosa brunonii*. As the season advances these are replaced by *Spiraea micrantha* and *S. bella*; the former powerful and erect with broad flattened heads of white flowers, the latter more gentle and displaying smaller heads of pink flowers upon arching branches.

In autumn, with shorter days and cooler nights, the deciduous shrubs make a last contribution with their dying leaves. Closer examination reveals an abundance of colourful fruits in which the species *Berberis Cotoneaster*, *Rosa* and *Viburnum* are generally well represented.

Winter comes, and woodland and glades are covered with snow leaving only suspicious-looking mounds and spikes of evergreens to indicate that life survives. All in all, the contribution of shrubs to the wild scene is not merely

significant but massive, and at least equal in detail to that of trees.

Shrubs in the garden

Likewise in a garden, shrubs have an important part to play. Their variety of shapes cannot be equalled by trees or perennials and they fill, in volume at least, those awkward gaps between the tallest perennials and the smallest trees. Not that shrubs are useful merely to fill gaps.

Shrubs contain in their ranks enough individuals of architectural merit to make otherwise sterile gardens enjoyable. This is perhaps the first and most important role for a shrub – to be used and admired as an individual, irrespective of its part in the grand design. Ideally a well-chosen, carefully sited shrub will dominate the garden for a short period (usually when flowering or fruiting) before blending in with the general order, giving way to some other singular display. Such a shrub is *Pieris formosa* (syn. *P. forrestii*) whose bunches of white puckered bells and rich scarlet, young growths electrify the garden for some weeks in late spring before rejoining the green throng.

In some shrubs however, the power to dominate is an all-year-round feature – for example the noble hybrids between *Mahonia japonica* and *M. lomariifolia*. Even the latter parent possesses a bearing which cannot easily be ignored. This characteristic has been passed on to hybrids such as 'Charity', 'Buckland', 'Winter Sun' and 'Lionel

Above: a well-matched rhododenron and azalea border, an effective contribution to the garden skeleton. **Below:** an abundance of colourful fruits from *Cotoneaster* x *watereri*. **Bottom:** *Mahonia* 'Charity', an ideal, cold-season accent plant.

Above: an informal shrub planting should explore variety of shape and size. **Below:** *Viburnum wrightii* 'Hessei' – in a small space, look for interest through the seasons. **Bottom:** *Rosa* 'Iceberg', a free-blooming, vigorous, fragrant floribunda.

Fortescue'. Place any one of these in the open where it can be seen from a busy room (such as the kitchen) and you will have a feature always worth looking at. Their bold deeply cut leaves are carried in huge ruffs on erect stems and their long racemes of yellow, faintly fragrant flowers usher autumn out and winter in.

One should choose and use shrubs thoughtfully to provide the garden with maximum interest for as long as possible. There are shrubs to provide flowers through each month of the year so this is rarely a problem. The essential consideration, as far as lasting effect is concerned, is a shrub's foliage. Leaves come in many shapes and sizes – broad, narrow, large, small, deeply cut or feathery and in colours ranging from green to gold, purple, red, grey, silver and variegated. Handsome or otherwise distinctive leaves are an asset and should be used boldly.

Then there are those shrubs with coloured or otherwise ornamental shoots during the dullest season of the year. A well placed shrub of this kind (see page 188) can maintain interest in the garden in that difficult period between the fiery tints of autumn and the first signs of spring.

Making another important contribution are those shrubs offering more than one feature in the year. So-called dual-purpose shrubs have always been popular, especially with the owners of small gardens who need to make the

most of every square foot of space. They include cotoneasters, viburnums, roses and thorns for flower and fruit, and some for autumn tints as well. Several deutzias have attractive flowers and bark whilst an evergreen such as *Mahonia japonica* offers ornamental leaves, flowers and fruit plus fragrance to boot.

One is so often blinded by the aesthetic effects of a shrub that its usefulness is sometimes forgotten. The uses of shrubs in the garden to provide hedges, shelter belts, screens, formal edges to paths and borders and, of course, ground cover, are limitless. If trees are the backbone of a garden and perennials, bulbs and annuals the flesh and blood, the role of shrubs is that of the skeleton without which the garden is, to say the least, an ill-balanced thing.

What can roses add to the garden scene?

Already we have seen the use to which roses can be put as climbing plants. All too often climbers and those modern bush roses, the hybrid teas and floribunda, are taken to be the pick of the genus. This is like flying to Agra for half a day to see the Taj Mahal and then supposing you have seen India. Like India, the genus *Rosa* is a wonderland of infinite variety which merits more than a brief exploration of one or two of its species. For just as an artist needs to know what colours are in his paint box, so the gardener should know what roses there are to provide colour in his garden.

Nor is colour their only contribution. Scent, obviously, has an important place. But it is in these things plus their continuity of flower – often underestimated by the beginner – and the sheer variety of shape and size that their unique position in a garden plan lies.

Planting times for shrubs, trees and roses

New deciduous shrubs and trees can be planted in autumn or late winter. Roses can be planted in late winter, early spring. Wait until early spring before planting evergreens, conifers and silver-leafed shrubs.

Growing conditions

It is of course important to know whether the trees and shrubs you choose prefer an acid or alkaline soil. But when planting a perennial of any kind it is always important to plan ahead for permanence. This necessitates sound judgement that the plant harmonizes well with surrounding permanent features, and thorough cultivation of the soil. Improve the soil according to the principles already laid down in Part I.

The plants in your garden

The changing role of herbaceous perennials in the garden

There are fashions in decorative gardening, not for frivolous reasons but because of a developing sense of the beauty and value of plants. Fashions change for economic reasons too. In the past forty years there has been a definite swing away from labour intensive modes of gardening. Ground covers and 'plant-them-and-leave-them' shrubs have supplanted border perennials because the latter are regarded as too troublesome.

The conventional herbaceous border *is* troublesome. The border does undoubtedly harmonize best with a background of greenery, a hedge or screen of trees, but their invasive roots often deprive nearby border plants of nutrition and moisture. Moreover, plants in a one-sided border are frequently crammed together for effect, despite the fact that this makes them lanky and weak as they vie with each other for light and air. Finally, tight planting, wide borders and the absence of a neutral space between border and screen makes access for weeding, staking and dead heading at best difficult.

The use of island beds has, in recent years, proved to be a much better way of growing perennials and has heralded a re-awakening of interest in them. Denying perennials a place in the garden is to deny the satisfaction which comes from continuity of flower, and a wide range of colour, scent and form which they make available.

Island beds reduce the need for staking – there is no need to plant tall subjects the full length of the bed. They provide much better access for maintenance and give you the opportunity to create beds which sculpt the land in interesting ways. We may think of islands as round, but of course such beds can be any shape you want, while preserving their essential advantages. See **Dressing up a small garden: Island beds.**

It must also be said that there is much scope for improving conventional one-sided borders. In the section about shade, Alan Bloom suggests ways to defeat the invasive roots of background hedge or tree plants. There are many dwarf varieties of perennials available now, and in **The Small Garden** he advises on heights of plants for specific widths of borders.

Although, in an island bed, the tallest plants are generally placed in the centre (and the height/width rule, page 107, still applies), there need be no formal grading of height from the smallest kinds to the tallest. An

Island beds at Bressingham, Norfolk.

undulating appearance is particularly effective there, and with no need for regularity one's choice is far less limited. When dealing with variety, some measure of skill is involved and that comes with practice. But the satisfaction it gives is beyond price. In gardening, satisfaction is in direct proportion to thought and effort, and a collection of perennials is one of the best ways to achieve it.

Growing conditions and planting times

As is the case when siting any plants, environmental factors are all-important. Most herbaceous perennials are very adaptable, but by far the most colourful kinds prefer a reasonably sunny, open position. Similarly, a majority prefer well-drained soil and all need freedom from perennial weeds such as couch grass, ground elder, nettles and creeping thistle. The best time for planting is early spring or autumn.

Bulbous plants

Not only do bulbs make flowers of great beauty in every season, but they require very little in the way of maintenance and they will, if left undisturbed, steadily increase in number over the years. The majority are suitable for use in semi-shade, where many other plants will not grow. They can be planted around the bases of trees, in rock gardens, on grassy banks, in lawns and as an edging or border around paths and beds. They can also be moved without difficulty.

Bulbs, corms, tubers and rhizomes store their food in underground organs. If it is the base of the leaves which swell, the plant is called a bulb. If the base of the stem swells, it is a corm. Typical examples of corms are the gladiolus and montbretia. Tubers,

such as the dahlia and tuberous-rooted begonia, are a combination of root and underground stem that swells. Rhizomes have thick, fleshy stems as storage organs which creep along the surface of the ground but are partly submerged so that the stem roots are below soil level. The bearded iris is a good example.

The bulb, therefore, is composed of a number of thinnish layers (see the tiny scales of a lily bulb), while both corm and tuber are quite solid. But it should be pointed out that these distinguishing characteristics are not always as easy to recognize as the above definitions suggest. The fritillary has a bulb, but it is composed of two rather solid scales more like a double corm, while the well-known florists' *Ranunculus aestivates* has a bundle of small tubers, which could be likened to a bulb if they were arranged differently. Where their distinction is immaterial, 'bulb' is used henceforth to include bulbs, corms and tubers.

Bulbs and corms appear to have evolved this capacity to store food in underground organs to avoid the effects of extreme climatic conditions. Many of them come from Mediterranean districts with their hot, dry summers and other places where the winter is very cold and the ground is covered with snow for a long period. Tubers, on the other hand, would seem to have less need to avoid harsh weather. Yams and the manioc have tubers, yet they are native to warm regions with ample rainfall throughout the year.

Bulbs and corms are a particularly economic investment because they propagate themselves. See page 222. It is, however, less usual for bulbs and corms to increase by offsets in the wild. One reason may be that there, bulbs and corms spend a lot of energy in setting seed. In the garden they are usually prevented from doing so. People wisely remove dying flowers at the point where a bulb's reserves are at their lowest ebb thus stopping energy going into seed setting and redirecting it into producing bulbils or, in the case of corms, cormlets. Their leaves, however, must be left untouched for as long as possible as these are responsible for restocking their underground food reserves. See page 181.

It is particularly important to remember to preserve bulb leaves when planting in lawns. Crocus, scilla and snowdrops all do well in this situation and one of the most beautiful spring sights is a lawn thickly covered with *Crocus tommasinianus*. But planting them delays mowing until mid to late spring. If you plant the autumn crocus,

C. medius, or even *C. speciosus* in grass there is less of a problem. Their leaves develop during the late autumn and winter when the grass is not growing.

Growing conditions and planting times

The majority of bulbs from Europe and western Asia are found growing in alkaline soil. However, lime does not seem to be essential for their well-being as most do equally well on slightly acid soils. Acid soils are essential for most North American lilies, such as *L. canadense* and *pardalinum* and the hybrids raised from them.

Chinese and Japanese lilies seem to be indifferent to soil reaction, but as a general rule lilies are plants of scrub and light woodland and appreciate some shade. The Regal lily is unlike others in that it appears to have no objection to continual sun.

Good drainage is the essential qualification for most bulbs, although there are exceptions. Most narcissus and daffodils react well to a wet situation during their growing season and dry out during the summer. The British climate suits their needs ideally. In the wild, *Scilla peruviana* grows in marshes and thus is an excellent bulbous plant for wet ground.

Although the foliage of spring-flowering bulbs may not appear above the ground until late winter, root production begins in late summer and the earlier they can be planted the better. The only exception to this is the tulip which is generally thought to be best planted in early winter.

Most of the summer bulbs should be planted in late spring (say late April/early May in temperate climates). These include such plants as the tiger flower (*Tigridia spp*), the tall hyacinth-like *Galtonia candicans* (and probably most popular of all, the autumn-flowering gladioli). The strongly scented *Gladiolus calliantha*, almost certainly sold under the name *Acidanthera bicolor murieliae*, is slightly tender and you would be advised to leave planting until a little later. Its corms may rot if the late spring is wet.

Apart from the so-called giant summer hyacinth (*G. candicans*), most of the summer bulbs are best lifted in the autumn, dried off and stored in frost-free, dry conditions. See *Spring and Summer bedding bulbs* on page 181.

Of the other gladioli available, the magenta *Gladiolus byzantinus* is summer flowering and perfectly hardy, so can be planted in the preceding autumn. The nanus group which flower

The lime-tolerant, popular *L. regale*.

in early summer is best planted in early spring. Finally there is a little treasure known as *G. tristis*, with lime-green, night-scented flowers, which needs planting in early autumn in a very well protected situation. It will flower as spring gives place to summer.

The autumn-flowering *Nerine bowdenii* is best planted in mid-autumn, immediately after it has flowered, but can be planted at practically any time when it is in growth. Its exotic appearance highly recommends it but frequently fools people into supposing that it needs the backing of a sunny wall or some such protective position. The other autumn-flowering bulbs such as the colchicums, crocuses and sternbergias are best planted towards the end of summer.

Lilies, which flower in the summer and offer a wealth of variety in both form and colour, make an exception to most generalizations about bulbs. Plant them as early as you can. The Madonna lily, for example – *Lilium candidum*, produces leaves in the autumn and must be planted as soon after it finishes flowering as possible. The roots of all lilies are inactive for a very short period, and if the roots are allowed to dry out, they take a long time to produce fresh ones. For this reason it is not unknown for newly-purchased lily bulbs to sulk for their first season, making no appearance above ground until the next year. So don't abandon hope. In fact you can increase your success rate by starting them off in pots for their first season, planting them out when you can see that they are making growth. It is particularly worth taking the trouble as lily bulbs are so expensive. What unfortunately tends to hamper the best-laid plans is that many bulb firms only sell lilies in the spring, which means that they have passed the winter in

store, become somewhat desiccated, and will take quite a time to recover from their traumatic experience.

Annual flowering plants

Annuals arrived quite late in the evolutionary time-scale, after the first ice age when they took advantage of the broken ground that was left exposed as the ice retreated. This soil was too unstable for perennials to establish themselves. Nowadays these conditions are most frequently reproduced in agricultural land which is subject to frequent ploughing (which explains why most agricultural weeds are annuals). Garden soil is often disturbed and is thus not only excellent for ornamental annuals but, alas, for such quick-growing annuals as chickweed, groundsel and shepherd's purse. At the moment annuals are somewhat unfashionable, but the time will surely come for their revival in popularity. The reason is that they are regarded as quite labour intensive, though their seeds germinate very rapidly.

Half-hardy annuals, such as zinnias and China asters, have to be started in heat, pricked out into boxes, hardened off, planted out and then, when their display is over, removed to the compost heap (see page 224). The whole process can be repeated the following year. With hardy annuals there are fewer problems as they can usually be sown where they will flower, but even so the seedlings must be kept free from weed seedlings and thinned out so that they have room to make decent plants. Sow either in spring (in which case they will flower in the summer) or in the previous late summer (in which case they will spend winter in a trance, to start growing again with greater intensity in the spring). Poppies, sweet peas, larkspurs, cornflakes, alyssum, clarkia and calendula – the pot marigold all do well sown in summer, but many other hardy annuals will produce superior plants sown at that time.

Given a good soil and ample space they can produce flowers over a long period. If they are given cramped conditions, with little room to expand, they will run to flower at once but produce very few blooms. Even when they make good plants and are flowering well, they need looking after – remove all flowers as soon as they have faded so as to prevent seed being set.

Although they require more attention than hardy perennials, annuals are remarkably useful in all parts of the garden that are not in shade. If you want scent, seasonal colour in beds and borders, or colour in tubs, boxes and other containers, annuals and biennials must have a place.

91

Making use of plants

Choosing plants to fulfil a purpose

Areas of your garden may be backed by walls which in themselves are necessary but unsightly to the eye. Look at the view of your garden from the house and other main focal points. If any scene is unpleasing, try to analyze why. This process should draw out positive ideas for using plants as clothing, to hide or disguise unsightly objects, make boundaries, soften existing shapes, give depth to a small garden, for example.

Disguising objects

In her own garden, Gertrude Jekyll had a problem with an unattractive north face of an eleven foot high wall with a doorway in it. The surrounds to the doorway on the south face were more interesting, having buttresses which died away into the wall top by easily-reclining roofing stones. She decided to keep that aspect visible by training a white-blooming *Clematis montana* along the top of the wall which hung down over the roofing stones but left the upper part of the buttresses bare. The lower parts of the buttresses supported the growth of a Mexican orange flower (*Choisya ternata*) on either side of the doorway. On the less interesting northern face she planted a white guelder rose either side of the door – a woody plant which thrust upwards to meet and intertwine with the clematis. This time, by choice, she had covered the stone masonry completely with blooms which were of the same colour, yet which provided a splendid contrast in their manner of growth. The rose stems pushed starkly upwards, the clematis hung down swinging naturally towards the door.

Clothing structures

There are many opportunities for making use of plants which have a natural, trailing growth habit. One is to clothe hard structures such as retaining walls. If brick, plants can hang down from the top and soften the clean outline of the wall's facade. If a dry-stone wall, consider interplanting it with rock plants such as *Alyssum saxatile, Campanula portenschlagiana* and *Phlox subulata*.

Loose-stone paths or patios interspersed with ground-level plants propose a natural marriage between structural and decorative features in all but the most formal plans.

Solving environmental problems

Barriers against the elements have been discussed on pages 40 to 45. In the section on dry shade (page 110) some of the difficulties associated with the more vigorously rooting plant screens or barriers are discussed, and

The south side of Gertrude Jekyll's garden door

On the southern side, two large bushes of Mexican orange flower, loaded with bloom, stop short of the clematis to reveal the wall's more interesting features.

they underline the importance of being aware of *all* of a plant's characteristics however successful one of them may seem in solving a particular problem.

There are also plants which can alleviate the problems of the time-pressed city gardener and others which will withstand the effects of dense shade, pollution and coastal climates.

In fact there are very few garden sites which cannot be planted effectively and this is the theme of pages 100 to 131.

Using plants to create an illusion of space

Using plants as view 'blockers' (page 58) is not the only way in which they can create visual illusions. Viewing a garden through a bold frame of foliage, for example, has the effect of making the whole plot seem longer and more mysterious. It is almost as if you are seeing a sumptuous stage-setting through a proscenium arch. If the plants in the foreground have large leaves and those in the distance small, perspective is increased still further.

Again, if you have a large house and a very small garden, sitting out in the afternoon can be an imposing experience. How do you reduce the impact of the house on the garden and so reduce the feeling that it is staring down at you? One practical solution is to place a

The north side
The guelder rose is a starkly upright plant, its stiffness relieved only by free-hanging white balls of flower. The clematis swings down to meet it with an exactly opposite way of growth.

tree between you and the house. (Remember that it doesn't have to be as large as the house, only tall enough to filter the view of it at eye level.)

Depending on where you choose to stand or sit, calculate the height of the tree or bush. The idea is to create an optical illusion which deceives you into thinking that the house is not as close to you as in fact it is. The more intense the filtering, the greater the attention will be upon the obstruction itself. The more open the filter, the more you will see through and, in fact, the greater the illusion. A solid heavy-leaved tree will look like a barrier and make the garden seem smaller, even more over-crowded, while a light-leaved, possibly small-leaved tree will break up the face of the house and cause it to 'retreat'.

Should your garden be surrounded by, or look onto, a natural landscape, give a thought to integrating the two. By treating garden and landscape as a visual entity (rather than blocking out the wider, natural view) the eye will pass easily from one to the other and create a feeling of continuity, an illusion that the garden isn't just a small slice of a richer scene.

Illusions with colour
If you have an uncomfortably long, narrow garden, plant pale colours near the house and gradually increase the colour saturation so that there is eventually a concentration of rich, deep colours at the far end. Clearly, a short garden can be 'lengthened' by reversing the process.

Colour also has strong psychological properties. Greens, for example, can provoke a sense of coolness, tranquility and restfulness. If you live in a hot climate you may well find bright, fiery colours oppressive and opt for predominantly blue, white and silver schemes which, with green, will give the effect of coolness. In colder climates (particularly in the northern hemisphere with its preponderance of blue light), pinks and pale orange shades provide a more successful illusion of warmth than bolder reds.

Laying out a bed or border
The shape and area of a new bed or border can be marked on site with sticks or lime (see picture page 52).

When sketching such a plan on paper it may help to give each kind of plant a number. It is a practical detail but very useful as you move the plants around deciding which groupings achieve the harmony or contrast you like. Alternatively, when moving from a drawn plan to a site you may prefer to write labels describing each plant's name, height, colour and season, and attach these to short sticks. These can be placed in the ground and moved around as your plan matures.

How much space between plants?
This depends of course upon growth rate, height, etc. Some tall or particularly robust growers will require 60 cm (2 ft) by 60 cm (2 ft) for a single plant, down to 15 cm (6 in) by 15 cm (6 in) for the dwarfs or slow-growing. When leaving space between groups of plants (separated, perhaps, for flowering times), it is best (as a rule of thumb) to allow 25% more between adjoining groups than between member plants.

Making use of plants

Choosing plants to create an effect

There is no need to have an encyclopaedic knowledge of the bewildering array of trees, shrubs, perennials, annuals and bulbs in order to make a success of your garden. By observation and experimentation you can learn to use plant characteristics to create pleasing effects and gradually, through experience, build up a useful storehouse of plant knowledge. It is in understanding how combinations of colour, form, texture, etc. work happily and productively together that the secret of plant planning lies.

Having an idea

'There is scarcely a garden where you cannot learn something, if only how not to do it. Once you start looking, it is surprising how many good ideas you will find.' Beth Chatto

Make visits to garden centres and botanic gardens; observe your friends' and neighbours' gardens too. And if the first step in plant planning is learning to look, be clear about what it is that you are looking for. Developing a good eye for plants depends upon being aware of some or all of the following plant characteristics:

Colour (not simply colour of bloom, but the subtler colour changes of foliage, bark, etc.)
Times of flowering
Texture
Scent
Form (shape and spread)
Height
Speed of growth
Preferred growing conditions

'It is important to train oneself to have a good flower-eye; to be able to see at a glance what flowers are good and which are unworthy, and why, and to keep an open mind about it . . .' Gertrude Jekyll

Colour, texture and time of flower

Decisions about colour should always be made with blooming times in mind. Too often gardeners remain satisfied with providing interest through spring and summer, leaving the garden monotonously dull during those months of the year when, admittedly, more time is spent inside the house. What of the vibrant effects of autumn and winter? Such are provided by leaves turning from green to an assorted range of browns, copper, orange, red and scarlet, and by the wood of trees running a whole gamut of colour from delicate silver grey to rich chestnut hues, and textures from gnarled to silky smooth. There are the berries too, more flower colours than

Arbutus andrachne

one might at first imagine, and the skeletal tracings of bare branches against a changeable sky.

If you do buy a plant whose magnificence is limited to a few weeks of the year, at least place it near a companion which will command attention as the first retreats into insignificance.

Simplicity and taste

It may help to think of your garden in a pictorial way. It doesn't matter what size the canvas is, the planner is searching for large effects first, and then lesser, beautiful incidents. The gardener's palette is full of the fantastic range of colours and textures that decorative plants afford, and the real joy of the garden 'picture' is that it is forever changing. The annuals and biennials disappear, the perennial plants mature, sometimes outgrowing the picture altogether . . . There is constant renewal. There is never a point when you can say, 'Yes, that's it; that is exactly what I want to see.'

Two guiding principles are worth considering at the outset. The first is that the simpler effect is always the most telling. A common fault is to crowd too much into the garden picture.

The second is not to be put off by others telling you what will or will not work. Ideally, you will experiment and come up with ideas of your own. So much of plant planning revolves around personal taste. This is never more true than in considering the highly subjective question of which colours work successfully together.

In spring and summer, the desire for continuity through the four seasons should not deny you the pleasure of a bed or border with plants which bloom simultaneously. The richest months of summer, when so much is in flower, shifts one's attention to arranging plants so that they harmonize or contrast effectively. Don't be dissuaded from experimenting.

Foliage plants can be indispensable in preventing colour clashes. Many of the summer bedders, so often placed cheek by jowl in public parks, create too busy an effect for a restful private garden. Spectacular colours need quiet companions to show them off and the many shades of green foliage can be useful for this purpose.

The colour green

In building colour combinations in the garden, greens are so often underestimated. Yet how varied they are. There is the full deep green of the holly – sombre, yet healthy and vigorous – then there are the lighter green lace patterns of the ferns, the variegated ivies and the tall, proud ornamental grasses which in their variegated forms can make superb accent plants backed by other shrubs and trees. The great thing about having a preponderance of green is that when you introduce another colour, however subtle, it immediately demands attention.

Texture is partly responsible for the pictorial impact of green leaves. By texture we mean the patterns and shapes of leaves and the way they would feel if we touched them . . . there is an endless variety of shape and form. Some plants even have different shaped leaves on the same stem. Leaf edges are different too, sometimes smooth, sometimes wavy, scalloped or bear sharp 'teeth'. Notice how form and colour of leaf conspire together to determine how successful a plant is as an accent. One fairly obvious example is the difference between variegated greens on an ornamental grass and similar colours on an ivy. The shafts of the grass 'upstage' the smaller, less dramatic form of the ivy leaves.

On closer observation, notice how the texture of leaf surfaces can stimulate reaction too. There may be a corrugated, waxy of smooth feel to a leaf; perhaps its network of veins is a further source of interest. When you see and enjoy such characteristics, remember the combination and note down the plants which display them, and what they achieve by being close to others.

Colour combinations

All colours are affected by the light conditions in which they are seen, and the intensity of light varies with the time of day, season and situation. A blue flower is intense in the morning (when there is a lot of crisp blue light about), but will appear appreciably paler in the softer, more yellow light of late afternoon and evening. Thus a cream or yellow coloured flower will look its best later in the day in warm light, but rather insipid in the blue early morning light. Aspect (page 13) – when and for how long a bed is in sun or shade – can thus have a bearing upon the plants that you choose.

The colours of plants (foliage as well as flower) tend towards warm or cold tones. The former range through cream, yellow, orange and peach shades to the brilliant red flowers. Warm foliage

colours range from yellowish green to yellow, and the vibrant autumnal shades.

The colder, blue-tinged flower colours range from a stark brilliant white and progress through shades of blue, bluish pink, magenta and purple to any reds with a strong element of blue. The cold-toned foliage progresses from bluish green to grey and silver.

There are no rules about mixing warm and cold colour tones. In a bed containing brilliant reds, for example, you may well find that apparently subtle tonal differences actually clash and that a cold-toned foliage plant, say of silver, makes a welcome foil.

Gertrude Jekyll liked to treat the warm colours (reds and yellows) in *graduated harmonies*. She suggested that the colours of many hardy azaleas can be treated successfully in this way, perhaps grouping creamy whites at the lower and shadier end of a bed progressing through pale yellows, pale pinks, to orange, copper, flame and scarlet-crimson, and finally softening this strongly coloured group with strong yellows and related colours.

Conversely, you may find the cool colours more effectively treated in contrasts, full blue and pale yellow, for example.

As a rule of thumb, it is helpful to select one base colour (yellow is a good choice as its close neighbours in the spectrum pose fewer problems than say pinks and reds, shades of which can so easily clash) and build upon it, experimenting with harmonies and contrasts in a continuous stream of colour groupings.

Again, the monochromatic scheme can be very successful and the famous White Garden at Sissinghurst is a fine example. Variety in a monochromatic scheme can be achieved by utilizing

different shades of the same colour or even tiny traces of another, contrasting colour. But remember that the paler the principal colour the more stress will be accorded traces of darker colours. Finally, as we have noted amongst green foliage plants, different forms and textures often provide variety within a monochromatic scheme.

Height, spread and shape

These characteristics are further useful clues to the best planting position for a plant. If this information isn't given on the plant label, check with a catalogue. Clearly it would be a mistake to plant a 60 cm (2 ft) hosta behind a 1.5 m (5 ft) delphinium, or a plant with a rapid or luxuriant spread where it would smother something with a lowly or compact habit. Indeed there is a case for confining favourite kinds with especially lusty habits to their own solus positions.

Interest should be sought at all levels in a bed or border. First decide upon an overall shape. In deference to the art of Ikebena, Beth Chatto shares her own delight in building irregular triangular shapes out of trees, shrubs and other plants, 'so that my eye will be led from low creeping plants through rounded shrubs to a fine feature tree. Even among small plants this principle gives each plant a setting, preventing some tiny thing being overlooked and overlaid.' See also pages 22–27.

Within the overall framework of a bed there is ample opportunity to experiment with plant form. One of the examples mentioned later is a specific suggestion by Alan Bloom to intersperse *Salvia* x *superba*, with its tapering spikes, with the flat-headed *Achillea filipendulina* 'Gold Plate' or 'Coronation Gold'. Similarly, and more generally, fastigiate shrubs (of columnar shape) can be offset to dramatic effect by globular, lower growing shrubs or heathers.

95

Plant purchase and nomenclature

Plant purchase
In the good old days when nurserymen still had time to meet their customers in the nursery and discuss their requirements, buying plants was both fun and an education. Those far off days were actually only the early 1960's. Then the first-time gardener could make an appointment through head office and arrange to meet the nursery foreman on site. Once the customer had confessed his or her ignorance, the foreman (who was an unpaid salesman as well) would quickly seize the initiative and proceed in a remarkably authoritative and impressive manner to tell the customer exactly what he or she was longing to know, and in doing so would 'plan and plant' the customer's garden with wondrously descriptive phrases about a great variety of trees, shrubs and flowery things.

Perhaps the customer only had in mind one or two nice shrubs for a particular gap but so persuasive was the foreman's tongue that he or she would eventually depart clutching a long list of unpronounceable but evocative names and a bewildering recollection of thousands of plants in serried rows.

Such luxuries, enjoyable though they often are for staff and customer alike, mean time and time means money. Those friendly conducted tours back in the old days sometimes occupied several hours in the day of a skilled foreman in return for an order amounting to a few pounds. Today, in what is a highly competitive market, the modern business of growing plants does not allow for conducted tours of the nursery unless the customer represents a large organization and there is a possibility of a substantial order. Some small nursery firms still manage to cope with visits from small private customers, however, and there is no doubt that a personal visit is a beneficial experience whether you are fairly knowledgeable or an absolute beginner. To see your plants *in situ* in a soil to their liking, and to have at the same time the advice of the man who has grown them is most reassuring.

Buying from a garden centre
In the last twenty years the garden centre has taken over the nurseryman's traditional, on-the-spot advisory role and on the whole they make a good job of it. One of the major problems in dealing with garden centres, however, is that their sales staff rarely have the knowledge to deal with the more searching questions and obscure problems that customers bring to them. Another drawback is that many tend to stock only a limited range of plants which may be easier on the beginner but is restricting, if not frustrating, to those looking for something a little different.

Having arrived in the plant area you will probably find that most of the trees and shrubs are in containers, usually plasic or polythene and standing on the ground in open frames. Smaller plants such as alpines and herbs may possibly be raised off the ground on a bench or shelving. Hopefully everything will be clearly and correctly labelled and each species or variety arranged in alphabetical order. Some garden centres help their customers by placing a code card by each variety indicating its requirements as to soil or aspect. Others store shrubs of a similar type, or having similar requirements, in separate frames or areas encouraging customers to go straight to the sunloving or the shade-loving section or to the acid soil section and so on.

When it comes to prices, buying plants is no different to buying food. In other words if you have a choice of several sources of supply it pays to shop around. Experience will prove which garden centres best suit your particular needs. Another point worth bearing in mind is that not all garden centres grow the plants they sell. Those run by nurseries usually do but many others simply buy in stock from one or several home or foreign growers. This need not affect your choice of course so long as the plants meet with your approval.

What to look for
If you are other than an impulse buyer you will have already visited public gardens and there noted plants which appeal to you. Alternatively, you may have had a plant recommended to you by a friend or have read a glowing description of it in a book or magazine article. Armed with a name you simply march up to a responsible-looking salesman and ask if he has it. If he doesn't, he might ask if you are prepared to have a substitute. Check it out in your catalogue or book and make absolutely certain that it will do the same job as your first choice.

Garden centres rely much upon impulse purchases. Cravenly, we are all too apt to take what is there rather than what we want. So let a less pliant mood prevail, and for the good of horticulture insist upon the best varieties and persevere until you find them. Local horticultural societies can be very useful in providing information about where to find what you want. Indeed, one would have to take Trappist vows to avoid eliciting priceless information from fellow members. Should a particular genus be of prime interest, why not become a member of the national society for that type?

Other retail outlets
During autumn and spring you will find a whole host of shops offering plants done up in polythene bags ready for prompt planting. The same insistence upon the best varieties should be maintained and it is, then, never more important to ensure that these plants are lively. The main problem is that the temperature of shops tends to be too high to store plants for any length of time. If the bark is smooth and the stems look plump, then the plant arrived recently; once the bark shows longitudinal ridges or looks wrinkled, or the stems shrivelled, the plant is dying. It is not unusual to find dead plants on sale in high street stores.

Buying by mail order
You will be expected to place your order based upon a catalogue or book description of a plant and to quote the catalogue code or full botanical name. You have the right to expect plants to be well-packed and of a quality in keeping with the price charged. Snags do sometimes occur, mainly due to delay through heavy bookings or inclement weather. Always unpack your order immediately. Should it arrive as autumn merges with winter place the plants in sandy peat or any light and open soil until early spring.

When to plant
Theoretically, any plant grown in a container can be planted out at any time during the year, as against one lifted from the open ground which is normally best moved during its dormant season. In practice this rule of thumb works fairly well, so long as care is taken to give sufficient water after planting. The main problem is the temptation to buy and plant container grown shrubs in late spring when everything in the garden is at its loveliest and when everyone else seems to be doing it. If the summer turns out to be really hot and dry, troubles can follow. It is always helpful if planting is followed by rainy periods and to assist this, it pays to know your local weather patterns.

Quality in relation to cost
Many a would-be investor has fallen for the seemingly cheap offerings in the press – they may be less than half the price of the same kind in a nursery catalogue or in a comprehensive garden centre. Indeed it is hard to find any other trade where both price and quality are so disparate. As a rule of thumb. you get what you pay for. Cheap perennials, trees, shrubs, border plants and alpines are, generally, immature stock, yet these plants can only give satisfaction if they have been carefully reared over a period of months or even years. With immature stock, the buyer

has to do the nursing instead of the nurseryman, and he seldom possesses the skill to bring it to a similar standard. This standard is reached when a plant, shrub or tree is mature enough to plant in an open garden without cosseting and to become effective in the first season after planting. Cheap substandard plants have an inadequate root system and are unlikely to please until the second or third year. It is quite likely they will fail to survive at all. Bonafide, conscientious nurserymen have always been up against cheapjacks who take advantage of gullible, ignorant or undiscerning buyers. It pays therefore to be suspicious of cheap sounding offers when buying perennial stock.

Recognising quality

It is of course very difficult to evaluate varieties upon the slender evidence of a single day. However, discernment does not rest solely upon grim experience.

In the growing season, look for evidence of lively growth and at all costs avoid plants with blind ends. Read up about the diseases which a particular plant you want is prone to, and walk straight out of that garden centre if they are present.

Healthy root system

Garden centres stocking plants ready for transfer to the garden are widespread because packing costs are increasingly high and purchasers are more mobile. Some stock, such as paeonies, will be root wrapped; others will be in pots or containers of some kind. Where a bare root is visible, choose those with several smallish roots in preference to those with one or two larger ones.

The more fibrous rooted plants are usually containerized. Then, a gentle wriggle with a finger will often tell you whether or not a plant is established and of good quality. There should be no heave or movement, and the soil medium should be firm but light.

Sometimes the roots of containerized plants become congested or, even worse, spiralled around the inside of

the container. This may be due to underpotting or being too long in the container. Actually these problems are less common than some would have one believe, but they do happen so check containerized plants for them before purchase. A congested root system requires careful teasing out before planting; one that has spiralled may be permanently retarded.

Occasionally the vigour of a plant causes its roots to push through the drainage holes of the container and into the ash or sand on which it stands. These escaping roots need to be severed, but if a tap root (the chief descending root) is visible, leave the plant well alone.

Choosing shrubs

If possible, choose a shrub of reasonable shape. Look for several branches of stems at its base or near to it. But bear in mind that all but a few sensitive shrubs will take pruning and once established, this painless operation can be employed to produce a healthy and shapely branch system without destroying its natural instincts.

Choosing trees

A tree is worth not a penny more than its leading shoot. If it has no leading shoot, high on a long thin stem, it is almost worthless and should in no case have money wasted on it. A good tree is sturdy, well furnished and with a strong, straight leading shoot dominating other shoots. The only exceptions to this rule are the Japanese cherries, which have to be bought as standards and a few other trees with globose or weeping crowns which must be grafted as standards.

With very few exceptions, a tree which is going to be strong in growth, tall and shapely, will start showing this in its second year from seed. Trees left for too long in crowded nursery lines lose their lower branches, become thin and need staking. Staking prevents trees from swaying, an action which might otherwise have stimulated compensatory growth in subjects which have been hanging around the nursery or garden centre for too long.

Avoid buying tall trees for unless they have been very expensively prepared over the years, they will leave most of their roots behind when lifted. A tree moved from a sheltered position in nursery lines, without its more remote, active feeding roots, cannot be expected to leaf out in a more open garden position where new leaves will rapidly lose moisture. Because leaves feed roots, neither will benefit from the move and may take years for the tree to establish itself properly.

For a tree to grow luxuriantly the year after planting and achieve great height and a good bole within say twenty years, it must be planted small. *Knee-cap height is a good guide.* But its smallness must be due to its youth, not because it is stunted or has been grown in shade.

Buying seeds

Preferably, purchase fresh seed. If there is a date on the packet then it is easy. Otherwise, buy from a reliable source and keep the seeds packeted until you want to use them. Pelleted seed is often available for plants with very small seeds. There are fewer in a packet and they are more expensive, but they can be sown more thinly and you save on wastage. The pellets broken down by the action of water on the clay coating, so keep the soil moist to ensure successful germination.

Choosing bulbs

Once again, avoid the cheap offers and look out for pests, fungus or any sign of rotting.

To sum up, the following are some of the main points to consider when contemplating a visit to a nursery or garden centre.

1. Obtain at least a general idea of what you want before visiting the nursery or garden centre. It will help you and the sales staff.

2. Resist impulse buying, decide on a planting position in your garden, and then look for the right shrub to fill it (not the other way around).

3. On arriving at the garden centre locate the plant area as soon as possible. Do not be waylaid by non-horticultural sundries.

4. Look for or ask to see the plants you have in mind. If they are not available and are not likely to be, try elsewhere. If you accept a substitute check it out in a dependable catalogue or book, which of course you should bring with you.

5. On finding your plant, check its root system.

6. Check for obvious signs of disease or pest infection.

7. Do not buy a young plant which has apparently only recently been potted unless you are prepared to grow it on before planting out.

8. Once you have found yourself a knowledgeable member of the sales staff stay with him; such people are worth their weight in gold.

Plant purchase and nomenclature

Guide to plant nomenclature

Chyrsanthemum, petunia, dahlia, delphinium are four common garden plants. All are known, at least in Britain, by these names and these names only. They frighten no one. Yet all four, and many more, are perfectly valid Latin generic names for which there is no alternative. In such cases they have passed into common usage without, it would seem, any of the difficulties normally associated with assimilating foreign words. Perhaps it is the lack of alternative, or even the failure to realize that they *are* Latin (a concept which is apt to cause a sort of mental constipation in both those who had the dubious pleasure of 'doing' the subject at school and those who avoided it). If the same careless or thoughtless attitude (in non-pejorative terms) could be held more generally, the 'problem' of plant nomenclature would be greatly reduced.

That there is a problem of a sort must be accepted. It is, however, not so much a difficulty with the forms of names as with their number. There are something like a quarter of a million different flowering plants as well as six thousand ferns, innumerable mosses and liverworts, fungi and algae. All, if they are to referred to and told apart, need names. Fortunately, none of us needs to know even a tithe of these. But for anyone, professional or amateur, involved in horticulture at any level, plants are the basis of the subject, and it must be possible to ask for this plant rather than that, once a particular visual or cultivational intention has been decided on.

Origins of plant nomenclature

It was, no doubt, just this need which led writers in classical times and earlier to record contemporary plants and their uses. Upon the work of Theophrastus (fourth century BC) Dioscorides, Pliny (first century AD) and others, that of Renaissance writers was built. Indeed, amongst the first books to be printed were herbals describing plants and listing their supposed virtues.

Leonhard Fuchs' magnificent folio *De Historium Stirpium* came out in 1542 and the illustrations are botanically exact (unlike the small woodcuts which accompanied so many other treatises of that century) and are named in both Latin and German. It is surprising to find the Latin names made up in a two-word combination which in some cases are still used today. It is a surprise because the custom of using two-worded names (known as binomialism) is commonly credited to the Swedish naturalist Carl Linnaeus in the mid-eighteenth century.

Before Linnaeus's binomialism became the norm, and in an effort to become as exact as possible, botanists coined for each plant a descriptive name sometimes of six words or more. Fuchs was considered altogether too simple.

In 1755 for example, an unknown plant was sent from the Jardin des Plantes to Philip Miller, then curator at the Chelsea Physic Garden in London. It had been collected in Madagascar. Miller recognized it as a periwinkle and named it, after the general fashion of his time, *Vinca foliis oblongo-ovatis integerrimis tubo-floris longissimo caule ramoso fruticoso*. To Miller it was an effective Latin polynomial name in that it belonged only to that plant. ('Periwinkle with oblong, oval entire leaves, a very long tube to the flower and a shrubby branching stalk' – some name!) With voyages of discovery and continuing colonial expansion the numbers of plants known in Europe continued to increase at what must have seemed an alarming rate.

Yet already this method of naming was out of date. In 1753 Linnaeus published his *Species Plantarum* which listed all plants known at the time, giving to each names we would recognize today. Miller's plant, sent on to Uppsala, was called simply *Vinca rosea* – still Latin, still an original name, but one convenient for universal use.

Thus it is on Linnaeus that all such nomenclature is based with 1753 as the starting point. Many Linnaean names (as shown above with Fuchs) already existed, but their appearance in *Species Plantarum* is taken as a new beginning.

The classification of plants

Nomenclature cannot be separated from classification. In order to deal with such a multiplicity of organisms, it is essential to group them into explicable categories and the search for a 'natural system' has exercised botanists for centuries.

While some Linnaean terms and categories are still used, their post-Darwinian concepts are inevitably very different. Fortunately the intricacies of botanical taxonomy need not concern us here beyond those categories in common horticultural use.

Every plant can be said to be of a certain *species*. Frequently, closely related yet distinct species can be grouped into a *genus* and, in turn, related genera (the plural of genus) are grouped into a *family*, the name of which is usually derived from the most important genus in the group.

Thus the families *Rosaceae* and *Ranunculaceae* have the 'type-genera', *Rosa* and *Ranunculus*. The '-aceae' suffix is constant for all but a very few

families which retain their earlier forms – e.g. *Compositae* and *Umbelliferae*, which have no 'type-genus'.

The diversity of the *Rosaceae* family entails considerable division, and though this will vary as to the authority followed, it can be said that in round figures the family contains 100 genera divided into 2,000 species. For example:

Rubus (brambles) – 250 species
Rosa (rose) – 100 + species
Sorbus (mountain ash, whitebeam) – 85 species
Fragaria (strawberry) – 10 species
Geum – 40 species

In order to refer to a species an epithet is added to the generic title. The combination of the two makes the unique binomial accorded to every plant. Examples of the combination are:

Rosa banksiae
R. bracteata
R. californica
R. moyesii
R. gigantea
R. koreana

It will be seen at once that the specific epithet describes the generic noun in a particular way (there are exceptions to this general rule which need not worry us here). The description may be commemorative (Lady Banks or Mr

Left: portrait of the Swedish naturalist Carl Linnaeus, credited with first using binomialism. **Above:** 'Silver Jubilee', a popular hybrid tea rose, is of multiple ancestry.

Moyes), botanical (with bracts or merely huge) or geographical (from California or Korea). The ending of each specific epithet – here predominantly 'a' to agree with the feminine *Rosa* – is governed by the gender of the generic name. (Problems of 'agreement' in English do not exist as they do in Latin, French, German etc.) So, other rosaceous genera must 'agree' according to the same principle.

Rubus cockburnianus (*Rubus* is a masculine noun)
   biflorus
Geum urbanum (*Geum*, a neuter noun)
   chiloense

There is one important exception to the general rule. For some unexplained reason most trees in Latin are feminine (like ships in England), and so if quite logically we expect a regular rhyming ending we can be confused by *Quercus petraea*, *Pinus radiata* etc.

It should be emphasized here that while it is interesting to understand the mechanics of nomenclature and useful as an *aide memoire*, these names are merely coined for convenience and should be used as such. (Further details of origins and the system can be obtained from many books: *A Gardeners Dictionary of Plant Names* by Smith & Stearn is excellent).

Other descriptive names
It will be noted that in some texts a plant name is followed by a letter or abbreviated name L. or D.C. or Mill. (Linnaeus, De Candolle, Miller). These are the authorities who coined, adopted, first published the name with a description of the new plant and usually a pressed specimen.

Hybrids and cultivars
Often, especially in gardens, plants grown are not true species. They may be hybrids or forms and this fact needs to be shown in their name. Hybrids may be bi-generic: e.g. x *Fatshedera lizei* (*Fatsia japonica* x *Hedera helix*), but more commonly they are bi-specific: e.g. *Rosa* x *alba* (*R. canina* x *R. damascena*). There are occasional graft hybrids such as the purple laburnum, + *Laburnocytisus adamii* (*Laburnum* + Cytisus).

Specific rank implies a wild plant and many plants we grow are chance garden forms or carefully bred variants. These are called 'cultivars' (cvs.). Any new cultivar name is not Latinised but written in the language of the producer e.g. *Camellia japonica* cv. 'Peach Blossom'. Older cultivar names still retained, however, are often in Latin (e.g. *C. jap.* cv. 'Magnoliae – flora'). These are shown to lack botanical status by being put within single quotes.

Updating nomenclature
One final vexed question must be mentioned – that of name changes. It is a common convention for gardeners to rail at botanists for what they consider are unjustified and arbitrary name changes. Certainly it is annoying that a plant well known as *Viburnum fragrans* becomes *V. farreri* apparently overnight. Names change for several reasons. An older (but post-1753) validly published name is re-discovered and takes precedence. New research shows differences or relationships hitherto unknown. Gradually, in theory at least, equilibrium will occur. All in all it should be remembered that plant names are made for use and are tools to be properly applied.

Only Latin can give universality and for that we can put up with a lot. Just think of the confusion in the European Common Market if every member country, as it does in other commodities, used its vernacular names for plants. Linnaeus was a better European than he knew.

The small garden

* In terms of planting a small garden, ultimate size (spread as well as height of plants) is the vital consideration. When studying catalogues it is important to remember that environmental conditions will affect a plant's growth in all directions.

* It is never more important than in the small garden, where one is by definition limited in the *number* of plants one can select, to go for plants which remain attractive for as much of the year as possible.

Small gardens bring with them environmental problems. They are often in cities, which may be polluted. Frequently they are surrounded by high buildings which create draughts and eddying winds; plants obviously have to be able to withstand these. City gardens have close neighbours and they must be borne in mind – roots as well as top growth can change a friend into a rebel with a cause (and could cost money – see page 49). Gardeners in the city may have little time to devote to their hobby and this helps narrow your choice to plants which will keep the weeds down, need little looking after, or take effect as soon as possible.

Shade is a characteristic problem of small gardens in built-up areas (though many country gardeners can experience the worst kind of shade – dry shade from low-lying trees with thirsty roots). Depending on the density of shade your choice of sun-loving plants (generally a rich source of colour in the garden) may be limited or virtually non-existant. The fact is, however, that nature has endowed a surprising variety of plants with the ability (or genetic characteristic) to grow with a minimum supply of energy from the sun. Large leaved plants are generally efficient, though finely divided leaves (such as appear on ferns) are also good. Irrigation becomes a vitally important factor, for unless plants have sufficient moisture in shade they will fail.

Sometimes, in their search for a suitable space, city gardeners mount impressive displays on roofs. There too a competent watering system is important, and although, as in most small gardens, planting space on the ground may be at a premium, vertical gardening (gardening up structures, backing walls, etc.) opens up a whole area of plant choice. Roof gardens are usually open and in full sun and firmly fixed vertical structures may be useful in protecting plants from the damaging effects of too much sun and/or wind.

Gardening in pots, sinks, troughs, etc. will involve you in the production of a

whole host of long and short-term plants and a deft handling of interesting subjects to ensure attractive containers through the year. Because you are planting in small quantities of soil be sure to give it your full attention. It will require adequate feeding and changing at regular intervals. Do not lift large or permanent plants of some maturity or you will damage their roots, but remove and replenish as much soil as possible.

So in small gardens certain elements of the environment need special attention, and certain plant characteristics become the object of your choice in preference to others. More people are interested in gardening than ever before, and most of them are having to come to grips with the principles of gardening in confined spaces. In actual fact one bonus which arises out of being unable to plan the meandering herbaceous borders of times past is that much of the drudgery has been removed from gardening. For beautiful as these borders are they involve a great deal of initial work and maintenance, which in bygone days were the province of a team of hired gardeners. Rarely did the house owner take on more than the role of the dilettante, or experience first-hand the supreme satisfaction that a more practical side affords today's amateur gardener.

Above: *Malus tschonoskii* can grow to 12 m (40 ft) but is pyramidal in form. **Right:** The red maple, *Acer rubrum* 'Scanlon', grows to about 10 m (35 ft) in 20 years. **Far right:** *Liriodendron* 'Fastigiatum'.

Trees in small gardens

When choosing trees for a restricted space, important considerations are the size to which a tree may grow and the shape of its unconfined crown. However, little reliance can be given to either the height or the spread figures seen in catalogues. Height is sometimes given, very misleadingly, as that achieved in the wild. One catalogue gives 70 m (230 ft) for the deodar (*Cedrus deodara*) which has indeed been found growing to that height in the Punjab, but in Britain it is more likely to grow to 38 m (125 ft), and in America few are even 25 m (82 ft) tall. At the other extreme, heights are frequently greatly *under*-estimated, either because the nursery does not wish to frighten away potential custom or because the writer has never studied big old trees. Typically, a catalogue will give say 12 m (40 ft) as the height that a ginkgo may achieve and 15 or even 10 m (50 or 30 ft) for the pagoda tree (*Sophora japonica*). In Britain, many ginkgos are over 25 m (80 ft) and in America many are around 30 m (100 ft), while in both regions pagoda trees are sometimes found up to 25 m (80 ft) tall. In the absence of

reliable information on height, it is best to visit collections where you can compare specimens.

Figures for spread of trees similarly give only a vague indication of what an open-grown tree may do. In catalogues, these are probably derived as a percentage of the height. Individual trees differ greatly within a species when unconfined. Some very old lindens are upright and relatively narrow, while others may have huge low branches spreading far. And beech, hornbeam and oak are as variable, making any figures rather meaningless. Most conifers, however, do grow to a fairly fixed pattern and a percentage of the height, usually about 30%, is often near the mark.

Action hint
* A small-garden technique popular in Scandinavia is to replace trees as they grow over-large with the new small ones. First, check local conservation laws.

A focal point for a small garden
In a restricted space, the safest trees are the truly fastigiate ones. All but two are clones (that is grafts from a single parent tree) and grow the same shape everywhere. The only widely known fastigiate is the Lombardy poplar, which is grown throughout Europe, in every state of the USA and

every southern province of Canada. But this is the least suitable, growing big too rapidly and having invasive roots.

The two exceptions to the rule that all fastigiates are clones, are particularly good as focal points. In central Italy, Lobel's maple (*Acer lobelii*) apparently grows wild, as it does in cultivation, with whorls of vigorous straight branches at a small angle from the vertical around a straight bole. It takes twenty years or so to reach a height of 15 m (50 ft) and then progresses rather slowly, the oldest trees bearing heavy crowns which open out at the top. The foliage is pleasant, if not striking. It resembles that of its close relative the Norway maple, *Acer platanoides*, but has bloomed grey shoots, few teeth on the lobes, and, unfortunately, not much autumn colour. The other wild fastigiate tree is the pillar apple (*Malus tschonoskii*) from Japan. Young trees are columnar but soon grow tall with narrowly ovoid crowns, occasionally approaching broad ovoid but still very upright and dense. It comes into silver leaf and, as it turns green, bunches of small but pleasant apple flowers open. But its real glory comes in autumn when it is a tower of orange and scarlet turning rich dark red. The fruit is small and is not unsafe if it falls on paved areas.

The fastigiate European beech is called the Dawyck beech, *Fagus sylvatica*. 'Dawyck' because the original tree was found in a plantation at the Dawyck Estate in Scotland, in about 1860, and moved down to the garden where it stands today 26 m (85 ft) tall. This makes a fine conic-columnar tree, very erect with normal beech foliage, bright fresh green in spring and yellow, orange and rich russet in autumn. It grows well in cities, as is shown by the four big trees by St John's College, Cambridge, and the younger, but as healthy specimens in Lincoln Street, Spokane.

The equivalent tree in the common oak family is the cypress oak, *Quercus robur* 'Fastigiata'. The parent tree of many of these was found in a forest at Haarenhausen near Frankfurt and was grafted in nurseries in 1783. This cultivar can be raised from seed and yields a mixture of upright shapes from that of a Lombardy poplar to a wine-glass outline. A grafted plant is safer if you want a narrow tree. It is a splendid and very robust tree of quite rapid growth. The pyramidal hornbeam, *Carpinus betulus* 'Fastigiata', is not truly fastigiate, having an upright ovoid crown when pruned 2 m (7 ft 6 in) up to stem (as it nearly always is). If unpruned it displays a very broad-

based bushy upright crown. It is a tree of great character in summer, autumn and winter, with a dense tracery of straight slender branches, and an always neat shape. It makes a superb, semi-formal avenue and street tree, and a single specimen of singular worth for the garden.

The tulip-tree or yellow poplar, *Liriodendron*, has a closely fastigiate form, 'Fastigiatum', with typically handsome pale green foliage. It is often said that this does not flower, but since tulip-trees need to be some twenty-five years old to flower in Britain – very few of the fastigiates are as old as that – this may prove to be untrue. Whatever is the case, it is the fine foliage that makes the tree.

The locust tree or false acacia (*Robinia pseudocacia*)has the form 'Fastigiata' but although slender, it is too thin to be elegant – rather gaunt in summer, more so in winter – and seems to be short-lived. The red maple, *Acer rubrum*, has a vigorous, slender-branched very upright form 'Erectum' seen more in America than in Britain. It is a good tree, if a bit thin in foliage, but the leaves are fine and give some autumn colour. In America there are two upright forms of sugar maple: the

first, *Acer saccharum* 'Temple's Upright', is distinctly bushy with multiple leaders but very erect. The other, *A.s.* 'Newton Sentry' is so slender and single-leadered that it can look absurd. One, in the Brooklyn Botanic Gardens, is just a leafy pole 16 m (50 ft) tall which has only ever grown one side shoot and that was pruned off. With the dazzling orange-scarlet that sugar maples assume in the American fall, both these are splendid trees. The fastigiate sessile oak, *Quercus petraea* 'Columnaris', is as narrow as any grown in Europe and has good foliage. 101

The small garden

Small trees that are attractive through the year

There are many trees which are of small stature at maturity and are thus suitable for confined spaces, but remember that in small places it is important for each tree to make its mark through the seasons. This proviso disposes of the cherries, laburnums and crabs, which are so depressing all through summer (though the gnarled form of some mature specimens can recommend them). Several maples rank among the best year-round trees. The paperbark maple, *Acer griseum*, grows slowly – even the earliest trees, now nearly eighty years old, have hardly outgrown a small garden. Several beautiful old specimens can be seen at Duffryn Garden near Cardiff and most gardens now have young ones. The bark is bright orange-brown and flakes and peels to leave smooth areas; the trifoliate leaves emerge pale yellow with yellow flowers hanging in threes. They turn dark green above and are blue-white with hairs beneath, until in autumn they become a spectacle of scarlet, crimson, then deep red. The closely related nikko maple, *Acer nikoense*, has a smooth dark grey bark and bigger leaves, but is otherwise similar. Both grow well on chalky soils. The trident maple, *Acer buergeranum*, is of similar growth and stature, but has a flaky, dull, orange-brown bark and a dense crown of pretty leaves, wedge-shaped at base. You may find some without lobes, but generally they grow three pointed lobes silvery beneath and, in autumn, crimson above.

Several snakebark maples fill the bill, but some of them flow out like fountains to fill a confined space. One snakebark is American and the rest come from China and Japan. The American one, called there the moosewood, *Acer pensylvanicum*, is the least spreading and indeed is rather upright. It has three-lobed leaves varying in size up to very big, broad, almost square specimens, 22 cm (9 in) across, emerging brilliant green and in early autumn turning to bright gold. The Japanese *Acer capillipes* is also fairly upright until mature, and has highly attractive, glossy green leaves with scarlet stalks and two small side-lobes toward the base of the long central lobe. The veins are in parallel parts and prominent autumn colours are orange, scarlet and crimson. Snakebarks add to their summer attractions by bearing great quantities of paired flower spikes of yellow-green flowers which rapidly mature into winged fruits. In winter their bark appeals with intensely white vertical streaks on an enamel smooth background of green or grey. Moosebark tends to be

Brilliant young foliage of *Acer rubrum* 'Columnare' and striped bark of *A. hersii*.

grey and *A. capillipes* bright green. Hers's maple, *A. hersii*, is particularly prolific of flower and of broadly winged fruit, pale green against deep matt green leaves which turn orange and crimson in autumn as the fruit takes on a pink tinge. Its bark is dark green and well striped. It is among the best of the snakebarks, but its remarkably attractive crown of long, drooping un-branched shoots, and its more marked vigour (9 m – 30 ft – in twenty years) does render it less suitable for very confined spaces.

The amur maple, *Acer ginnala*, is often only a bush but can be a small tree and is exceptionally hardy. It is used in tubs in Montreal streets, and in the ground in many northern and prairie cities. One with a big bole grows on a street corner in Revelstoke, BC. It flushes yellow, and as the leaves turn dark green, the flowers open in erect broad white heads. The leaves are small with three deeply toothed lobes and turn from bright to deep red through autumn. The dull-brown winter fruit droops down in bunches.

A black mulberry, *Morus nigra*, provides character where there is room for only one or two trees. But it does like to spread somewhat and should not overhang paved walks for its fruit will make the path a mess if it escapes the attention of blackbirds and humans. Apart from its red fruit which ripens into black, it has a leafy crown of big bright green leaves turning pale yellow in autumn, and an orange and grey stripping bark.

Two of the host of thorn trees have some merit beyond their ability to

thrive anywhere in any soil. The broadleafed cockspur thorn, *Crataegus x prunifolia*, is best grown on a clean stem of 1.5 or 2 m (5 or 7 ft 6 in), otherwise it may be a spreading bush. It is of no attraction in winter but it has a long and varied season. The glossy purple shoots bear 5 cm (2 in) spines of the same colour, and broad, glossy dark green leaves which highlight the flat heads of pretty white flowers. The flowers ripen to dark red fruit before the leaves turn to a remarkable blaze of copper, orange, scarlet and crimson, lasting well through the autumn.

The hybrid cockspur thorn, *Crataegus x lavallei*, is somewhat better in winter. Its pale grey cracking bark and level branches, clustered on their upper side with bunches of twigs, are very distinct. Its narrow, glossy, dark leaves are inundated in late spring with masses of heads of white flowers. The leaves stay glossy and dark well into autumn, then in winter they turn deep red and the fruit remains orange red through the winter. A third thorn, the Washington thorn, *C. phaenopyrum*, makes a small bushy tree with small deeply lobed leaves and heads of white flowers. But its main value is its clusters of scarlet berries which remain after the leaves have fallen.

Several rowans are good in confined spaces. *Sorbus* 'Joseph Rock' is quite narrow, has fine foliage turning fiery crimson in autumn when its lemon yellow berries are at their best. Vilmorin's rowan, *S. vilmorinii*, is a low tree with arching branches bearing feathery, dark green leaves which turn deep red late in the season; its flowers mature into little deep red

Right: *Crataegus* x *lavallei* for fruit.
Above: shows its leaves turning bronze.

berries that slowly turn pale pink. Sargent's rowan, *S. sargentiana*, has stout shoots and big pinnate leaves, handsome at all times but notably so when turning orange-pink then mottled red then scarlet to deep red. Broad heads of some two hundred small red berries add their share. It has a low, domed crown. The crab, 'John Downie', scores over most of the other crabs by its upright early growth and, more particularly, by its show of conic fruit glossy bright yellow and scarlet.

The hollies include many superb foliage plants and being evergreen, they remain good value in winter. The Highclere hybrids withstand any conditions, and the form *Ilex* x *altaclarensis* 'Camelliifolia' makes a splendid conic tree with big glossy bright leaves. 'Lawsoniana' is a striking form with leaves variegated in yellow and shades of green. Of the forms of common holly, *Ilex aquifolium* 'Pyramidalis' is perhaps the best as a single tree, being shaped with bright green, smooth-edged leaves and copious red berries.

Of the stewartias, the best here is *S. sinensis* because of its midsummer white flowers, good autumn colours and year-round smooth pink or grey-pink bark.

The pittosporum, *P. tenuifolium* is very good value as a fresh evergreen with crinkled leaves. In the far west of the British Isles it can be 15 m (50 ft) tall, but in the east it remains a shapely ovoid scarcely 6 m (20 ft) tall and surprisingly hardy.

In eastern North America the flower-

ing dogwood, *Cornus florida*, is almost universal as a small tree with masses of white flowers and bunches of glistening scarlet berries, which with its interesting checkered bark make it a year-round tree. In Britain it is less reliable in flower and rarely seems to fruit, but the form 'Rubra', usually bears showers of soft pink flowers. The Japanese *Cornus kousa* is more reliable in Britain for densely held flowers and the variety *chinensis* is taller, to 9 m (30 ft), more floriferous with a long season of flowers which fade to pink and are followed by fruit like little strawberries standing up in lines on matchsticks. It is often called the 'strawberry tree', but this is misleading as true strawberry trees are the very different, evergreen *Arbutus* genus.

The best for a very small space is the rare Eastern Mediterranean strawberry tree, *Arbutus andrachne*, a neat little

Ilex x *altaclerensis* 'Lawsoniana'.

tree with spring flowers in nodding bunches. Its great feature is its bark of rich orange, flaking to reveal pink and yellow smooth areas. These areas turn slowly orange and in their turn, flake away. Unfortunately this tree is hardy only in southern parts.

The hybrid strawberry tree, *A.* x *andrachnoides*, is hardy enough and has dark red, scaling bark, but grows to be quite big and spreading. The Pacific strawberry tree, *A. menziesii*, also grows tall, to 19 m (60 ft), but remains quite narrow. Frequently overlooked, its bark is dark red, stripping to leave smooth pink and yellow patches. It has good flowers in late spring and small fruit, ripening red in early autumn and is a thoroughly good all-the-year tree.

Sorbus 'Joseph Rock'

Bright colour in small spaces
No garden is too small (excepting a trough-garden) to take one of the two most compact and brightest coloured trees, which are forms of the big, dull and rugged sycamore, *Acer pseudoplatanus*. The one of English origin, 'Brilliantissimum', is the more compact and makes a mop-head if grafted high, a rounded bush if grafted low. The other is 'Prinz Handjery' and is more open. Both come into leaf bright red, soon fading to rose-pink. This then turns to a subtle orange with some pink and yellow. By now the leaves have been fully expanded for two weeks or more, but there is more to come. They turn a good yellow for another two weeks and then white for a little more before becoming a not very attractive slightly bronzed green. In mid-glory, somewhere about the red and orange phase, older plants grow numerous and stout yellow catkins. No tree has such a complete crown of good colour for so long, nor does any, except the sunrise horse chestnut, go through such a range of colours. 103

The small garden

The sunrise horse chestnut, *Aesculus neglecta* 'Erythroblastos', follows much the same pattern, but more rapidly. Each phase is, at most, a week long. It may be broad and 5–8 m (15–25 ft) tall; if narrow it will grow taller. Its leaves have slender tapering leaflets, finally a good green, some retaining white centres.

The Chinese or glossy privet, *Ligustrum lucidum*, is a winner in several respects, only it can eventually become quite big and shady. It thrives in warmth, running wild in Georgia and making fine trees in Jackson Square, New Orleans. In England it does best in London and the south but is also hardy enough for the north. Its glossy, dark, cupped leaves are bedecked with erect plumes of ivory-white buds from early spring which open and spread their rich sweet fragrance in the autumn and stay until the end of the year. Then it's only a few months before the buds are there again. Its neat rounded crown is always attractive and it has grown splendidly in Enfield as a street tree with scarcely any open soil for its roots.

Conifer trees and shrubs as feature plants

In the very small garden, shrubs may well supplant trees as focal points. Not all large shrubs are broad and bushy, and one or two of slender proportions might be included to provide otherwise absent elements of height and even perspective.

They need not be fastigiate, although several conifers of columnar habit such as *Juniperus virginiana* 'Skyrocket', *Taxus baccata* 'Standishii' and the more tender *Cupressus sempervirens* 'Swane's Gold', are excellent for this purpose. The last two are fairly slow growing, especially 'Swane's Gold', and can be kept pencil slim by careful and regular pruning. One tall and elegant shrub, *Genista aetnensis*, is, despite its later spread which can be checked, graceful and open in growth permitting mass planting beneath. A more compact shrub is the Tasmanian *Ozothamnus rosmarinifolius* which might also be useful, for its bold appearance belies its natural neatness. Its shoots are closely packed, erect, and densely clothed with dark green rosemary-like leaves. In summer, the terminal clusters of red buds open to white flowers which cover the outside of the shrub and last for a considerable time. Closely related, but smaller, is *Ozothamnus ledifolius*, whose yellow-green domes are covered with white flowers in summer preceded by buds of a rich burnt sienna. Even in seed this draws attention to itself with a sweet honey-like aroma.

The variety of combinations and effects that are available make dwarf conifers an ideal choice for a small garden. (See also page 109.) There are, however, a great many semi-dwarf or slow-growing conifers which could form a part of the structure of a small garden.

The Irish juniper, *Juniperus communis* 'Hibernica', is invaluable as a vertical mark to offset rounded forms of shrub plantings. It is a slender cone, very slow to 8 m (25 ft) and bluish grey-green. The Chinese juniper, *J. chinensis*, also has several forms useful in this respect, notably the golden 'Aurea' and the blue, fuzzy 'Blaauw'.

The *Chamaecyparis* group of false cypresses is a treasure-house of dependable, tough, tolerant trees of small-medium size and good foliage. *C. thyoides* 'Andelyensis' is a very dull green but it makes slender tapering spires, and in season is relieved by masses of male flowers at the shoot-tips. *C. pisifera* 'Filifera Aurea' is among the brightest golds available, slender threads hanging from level branches. It remains tub-plant size for a long time and needs about a hundred years to exceed 9 m (30 ft). *C. p.* 'Boulevard' is among the brightest metallic blues, best in slight shade as strong light can fade or scorch it.

Easily raised from cuttings it is a broadly conic, fuzzy bush which grows a little too fast for the smallest garden. You could, however, replace it with a new cutting every ten years. *C. obtusa* 'Crippsii' is, in full light, as bright gold as any tree. It is sturdy, conic and grows fairly slowly but steadily and may be 15 m (49 ft) tall in fifty years. *C. lawsoniana* has no equal for the number and variety of foliage forms. Apart from a wide range of true dwarfs, a large number of the best grow slowly and although they may inch their way to considerable size, they take long enough to do so to have a useful period in a very small garden. Be careful about a few which look like dwarfs, and for a few years grow very slowly, but then take off like a rocket. The prize example is 'Wissellii', which has congested, tufted, dark blue foliage as if it were very dwarf, but can, within twenty years, be 12 m (39 ft) tall, and in seventy years some are 25 m (82 ft) tall and 1.1 m (3 ft 7 in) through the bole. 'Ellwoodii' is not so bad, but all are still growing steadily, and one forty years old is 13 m (43 ft) tall. It is, however, still a very neat, narrow column of dark blue-green. 'Fletcheri' has grown to over 15 m (49 ft) and tends to be a multiple column of juvenile, dark blue-grey foliage. 'Green Spire' and 'Green Pillar' are very alike, being neat, strictly upright, bright green trees, of

Left: *Chamaecyparis lawsoniana* 'Wissellii' is vigorous after a rather slow start. Above: *Thuja occidentalis* 'Rheingold' – copper gold in winter, remains small.

handy size so far (an immense improvement on the untidy, big-growing old 'Erecta Viridis') but of unknown final size. 'Erecta Aurea' is quite safe, being very slow and never big. It is a reasonably broad, erect plant of rich golden foliage. Of the blues, the outstanding colour form is 'Pembury Blue', a unique, smoky pale blue. Slow growing and rather bushy, at length it makes a broad conic tree up to 10 m (33 ft) tall. 'Lutea' is a rich gold, narrow tree, slightly pendulous, but can grow to be 18 m (59 ft) tall.

Among many thujas, the best for the small garden are *Thuja occidentalis* 'Spiralis', a narrow column with short level branches and soft green foliage, and *T. o.* 'Rhinegold', a broad bush of pale yellow becoming orange-tinged in winter and seldom more than 3 m (10 ft) tall. *T. plicata* 'Zebrina' is a fine sturdy, conic tree with golden-barred foliage. It is a steady grower, and the older trees now seventy to eighty years old are 20–25 m (66 ft–82 ft) tall. 'Stoneham Gold', however, stays small and is rather erect and bushy with bright gold tips paling through yellow to a deep green interior, and very attractive.

In general, the silver firs, *Abies spp*, tend to set out fairly early to their 40 m (130 ft) height, and very few have a place in the small garden. One that does, is the Korean fir, *A. koreana*, but make sure that it is derived from the trees on Quelpaert Island off Korea. The mainland form grows more normally, while the island form makes a broad low tree. Both bear flowers when the plants are only 2 m (7 ft 6 in) tall, the females stand in dense lines along the shoots, slender, conic and varying from bright pink to yellow or pale green. These mature into tall cones with purple-blue scales, later mostly hidden by downward-bent, brown bracts. Several other Asiatic species grow sufficiently slowly to give many years service in quite a small space. The Manchurian fir, *A. holophylla*, has long bright green needles and a good shape and Maries's fir, *A. mariesii*, has dark green, shining leaves on an elegantly conic crown. The best of the American species is the cork fir, *A. lasiocarpa* var *arizonica*, which is narrow and has bright metalic blue foliage, and is hardly enough to grow in Morayshire, but does not always thrive.

Several spruces, *Picea spp*, are suitable. The most popular are some very blue forms of the Colorado spruce, *P. pungens*. A mixed group of bright blue or blue-white selections is sold as 'Kosteri', which slowly reach 20 m (65 ft), but can be thin and unhappy unless in damp soils. The brightest is fairly newly arrived in Britain from the USA, where it is common in small gardens. Called 'Hoopsii', it is a peculiarly bright silver-blue and, so far, has remained bushy and quite small. The black spruce, *P. mariana*, is slow and never of great stature. It has a dense crown, often bushy at the base, but exceedingly slender from top to bottom in the wild, with fine blue-grey needles. The Serbian spruce, *P. omorika*, is the best for most purposes. Although varying in crown width (sometimes necessitating planting three from varied sources for every one required), the best have very slender, long spires. This grows on limestone, peat or any other soil, and even in towns it is better than other spruces, if a little thin. It grows quite rapidly, sometimes 1 m (40 in) a year, but it is so narrow that it rarely inconveniences anyone.

The very tiny patch

Here the gardener has two great advantages. He can devote more care and attention per square foot than he can to the same area in a larger garden. Secondly, the garden is easily kept under control. So, rather than complaining at having a small garden, enjoy it! Sympathize with those whose extensive lawns are constantly screaming to be cut, and whose broad borders are under perpetual attack by all sorts of insidious, creeping weeds.

Even a narrow strip of soil 60 cm (2 ft) wide and 4 m (12 ft) long can provide colour for most of the year. Such a strip might be found in Britain in the front of houses, making a brief Eden between home and public pathway. You can of course extend the plot by means of window boxes (which do not necessarily sit on window sills) and other containers which can either be free-standing or lodged on brackets attached to the boundary or house walls.

In such a narrow patch one can plant snowdrops, crocuses and daffodils in the ground and early spring flowers in the containers (for example wallflowers and tulips). One of the climbing plants mentioned on pages 44 and 45 could also be incorporated into the scheme. Three rose bushes could be planted to follow the early-flowering containers, and the containers could be replenished with summer flowers (among which petunias and snapdragons are extremely useful) and a grey-leafed plant or two. Have a hardy fuchsia at one end of the strip, a fern at the other, and a miracle is made – colour from a tiny piece of ground for more than three-quarters of the year.

The choice of roses for the strip will be decided by its environment. Nothing lanky and upright is wanted because the house wall (with climber) is already a dominant upright factor and the shade it casts is likely to encourage lankiness. A rose of rounded bush growth is ideal; choose one variety for all three subjects. 'Iceberg' would be first-rate but for the fact that a warmer colour than white is probably called for. Perhaps the best colour to choose is rose-pink. It is unintrusive, natural to roses and a pleasing colour at the base of a garden picture. Among floribundas these qualities can be found in 'Letchworth Garden City', 'Busy Lizzie', 'Dearest' and 'Pink Parfait', the last being perhaps a bit pale. Alternatively, you could use the rugosa, 'Frau Dagmar Hastrup'.

The ideas behind making a success of so mean and uncompromising a strip are even more effective when applied to a larger space.

The small garden

The land developer's plot

Many present-day gardens designed to go with new houses are of a regular pattern. The original area is often sited on agricultural land, which the developers carve up into plots of roughly equal size and rectangular shape with at least two straight boundaries. (A fence, green hedge or border of shrubs as a screen generally serves this purpose.) In front of the screen there is usually a flower bed and then a central lawn. Elsewhere a bed for roses or annual bedding plants is squeezed in or perhaps located in the front garden.

This somewhat stereotyped pattern of the modern small garden goes only part way to fulfilling the need for privacy and at first sight allows little scope for environmental harmony and individuality.

However, the greatest delight is in creating an oasis of colour (however small) within otherwise harsh terrain and the first job is to choose the best enclosure.

Barriers and screens

In a small garden, if there is so little to hedge in, you may prefer to mark its boundaries as unobtrusively as possible. Low walls or fences could be erected and hidden by plants for most of the year. If you need a more substantial barrier, for privacy or other reasons, a screening hedge or row of conifers might be preferable. In that case bear in mind the speed with which they will grow. A screening which grows too fast may put the whole garden in shade and grow too wide for the bed at its foot. The rose hedge (page 134) and privet should be avoided, as should such fast and tall growing trees as poplar or willow, whose foraging roots can play havoc with nearby plantings.

Clothing low walls

In a small garden even a low wall cannot be ignored as a planting space. In fact it is one of the most natural positions for a variety of plants. Both dry-stone walls and brick retaining walls can be interplanted (page 70).

Many species of the genus *Sempervivum* are suited to soil pocket planting as are a number of campanulas, especially *C. portenschlagiana*, *C. poscharsky-ana* and *C. garganica*. So are the easier alpine plants, provided due care is taken to provide the environment they like.

Trailing plants which you might care to consider are: *Alyssum saxatile*, a sprawling alpine perennial with grey leaves and yellow flowers (cut it back after flowering to forestall its eventual lanky appearance); *A. maritimum* (syn. *Lobularia maritima* – sweet alyssum) with its fragrant pale blue and white flowers; the rock cresses (*Arabis* spp) whose foliage and white flowers are too invasive for the rock garden; the purple-flowered *Aubrieta deltoidea*; the various forms of rock rose *Helianthemum nummularium* (syn. *H. chamaecistus*); and *Phlox subulata* (which again needs trimming to keep compact). All these are spring-flowering sun-lovers.

Banks of colour on terraced beds

Many town gardens appear to restrict planting, yet as the illustration shows, there is usually ample opportunity to utilize space upwards.

Hypericum empetrifolium and *Rubus calycinoides* are spreading evergreen shrubs suited to a similar position.

In more shady positions you might choose *Haberlea ferdinandi-coburgi* and *H. rhodopensis* which have hairy leaves toothed in a loose basal rosette. *Ramonda myconii*, with two or three pale mauve flowers on each stem, also likes a cool position.

Beds and borders as focal points

There is no reason why you should be satisfied with a rectangular piece of lawn surrounded by very narrow, straight borders at the base of the garden boundaries. Even if the site is 6 m (20 ft) wide by 12 m (40 ft) long the narrow borders will look thin and cold.

The island bed

This is one way of breaking out of the stereotyped small garden with its central lawn and hopelessly narrow borders. It allows great scope for individuality: it is suitable for a wide range of different plants; it can be rectangular, oval, circular, or whatever shape is in keeping with the shape of the plot; it need not be at ground level. In practical terms, because they are accessible all round, they are easy to maintain. If in grass, however, they should be planned for the convenient and economic use of the mowing machine. You should never have to mow narrow strips or back a mower out of a narrow 'dead-end'. Rounded corners are usually easier to 'edge-cut' than angled ones. A raised island bed could be made of stone, brick, concrete blocks, or even railway sleepers (ties), and filled with peat or a clean soil mix to suit the plants you choose.

Most dwarf shrubs, as well as conifers, will flourish in a peat bed, as of course will heathers and a wealth of alpine plants. You may even decide to line a raised bed with peat blocks. See **Ideas for an acid soil garden.**

The traditional border

If you decide to keep the one-sided border, make life easier for yourself by 1. introducing a neutral space between plantings and boundary, and 2. giving the border itself as much width as the garden will take. Turn it into the main feature.

Breaking with tradition

There are pros and cons for all border and bed designs. Be aware of the possibilities that island beds present, both in planting and sculpting the garden with interesting shapes.

Tall-growing plants look unhappy in very narrow borders. If a border is only 1.8 m (6 ft) wide, it should contain nothing over 90 cm (3 ft) high when in flower. This proportion can be applied to any specific width. With adequate space there is ample opportunity to include a whole variety of dwarf shrubs, and some of the bolder perennials such as kniphofias (pokers), lupins, yuccas and grasses; all are effective against a tall backdrop.

Raised planting designs

These are of interest not simply because they elevate the work surface and facilitate planting for the elderly or disabled. In a small garden, one of the most effective displays might consist of a terraced planting with several levels created within the basic raised bed to produce a 'wall' of colour.

Rose beds for small gardens

Roses can be mixed in small beds and borders, but here in the small garden the problem is which varieties to select for a necessarily limited display. If a bed will only take six plants, the choice must be whether to plant six roses of one variety, for effect, or six different varieties for interest. To plant two's or three's fails to make the best of either objective in a restricted area.

This policy holds good up to a bed of say fifteen bushes, when the decision is either to plant fifteen of one variety or to work in threes and fives. The reason is that there comes a point when a single plant of a variety appears insignificant in relation to the bed as a whole, whereas a group of it looks more in proportion.

If space permits, a rose border can have pillars or upright shrubs at the back, each plant of a different variety perhaps. A middle row of smaller plants could stand different varieties for each group of three. Dwarf subjects in the front might be best grouped in fives or sevens of one variety.

107

The small garden

There is scope, then, for some of the short, bushy miniatures like 'Baby Masquerade' and the short floribundas, like 'Anna Ford'. Ideas for the middle row are a Scotch rose or two to flower early, a conversation piece like the green *R. chinensis viridiflora*, the invaluable 'The Fairy' to flower late, and perhaps the lovely bourbon, 'Souvenir de la Malmaison'. For the taller plants make use of the available contrast between 'spires' and 'domes'. Suggestions include another bourbon, 'Boule de Neige', and the early flowering 'Golden Chersonese'. 'Aloha' could be grown as a shrub, 'Sander's White' and 'Crimson Shower' could be tied to pillars.

Roses for a vertical wall of colour

For a steep bank or a terraced raised bed, where one mainly sees the tops of the plants, a delightful rose pattern can be made by planting rugosa roses and *R. rubrifolia*. The rugosas should form the main body of the design, but let veins of *R. rubrifolia* run through them. The resulting display is most effective; young purple shoots against white; feathery growth against dense growth. A bonus comes with the hips of both kinds.

Choosing shrubs for a bed

Some people, when faced with planting in a confined space, pack in as many of the smallest shrubs they can find. Most shrubs can be kept within bounds by trimming them back when they have flowered. In any case, cluttering a small garden merely emphasizes its restrictive dimensions. It is far better to have a few well-spaced, choice, permanent subjects and to plant the intervening spaces with less durable flowers or hardy perennials.

Early flowering 'Canary Bird'.

Using roses in a mixed shrub bed

Choose with a very careful eye to their health, and go for something of character.

'The Fairy' recommended for the middle row of a rose bed.

One of the early-flowering members of *Pimpinellifolia* answers these requirements – preferably 'Canary Bird' or 'Golden Chersonese'. They are in flower about tulip time or a little later, are indescribably lovely, and their foliage is an asset afterwards. They grow about 2 m (5 ft) tall, and about as wide. Choose 'Alexander' as another shrub; it has a lustrous vermilion flower against dark leaves and flowers freely from midsummer to late autumn. It grows about 1.75 m (5 ft) tall and not very wide. 'Iceberg' is best grown as a shrub when it forms a rounded plant about 1.25 m (4 ft) high, marvellously clad in glistening white flowers in both summer and autumn. For some reason it seems much healthier when treated as an individual plant than when grown by the yard.

A most useful rose to grow as a shrub is *R. chinensis mutabilis*, which has creamy single flowers changing to pink and finally to magenta red. Far more charming than it might sound, this plant has an extremely long flowering season. Its development depends more than most on a congenial environment, when it will grow to about 1.75 m (5 ft) high and fairly rounded.

If short roses are required, then there are many choices, including some floribundas and miniatures. Particu-larly delightful among the former are the white 'Yvonne Rabier', the pink 'Nathalie Nypels', the yellow 'Kim' or 'Bright Smile'. Miniatures need to be chosen with caution, however, for sometimes they can be unhealthy. Among the more reliable are 'Pour Toi' and 'Easter Morning', both white, the pink 'New Penny', the yellow 'Rosina' and the orange-scarlet 'Darling Flame'. A fairly low white rose of great charm is the sempervirens hybrid, 'Little White Pet'.

The brightest of these short roses are 'Topsi', 'Meteor' and 'Marlena' with vermilion and crimson colours. Effective as they are, they do grow very close to the ground.

Making use of a variety of form in shrub beds

You might consider little informal groups of hummock-shaped shrubs or, better still, use them in isolation swelling amongst lower growing or prostrate plants. The best of these shrubs include *Spiraea japonica* 'Nana', *Ilex cornuta* 'Rotunda' and *Hebe rakaiensis*. The last named rising out of a carpet of *Acaena microphylla* is very effective. Many hummocks are to be found amongst the rock roses (*Cistus*) group and conifers. And no garden, large or small, should be without conifers of one kind or another.

Hemerocallis spp good when root competition is a problem.

Sculpting shapes with conifer shrubs

Small and slow-growing conifers give a superb effect when several of different shapes and colours are planted together. The blue or grey carpets of *Juniperus horizontalis* and its varieties can be used as a base on which to build an interesting group which might include two or three of globular form. Three of the best are the golden bronze *Thuja plicata* 'Rogersii', *Picea abies* 'Gregoryana' (absolutely dense and compact with grey-green needles) and *Cryptomeria japonica* 'Globosa', which is pale green in summer turning to an attractive rust-red in winter. There are innumerable others which can be planted to create different colour and textural effects. To give the group height, one might add a conifer of columnar growth. Perhaps the slowest growing and ultimately the smallest is *Juniperus communis* 'Compressa' (an essential for miniature landscapes).

Two of the best blue-grey varieties of *J. horizontalis* (suggested as a carpet from which these shrubs can rise) are 'Bar Arbor' and 'Marcellus'. Sometimes a low-spreading, but not prostrate conifer will add another dimension to the group without detracting from its unity. Such suitable subjects are also to be found in the juniper clan –

J. communis 'Repanda' and *J. communis depressa* 'Aurea'. Both form somewhat higher carpets than the horizontalis and differ in both texture and colour (the first being bright green, the second yellow in summer turning to bronze in winter).

Also associating well with dwarf conifers are the heathers and heaths, though in America, outside coastal areas or the north-east and north-west, they are short-lived. These mostly low-growing shrubs are available in bewildering variety, but a selection taken from the interest-through-year garden (pages 176 and 188) will provide colour even in the most difficult season. A bed of these together with dwarf slow-growing conifers makes a fine feature for the smaller garden. Certainly you will have to forego planting the summer and autumn varieties if gardening on a chalky soil, but you can enjoy winter and spring species.

Combining perennials with shrubs

Depending on the spacing between shrubs the variations for planting are endless. When root competition is a criterion of choice, the summer flowering *Hemerocallis* genus (day lily) is highly recommended as being able to look after itself. Thanks to plant breeders there is now a large range of hybrids

which includes a wide variety of colours. In shady dells you will find that the hostas hold their own, and the creamy or white, pink-tinged tiarellas make attractive groupings with clumps of rhododendrons or azaleas. *T. polyphylla* flowers in the summer, *T. wherryi* between late spring and mid-summer. Both prefer semi-shade.

If the shrubs are well-spaced the choice of perennials widens to include many alpines which could trail over the wall of a raised shrub bed or grow on the flat. They associate particularly well with shrub roses but could as easily be selected to give a display when the roses are out of season.

Ringing the changes with seasonal colour

Annuals, biennials and bulbs play a very important role in the small garden. The bedding annuals are of course prime subjects for planting *en masse* in swathes of colour. See page 180. Fortunately, catalogue descriptions about the height, spread and colour of annuals are generally accurate, so harmony within a bed or border arrangement should present few problems. When planting them between shrubs and perennial plants in mixed borders, it is a good idea to cluster a fair number of them quite close together to create the effect. Think too about choosing flowers for scent; in a small space this really is a good deciding factor in your choice.

Shade in a small space may well limit your choice of both annuals and bulbs, but as we shall see this depends entirely upon the degree of shade.

Of course, bulbs and tubers vary greatly in height. At one end are the spring dwarfs, such as the crocuses and scillas; at the other extreme there are the great spikes of some of the foxtail lilies (*Eremurus spp*), which can reach over 2 m (6 ft 6 in). In fact even the small eremurus, such as *E. bungei*, will exceed 1 m (3 ft), and the Shelford hybrids, which present pastel shades between the yellow of *E. bungei* and the pink of *E. himalaicus*, are also midway in height. They all flower in early summer. Many of the florist's gladioli reach over 1 m (3 ft) high, and so may the hardy *G. byzantinus*, though 60 cm (2 ft) is more likely. The hybrid *Crinum powellii* makes a massive plant with both leaves and flower spikes exceeding 1 m (3 ft) and looks so unkempt during the winter that it is really not suitable for the small garden.

Some planning care is therefore required in siting some of these taller bulbs if you choose them as sources of colour in a confined space.

Solving problems with plants

The shady garden

What sort of shade?

Shade is the most common problem in small gardens. Each plant has its own light requirements, and this influences the type of shade it can tolerate. Some parts of the garden may be in shade only at certain times of day; the density of shade also depends on how much light filters through trees or is blocked off by large structures such as walls, fences and buildings. Before you think about planting for shade you should carefully note which kind of shade you have in your garden and how this is affected by the time of day, the seasons, and above all the nature of the obstruction.

Areas of very dense shade usually occur in the vicinity of large vertical enclosures, but planting is most difficult under trees with thick, low-lying foliage. The fibrous root systems of mature trees will take away much of the moisture and nutrients from surrounding soil, causing what is known as *dry shade* in which only a very limited number of plants (of a very restricted colour range) can survive. Rain-drenched branches, hanging low over the soil, drip and have a detrimental effect on plants placed on the perimeter line of a tree's crown.

Alan Bloom explains how he tackled dry shade: 'My own garden was once a park-like meadow, with some large deciduous trees. I dug out an island bed to make use of the shade of an oak and an ash growing on a bank above it. Some tree roots, especially from the ash, had to be severed, but in the very first season they penetrated far into my newly planted bed of shade and moisture-loving plants. Hoping to defeat the tree roots for good, I dug a narrow trench, lined it with strips of asbestos sheeting and filled it in. But within a year or two, dry patches appeared and flagging plants were evidence that hungry ash roots were determined to find the moisture and goodness I had provided. It became an annual task every winter to keep tree roots cut back, until after the 1976 drought. This so accentuated the nuisance that I had to dig another trench further back from the bed and nearer the tree. It had to be about 75 cm (2½ ft) deep and this time I lined it with overlapping polythene fertilizer bags, taking care to leave no gaps. This foiled the roots so thoroughly that not only have the choice inhabitants of the bed thrived, but even the grass strip between the bed and the barrier has remained green during dry periods.

'This method can be recommended to anyone who wants to make a bed for plants between trees, more or less clear of overhanging branches. It could also

be used to overcome root penetration into a bed backed by a hedge or conifers. It is a matter of discretion as to how close to place the polythene barrier, but its top edge should be only just below the surface level of the soil. It would have to be *very* close to a hedge or tree to have a detrimental effect on them, though one may be sure that if roots are barred from spreading in one direction, they will soon find another to exploit.'

Things are much easier if light can filter through the leaves of tall trees, producing an alternating play of light and shade. This dappled effect is not only pleasing to the eye, but creates a suitable environment for a far greater number of plants than does dense shade. Under high, open-leaved trees, plants are sheltered from direct sunlight, but still receive full daylight. Deciduous trees, of course, lose their leaves in autumn and then permit a much greater proportion of light to reach the plants beneath. With broad-leaved evergreens and conifers, on the other hand, there is no such seasonal sympathy for underlying plants.

Bear in mind the following points when planting in the shade:

* The chosen plants must not be sun-lovers. If you plant these in the shade of

a wall, they will grow tall and lanky in an effort to reach the sunlight.

* Some plants are nominally sun-lovers but will tolerate a degree of shade. They may not fruit or flower as well as they would in direct sun.

* Watering is vitally important. Unless plants in shade have sufficient moisture they will fail.

* Shady soil under thirsty trees or very close to buildings is anathema to most plants. Competition from tree roots must be allowed for, or if possible solved.

Only shallow-rooting small trees will not tolerate some root disturbance. But if you do underplant these with shade-tolerant shrubs, use mulches rather than digging in compost.

Growing trees in a shady garden

Every tree – however tolerant of shade when young – requires open sky above it to mature to its proper shape and to flower and fruit. No tree can grow under the shade of its own kind; those which can grow under shade when young do so by having dense, large-leaved crowns which are efficient at intercepting what light there is. Consequently there is little grown beneath them.

In shade there is a first-rate opportunity to experiment with the variety of foliage forms, but colour is possible too from many bulbs and shade-tolerant perennials.

In a natural environment there is a regular progression of species from the light-demanding pioneers which spring up first on bare land (propagated by small wind-borne seeds) through to species more tolerant of shade, then finally to shade-bearers which grow up beneath and replace the other trees. At this point the wood is said to have reached its 'climax', and regenerates only in gaps caused in nature by the falling of old trees.

Shade from buildings can only be side-shade, and is rarely serious to trees. Beneath a tree canopy, however, no other tree will grow at its best. The approach, in that situation, must be to grow those that in the wild start in shade. But in a garden setting you should expect to have to replace them in succession, perhaps planting them with some semi-dwarfs that can make a more permanent display. In nature, oak and (where the soil is sufficiently well-drained) beech are shade tolerant to a degree and will grow up to replace the wind-borne seeded, light-demanding pioneers. But even the holly, yew and hemlock, which are known to grow wild in partial shade, do not excell in form, flower or fruit, when so planted.

Conifers in shade
Of the many conifers that can start in shade, not many are really suitable for the long-term. Douglas fir survives, but it soon needs full light or it will become covered with the sticky white wool of the adelges green-fly and lose colour and vigour. Silver fir, *Abies alba*, grows for thirty or forty years in quite dense shade, but grows exceedingly slowly and is rather dull. For many years most of the Asiatic silver

firs need light overhead shade to ward off spring frosts when their buds are sprouting. But they all need open sky after some fifteen years. For about the same time the Nikko fir, *A. forrestii*, and the Caucasian fir *A. nordmanniana* make vigorous and shapely trees in light shade.

Lawson cypresses can grow well in considerable shade and have a drooped leading shoot which enables them to thread their way through the branches of other trees without damage to their growing tips. The coloured forms which are the most desirable are more sensitive to shade and lose their brightness – some of the golden ones are quite green in moderate to severe shade. The smallest-growing coloured forms are probably the best.

Shade is about the only thing that will slow down the growth of the Leyland cypress but it will tolerate quite a degree of it. The form 'Leighton Green' becomes very narrowly columnar; the golden forms will probably lose a little of their colour.

No spruce or pine is of any use in shade. Western red cedar, *Thuja plicata* can grow quite well but is thin. The Western hemlock, *Tsuga heterophylla*, is able to grow fast in fairly dense shade and like the Lawson cypress has a drooped leader for growing through other trees. It has elegant, small foliage, but like the yew it is a very dark, dull green.

The broadleaves in shade
Among the broad-leafed trees, the hollies stand out as shade-bearers. The many variegated and coloured leaf

forms only lose a little of their colour from not being fully in the open. The Highclere hybrid holly, *Ilex* x *alta-clarensis* 'Golden King', is vigorous and bright and may be best in shade but it cannot be expected to carry many berries away from full light. Of the *Ilex aquifolium* forms, 'Handsworth New Silver' is among the most attractive. The strawberry tree, *Arbutus unedo*, survives in some shade and may even flower, but the other *Arbutus* species are not likely to thrive. The box, *Buxus sempervirens*, will grow, but only as a shrub. The variegated form is too feebly coloured to be effective in shade.

Of deciduous trees, very few can be used in seriously shady conditions. The hornbeam, *Carpinus betulus*, is among the least unhappy but makes an impressive crown, even the splendid form 'Fastigiata' loses its good shape in time. Beech, *Fagus sylvatica*, is thin and straggling but both these species are excellent where there is side shade only. So are a whole range of deciduous trees, including many flowering ones like the *Sorbus* species.

As a general rule, gardens shaded by big trees should not be planted with more trees beneath them. They will look better under-planted with ferns, hostas and other shrubs.

Shrubs in dry shade
There is a limited number of shrubs which can prove satisfactory in dry, shady conditions, provided you maintain a good mulch of well decayed compost or leaf-mould. These are *Rubus tricolor*, *Ruscus aculeatus*, the ivies and the sarcococcas. The rubus and the ivies it should be noted, are vigorous growers and have little respect for plants which are smaller and weaker than they are. (It should also be noted that many varieties of *Hedera*, *R. aculeatus* and the sarcococcas are likely to be less successful in colder parts of the U.S.A. than the shade tolerant, variegated *Kerria japonica* 'Picta', *Kalmia latifolia* and various rhododendrons.)

The first of these, *R. tricolor*, is a Chinese non-thorny bramble. It has long trailing hairy stems and handsome evergreen leaves which are glossy on top and white underneath. Neither the flowers nor the fruits are of much consequence – in temperate climates at any rate – but in a large garden the plant makes an excellent ground cover, throwing a blanket several yards long over the ground that gleams in the gloom. It is not suited to small spaces unless you are prepared to keep its prodigious growth in check. Like any shrub in dry soil, *R. tricolor* should be planted in a generous-sized 111

The shady garden

hole filled with peat, leaf-mould or any other water-absorbant material.

Ruscus aculeatus, butcher's broom, is an erect, tough-stemmed shrub which grows from 60 cm to 1 m (2 to 3 ft) high. The foliage is in the form of small, dark, spine-tipped cladodes -- branches closely resembling leaves – while the actual leaves are diminutive and scale-like. Female plants, if pollinated, bear occasional cherry-sized red berries, though some forms are more generous than others with their fruit. There are other species of *Ruscus* which are less often seen but have a much greater ornamental value. The best of these is *R. hypoglossum*, which differs from the common species in having larger, pale green, spineless cladodes on short stems in low-spreading clumps. It grows wild in the Belgrade forest to the north of Istanbul, where it shares the shade with *Euphorbia robbiae, E. amygdaloides, Hypericum calycinum* and various ferns – a highly effective combination which you might like to try for yourself in your garden, provided you bear in mind the vigorous nature of hypericum and that the euphorbias are not easy in cold climates.

There are several species of *Sarcococca*, all of which tolerate dry soil in shade (especially on chalk). They have dark evergreen leaves, are low in stature and produce clusters of small white, sweetly scented flowers early in the year. Two to note particularly are *S. humilis*, which is the lowest growing – up to 25 cm (10 in) – and can be used to form carpets, and *S. confusa*, which forms a bold single clump up to 90 cm (3 ft) high, with glossy dark green privet-shaped leaves.

Ivies are very useful and adaptable and could be planted to grow up walls, fences or the trunks of large trees, or simply left to cover the ground. Once established they will do as good a job as the rubus. The bold-leaved, exceptionally hardy Irish ivy, *Hedera helix* 'Hibernica' and the Persian ivy, *H. colchica* and its variety 'Dentata', form a close ground cover which will associate well with walls and tree stumps. The variegated form 'Dentata variegata' has leaves which are streaked and bordered with creamy-white and this will provide a striking contrast with the dark green of the others (though in dense shade its colours will fade). The various cut or coloured leaf forms of the English ivy, *H. helix*, are legion, but a selection of the best would include 'Goldheart', for its yellow blotched leaves; 'Cavendishii', for white-margined leaves; and 'Buttercup' for the bright yellow of its young leaves (though it needs more moisture than most varieties). These varieties are more

Variegated *Hedera colchia* 'Dentata'.

suitable for climbing positions than as ground covers.

Two green-leaved ivies worth special mention are 'Caenwoodiana', with its small fingered leaves, and the hardy 'Ivalace', with deeply-lobed leaves.

Any combination of the above will have pleasing results though the less vigorous sarcococca, ruscus and ferns such as hart's tongue, *Scolopendrium vulgare*, are thus preferable bases for interplanting colonies of bulbs. In particularly cold climates choose *Hedera helix* in preference to its cultivars and other ivy species, and look to the rhododendrons, *Kerria japonica* 'Picta' (a silver variegated dwarf form of the deciduous shrub) and *Kalmia latifolia* for variety and interest.

Shrubs in light shade

For shady areas which are not so treacherously dry, a much wider range of shrubs is available. A special mention must be made of *Daphne bholua* 'Gurkha', a superb Himalayan shrub which during late winter and early spring is alive with terminal clusters of sweetly scented, purple-stained flowers. Some hydrangeas do well in light shade: *H. serrata* 'Grayswood' provides late summer and autumn colour with its lacecap heads. These are white at first, changing to pink and finally to deep crimson, while the more erect *H. macrophylla* 'Preziosa' has globular heads of sterile florets which exhibit a wide range of tints.

For late summer flowering, the yellow cups of several hypericums are useful. If you feel that the ubiquitous 'Hidcote' is a little too familiar try the more robust and rounded *H. forrestii*, which is both floriferous and easy to grow. *H. kouytchense* is slightly smaller, with larger, more open flowers crowded with long stamens.

Most shrubs growing naturally in forests or woods are of course suitable for dappled shade in the garden. These include the dogwoods, *Cornus spp*, the viburnums and many rhododendrons and azaleas. The scarlet, almost crimson colour of young *Cornus alba* stems are most attractive in 'Sibirica' (sometimes known as 'Westonbirt Variety'). Prune it to base in spring to make the most of this feature. But the North American dogwood, *C. florida*, is arguably the most beautiful, especially *C.f.* var *rubra* with its rose-pink petals. The rhododendrons and the related azaleas have, of course, long been favourites among those who garden on acid soil, both for their flowers and for the ability of some to tolerate semi-shade. The range of colour, height and habit is enormous and some expert guidance may well be necessary before you can choose a selection best suited to your own needs. Broadly speaking, the larger leaved species flourish most successfully in shade. See also **Ideas for an acid soil garden**.

Rose beds in shade

It is the natural habit of roses to produce their leaves and flowers in the sunlight. It is easy to tell when roses have been positioned in too shady a bed; in their search for light, they will have become elongated and thin, and the blooms will be small and pallid. To decide whether a place is too shady, see if it has half a day's sun on a fine summer day. If it has less than six hours, the conditions will not be good for roses.

In spite of this, bush roses may be planted in the shade of a low wall, provided they can easily lift their leaves into the light above it. By the same token a climber or trailer can be planted in the shade of a higher wall, to flower on top of it or to trail over the other side. Inevitably, on the side of the wall where the plant is in constant shade, a rose will look somewhat bare.

Another way to lift roses out of the shade is to plant standards. The rose likely to prosper in shady places better than any other is *R. rubrifolia*. This species grows fairly tall and narrow and is famous for its red-purple leaves. The flowers are small and fleeting, but the hips make a fine show in autumn.

Ferns in damp shade

Damp, shady conditions in woodland, hedgerows, marshes and rocky outcrops form the natural habitat of many kinds of fern. Though there are varieties which will grow in open sunlight, the overwhelming majority look for filtered sunlight, dappled shade or a north-facing aspect. They prefer a soil which is moist (but not waterlogged – this will cause the roots to rot), cool, rich and slightly acid. If necessary some peat, leaf-mould or other humus-forming material can be worked in, along with sand to improve drainage if the soil is heavy. Many ferns will benefit from a good mulch. Avoid very deep shade or a position close to the drip line of tree crowns, walls or buildings.

Ferns come in a wide range of greens, from pale yellow-greens to a dark blue-green, which gives a cool, restful effect. They complement the brighter colours of other plants, particularly if you follow some of the planting suggestions discussed in **Ideas for a wet garden.**

Some ferns are tall and stately, others delicate and diminutive, and planting in variety can emphasize the differences in shape, form and texture. The smaller varieties can be used in rock gardens or walls.

Osmunda regalis (royal fern) is a tall, stately fern with good autumn colour, reaching well above 1.2 m (4 ft) in more moist conditions, but less (around 90 cm (3 ft)) in drier soils. It is suitable both for water-side conditions and in open beds. Plant individual specimens 90 cm (3 ft) apart in a good mulch.

Osmunda cinnamomea (cinnamon fern) gets its name from its brownish scales. In the wild it grows 1–1.5 m (3–5 ft) and has fronds 15–25 cm (6–10 in) across. It is suitable for planting on the banks of ponds and streams.

Matteuccia struthiopteris (ostrich fern) has tall, pale green fronds extending some 60 m (2 ft). This elegant fern is deep-rooting, making it useful for growing on slopes or other areas where soil erosion may be a problem. In marshy conditions it can spread rampantly by means of underground runners.

The Dryopteris species (buckler ferns) are usually about knee-high and very robust, but do not have a particularly spreading habit.

D. aemula, with fronds between 15–60 cm (6 in–2 ft) long, produces a scent very like that of new-mown hay when the fronds are dying, and is commonly called the hay-scented buckler fern.

D. marginalis is a robust evergreen fern. Its fronds, yellowish in spring, turn a dark blue-green in summer.

D. filix-mas (male fern) comes in many varieties with fronds between 40–90 cm (15 in– 3 ft) long. Magical properties are ascribed to it in folklore.

D. spinulosa has more finely-cut, pale leaves, between 30 cm–1.2 m (1 ft–4 ft) long. It looks for a deeply mulched, rocky soil, and can be grown successfully at the base of rocks or tree stumps.

D. borreri (D. pseudomas), the scaly male fern, comes in many forms and is evergreen in good conditions. It has 60–90 cm (2 ft–3 ft) fronds with orange scales on the stems. It looks for a humus-rich soil.

Adiantum pedatum is the botanical name for the very popular maidenhair fern. Its light green, 30 cm (12 in) fronds are delicate and arching. It prefers a loose soil, well mulched with compost, peat moss, leaf-mould or other organic material to which some gravel has been added.

Athyrium filix-femina, the lady fern, is another very popular fern, coming in many varieties with delicate feathery fronds ranging in length from 75 cm–1 m (30 in–40 in). It dislikes lime and should be grown in well-mulched soil, where its tendency to spread can be curbed by trimming or by confining within natural barriers.

Thelypteris phegopteris, the oak fern, has delicate pale green fronds 15–30 cm (6–12 in) long. It dislikes lime but can be grown very successfully in rock gardens or on the banks of a stream or pond.

Polypodium vulgare, the common polypody, has 10–40 cm (4–16 in) fronds and comes in many varieties. Often recommended for the tops of walls or the rock garden, it is an evergreen fern which is at its best in winter.

Polystichum aculeatum, the hard shield fern, is lime tolerant with 30–60 cm (1–2 ft) leathery fronds. It can be used to prevent erosion on banks and slopes.

P. setiferum, the soft shield fern, has lighter coloured, softer leaves, up to 1 m (40 in) long.

The shady garden

Perennials

Beds in the shadow of a house are common flower planting 'problems'. To minimize the risk of weak, elongated stems, choose plants which do not grow more than 60 cm (2 ft) high. Spring-flowered pulmonarias, primroses and bergenias might be ideal. But look too at the many subjects whose handsome foliage provide compensation for a shady garden. The hostas, now available in great variety, are at home in shady places, especially where the soil is unlikely to dry out. It is possible to have luxuriance for much of the year from a collection of hostas. They range in height from quite small to 1.2 m (4 ft) in flower and with leaves egg-size to those of a tennis racket. There are many shades of green and differing variegations amongst them.

Many perennials with variegated leaves actually prefer shade. The golden-leaved filipendula and the brightly variegated *Brunnera macrophylla* (as well as most variegated hostas) will become sun-scorched in fully open positions. The stately cimicifugas, the brilliant astilbes and the creamy white plumes of aruncus are all best in shade. Amongst the range of plants adaptable for either sun or shade there are several hardy geraniums, in soft blues and pinks, and in spring you can have a bright display with yellow doronicums and blue pulmonarias to precede the summer flowering beauties.

A shaded peat bed offers great scope. Even if the natural soil is alkaline, calcifuge kinds can be grown in a raised peat bed. Many alpines and dwarf shrubs, such as azaleas and daphne, will be content with about 30 cm (1 ft) depth of peat, though Alan Bloom prescribes a mixture of peat and shredded forest bark plus 10–15% sand and 10–15% lime-free soil. In such a mixture an entrancing range of plants can be grown, including some of the best lime-tolerant kinds.

In dry shade one can only suggest trying vincas, lamiums and a few other ground coverers (see **Low-maintenance planning ideas**), none of which will make a particularly bright or prolonged display, even if they flower at all. Autumn is a better time for planting these than spring, not only when the shade is caused by deciduous trees, but because when the soil is damp for a long period plants have more of a chance of taking hold.

Planning beds for shade-tolerant perennials

The ideal is to have separate beds, or two parts of a large bed or border designated appropriately for sun-loving and shade-loving plants. There need be no inflexible rules – leave room for modest experimenting and the very adaptable kinds, such as the spring-flowering, evergreen bergenias and the primrose-polyanthus type of primula, to succeed where they will. It's worth remembering that most spring-flowering plants depend upon the accumulated moisture from previous winter months to produce their display. Many can withstand dry summer spells since they have learned to accept that in their natural habitat.

'When extending my garden,' recalls Alan Bloom, 'I was up against the problem of how to place early spring plants which preferred some shade. In my zeal for island beds I saw no place for a north-facing, one-sided border, though there was an evergreen shelter belt which obviously could be utilized. This was about 4.5 m (15 ft) high, curving gently in its 55 m (60 yd) length. A compromise occurred to me and I dug out two new kidney-shaped beds, leaving a narrow path close to the

114

Far left: mixed bed of foxgloves. Top left: the wax begonia. Bottom left: a carpet of periwinkle. Above: *Cyclamen neapolitanum*, noted for its ability to grow under the shade of beech. All do well in some shade, the periwinkle survives quite deeply shaded areas.

evergreens and another between the two beds, each up to 5 or 9 m (6 or 10 yd) wide.

'This allowed part of each bed to be shaded for most of the day. Planting followed the usual island plan of having the tallest kinds in the middle, which was largely in sun. In the rear shady side the spring-flowering kinds were planted, interspersed with shade-lovers which came into their own later on. It worked well. During the spring this shady strip was a great attraction, but with the spring over the beds were best seen from the sunny side. Indeed the view from this side back to the shelter belt gives an initial impression that they are one-sided beds, as the taller-growing centre groups tend to hide the now resting spring subjects.

'It is worth mentioning that most tall-growing, shade-loving perennials flower after midsummer and on into the autumn. It would be a mistake to plant them too close to a shade provider lest they become drawn up and spindly. In any case, almost all are happy in partial shade and some will grow quite well in a mainly sunny position, provided the soil is good and does not dry out.'

Annuals, biennials and bulbs in shade

Annuals are particularly difficult in shady conditions, although you may have more luck in growing biennials and bulbs, corms and tubers. Remember that you can always grow these temporary plants in containers in the sunnier conditions they prefer and move them into shadier parts to add a little colour for a day or two. This will not place too much stress on the plants, although they will probably be glad to get back into the sun.

Except where noted, the plants suggested here need conditions in which a reasonable amount of light can reach them (dappled or light shade, for instance). Recent developments in hybridization have meant that there are now appreciably more shade-tolerant plants available. Nevertheless the point should be made that plants grown in conditions which are not absolutely ideal for them can often be unpredictable.

Of the hardy annuals, the following can usually be grown reasonably successfully in moderate shade: hollyhocks (*Althaea rosea*) in white, red, yellow and pink; woodruff (*Asperula orientalis*) in blue; the yellow or orange pot marigolds (*Calendula officinalis*); violet cress (*Ionopsidium acaule*) in white or purplish shades; lupins (*Lupinus hartwegii*) in blue, red, mauve and white; and the assorted colours of virginia stock (*Malcomia maritima*). Of the half hardy species, there is the snapdragon (*Antirrhinum majus*), wax begonia (*Begonia semperflorens*), in white, red or pink; the yellow orange or red *Gaillardia pulchella*; the faithful balsam or busy Lizzie (*Impatiens walleriana*) in many reddish shades; and *Lobelia erinus* in blue, white and red.

The better the conditions, the more chance you have of being successful. But you should have few problems with three hardy biennials: the foxglove (*Digitalis purpurea*), which comes in white, red and mauve varieties; Dame's violet (*Hesperis matronalis*) in purplish tints; and honesty (*Lunaria spp*) with its white or mauve flowers and the transparent silver flattened seed pods which look so well indoors when cut.

It is not difficult to grow many bulbs in shady conditions, provided they have light when their foliage is in active growth and are warm and dry in their summer rest period. This means that spring bulbs (including tulips, daffodils and crocus) will be quite happy under deciduous trees and shrubs which, until they have grown their own new foliage, will let quite a lot of light through to the bulbs beneath. The severity of root competition from trees depends upon whether, like oaks, they are deeply rooted, or whether, like beeches and maples, they are shallow rooted. Test dig if in doubt and should there be roots close to the surface do not plant within the compass of the tree crown. The very early bulbs such as snowdrops and winter aconites will grow where there is less light, making them the first choice where there is permanent shade from a building or evergreen tree. Cyclamen also seem to be tolerant of quite dense shade, and appear to prefer a little shade to permanently open sites. You might not expect the *reticulata* irises to do very well in the shade, but in practice they seem to take very little notice of what the text books say about them and they can sometimes be found thriving in what would seem to be quite unsuitable conditions. 115

The seaside garden

Two great problems face the seaside gardener: wind and salt. The wind buffets the plants, while the salt scorches their young leaves. On the other hand, there are generally a number of advantages not enjoyed by inland gardeners: a sunnier climate, with better light quality and less atmospheric pollution, and a reduced severity of frost in winter.

Enclosures

The first requirement is to protect the garden from the ravages of salt-laden winds and drifts. An evergreen screen will be needed for year-round effectiveness. Its foliage will trap much of the wind's impact, giving shelter to the plants behind it. Holm oak, though not the most visually exciting of trees, is ideal for most soils. If the soil is thin, sandy or rocky and the climate not too severe, then Monterey cypress will be dense enough to provide a fair amount of protection for a small garden. In colder conditions, the Japanese pine can be used and if you are on chalk or lime the Austrian pine. If you use pines as a screen you will need to plant them two or three deep to achieve the same amount of protection afforded by the two first-named trees. For general planting rather than as shelter, cedar, leyland cypress, monkey puzzle, sycamore, white poplar and white beam are salt-tolerant.

In large gardens where space is no object one of the most successful shrubs for screens or informal hedges is the evergreen *Griselinia littoralis* which has large yellow-green leaves and reaches 6 m (20 ft) or more when happy. This is very successful in southern and western coastal areas where another New Zealander, *Coprosma nitida*, is also popular. It is a vigorous evergreen used to excellent effect too in the Isles of Scilly.

Along eastern coasts, the most commonly used shelter and screening shrubs are the feathery-branched tamarisk and the silver-leaved *Hippophae rhamnoides*. Both are deciduous but can withstand almost any amount of salt and wind. Tamarisk has colourful pink or reddish-purple flower plumes (but no fruit of merit), whilst *H. rhamnoides* (or sea blackthorn) is the opposite, the female shrubs producing dense clusters of bright orange, bitter-tasting berries.

The *Escallonia* genus, in one or other of its species or hybrids, comes near to being the perfect seaside hedge for mild climates. All are evergreen and of dense habit. In addition to this they produce clusters of attractive, white, pink, rose or red flowers during the summer. They dislike root disturbance and are usually

grown by nurserymen in containers. They are tolerant of regular clipping or even an occasional hard pruning, best done after the flowers have finished.

In some parts of western Ireland the common *Fuchsia magellanica* is found thriving as a coastal hedge, which is hardly surprising when one considers that it grows naturally in the cold, blasted regions of Tierra del Fuego in South America.

There was once a garden on the hills of Zennor on the north Cornish coast which boasted a large number of shrubs from New Zealand more surprisingly suitable for their new home. It was planted by the late Arnold Forster whose favourites included the numerous species and varieties of *Olearia* and *Senecio*. Popularly known as daisy bushes, these were incredibly resilient in the teeth of Atlantic gales and are equally successful in a more sheltered situation. *Senecio* 'Sunshine', a hybrid previously and incorrectly known as *S. greyi*, is perhaps the most commonly planted, and there is no doubt that its bold mounds of soft grey leaves, plastered with bright yellow daisy flowers, are as satisfying a summer spectacle as can be found anywhere. The larger, more leathery-leaved *S. reinoldii* is even more tolerant of salt spray and wind, though its

flowers are inferior to *S.* 'Sunshine'. Its large, compact, leafy domes up to 2.4 m (8 ft) high do, however, look spectacular in the right position.

Shrub planting ideas

Olearia haastii and *O. nummulariifolia* both grow well in the north of England, where they are exposed to high, chilling winds in hillside plots. The former species sports grey leaves and a neat, erect habit whilst the latter has smaller, more leathery, yellowish-green leaves and a stiff, globular habit. Both have white daisy flowers in clusters during summer. They are dwarfed however by the much bigger mounds of *O. macrodonta* and *O. ilicifolia*, whose grey prickly-toothed leaves add an extra dimension to the ornamental attributes of the genus. All these daisy bushes, with the exception of one, thrive in full sun. The exception is *O. cunninghamii*, which is one of the best flowering shrubs for a woodland garden by the sea. For anyone with sufficient space, a group of olearias interplanted with some of the mound-like hebes, such as *H. rakaiensis*, *H. anomala*, *H. subalpina* and the golden *H. ochracea*, would make an exciting and most effective display. Additionally for general garden use or in tubs, all hydrangeas grow well by the sea.

In Mediterranean regions of Europe

Left: *Senecio* 'Sunshine' that grows to 1.5 (6 ft) with thick grey-green leaves and daisy-like flowers. **Above:** *Spartium junceum*, fragrant, yellow blooms.

the wild, scented hillsides above the sea are full of many good plants which are suitable for seaside gardens, especially those in milder climates. *Cistus, Lavandula, Santolina, Linum spp* and numerous members of the broom tribe - *Genista, Cytisus* and *Spartium* genera - are just a few of the shrubs found in such associations. Most produce yellow pea flowers in abundance and cover a range of forms from dwarf, spiny hummocks to large open-branched shrubs with reed-like stems. All these shrubs love sun and warmth and are worth considering as a collective planting if you take the care to select those which will provide a flowering sequence from spring through summer.

Spanish broom, *Spartium junceum,* is one of the last of the pea flower shrubs to bloom. Your selection might also include *Genista tenera* or *Genista aetnensis*, both of which attain an average of 3-4.5 m (10-15 ft) in height and as much (or more) across. The slender, whippy branches bring an element of movement into the garden and are sufficiently open in growth not to suggest an overcrowded plan.

Groupings and associations

Grey foliage is worth having if only for the pleasing contrast it makes with green. One of the most satisfying of this group is the semi-evergreen *Atriplex halimus*, whose erect 1.8-2.4 m (6-8 ft) stems are densely clothed with silver-grey, downy leaves.

A. canescens is a similar shrub, more lax in habit and with narrower greyish white leaves. For those who enjoy grey and silver associations these two combine well with *Buddleia fallowiana* or even *B. davidii*, the latter's taller, arching habit complementing the stiffer, more compact arrangement of the atriplex. Buddleia is surprisingly adaptable to coastal conditions, despite the fact that its native habitat is deep in the interior of China. One of the happiest grey-based colour arrangements you could make is to group together four or five *Atriplex hortensis* 'Atrosanguinea' between them. The rich red-purple of this hardy annual known as orach is particularly startling against the grey of the shrub.

Bamboos as accent plants

If you can provide them with adequate protection and the rich, moist, loamy soil they need, bamboos will enjoy the mild, moist atmosphere of coastal regions. They are evergreen and very durable. Young clumps should be well

mulched for the first two or three years while they are becoming established.

Two of the most popular are *Sinarundinaria murieliae* - a dense, compact plant reaching 2-3 m (7-10 ft) tall, with elegant, soft green foliage, and *Pseudosasa japonica*, the metake bamboo, which has tall, erect stems some 3.5 m (12 ft) or more high with glossy, arched leaves. Some bamboos will reach much higher than this. The very decorative *Phyllostachys viridi-glaucescens* readily grows to a height of 5.5 m (18 ft) or so - but there are a number of much smaller kinds, such as *Sasa veitchii, S., disticha* and *Shibataea kumasasa*. Few bamboos will flower in temperate climates.

In harsh, unprotected sites, your choice is more limited, though some of the leguminous shrubs are certainly worth trying. They are not always long-lived but are very tolerant of wind. Recommended is *Cytisus scoparius* var 'Maritimus' (syn. 'Prostratus'), which creeps along the ground and has been seen cascading like a golden waterfall over cliffs, and the Mount Etna broom, *Genista actensis*, which stains the mountain yellow in summer with pendulous flowers. Also consider the species of the *Lespedeza* and *Indigofera* genera.

Roses by the sea

Roses can readily be grown by the sea, provided they are protected from the worst of the wind and salt. Their continued popularity in municipal seaside plantings throughout Europe, where they can be seen in parks and gardens in their thousands, is a testament to their adaptability to these conditions. There are, however, two varieties which will stand up to coastal conditions better than any others.

The Scotch or Burnet rose, *R. spinosissima*, is a short, suckering bush, with white flowers in early summer, black hips in late summer, and many thorns. It can be found growing wild on cliff tops or towards the beach, and seems to withstand the wind. It lives by early dormancy, shedding its leaves quickly so that there is no soft growth to be blasted by the winter winds. Scotch roses can be invasive if grown from seed or cuttings, because they freely propagate themselves by suckers. The budded plants supplied by most nurserymen are less invasive, but usually after a few years they will send out colonizing runners.

The seaside garden

The Scotch roses are normally dense cushions of plants. They flower very early, and have some spectacular colours: the purple of 'William III' and 'Mrs Colville' is, at first sight, a magnificent revelation. There are also some good yellows in the group, and many shades of red and pink, often marked with white. It is from the Scotch rose that the intricate, marbled red and white patterns of the 'hand painted' roses have come.

From the coasts of China, Korea and Japan comes another seaside rose, the robustly healthy *R. rugosa*. Its name means 'wrinkled' and is explained by its thickly veined leaves. The Scotch rose drops its leaves in a hurry, but *R. rugosa* hangs on to them. The rugosa rose halts transpiration – the exhalation of moisture in vapour form from its leaves – by putting a tough cuticle around them. This has the added bonus of making it difficult for blackspot to break in. Its flowers are borne over a longer period than those of the Scotch rose, and their hips are redder and more lustrous.

R. rugosa 'Scabrosa'.

The pure, original species is hardly ever offered for sale. Instead, there are some excellent varieties: the white *R. rugosa alba*, the red *R. rugosa rubra*, and the mauve red 'Scabrosa'. Another superb variety, but one which has no hips, is 'Roseraie de l'Hay'.

R. rugosa is frequently advertised and sold as a rose hedge; and a good strain does make an excellent hedge. But there is one selection, 'Hollandica', which is the stem upon which standard roses are budded. This is not a good plant for hedging or any other garden purpose, being unpleasantly lilac pink, leggy in growth, and often crippled with what is called the 'Dutch rugosa disease', which is probably a virus and certainly curtails its growth.

R. spinosissima 'Scotch Yellow'

R. Rugosa 'Roseraie de l'Hay'

Perennials, annuals and bulbs

One source of loose, light soil which, as we have seen, suits annuals, lies in sand dunes near the coast. The Virginia Stock, for instance, can often be found in sand dunes by the Mediterranean coast, while the ancestors of our garden stocks grow in similar conditions further north. Many ornamental annuals are tolerant of salt spray. Most bulbs can be grown with little trouble too, but you may have difficulty with lilies, which are woodland plants in nature (though the Regal lily will tolerate salt in moderation). Among perennials which will enjoy the light soil of a sea-side garden are lavender, scarlet lychnis and loosestrife. But provided that your enclosure blocks severe winds without blotting out the sunshine, the choice is quite wide. Red-hot pokers (*Kniphofia spp*) are often recommended for seaside gardens, as are carnations and pinks (*Dianthus spp.*), sedums, *Gazania splendens* and the evening primroses (*Oenothera spp*).

The advice of local gardeners and nurserymen should be sought on the best varieties for the prevailing conditions, their salt tolerance and sympathy with local soil.

Californian poppies and lavender enjoying the soil and climate of the Mediterranean.

The city garden

Special problems

Shade and size are typical problems with which the city gardener must cope, but there are others.

The first of these is soil. Over the years city soil very often becomes compacted and starved of nutrients. It is therefore important to give special attention to cultivation, feeding the soil with generous quantities of compost or manure and fertilizers. Ideally, these improvements should be made in the autumn of the year prior to planting.

Pollution from industry and traffic has a detrimental effect upon many plants, though there are relatively few which do not perform satisfactorily in city environments. Generally, waxy, broad-leaved evergreens are more suitable than the needle evergreens. Typically the hollies do well, but no tree sits better among buildings than the ginkgo nor tolerates better the most extreme street conditions. Not only is it the downtown tree *par excellence* from Sherbrook Street, Montreal, to Meeting Street, Charleston, and in Chartres Street, New Orleans to Tulsa, Oklahoma, but in southern England, it is the tree of cathedral closes, bishops' palaces and deans' gardens. The fresh green new leaves are equally pleasing against concrete, grey or dark grey Portland limestone, red sandstone and old red brick. The ordinary ginkgo, although highly variable in form, is usually rather erect. But for small courtyards and gardens, the sentinel ginkgo, *Ginkgo biloba* 'Fastigiata' is ideal with a slender, shapely tapering crown. In Europe, this is scarce and slow growing (as befits a small space) but in North America, it is really only evident in Pennsylvania and New York State. There, it is probably quite rapid and can be seen 30 m (98 ft) tall. The bright gold autumn colours assumed in those areas are less reliable in England but go well with typical building colours.

While on the subject of autumn leaf colours, it is an unfortunate fact that many of the more subtle visual effects are less appreciable in polluted atmospheres.

Tilia x *europaea*, the common lime, has been described as a valuable street tree but it can cause no end of problems for the city gardener. It plays host to aphids, tiny, soft-bodied insects that suck the juices of many trees, including spruce, elm, and poplar. Most aphids, and certainly those which are attracted to the common lime, produce a sweet fluid called honeydew. Sooty mould settles readily upon the tacky substance, and when the honeydew drips from the lime tree's leaves it causes a

Where space is at a premium, it may be best to dispense with grass altogether, for no species will stand up to very concentrated use. Hard surfaces provide a good base for year-round container

plantings which will, if properly maintained, obviate the problem of compacted soil typical of city gardens. Colour and scent can be chosen to be specially effective after office hours.

mess on the ground within the compass of the tree's crown which is very difficult to remove. The best advice is not to plant *Tilia* x *europaea*, and if you do, refrain from underplanting it.

In less problematic situations soot particles on leaf surfaces can be removed with a fine spray from a garden hose. You will need to do this regularly (but beware of over-watering the plants' roots). Advice as to when to do this was given in the watering section of the book and in the roof garden feature. It is not simply that soot particles dull the visual effect of plants, they actively hamper the process of photosynthesis.

Two final points. Flowering times can be earlier (page 14) and you may be able to plant subjects north of their usual hardiness limits, particularly if they are positioned in a sunny aspect with their backs to a wall. Secondly, city gardeners are often week-end or evening gardeners, so consider the time of day when you will be able to appreciate the garden. We make the point in **Creating a perfumed garden** that tobacco plants, *Nicotiana spp*, are strongly fragrant in the evening. Also, warm and light colours show up better at dusk. So you may, for example, choose yellows in preference to blues. See page 95.

119

The roof garden

Not surprisingly the problems associated with roof gardening are environmental. Leaving aside the provision of suitable soil in suitable containers with adequate drainage and irrigation, there may be severe problems of wind and sun. Planting a garden on the top of a tall apartment block can be like planting atop a rock pinnacle. The summer sun when it shines seems to be hotter and the wind, when it blows, seems to be stronger, and in winter, colder. Apart from direct winds, there are various side winds – downdraughts and updraughts – caused by the close proximity of other buildings.

The advantages of roof gardens, well-equipped to withstand these problems, are many. Roofs provide probably the most secluded sort of garden, and since they are almost always in towns or cities the contentment they give is all the more welcome. Given suitable conditions, and this is not impossible, there are great possibilities for both sun-loving flowers and many foliage plants. Finally, they can be, as we shall see, a sanctuary for birds and fowl.

A good soil mix is the first essential. Quite probably the patient roof gardener will allow his haven to evolve gradually and not expect it to be complete overnight. He or she will add one or two containers at a time to the collection and buy and convey the soil to the roof as it is needed. If the house is to be newly built, it is hoped that the topsoil from the house site will be retained, stored properly and used as the basis of the garden soil. Plenty of manure or compost is required and for some of the shrubs, a good peat mix will be useful. Make sure that the soil is at least 22 cm (9 in) deep. Trees and shrubs will need much more.

Starting from scratch

The roof garden illustrated here began as an idea; there was nothing there when the owner moved to the house other than a pointed, slated roof. In discussing his idea with the architects, it became clear that a structural engineer would be required to calculate the weight of the garden and thence the number of beams and size of the joists. There was no problem with planning permission as the idea did not involve spoiling the line of the building as seen from the street.

The floor of the garden sits at the level of the apex of the original roof and is situated on the west side of the house. Balancing this, on the east side, is a conservatory where he houses some sub-tropical plants and derives a great deal of colour from potted annuals. Between the two is a sitting room, which is naturally very quiet and well

insulated by the flanking gardens. During the construction of the complex, the roof slates were preserved and used to clothe the water tank (which supplies the house and would otherwise be an eyesore as seen from the roof garden) and the garden walls situated either side of french windows opening out to the garden from the central room.

The virtue of the plan, in terms of the environmental problems which roof gardens suffer, is that the plot now nestles snugly between two substantial chimney stacks (on north and south faces). It is protected from severe westerly winds by a frosted glass screen, which also enhances its privacy. There is a door in this screen which opens out on to a 1.8 m (6 ft) wide strip where the owner grows vegetables in pots – beans, lettuces and parsley – and a strawberry plant. Although the screen serves its purpose well, it does tend to heat up in the summer and has caused leaf scorch on two plants – a rhododendron and a laburnum – which were originally placed near it. The owner has the advantage of having all his plants in containers so that any mistakes of this kind, or of plant association, can easily be rectified.

Provided the plants are watered adequately there should be no immedi-

The London-situated container garden, above, and the Monaco garden pictured on page 121, give an idea of the range of possibilities that roofs afford.

ate likelihood of their becoming 'pot-bound', particularly as the containers are large. If, after about ten years, vigorous plants do show signs of deterioration (and have been well fed and watered) then really the only solution is to transfer them into still bigger containers. 'Coring' the soil – digging round the inside of a container to curtail root growth – is extremely dangerous because the roots may have coiled round the sides and important feeder roots can easily be cut. However, soil can be scraped off the top and containers top-dressed with a good mix.

Planting a roof garden

Perennials and alpines can play an important role. It may be that a rock garden as such is discounted for practical reasons, but there is ample opportunity to provide planting beds to suit a wide variety of such plants, whether they be happiest in semi-shade, damp or dry and stony soil, or a peat mix. Be aware of the path of the sun and employ shrubs and small trees to help protect subjects sensitive to too much sun. With winds a problem, resist plants which need staking; plants with shorter, sturdier growth are more

suitable. However, in temperate climates you can make use of vertical space by introducing climbing and rambling plants provided they are firmly secured to a wall or trellis. The common grapevine, *Vitis vinifera*, and its ornamental varieties would be particularly happy. The featured garden contains window boxes above the two french windows from which a variegated ivy and a periwinkle spill down over the garden's east wall. The periwinkle has failed to flower, possibly because it is in a line above the protective glass screen and gets the full force of the westerly wind.

Shrubs with delicate leaves, such as the Japanese maples, may be scorched. As in other garden situations, it helps to be aware of the natural conditions in which plants thrive or survive. There are several junipers which tolerate wind and drought in their native state, and *J. oxycedrus* and *J. phoenicea* are well worth considering it. In some northern American states few evergreens are successful because of dryness and wind, though *Thuja occidentalis*, *Pinus thunbergii* and *Juniperus virginiana* are well worth trying.

Many conifers, especially dwarf and slow-growing varieties, are suitable in temperate climates so long as watering is carefully monitored. Watering is a critical factor in the successful cultivation of all plants on roofs. In the illustrated garden the source of water is a tap concealed behind an open-mouthed lion's head, positioned centrally on the north wall. The water spills into a large tub below and is re-cycled by a pump. A hose pipe is connected to this and is brought round the garden to water the containers. There are many alternative methods of watering suitable for all kinds of roof garden described on pages 38–39. The water drains through the containers to the front of the build-

ing and, by prior arrangement with the next-door neighbour, onto his roof and down the gutters and drain pipes. Should you decide to employ a sprinkler watering system, remember that water reduces temperature and if applied during freezing spells could damage the plants. Sprinkling when the sun is high can scorch leaves because the water acts as a magnifying glass. In summer, the best time to water is in the late afternoon or early evening when there is still enough heat to evaporate the water from the leaves but the sun is no longer sufficiently strong to damage them. In this garden a very attractive weeping birch occupies a central position in a 75 cm (2 ft 6 in) square tub, and there is a mimosa on the south facing wall which produces beautiful, scented flowers in spring. Both must be watered daily. If the owner misses even one day, the birch will lose some of its leaves – it won't go bald, but it will not be as green and lush as it should be.

Many popular flowering shrubs can be grown, including *Philadelphus spp*, *Deutzia spp* and the lilacs (*Syringa spp*). And for the sunny aspect, you should consider *Elaeagnus macrophylla* and *E. pungens*, the lavenders, and *Senecio* and *Olearia spp.* from the *Compositae* family. Also, *Cistus*, *Ceratostigma*, *Buddleia* and *Escallonia spp* are outstanding.

The featured garden relies mainly upon shrubs and the owner co-opted the help of a local garden centre in choosing plants which were added slowly over a period of about five years. It had modest beginnings – a laburnum, a honeysuckle and an apricot rhododendron. He explains how it evolved:

'I tried to get one plant of each variety as against six all of one kind. By doing that you get different flowering seasons and many different colourings. The original arrangement of foliage plants was fairly haphazard. I paid attention to their needs in terms of light and soil, but moved the tubs around for the best arrangements. Now the plants have grown into tiers, undulating waves of foliage which is effective.'

Key plants, other than the mimosa and weeping birch already mentioned, include rhododendrons, camellias and a creeping maple ('which is not at all keen on strong sunlight'), all on the north-facing wall. There is a large Pampas grass ('which multiplies like mad and I have to keep dividing it'). This is near the weeping birch and its thrusting, upwards growth contrasts well with the birch's weeping branches.

With the mimosa on the north wall is a winter jasmine.

'It is mainly a green garden; I like green. But in spring there are masses of colour from bulbs. I don't know whether I should admit it, but I bought a lot of narcissi and daffodils from Woolworths, which turned out to be marvellous. Many others of my bulbs came from the parks. When their season is over the park gardeners throw them away, along with the other bedding plants, because they cannot guarantee that they will all come up the following year. I avoid sowing hardy annuals or raising anything from seed, not because I am an instant gardener but they always seem to come up and then die from damp rot or something. I can nurse a sick plant back to health, but when it comes to seeds, I'm hopeless. One great advantage of this predominantly green garden is that my roses really do stand out. The roses I have are not chosen for their particular species, but are very successful in a sunny position. I also have masses of wallflowers just in front of the fountain, but not solely for colour and scent. I leave them to bloom through two or three years (though they do get a bit spindly and I revitalize the collection every year). But I like their greenery which can be kept right through the winter.'

One interesting point is that in the process of building the garden, metal wall brackets were cemented into the walls to take pots of colourful blooms in appropriate seasons. Colourful alpines which might have been interspersed amongst dwarf shrubs include campanulas, aubrietas, helianthemums, sedums and sempervivums.

A sanctuary for birds
One of the most delightful aspects of this garden is the life it attracts to it. Two ducks arrived one day and produced twelve ducklings. One nested under the mimosa which meant that the daily watering could only be done when she'd flown off to eat. 'We built a little pool for the ducklings when they hatched. Then tragedy struck. A magpie or similar bird took the eggs and placed them the other side of the screen and drowned the firstborn ducklings who will have ducked under the water to escape the bird, as they do in the wild. In so small a space they were unable to avoid the bird. I can only assume they got waterlogged trying to escape.'

Blackbirds nested and produced three offspring very successfully, and bluetits, sparrows (both hedge and town varieties) and a kestrel have also been uninvited though welcome guests.

The suburban strip

On page 58 a fleeting visit was made to Anthony Huxley's garden specifically to examine how he had made the most of its long narrow shape by utilizing the 'blocking' principle which masks views and provokes elements of surprise. The illustration here depicts the same garden fully clothed with plants.

The first planting decision was to have little grass and plant intensively. One piece of turf was left in the form of a part-eclipsed circle adjoining the round terrace, and to make the purple plum seem less central an oval turf area was retained but raised with surplus turf into a low mound around its trunk and to one side. The only other grass is on the sloping bank, which separates the vegetable area from the rest of the garden and was described earlier.

Planting a long, narrow strip

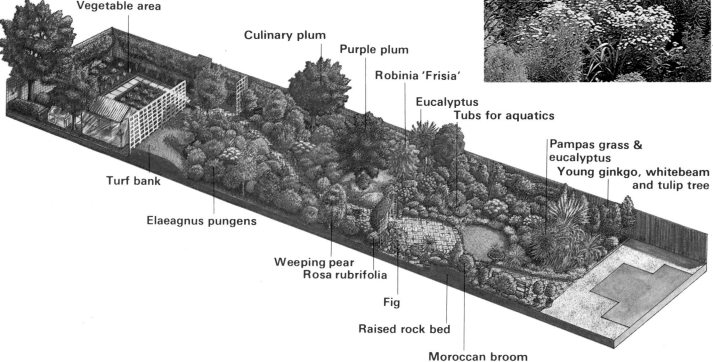

Vegetable area
Culinary plum
Purple plum
Robinia 'Frisia'
Eucalyptus
Tubs for aquatics
Pampas grass & eucalyptus
Young ginkgo, whitebeam and tulip tree
Turf bank
Elaeagnus pungens
Weeping pear
Rosa rubrifolia
Fig
Raised rock bed
Moroccan broom

Most of the shrubs he inherited were early summer flowering with no other seasonal appeal. These were eliminated by degrees. Amongst the plants retained were the well-sited purple plum (*Prunus cerasifera* 'Pissardii'), an amelanchier, a large forsythia, and a culinary plum, mainly because they helped to extend the wooded effect of the southern fence created by the neighbour's old fruit trees.

Once the rough plan had been worked out (the garden 'divided' into two distinct parts plus the vegetable plot), and the path and circular terrace laid in brick, irrigation works were installed: 'Laying a long-life reinforced hose underground the length of the garden has proved very worthwhile. This can be attached to the end of the "local" hose-reel by the garden tap at the side of the house and runs to another by the vegetable plot. Both hose reels are of the invaluable "thru-feed" type. Had I known of it then I would have installed a German system involving several plug-in watering points at intervals. But the existing system saves me having to drag an unwieldy length of hose all the way up a long curving path when the far end needs watering.'

The planting plan

'Next to the sitting circle I built a small rock bed of flat reddish stones. Behind it is the Moroccan broom *Cytisus battandieri*, which keeps its silky grey foliage all year and is easily trimmed of forward-growing branches. Between rock bed and house a cartwheel herb bed repeated the circle theme of terrace and grass areas. At their junction I made a water garden of closely positioned tubs of various sizes, the largest being half-barrels, those at the back being slightly raised above ground level. The remainder of this half-garden (on its south side) now formed a wide, long bed stretching from conservatory to purple plum. This bed is mainly planted with fairly low shrubs and herbaceous plants with some tall shrubs and trees positioned by the fence.

'Beyond the plum, two unequal areas separated by the main path are planted with larger shrubs and several trees above herbaceous plants. They have a very different character from each other and the "open" bed; the one in the lee of the south fence, much shaded by trees, forming a miniature woodland, the other devoted more to sun-lovers.

Stepping-stone paths through each bed allow access and add further to the surprise element.

'Many of the shrubs and trees are planted close to the boundaries to enhance the garden's self-contained, enclosed effect, and climbers grow up the fences, including roses, honeysuckles, clematis and, on the shady side, the invaluable variegated ivies. These twine on or are attached to brown semi-rigid plastic netting stapled on to the fence, almost invisible once climbers are established.

'Planting cannot be described in detail but in principle we have chosen markedly erect trees and those which can be grown clear-trunked before bushing out, so that there is plenty of scope for plants beneath them. Trees with interesting trunks like snakebark and paperbark maples, green *Acacia dealbata*, gun-metal eucalyptus and twisty-stemmed *Salix matsudana* 'Tortuosa' are included among some twenty-five kinds. All-year contribution is prized far above a three-week flush of bloom such as a lilac can provide. The same applies to the shrubs. Included in key positions are

Right: golden yellow leaves of *Robinia pseudoacacia* 'Frisia' contrast with *Prunus cerasifera* 'Pisardii'.

such evergreens as photinia and pieris with new leaves in red, variegated elaeagnus and rhamnus with perpetual bright interest, a spire-shaped golden conifer, and yuccas and mahonias with very distinctive foliage. Deciduous shrubs are also chosen for good leaf effect, including purple smoke-bush, *Cotinus coggygria*, and golden catalpa kept low by annual stooling. We are also growing hydrangeas of varied kinds primarily to give flowers in late summer and autumn.

'Herbaceous and sub-shrubby plants are again selected with a bias towards all-round value, including rue, *Euphorbia wulfenii* and its relations, ballotas, variegated irises, hellebores especially the early *H. orientalis* hybrids. Many are bluish, grey or silvery, or have bold leaves like acanthus, giant montbretia (*Crocosmia pottsii*), plume poppy (*Macleaya spp*) and not-to-be-despised "elephant's ears" (*Bergenia spp*). I am no plant snob: if I like a common plant I will have it.

'The circular brick terrace was later divided from the border behind it by a short section of square trellis, and its sunny, Mediterranean feel is enhanced by a rapidly developing fig tree. Round the terrace in summer we crowd pots of geraniums, lilies, agaves, palms and the like, some having had winter shelter in the conservatory.

'Beyond the sitting terrace, its trellis and the purple plum are reinforced as view "blockers" by the grey weeping pear *Pyrus salicifolia* and blue-leaved *Rosa rubrifolia* on either side of the path, and the golden-leaved *Robinia* "Frisia" in front of the plum – a rather corny but effective contrast. The final trellis, on which annual climbers are grown, looks like the end of the garden but a gap at one side reveals the vegetable plot, garden shed, compost heap and a utility greenhouse.

'I must stress that we never worked out a detailed planting plan. The ground was at first filled largely by quick growers such as hardy geraniums, miscanthus and pulmonaries, which are being discarded or greatly reduced as better plants are obtained. Trees and shrubs were mostly selected early on and carefully sited, though some have been added recently; these of course form the basic structure of the layout. Herbaceous material can, after all, be moved around readily if it does not fit well at first. Each set of layout or planting decisions certainly influenced the next stage of development.

'Certain short-lived plants are allowed to seed themselves and help to remove any feeling of over-planning. These include white double feverfew, silver-leaved *Lychnis coronaria* with crimson-magenta flowers and its white form, honesty, the odd foxglove and opium poppy, and in the "woodland" the yellow Welsh poppy *Meconopsis cambrica*. Self-seeding forget-me-not has proved rather a nuisance.

'The garden was *not* designed for children, but a change in our feelings towards the possibility has now resulted in a daughter. In order to provide her with a play area the herb bed was dismantled (the plants being established just beyond the conservatory) and its brick surround being filled in to form a sizeable flat area with room for a sandpit and paddling pool in due course. Bricks can be removed later to form a plant bed if gardening aspirations are apparent!

'Six years on, the garden is beginning to settle down though I am still replanting certain unsatisfactory areas. The growth of trees and shrubs has been remarkable, and it is clear that this will prove a problem in due course. Trimming these to fit is an essential task, and I shall have no hesitation in applying the Scandinavian small-garden technique of replacing over-large specimens with new small ones. As it is, I have already removed two trees which rapidly grew out of proportion to the overall planting scheme.' 123

Solving problems with plants

The low-maintenance garden

The overall reaction from experienced gardeners is that the no-maintenance garden is a fallacy. But they would concede that it is possible to plant a garden in which maintenance is kept to a minimum. It is certainly true that most city gardeners would be hard put to find sufficient time for maintaining gardens containing lawns, hedges, beds and borders, rock gardens, grassy banks, fruit and/or vegetable plots.

Weeding is generally regarded as the biggest and most laborious task. The other major maintenance activity is associated with grass and its care. Trees and shrubs are some of the least demanding plants to grow, and there are many shrubs and perennials which actively suppress weeds.

Weed suppression

Avoid areas of open soil. If left untended they will soon provide a home for a variety of weeds. There are two particularly effective labour-saving methods of smothering weeds. One is by mulching (see page 32), though this is not effective in getting rid of perennial weeds. These must be eradicated first; low-maintenance assumes thorough preparation.

The second method is to plant ground coverers, low-lying plants which spread widely in proportion to their height to form a ground-hugging carpet which, if sufficiently dense, will inhibit most weeds. They may be chosen for their foliage and in many cases for their conspicuous flowers.

Some spread by means of stolons or runners, others need to be planted close together so that they will eventually intertwine. Some are shade-lovers; others prefer ground open to the sun; a few will survive in either situation. Good drainage is essential and when cultivating, work in some peat moss or leaf-mould to attain a friable soil. Cultivate to 15 cm (6 in).

Most ground covers should be planted about 15 to 30 cm (6 to 12 in) apart. The following are exceptions:

30 to 45 cm (12 to 18 in)
Vinca
Cerastium
Phlox
Hypericum
Helianthemum

60 to 90 cm (2 to 3 ft)
Heathers

90 cm to 1.2 m (3 to 4 ft).
Cotoneaster
Juniperus
Taxus
124 Roses

Sedum spathulifolium 'Purpureum'

Ground covers for shade

Hedera, vinca and pachysandra are three of the most popular shade-tolerant coverers. The *Hedera* genus includes the English ivy, *H. helix*, which is perhaps better suited to cooler conditions than the very attractive variegated form, *H. canariensis,* whose roughly triangular leaves have dark green centres and creamy edges. *Vinca major* and *V. minor* (the periwinkles) are amongst the evergreens recommended for planting in hanging baskets, but they are efficient ground covers too, though the latter is best suited to temperate climates. With the species *P. terminalis* of the *Pachysandra* genus (saw-toothed leaves and small white spring blooms) these three provide an interesting choice for an open stretch of soil shaded by thirsty trees.

In less serious shade conditions, the choice widens considerably. The wild gingers, *Asarum caudatum* and *A. europaeum*, are a special treat. When trodden on they will release their characteristic aroma. The creeping mahonia, *M. repens*, has tiny yellow blossoms and black berries which remind one of a whole range of possibilities amongst fruiting ground covers. *Rubus nepalensis*, one of the creeping raspberries is well worth tracking down. Roy Lancaster was a member of the expedition to Nepal in 1971 which collected its seed and the plant is now in cultivation from several sources. It has small, shining green clover-like leaves followed by white flowers and later still, red fruits.

Ground covers in the sun

Here we find many plants which will provide the colour that is, typically, absent from a low-maintenance garden. *Cerastium tomentosum* is known as snow-in-summer because of its mass of tiny white flowers which rise in spring and early summer out of a mat of silver-grey leaves. It will cover a large area of ground very rapidly. *Armeria maritima* grows in grass-like clumps and in spring and summer develops tiny pink flowers on 30 cm (12 in) stems. It is specially useful as an edging plant for borders provided it is in full sun and the soil is light and well-drained. *Cotoneaster dammeri* might be chosen for its spring blooming white flowers which give way to generous quantities of bright red berries. It is not as fast a grower as some but is particularly successful in rocky areas and on steep banks. The maiden pink, *Dianthus deltoides*, is another slow spreader, but its pink, white or red flowers make it a strong contender. The many forms of *Helianthemum* root as they spread, intertwining to produce a dense mat over quite a wide area and spring/summer flowers of yellow, white, red and pink. *Phlox subulata* can be used outside its rock garden environment to cheer up fronts of beds and borders. Its abundant flowers range over the whole spectrum of red, and its evergreen foliage forms large, tufted mats of tiny, arrow-shaped leaves.

There are roses too which make effective ground covers. *R. wichuraiana* has small dark leaves and waxy, white

Ground covers suppress weeds, but take care to eradicate perennial weeds first. **Right to left**: hostas, saxifragas, and the slightly tender periwinkle.

flowers, and although it does not grow sufficiently dense to smother all likely weeds, it is an attractive trailer that creeps naturally along the ground. It is important when using any rose as a ground cover to make sure that it is resistant to blackspot and other diseases which cause premature leaf fall. In recent years breeders have diverted resources into ground cover roses and some which can be recommended are 'Temple Bells', 'Nozomi', 'Snow Ballet', 'Red Blanket' and 'Fairyland'.

Among the sedums which form large mats are *S. acre* with succulent green leaves and clusters of yellow, star-like flowers, and *S. spathulifolium* with similar flowers on reddish stems and leaves which grow in compact silvery rosettes.

Of the herbs, *Thymus serpyllum* is very good. Its small aromatic leaves provide the mat from which flowers come in subtle shades ranging from deep purple to pink.

Elsewhere, both *Juniperus horizontalis* and the heathers and heaths are recommended carpet shrubs from which shrubs of a globular form can rise to create an interesting effect that requires very little maintenance work. See also *Acaena buchananii* below.

Larger spreading shrubs
On a larger scale, the selection might include *Taxus baccata* 'Repandens', *Cephalotaxus fortunei* 'Prostrata' and *Picea abies* 'Procumbens'. There are other shrubs too which are wider than they are high, slow-growing, dense and compact in habit, and thus ideal for this garden. Of the non-conifers that are equally effective at this level you might consider the merits of two laurels: *Prunus laurocerasus* 'Otto Luyken' and 'Zabeliana'. Both have glossy, dark green, leathery leaves and produce spikes of white flowers followed by glossy black fruits. The first is comparatively neat and erect,

though not too tall; the last named is quite the opposite in habit, being wide spreading like certain junipers.

Two evergreens which can develop a dense leafy habit and cover a large space with their spreading branches are *Mahonia aquifolium* and *Skimmia japonica*. The mahonia has beautifully polished prickly leaves and a bonus of yellow blooms in spring. The skimmia must be planted in both male and female forms if you want the plants to produce their bright red berries. Recommended varieties are 'Fragrans' (male) and 'Foremanii' (female). On a larger scale still you might consider the Mexican orange blossom, *Choisya ternata*. It forms a bold mound up to 1.8 m (6 ft) and in spring it is covered with sweetly fragrant white flowers. (See also illustration in **Choosing plants to fulfil a purpose**.)

Shrubs as relief to low level plantings
Among the several rosette or spikey plants which, although not woody in the strict sense, have the shrubs' sense of permanence are the yuccas. There are two main groups: those which are stemless and those which develop a short woody trunk. Of the latter, *Yucca gloriosa* and *Y. recurvifolia* are most commonly cultivated in northern

climates. The former, with its stiff bayonet-pointed, blue-grey leaves, and the latter with reflexed grey or green leaves are superb 'feature' plants and can be used very effectively with a number of carpeting shrubs.

The stemless yuccas, *Y. filamentosa* and *Y. flaccida* create substantial clumps of green or grey-green erect or reflexed leaves and make effective companions for the larger species. They also flower more freely, their spikes producing crowds of nodding ivory-white bells.

You might use sedums in association with *Y. gloriosa* and *Y. filamentosa*. The grey species *S. hispanicum* and *S. dasyphyllum* are especially compatible as are the various species and hybrids of *Sempervivum*. Then again a bold clump of *Y. filamentosa* would look outstanding with a ground cover of *Acaena buchananii*. The acaenas are mainly native of New Zealand. Chosen carefully for colour and texture of leaf they can create the most spectacular effects, but they are without scruples and will overcome and swamp lesser plants within their extensive sphere of influence. Prune them back during spring or summer in order to contain them. Of the many kinds, *A. microphylla* has brownish-green leaves and red spined burs, whilst *A. caesiiglauca* is more robust and leafy with stems and leaves of a charming sea green colour. An unusual trio could be completed with *A*. 'Blue Haze', whose blue-grey leaves on red stems create a misty blue haze effect at a distance.

Similar to a yucca in its large rosettes of blue-grey leaves is the Mexican *Beschorneria yuccoides*. What sets it apart is a massive coral-red flowering stem, spectacular when bearing its red and green, tubular bell flowers. It associates well with yuccas except when in flower. Possibly a bank is the best setting for its leaning flower spike or at the foot of a sunny wall. 125

The low-maintenance garden

Deciduous shrubs for the low maintenance garden

This may seem a contradiction in terms. The beauty of evergreens in this respect is that throughout the year they make it difficult for any plants, including weeds, to grow beneath them. But even the time-pressed gardener would agree that a garden consisting purely of evergreens would be lacking in spirit. The following suggestions associate well with ground covers, and the chore of occasional leaf sweeping is a small price to pay for the pleasure gained.

Spiraea japonica 'Little Princess' is a low-mounded shrub up to 90 cm (3 ft) tall, which is covered in summer by a succession of rose-red flower heads. It is dense and compact and associates well with cistus and *Potentilla fruticosa* and its hybrids, all of which provide a variety of lovely flowers in addition to their ground cover qualities. Another mound-forming shrub with small neat leaves and heads of pale lilac flowers in late spring/early summer is *Syringa velutina*.

For its low-growing, wide-spreading habit, few deciduous shrubs can better *Cotoneaster horizontalis* with its herring-bone pattern branches. The variegated form is even more attractive. *Lonicera pileata* associates well with cotoneaster and is especially useful in shade, but wherever it is used, its horizontal branches are effective ornamentally too.

Trees for low maintenance

Once they are properly established, trees look after themselves; very little need be done beyond cutting out some to leave room for others, and cleaning them up after about their fifth year. Evergreens are the most maintenance-free items in the entire garden.

They must be planted small with their roots well spread into large holes of good soil cleared of perennial weeds to a 1 m (3¼ ft) radius. On sandy soils some fertilizer will be needed in late spring to encourage the establishment of roots. In the first season (the second season too on light soils) generous watering is required during dry spells and some at all times.

Innumerable and otherwise fine collections of well-planted and well-spaced trees are largely ruined through the lack of one other item of care. Forked leading shoots and *any* multiple stems need singling, and strong low branches need cutting off at the bole. Beautiful clean boles with attractive bark can be admired for the price of an enjoyable hour with secateurs in the early years.

Lonicera pileata in the foreground, *Bergenia cordifolia*, top right.

Potentilla fruticosa 'Tangerine'; it goes well with *Spiraea japonica* 'Little Princess'.

The paved garden

This rids the gardener of the need to maintain a lawn, and in dark, poky town gardens or where the soil is an intractable clay (or otherwise unworkable), a hard surface is a practical alternative.

Paved gardens are also an advantage to the old, infirm or disabled, for by using tubs, troughs and raised beds, the 'working surface' can be brought to a more comfortable level.

Furthermore, if you opt for container plantings on the paved area you can import soil to grow plants which would not be suited to the native soil. Even if you live in an area where the native soil is alkaline, you can still grow azaleas, camellias, rhododendrons and all those other shrubs which abhor lime. Do remember, however, that 'hard' water is anathema to such shrubs, and to avoid chlorosis setting in you should install a butt or drum in which to catch rain water and 'run off' from roofs.

Interplanting a paved area

Container planting restricts one's choice of shrubs because some of the more desirable tall or spreading varieties have root systems commensurate in vigour and spread to their crowns. Although such shrubs can be

Above left: *Thymus vulgaris* 'Silver Queen'. **Above right:** the wide-spreading *Salvia officinalis* 'Tricolor'. **Below:** the purple-spiked *Liriope muscari*.

contained for a number of years they must eventually be released or suffer regular root and branch pruning.

One way to avoid this problem altogether is to remove a slab of paving or a few bricks and plant directly into the ground. If the soil is in any way unsuitable, excavate a good sized hole and fill it with a more suitable mix from elsewhere. This method of planting is particularly effective with those conifers of columnar shape

mentioned previously – *Juniperis virginiana* 'Skyrocket', *Taxus baccata* 'Standishii' and *Cupressus sempervirens* 'Swane's Gold'.

The same method can be used in a limited way for neat, dome-shaped shrubs such as *Ozothamnus ledifolius, Daphne collina, D.* 'Neapolitan', *Hebe rakaiensis, Fabiana imbricata* 'Prostrata' and many dwarf or slow-growing conifers.

Small chinks left between paving slabs can make a home for a charming selection of small hummock or prostrate plants, including French lavender (*Lavandula stoechas*), the suckering hardy plumbago (*Ceratostigma plumbaginoides*), the common sage (*Salvia officianalis*), especially in its purple leaved form, 'Purpurea', and the equally attractive tricoloured 'Icterina'.

These combine well with the late-flowering, violet-purple spiked *Liriope muscari* and *Thymus vulgaris* 'Silver Queen', provided there is room.

Many alpines and low perennials are also very suitable for these positions. But whatever you choose to plant, bear in mind, particularly if infirm or disabled people will be using the garden, that fleshy leaved plants can be a hazard if trodden on.

127

The container garden

Container gardening

Experienced gardeners are wary of hearing how easy it is to grow gardens in containers. The fact is that plants are much happier in their natural environment, a soil bed, than they are in containers. However, practical considerations are of obvious importance. In town and city, and wherever space is limited or there is a need to decorate hard surfaces, container gardening is important and very effective.

Dull or bland areas can come alive with a few geraniums carefully graded in colour tones. Indeed it is not unknown for property sellers to use the facility to dress up a house for sale.

Container plants are especially useful in detracting from the glare and sheer ordinariness of paved areas. Sometimes, containerizing plants is the most effective way of growing plants – bamboo for example - in order to admire their foliage without having to worry about their roots spreading without control. Hanging containers can also be used to decorate vertical planes and to enjoy the effect of trailing plants. Finally, balcony and roof gardens would be lost without the possibility of container gardening.

Container gardening in the north

In regions where container planting is severely limited on account of the cold, it pays to have a conservatory and take container plants outside when the weather permits. Another suggestion is to choose trees or shrubs from at least one hardiness zone north and plant them out in large containers which can to some extent be protected from alternate winter freezing and thawing by lagging them with sacking, straw or bags of salt.

In these places you can discount virtually all evergreens. Box, holly and bay are definitely out. Some of the cherry laurels might be worth a try. For a compact laurel you could consider *Prunus laurocerasus* 'Otto Luyken'; a fairly spreading variety that might be suitable is 'Camellifolia'.

Some bush ivies are useful. Try *Hedera helix* 'Baltica' and the forms of 'Baltica', 'Poetica' and of the common ivy itself. Conifers often take over where broad-leaved evergreens are unsuitable: the Canadian yew is very tough as are some junipers. In the north east and east of the U.S.A. and similarly exposed climates you might try the dwarf forms of *Thuja occidentalis*, if not *T. plicata* more widely distributed along the Pacific coast of North America and western Canada. When consulting your local nursery, ask too about pines and white spruce.

Maintenance
Action hints

*Keep plants well watered, especially in the growing season. Small quantities of soil dry out very quickly. Set hanging baskets within reach and use the 'spaghetti' watering system suggested on page 39. Sphagnum peat or holed plastic sheeting can make hanging baskets more water-retentive.

*Use liquid compound fertilizers to feed containerized plants. Nitrogen, phosphate and potassium are easily leached from the soil.

*Replenish half the soil every one or two years. Give it a complete change every three years. A good mixture for most plants is equal parts of loam, sand and organic matter such as leaf-mould or peat.

*Ensure adequate container drainage and a way for the water to drain off the patio.

*Raise or lower pH to suit plant needs.

*Dig around the soil surface periodically to prevent it becoming compacted. Any old roots can be removed at the same time in order to stimulate growth rate.

*Container soil heats up and cools down very quickly. In very extreme conditions it is important to give some protection. Foliage covering the soil will of course help keep it cool; mulching is also useful in maintaining an even temperature.

Roses for continuity of display in the container garden

One of the great advantages of container planting is the ability it gives you to introduce colour, however temporarily, into otherwise bland areas of the garden plan. Roses can provide that spark of life during as many as eight months of the year in temperate climates.

See pages 176 to 177 and 186 for advice about continuity. Practically any rose can be container grown. One plant plan suited to these conditions is suggested here.

Roses in containers

Roses are excellent plants to grow in tubs and pots, and they can live to a ripe old age if they are properly cared for. As ever the vital element, which makes the difference between a rosy life and a death sentence, is water. If too little is given, the young growths start to droop, the leaves point downwards, and the plant slowly dies. If too much is given, the leaves turn yellow and fall off. The tub or pot should drain well, because roses will not flourish when their roots are in pools of water or soggy mud.

Today it is easier than ever to grow roses in tubs or pots, because so many convenient feeds are available. Nevertheless, it will be as well to use some really good soil when first planting the rose. It is not necessary to plant a subject in a huge tub straight away; better put it in a pot, and move it into larger quarters when the pot is a ball of roots. Roses can live for many years in a large flower pot.

In the years when a rose is becoming established, it is as well to scrape off the surface soil annually, and replace it with some fresh, rich soil. This operation should be carried out, as far as possible, without disturbing the roots.

Practically any rose can be grown in a pot or tub, even trailers and climbers, although one can scarcely expect those to cover vast distances when their roots are kept in confinement. It is better to keep their tops firmly trimmed, thus concentrating the area of flower. It is even possible to grow 'Banksian Yellow' in a pot this way, and highly delightful it is. The most difficult are standards because their growing points are separated from the roots by long single stems. A shorter stem gives a better chance of errors in watering being corrected in time to save the

Dainty and perfectly in scale, miniature roses are ideal for planting in small containers or *en masse* in troughs, using miniature standards to provide height.

plant, and some delightful choices are miniature roses budded on short standard stems.

One pleasure of pots and tubs is that they are movable. You can shuffle plants about to give prominence to those which happen to look beautiful on a particular day. It is tempting to take roses into the house, but a week is long enough for them to start reacting against the lack of light.

Their proper place out of doors is in little gardens paved with stone, by a door or window, or on a sunny balcony. Roses are also rewarding in a glass house; the flowers are usually of wonderful purity and quality, and very welcome some weeks before the rose season begins. After they have flowered they can be put outside, an excellent and trouble-free method

being to plunge them in the soil, pot and all, to remain until they are brought under glass in late autumn.

If the tub is large, then the rose needs to be in proportion, say 'Celestial' or *R. chinensis mutabilis*, a most rewarding pot plant. Smaller roses should have smaller containers in proportion.

It is good to have a collection of roses to cover different flowering times; take 'Williams' Double Yellow', which is a Scotch rose, to start the season; 'Mme Legras de St. Germain', which is an alba, to continue it; remontant roses such as 'Cécile Brunner', 'Iceberg', 'Silver Jubilee' and 'Grandpa Dickson' to bear the brunt of the flowering time; 'The Fairy', 'Anne Harkness' and 'Crimson Shower' to take over, fresh, as the others are resting. Either 'Doncasteri' or 'Geranium' would provide hips for good measure in autumn. This recipe will give roses in bloom for at least eight months of the year in a temperate climate from a very small number of plants.

129

The container garden

Plant planning in hanging baskets

Do remember that your choice of plants for any container depends upon the environmental conditions which they prefer. Full of soil, water and plants, hanging baskets are heavy, so ensure that they are firmly secured to the wall. Many baskets can be planted so that flowers appear through the mesh as well as spilling over the top.

One plan is to layer the base of the basket with moist sphagnum peat, followed by a layer of potting compost. Seedlings can then be placed on the potting mix so that the leaves appear through the wire. Repeat in this way throughout the basket, but concentrate the sphagnum in the centre of the planting and make sure that the plants have plenty of room to grow.

Any trailing plant, whether flowering or foliage, is suitable. Lobelias, nasturtiums, fuchsias, begonias, ivy-leaved pelargoniums are very popular. *Vinca major* and *V. minor*, trailing evergreens which produce large or small blue-purple flowers on erect shoots, bloom from spring to early autumn. Other long-term plants include the spider plant, *Chlorophytum comosum* var *variegatum*, many variegated ivies and other smaller ferns, such as *Polypodium vulgare* and the very popular maidenhair fern *(Adiantum pedatum)*. These would be more suitable for a shady spot.

Window boxes

Although they are available in a wide range of materials, you can make these yourself quite easily. The minimum depth and width should be about 25 cm (10 in); the length will of course depend upon available space, but 1 m (3 ft) provides plenty of scope. If you use wood, protect it with a preservative such as Cuprinol, which will not harm plant roots. Make sure that the box can drain properly - it may need to be slightly raised - and that it is firmly secured in position.

Petunias look far better in window boxes or tubs than in flower borders. But think in terms of continuity of flower. You may like to start with spring bulbs and then let suitable annuals (such as petunias or trailing lobelias - try 'Pendula Blue Cascade' and 'Pendula Sapphire') take over the spaces in between, cover the bulbs' residual foliage and go on to maintain colour throughout the summer. Annuals are indeed among the best plants for window boxes.

Sources of colour in shaded window boxes include begonias, impatiens, pansies, fuchsias, coleus and browallia

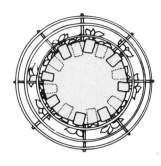

The illustration depicts a planting of wax begonias that will form a cluster of blooms to cover the hanging basket. Build the planting in layers of potting mix on a base and with a central core of sphagnum. Alternate the plants as shown above to give them plenty of room to develop.

and ferns may make a useful background foil. Most popular in sunny conditions are geraniums, nasturtiums, short chrysanthemums, lobelia and alyssum. But there are many others. As far as bulbs are concerned, it might be a good idea to lessen the problem of persistent foliage and opt for the smaller bulbs such as crocus, snowdrop and scilla which do not cumber the ground for long. You may prefer to interplant the bulbs with wallflowers or forget-me-nots, remove both bulbs and biennials in late spring or early summer and put summer bedders in their place. These could be followed by chrysanthemums. Best types are early flowering varieties of charm chrysanthemums which form a carpet of autumn flowers. Whatever you decide, bulbs in outdoor containers can be regarded as a permanent planting, if convenient, or they can be lifted and planted elsewhere in the garden once they have completed their growth. Window boxes are liable to look rather dreary in the winter months but

provide excellent sites for some of the smaller bulbs which flower in late autumn and winter, and which are very often swamped in other places. These and other bulbs are described in the section about planting for interest through the year.

Selected dwarf conifers together with miniature roses will provide a more long-term solution.

Other containers

If you mount sinks, troughs, baths, chimneys, etc. upon some kind of pedestal, they will suffer less from the attentions of garden pests such as slugs. Raised containers are especially suited to the handicapped gardener, and all sorts of containers are an excellent way of introducing children to the delights of gardening. Roy Lancaster's own conversion to gardening followed a visit to his uncle whilst a small boy. 'He had an old stone kitchen sink in his yard filled to overflowing with sedums, saxifragas, sempervivums

Containerized plants may be effectively displayed as single features or small groups. **Far right:** combinations of colour and form, similar to that obtainable in plant beds, are the mark of well-planned larger groups; feature plants in attractive containers heighten interest.

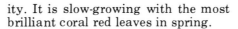

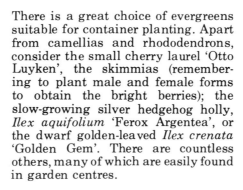

and a glorious *Daphne cneorum* in full flower. I remember also a sentinel cypress in that sink which greatly impressed me. It seemed a perfect replica in miniature of ones I had seen in a painting in my grandfather's home. Years later I learned that my mini cypress was in fact *Juniperus communis* 'Compressa', referred to by some gardeners as the Noah's Ark Juniper, quite why I am not sure. But this neat juniper is a perfect shrub to give height to your trough garden.'

Containers are ideal for the cultivation of alpines and dwarf shrubs. *Sorbus poteriifolia*, the world's smallest rowan with its red-turning-to-white berries set amidst tufts of glossy green leaves, is a good choice. You might also consider *Ceanothus prostratus*, with its small evergreen leaves and blue flowers, and *Cotoneaster congestus*, the true plant with little green molehills studded with white flowers followed by red fruits. A miniature maple called *Acer palmatum* 'Corallinum' is another possibil-

ity. It is slow-growing with the most brilliant coral red leaves in spring.

There is a great choice of evergreens suitable for container planting. Apart from camellias and rhododendrons, consider the small cherry laurel 'Otto Luyken', the skimmias (remembering to plant male and female forms to obtain the bright berries); the slow-growing silver hedgehog holly, *Ilex aquifolium* 'Ferox Argentea', or the dwarf golden-leaved *Ilex crenata* 'Golden Gem'. There are countless others, many of which are easily found in garden centres.

For a real Mediterranean flavour, try a few bold, sword-leaved perennials in a warm, sunny position. We suggest the grey-leaved *Sisyrinchium striatum*, *Beschorneria yuccoides, Kniphofia northiae, K. caulescens* and the green-leaved *Eryngium serra, E. bromeliifolium* and *E. agavifolium*. Most are tender in northern regions where the *Yucca* combination described in the

low-maintenance garden could be more successful.

Creating an illusion of space with containerized plants

By a careful choosing of plants and shrewd planting, you can create an impression that the garden area is larger than it really is. Foliage has much to do with this illusion – shrubs can contribute to it if used in combination with bold-leaved perennials such as hostas, bergenias, hellebores, ferns and rodgersias. One of the boldest shrubs is the deciduous *Aralia elata* known as the Japanese angelica tree. It can reach 3 to 4.5 m (10 to 15 ft) tall, but hard, annual pruning will encourage the production of strong prickly shoots bearing huge, divided leaves similar to those of the herb angelica. Unpruned, it produces terminal heads of creamy white flowers in autumn. If kept to a single stem this naturally suckering plant will provide a notable feature either in a large tub or in a hole in the paving. 131

The natural garden

The traditional English cottage garden offers an opportunity to break away from the rules and conventions of formal garden design and use your own initiative and instinct for improvization. Informality is the keynote, but you should never forget that the growing requirements of plants remain the same whether they are planted in a cottage garden or in a more formal arrangement. Don't fail to allow plants their due amount of light, air and water, or to take into consideration factors such as shade, soil and growth habit.

The first cottage gardens were the preserve of farm labourers and other workers in the English countryside. With little time, space or money available for more elaborate schemes, they raised plants with an eye to their usefulness – as food, for instance, or for their medicinal properties – rather than for their aesthetic appeal. Of course, some flowers were grown for pleasure, but if this meant that hollyhocks were planted next to cabbages, then this was perfectly acceptable. In time – particularly as a result of the efforts of the cottage garden enthusiast Gertrude Jekyll and the even more wild and natural approach advocated by William Robinson – the purely decorative aspect came into its ascendancy. Now, the principle of the English cottage garden is to display in a natural, free and harmonious arrangement those characteristics of plants which stimulate the senses and provide enduring interest.

A cottage-style garden can be adapted to suit modern dwellings in temperate climates as long as you're careful to make them look as though they belong with each other. Use natural materials wherever possible in making walls and fences and avoid cluttering the garden with too many ornaments and furniture.

A cottage garden should be informal, but it should not be chaotic. Plants may be scattered seemingly at random, but in the end, harmony depends on imaginatively planned combinations. The aim of the cottage garden is to soothe, refresh and revitalize the spirit, but to do so without it appearing to have been achieved by conscious effort. Gertrude Jekyll was an artist before she turned to gardening, and the development of the mixed border (which in time gave rise to the mainly herbaceous border) is largely the result of her sensitivity to colour and form.

The choice of flowers for a cottage garden is enormously broad, but many people opt for those which they feel give something of an 'old fashioned'

Cottage gardens can adorn modern dwellings but intimations of rusticity do help.

aura: hollyhocks, daphne, lavender, delphiniums, aubrietas, periwinkle, heleniums, primroses, sunflowers, violets, lilies, crocuses, tulips, snowdrops, aconites, narcissi, campanulas, pinks, carnations, phlox, snapdragons, Michaelmas daisies, sweet peas and sweet Williams, love-lies-bleeding, scillas, honesty, fritillarias and so on. For best effect, intersperse these plants instead of segregating them as you might do in a more formal bed or border. In time many will form pleasing clumps, though these will need occasional dividing and replanting. The more you are aware of their growth habit and blooming times, the more successful will be these massed banks of colour. By growing in abundance in crowded beds you will, incidentally, keep the weeds down, though you should always try to start off with a well-prepared and thoroughly weeded soil.

There is little space in the cottage garden for labour-intensive flowers such as bedding plants – the style of gardening is essentially a low-maintenance one – though there is no reason why you should not go in for this if you wish. On the other hand there is always a place for plants with a purpose as well as aesthetic appeal – herbs, for instance, or fruit trees such as apples and crabs.

Roses in the cottage garden

Though you can plant annuals and bulbs fairly indiscriminately, some discretion is needed when choosing larger plants such as roses and shrubs. Because of the nostalgic associations of the cottage garden, many people feel tempted to plant old-fashioned roses. This, however, may well be shortsighted, because many grow too wide – and are out of flower too long – to justify their inclusion. The ideal cottage garden roses are those which grow resolutely upwards and flower above the surrounding plants without sprawling over them.

Aconites and snowdrops

'Golden Wings' is almost the perfect choice, a spinosissima hybrid with creamy yellow, single flowers, more deeply coloured in the centre. Its soft colour cannot be out of place anywhere, its flowering season is long, and it has the virtue of compelling admiration even at times when only a few flowers are showing.

The well known 'Queen Elizabeth' is the right sort of pink for a cottage garden and a single plant can make a fine shrub. If something not quite so tall and commanding is needed, then the older 'Dainty Maid' is to be recommended, especially as its single flowers withstand rain very well. One of the best red hybrid teas is 'John Waterer', deep and dark. Additionally, 'Red Planet' and 'Precious Platinum' are contenders, being bright crimson with the ability to lift up bright leaves and flowers. Many popular hybrid teas and floribundas must be relegated to also-ran status for the cottage garden, either because they are liable to be overgrown by other plants or because their colours are too garish. Most people would agree that the cottage garden is no place for vivid orange-scarlet and salmon roses, and it is most desirable that the roses chosen should mature in an agreeable way.

One glorious shrub which might be suitable for the cottage garden is 'Sally Holmes', with its wide white flowers in great heads, and the whole plant clothed in sparkling foliage.

If the temptation to plant an old rose or two cannot be resisted, then the gallica 'Tuscany' is a good choice. It grows upright, and has bold crimson flowers in summer. 'Buff Beauty' could well inhabit a corner; this hybrid musk has double flowers of light apricot, the very essence of a peaceful summer afternoon. *R. gallica versicolor*, also known

Dimorphotheca aurantiaca 'Glistening White' and *Salvia pratensis haematodes*, useful in the 'cottage garden'.

as 'Rosa Mundi', is the famous striped rose, red and blush, flowering in summer. Although it does not grow very tall, it is the obvious candidate for a traditional cottage garden, being interesting, old and English.

The art of putting the right plants together is, as always, a matter of practice, trial and error. What will please one person may displease another. In a cottage garden scale is particularly important. One variety of plant must not dominate; nasturtiums for example, can very easily take over too large an area to the detriment of other plants. That is why we have written of the roses in the singular, as making 'a shrub'. This is a place to ignore the usual advice to plant roses *en masse*, for nothing could destroy a cottage garden more thoroughly.

Shape is particularly important in the mixed bed. Along with the spires of foxgloves, lupins, delphiniums and

Planning a billowing, unregimented rose hedge.

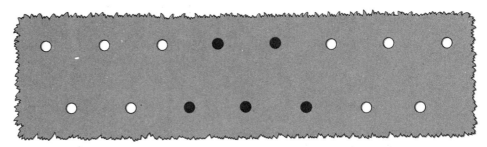

hollyhocks, one needs some domes. Roses can provide both features. Some of the spires are 'Queen Elizabeth', 'Alexander', 'Buccaneer', 'Anne Harkness' and 'Tuscany', while among the best domes are 'Sally Holmes', 'Golden Wings', 'Iceberg', 'Nevada', 'Marguerite Hilling' and 'Escapade'.

Rose hedges and informal lines
Straight lines are self-defeating in a cottage garden. Being the shortest route between two points, they provide the shortest amount of colour. Compare hedgerow and clipped hedge. The one is uneven, full of grace and interest; the other is a sharp line, admirable if it points towards a distant goal, but in a short stretch there is little to stimulate the mind. There is, therefore, a good argument for using roses as hedges. Being unclipped, they provide a soft, natural, undulating line. Indeed a mixed rose hedge and sun-soaked walls suggest themselves as a heavenly frame for a cottage garden. The main requirement is to give the roses sufficient elbow room - as one would with any other shrub - for roses are not intended to be clipped, but rather to be grown in billowing, unregimented curves.

The sense of freedom and naturalness is increased if the varieties are mixed. The roses should be shrubs, or grown as such. If the path or boundary is, say, 18-36 m (20-40 yards) long, you should plant in groups of three plants per variety. Beyond this, increase the number to five plants per variety. Each variety will cover about 2-2.5 m (7-9 ft), giving an agreeable and interesting range of choice without any one variety dominating the scene. The best way to make a hedge is to plant in two rows, as shown in the illustration.

The plants are about 1.2 m (4 ft) apart, the rows 90 cm (2½ ft). The width of ground that will eventually be covered by the hedge will probably be 3.6 m (12 ft). It is important to remember this when planting, so that the path or roadside verge is kept clear.

The choice of varieties is of course a delight; they can be mixed quite freely, the most important considerations

Above: shows informal pattern of rose varieties, each intermingling with the next. **Below:** *Rosa* 'Nevada', a creamy white, dome-shaped shrub.

not being the colours, but the times of flowering. It is bad planning to have one section of the hedge flowering early, and another section later. The ideal is for the colour to be sprinkled freely about through the year. Thus each component of the whole calls attention to itself in turn, and then shyly retreats into the general greenery while another holds the floor.

Creating a haven of tranquility

The natural garden

Here is a proposal for such a hedge, in planting order, with comments, and times in bloom. Note the following requirements:

* They must grow to cover their space easily.
* They must grow at least 1.2 m (4 ft) tall.
* They must have good foliage.
* They must not get diseases easily.
* They must be beautiful and interesting.

These thirty-two varieties would, at five plants each, hedge both sides of a 45 m (50 yd) driveway or boundary in the most beautiful and interesting way imaginable. Even in a small cottage garden, on a much reduced scale, the effect will be most pleasing. The hedge would vary from 1.5–2.75 m (5–9 ft) tall in the way of a natural hedgerow. If some other plants are needed to fill in at the front, there is much to be said for German irises, which can flower against the rose foliage, with leaves in sharp contrast to those of the roses.

Pruning is kept to a minimum; mainly it is a question of taking out old parts of the plants as they become noticeable. Most weeds will be smothered by the roses, provided they are kept down while the plants are becoming established and that there are no rough areas behind the hedge. Herbicides can provide a clean start, and can also control weeds that do manage to intrude later.

We have described but one hedge; many others are possible, as 'Queen Elizabeth' demonstrates all over England. A short rose hedge is best composed of one variety because there will not be enough of each variety to make a proportionate spectacle, and the result will be spotty. Those who want a bright hedge could plant 'Alexander', which is marvellous when grown in this way. In a small garden prune such hedges to keep them within bounds.

Mixed hedge of roses

Variety	Flowering time	Characteristics
Canary Bird	Late spring	Soft yellow, graceful Chinese type.
Fritz Nobis	Midsummer	Pink, spectacular; bred from sweet briars.
R. spinosissima hispida	Early summer	White, Scotch type; black hips.
Scabrosa	Remontant	Mauve red rugosa; red hips.
Frühlingsgold	Early summer	Cream hybrid from Scotch rose.
R. rubrifolia	Midsummer	Fine leaves and hips; European species.
Sally Holmes	Remontant	White hybrid musk type; spectacular heads.
Geranium	Midsummer	Red; Chinese: spectacular hips.
Marguerite Hilling	Midsummer	Pink; Scotch rose hybrid.
Golden Chersonese	Late spring	Brilliant yellow; hybrid of *R. ecae.*
Alexander	Remontant	Vermilion hybrid tea; tall.
Celestial	Early summer	Soft pink alba.
Golden Wings	Remontant	Yellow hybrid from Scotch rose.
R. roxburghii normalis	Midsummer	Pink; hips like chestnuts.
R. virginiana	Late summer	Pink; red hips: American.
Queen Elizabeth	Remontant	Pink; floribunda.
R. x dupontii	Midsummer	Blush white musk type.
R. chinensis mutabilis	Remontant	Cream to red Chinese rose; not for harsh cold places.
Mme Legras de St Germain	Early summer	White alba.
Buff Beauty	Midsummer	Light apricot hybrid musk.
Roseraie de l'Hay	Remontant	Purple rugosa.
R. x cantabrigiensis	Late spring	Cream hugonis hybrid.
Chinatown	Remontant	Yellow floribunda.
R. farreri persetosa	Midsummer	Pink; fascinating, tiny flowers.
R. rugosa alba	Remontant	White; Japanese variety.
Nevada	Midsummer	White; Scotch rose hybrid.
Doncasteri	Midsummer	Rose red; splendid hips.
Semi-plena	Early summer	White alba; Bonnie Prince Charlie's rose.
Marjorie Fair	Remontant	Red and white; polyantha.
R. primula	Late spring	Cream; the incense rose.
Félicité Parmentier	Early summer	Blush alba.
Ballerina	Remontant	Pink polyantha.

Shrubs for colour and aroma

In the long history of English cottage gardens the shrubs which have probably played the most consistent part have been those which we commonly refer to as herbs – lavender, thyme, sage, rosemary, rue and others – planted for their usefulness in cooking, as folk medicine and so on. But even the *doyenne* of cottage gardeners, Gertrude Jekyll, saw nothing wrong in planting her garden with such exotic decorative shrubs as *Abutilon vitifolium*, *Solanum jasminoides* and *Magnolia stellata*. Roses are only one of a number of shrubs traditionally associated with the cottage garden.

There are no strict limits to the kind of plants to use in the cottage garden. The aim is a soothing, informal miscellany of colour, fragrance and form. Let the plan evolve gradually as you discover the value of particular combinations.

The natural garden

Climbers popular in the cottage garden

A popular 'old-fashioned' plant is the climbing honeysuckle. Apart from the typical wild form *Lonicera periclymenum*, the ones most often seen are 'Belgica' and 'Serotina', known by the names 'Early' and 'Late Dutch' respectively. Just as common is the early cream honeysuckle, *Lonicera caprifolium*. All three are floriferous, fragrant and suitable for growing up poles, trellises, walls or in hedges.

Climbers have always figured strongly on walls, fences and porches in the cottage garden and apart from rambler and climbing roses – of which the fragrant pink 'Albertine' is one of the most famous – there are at least three others which have a special place in the cottage garden.

First comes the winter-flowering jasmine, *Jasminum nudiflorum*, introduced by Robert Fortune from China in 1844. The scentless yellow flowers on the leafless green stems provide one of the few splashes of colour in the winter season, and this makes them doubly appreciated. In spring and throughout summer the scrambling growths of *Jasminum officinale* are thickly set with deciduously fragrant white flowers, often pink tinged in bud. This is a well established resident of the garden, having been introduced to Britain some time in the sixteenth century.

The large, violet-purple flowers of *Clematis* 'Jackmanii' are the result of a union between the Chinese *C. lanuginosa* (now sadly lost to cultivation) and the South European and South-West Asian *C. viticella*. It introduced a new race of clematis hybrids to gardens and now there is a wealth of named varieties in a fine range of colours from the petunia red 'Ernest Markham' to the mauve-pink, red-striped 'Nelly Moser'.

Coloured borders

Grey foliage plants figured prominently in Gertrude Jekyll's gardens and for those who dream of planting a grey or silver border or bed, the following shrubs are worth considering. Firstly, there are those which are dwarf or prostrate: *Santolina chamaecyparissus*, especially in its variety 'Nana', and the more feathery-leaved *S. neapolitana*, which makes neat hummocks topped by the bright yellow buttonhead flowers on slender stalks. These should be cut away immediately after flowering to maintain the shrub's tight growth. A little higher in growth is *Senecio maritimus*, of which there are several named forms including 'Ramparts'. It can be a brilliant grey – almost white – and preferably, in order

Jasminum nudiflorum has a special place in the cottage garden.

to keep the shrub's compact habit, the flowers should be cut away as they develop. If it is allowed to flower, the weight of stem spoils the shape of the plant, and the yellow flowers – not very inspiring at their best – are downright ugly when finished and spoil the overall effect. Taller than any of these is *Artemisia arborescens*. This makes a superb mound of filigree silver foliage but unfortunately, being a native of the Mediterranean, it is not hardy in cold northerly regions. Its place in cold gardens can be taken by one of the herbaceous kinds such as *A.* 'Lambrook Silver' which has neither quite the same shape nor lasting effect. Of similar size but more spreading in growth are the various forms of *Caryopteris* x *clandonensis*, of which 'Arthur Simmonds' is perhaps the most common. Its blue flowers in late summer and autumn are a lovely contrast to the grey-green of the leaves. As a taller member of the group the spire-like *Perovskia atriplicifolia* is a must, although *P.* 'Blue Spire' will do just as well. The tall slender stems – 1.8 m (6 ft) – help break up the general uniformity of the low mounds and hummocks. Those in mild areas or with warm, sheltered, sunny gardens might like to add *Teucrium fruticans* which has a lax habit of growth and, like the *Caryopteris*, produces blue flowers through summer.

To add purple contrasts to the grey, there are several shrubs which are easy to cultivate. These include *Berberis thunbergii* 'Atropurpurea' or one of several dwarf versions such as *Salvia officinalis* 'Purpurea' and the taller, more robust *Cotinus coggygria* 'Royal Purple'. There are several non-woody purple plants which could be used, including the annual *Atriplex hortensis* 'Atrosanguinea' and *Sedum maximum* 'Atropurpureum'.

There are a wide range of shrubs which may be used as individuals in the cottage garden, either in association with other plants or with non-plant features such as steps, low walls, a sundial, etc. Of these one of the most popular is undoubtedly *Euphorbia wulfenii* or its relative *E characias*.

Both make bold clumps of erect stems clothed with narrow grey-green leaves and crowned in summer with a handsome head of green flowers with or without black or maroon eyes. These two are better off in isolation where their poise and colour can best be seen and appreciated. The tree lupin *Lupinus arboreus* is another such shrub. Its fingered leaves are very effective, particularly before the flower spikes appear in summer. The common self yellow is by far the best of the several forms.

Evergreens

Most cottages would, traditionally, have either holly or box. Both make excellent hedges. Two favourite specimen evergreens, however, are the bay and the laurustinus. A bay tree or bush, *Laurus nobilis*, can be made to serve ornamental, utilitarian and culinary purposes and there are few other evergreens that can match that. Even better, ornamentally, is the golden form 'Aurea', but it is particularly susceptible to scorching by severe frost. The laurustinus (*Viburnum tinus*) like the bay, hails from the Mediterranean regions of Europe but it is a long-established favourite in cottage gardens. Sometimes, particularly in coastal areas, it is used as a boundary hedge. The white flowers are without fragrance, but they cover the bush from one end of winter to the other. There are several named forms, of which 'Eve Price' is notable for its compact habit, small neat leaves and red flower buds.

Natural gardens

You further reduce the degree of artifice and the obvious presence of the hand of man by opting for a natural garden. The idea was pioneered by William Robinson in Victorian times, although few gardeners today have the space in which to match what he achieved at Gravetye. Effectively, the natural or

Viburnum tinus, another great favourite.

wild plan is a little piece of the countryside brought into the garden, a home for plants which are encouraged to grow in conditions similar to those of their natural habitat. In many respects it can be labour-saving. It is devoid of formal beds, borders, terraces and other engineered features. Shrubs are grown in conditions more akin to a thicket than a shrubbery; lawns grow long and are planted with bulbs and annuals so that in season they resemble meadows or woodland glades.

It is best to start the grass and flowers at the same time. Under the canopy of trees, a miniature woodland landscape of shade-tolerant shrubs, flowers and ferns will grow up according to the natural order of things. Paths become simple tracks, and maximum use can be made of natural features such as a stream or rocky outcrop. The natural appearance also comes from letting plants grow pretty much as they please, without trimming or pruning, by tolerating weeds as long as they don't overrun or harm the more interesting plants, and by incorporating wild plants, provided you do not dig them up from the wild. Cowslips and primroses used to be widespread in England, but they are now quite rare. Wild flower seed can in any case be obtained commercially. How tidy the garden is depends entirely on your own inclinations and the way you want your garden to look.

A natural garden isn't quite the same as wilderness (or even a cultivated garden that has been neglected) because in nature you would rarely find quite the same concentration of plants growing happily together. Therefore, a modicum of plant planning and garden design is necessary to combine all the elements of what, to you, seems 'natural'. If you look mainly to varieties which can be found growing wild in your locality you will involve yourself in far less cultivation than if you try to introduce non-native species. And if you are interested in the fauna as well as the flora of your garden, you may well find that your garden will be visited by dozens of species of insects, birds and mammals which can establish food chains there, with many paying more than an occasional visit to this peaceful, undisturbed habitat.

The ecological garden

In the wild, woodland trees, shrubs and flowers have an attraction for animals, birds and insects of all kinds looking for food, water, shelter and a place to breed. The domestic garden fulfils a similar need if it contains suitable plants. Living creatures will travel a long way in search of food and if a ready supply can be found in a garden, then it will become a hive of activity for many species and a fascinating source of interest and pleasure to onlookers.

Attracting insects

The flowers and shrubs which are especially attractive to insects are those which collectively produce abundant nectar or pollen. No better example can be found than the shrub buddleia, especially *B. davidii* which is sometimes referred to as the butterfly bush. Its long flower heads in late summer/early autumn attract a rich variety of 'long-tongued' insects, among which butterflies and moths predominate. The orange-flowered *Buddleia globosa* flowers earlier than *B. davidii* and is just as eagerly sought after, especially by bees who find the nectar easier to reach. If you haven't the space to grow a buddleia it might be worth considering growing it espaliered against a wall.

The rich rose flower heads of *Clerodendron bungei* are also attractive to butterflies in late summer and autumn. Lacking the mobility of bees, butterflies generally prefer flowers which are produced in large clusters of heads. They are easier to work over and more productive.

One group of late-flowering shrubs which provides ample nectar and attracts a wide insect clientele is the ivy family *Araliaceae*. The ivy itself is well known for this reason but other members of this family, such as *Fatsia japonica* and *Aralia elata*, are equally attractive. Their flowers are extremely decorative and have bold foliage (evergreen in the former, deciduous in the latter).

Some of the most important sources of nectar and pollen are found in the *Rosaceae* family. Many genera have small white flowers in crowded heads. Try *Cotoneaster, Pyracantha, Crataegus, Chaenomeles* or *Spiraea spp.* Heaths and heathers are famous for their pollen and many bee-keepers still take their hives out into the hills when these plants are in flower. In the garden all heathers and heaths are visited by insects, including bees and butterflies. The early-flowering heaths such as *Erica carnea, E.* x *darleyensis, E. mediterranea* and the tree heaths *Erica arborea* and *E. lusitanica* attract the first insects of the year which then move on to crocuses. Spring-flowering shrubs attractive to insects include the flowering currant *Ribes sanguineum* and the many berberis species. Herbs like rosemary, thyme, marjoram and lavender will also attract bees.

For gardens in warmer regions there is a genus of Tasmanian and Chilean shrubs known as *Lomatia*, whose long-tubed, nectar-filled flowers are attractive to bees and butterflies. Perhaps the most readily available is *L. myricoides*, a large shrub with long narrow evergreen leaves and showers of white flowers in summer. Also from Chile comes *Abutilon vitifolium*, a tall powerful shrub whose large, mallow-like flowers in white or lavender blue will attract insects from miles around. In many coastal gardens where tamarisk is grown its plume-like inflorescences in spring or summer are a great attraction to insects.

The natural garden

Some commonly planted hedge shrubs are popular with insects, especially bees. The box (*Buxus sempervirens*), holly (*Ilex aquifolium*), hawthorn (*Crataegus monogyna*) and privet (*Ligustrum ovalifolium*) come into this category, but clipping must be kept to a minimum to allow flowering.

Most of the pea-flowered shrubs – cytisus, genista, spartium, etc., are attractive to bees and other insects, either for nectar or pollen, and so too are many summer-flowering shrubs such as caryopteris, perovskia and elsholtzia.

The family *Compositae*, in which the small tubular or rayed flowers are densely crowded into daisy, dandelion or thistle-type heads, generally provides a feast of nectar for insects.

Most of the important members of this family are perennials or annuals but there are some shrubs amongst them. These include the rich yellow knapweed heads of *Grindelia chiloensis* which flower continuously and are popular with butterflies, *Aster albescens*, a shrubby michaelmas daisy with yellow-eyed purple or lavender blue flower heads, and *Eupatorium micranthum*, another late flowering shrub for milder areas. Add to these the collective potential of the *Olearia* and *Senecio* clans and the choice of shrubs for insect appeal widens enormously.

The old-fashioned cottage garden attracted many varieties of butterflies and other insects because the flowers growing there were rich in scent as well as nectar, while the weeds provided food for caterpillars. Butterflies are found less often in today's gardens, due – among other things – to the development and cultivation of hybrid flowers whose scent and nectar content has been sacrificed for bigger and better blooms, the increasing use of pesticides and insecticides, and the attentions of diligent gardeners in removing 'undesirable' weeds on which caterpillars feed. Some traditional plants are still available, however, which provide nourishment for many adult butterflies - honesty, for instance, *Hesperis matronalis* (sweet rocket), and almost all members of the daisy family.

Butterflies, bees and flowers

After the crocuses have flowered, the early butterflies will move on to visit yellow alyssum, arabis, aubrieta, polyanthus, and wallflowers. In summer annual alyssum, phlox, petunia, nicotiana, sedums, origanum and dianthus will attract different varieties by virtue of their abundant nectar, while in

Above: *Sedum spectabile* 'Carmen'.
Right: 'H. E. Beale', one of the best, free-spreading varieties of *Calluna vulgaris*.
Below right: *Viburnum opulus* 'Compactum'.

autumn Michaelmas daisies and the late-flowering sedums and single varieties of dahlias will be much in demand. Bees will also be attracted to these flowers – provided other environmental conditions in the garden are sympathetic to their needs.

If you want to attract more than just a passing interest from butterflies, you will need to make your garden into a suitable breeding site for them by providing food for their caterpillars.

Though it may go against the grain, a few clumps of dandelions, nettles and thistles could be tucked into some out-of-the-way spot to provide food for a variety of species. Remember, of course, that these plants are very invasive and you will need to keep them in check to prevent them overrunning your garden.

Roses and insects

As every gardener knows, roses attract greenfly; but no sooner is this pest seen, than it is slaughtered. It is no pest to ladybirds, hover flies or lacewing flies, for to the larvae of those three attractive insects, greenflies are food. Ladybirds may spend the winter clustered closely around the older stems of roses, especially on some large shrub or climber. Hover flies, like slim and benevolent wasps, flit fast and then stay poised in the air above the flowers. The lacewing fly, with its light green, lace-patterned wings, is a pretty insect related to the dragonfly. (Its larvae cover themselves with the skins of their dead victims.) Some small birds, especially tits and sparrows, also feed on greenfly; nesting boxes for tits can be an important part of a rose garden's ecology.

Bees are attracted to all those roses which open to show their stamens. Roses flower at a useful time for bees, after the great burst of spring and early summer is over, but do not spray insecticide on roses when they are in full bloom, otherwise many valuable bees may die. A particularly interesting insect is the rose leaf cutting bee. It does little harm to the rose, for all it requires is a piece of leaf for its nest. The patient observer may see how cleverly the bee works. It lights upon the edge of a leaf, swivels itself round, and cuts a piece of leaf in a perfect arc. As the piece falls, the insect catches it and flies off to its nest, a favourite site being the crumbling mortar of a brick wall.

Attracting aquatic life

Frogs have been steadily declining in number in many parts of the world as the ponds where they find a home in the wild become polluted with pesticides or filled in to provide land for building and agriculture. They are capable of travelling some distance to colonize a domestic pond. Ponds also provide a home for numerous insects, of which the dragonfly is the most immediately attractive, and a population of newts and toads may well develop if the pond is large enough and left sufficiently undisturbed. Notes on stocking a domestic pond with fish are given on p. 164.

Top to bottom: dragon-fly, toad, frog, damsel-fly, newt.

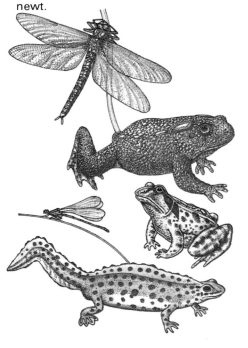

Attracting birds

Apart from finding nesting sites, birds take food from the garden in the form of fruits, the most popular being those of a succulent nature such as berries. The guelder rose, *Viburnum opulus*, carries large bunches of bright red, very succulent berries: birds are also attracted to *V. betulifolium*, *V. trilobum*, *V. lantana* and for smaller gardens, *V. wrightii hessei*. Barberries are also producers of succulent berries while those of the cotoneaster, though produced in abundance, are generally drier and tend not to be eaten if anything better is available. *Sambucus, Rubus, Crataegus* and *Sorbus spp*, on the other hand, are sought after for their fruit.

Under normal circumstances, birds go for red or black berries first, leaving those of other colours until later. Thus the fruits of yellow-berried forms of the cotoneaster, holly and *Viburnum opulus* and of white-berried *Sorbus* and

Symphoricarpus spp tend to linger on long after those of the red and black varieties have been eaten. As well as being attractive to insects, most members of the daisy family – even sunflowers – will provide seed for birds, as do evening primroses and poppies. Remember, though, that a newly seeded lawn will also act as a magnet for birds. criss-cross strands of black thread positioned between stakes a few inches above ground level will deter this invasion.

Building bird tables

You can easily make a bird table from any wood suitable for outdoor use. Try to make the base at least 60 cm (2 ft) square – this way, more birds can get on to the table at feeding time. Make a raised edge to stop the food blowing away by screwing lengths of stripwood 25-50 mm (1-2 in) wide around the sides but leave gaps at the corners to allow rainwater to drain away. Of course drainage is easy with a bird table roof.

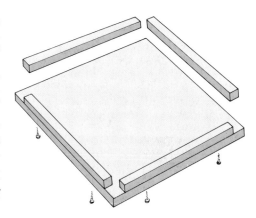

Whether you hang the table from the branch of a tree or raise it above the ground (a pedestal about 1.2-1.5 m (4-5 ft) high would be ideal) make sure that it is out of reach of cats. Birds won't come to feed if they know a cat is going to leap out at them. Keep the table clean and free of possible infections by washing it down regularly with disinfectant.

You can buy packets of seed for wild birds from pet-shops, or you can make your own food for them. Mix together seeds, raw oatmeal, chopped nuts, dried fruit and any odd bits of cheese or bread, and pour melted fat over it. When the concoction has hardened you can put it out on the table. Many birds are also fond of bacon rinds and, of course, peanuts – as long as they are unsalted. These can be threaded together on a string and hung in a suitable spot. Remember, though, that once you have started feeding birds they will regard your home as a regular port of call and come to rely on you for food, particularly in winter – so carry on feeding them every day.

139

Creating a haven of tranquility

The perfumed garden

In search of a perfumed garden

Of all plant characteristics that of scent can be the most evocative. The merest whiff can recall a place or a moment which has for months or even years been lost to conscious thought.

Successful plant planning encourages enjoyment through all five senses. The emphasis may well be upon visual satisfaction, but appreciation of scent follows close behind. There is a popular argument that plants, and roses in particular, are not as fragrant as they used to be. It is hardly justifiable, and quite possibly arises from the damage which tobacco-smoking and pollution have done to our noses rather than anything that has happened to the plants. We still have rose species that were enjoyed in the seventeenth, eighteenth and nineteenth centuries. Some of them are fragrant and some are not; and so it is with modern hybrids. Indeed, possibly the most beautifuly fragrant rose in the world, after the sweet briar, is the white 'Margaret Merril' which was introduced in 1977.

The ecology of scent

You may be surprised to learn that plant scents do not exist solely to please man's aesthetic sense. Each is a clearly evolved part of a plant's effort to succeed as an organism in the habitat in which it lives. The aromatic oils of lavender and rosemary, for example, evolved as a defence against browsing animals. We happen to like them. Similarly, floral scents have developed with the aim of attracting pollinating birds, bees or blow-flies upon which they depend for reproduction. Nor is their evolution in any way haphazard. There would be no point in wild arum developing a scent like Chanel No. 5; it is pollinated by flies and its scent, like rotting meat, fulfils its needs admirably.

Even among human beings flower scents are attractive to some, of little interest or even positively repellant to others. For example, to some people the heavy summer scent of *Lilium auratum* is altogether too much of a good thing; to others, the brisk smell of freesias is barely appreciated, if at all.

It is, therefore, not a simple task to recommend scented plants that will appeal to everyone, though everyone would agree that scent plays an important role in every garden plan. Additionally, the production of scent depends upon many vagaries.

Positioning scented plants

Garden environment affects the efficacy of scented plants. They are

aided by shelter from dissipating wind.

Often the weather plays the major part – a soft rain and a kind warmth make the plants swell with fragrance. Apple-scent from sweet briars is stronger when exposed to rain, and carries further. But where you place scented plants in your garden should also take cognizance of how they dispense their fragrance.

The scent of balsam poplars (particularly strong as the young leaves are unfolding in spring) is carried upon the air for considerable distances. Not dissimilar, but local by comparison, are the sudden fleeting drifts from *Cistus* x *skanbergii* (authentic evocation of a Mediterranean maquis even on the darkest winter day). Additionally, some of the tree-climbing synstylae roses distil their scent for a considerable distance – *Rosa filipes, R. longicuspis* and *R. helanae* are alluded to on page 44. The scent of these roses comes not only from the petals, but from the stamens as if they were an extra advertisement for pollinating insects to travel into the tree tops.

Whereas flowers dispense scent unaided by man, most foliage scents are released only when touched. Sometimes the merest brushing by is sufficient, whereas others react to

Above: *Rosa* 'Fragrant Cloud', a hybrid tea. **Right:** *R. Filipes* 'Kiftsgate'. **Below:** *Daphne adora* 'Aureomarginata'.

actual bruising of their tissues. This group includes all the herb shrubs – lavender, rosemary, santolina, myrtle, helichrysum, and so on – as well as lemon balm, lemon verbena, bergamot, and basil, to name but a few. It is advisable, therefore, to plant these in places where they *can* be touched (a fair-sized raised bed could be an answer). After all, with no large-scale beauty of flower to recommend them their fragrance becomes all the more important. In *Magnolia salicifolia*, incidentally – a sadly underused plant – the lemony fragrance of the leaves extends to the twigs and bark as well.

mollis, Viburnum farreri and *Mahonia japonica.*

Planning for scent in town gardens, where seasonal plantings in tubs and urns are popular, is no problem. For spring, there are wallflowers, Brompton stocks and polyanthuses which can be effectively mixed with hyacinths. For summer, nicotianas (tobacco plants, which will grow in light shade), ten week stocks, petunias (related to nicotiana, their scent too is especially fragrant in the evening), mignonette (*Reseda odorata*), so distinctive in its scent that it is used as a scent name and cherry pie (*Heliotropium peruvianum*) which also produces a highly individual perfume.

In addition to the aromatic shrubs already mentioned, less secretive in their fragrance are some scented flowering shrubs. In high summer, philadelphuses (known as mock orange) can fill a whole garden with their characteristic scent, and there is the honey-scented *Spartium junceum.* You might underplant these with lily-of-the-valley (which prefers shade), sweet woodruff and lilies. Later in the summer consider planting *Hosta plantaginea with the golden-rayed lily, Lilium auratum,* an exquisitely scented pairing. Unlike others, this lily is a lime-hater.

By far the widest range of scented plants deliver their fragrance only to a close observer. And while it is a pleasure to visit a particular part of the garden in order to enjoy some plant or other in flower, the concept of an area especially devoted to scented things inevitably suggests a place to sit and relax. A terrace is ideal. Very probably it will be sheltered and because of its proximity to the house and hard floor surface, a terrace is more likely than anywhere else to be continually used. In a small town garden there may be nothing other than 'terrace' or, more exactly, courtyard. With its surrounds – the buildings, walls and/or fences – and its role as an outdoor room to sit and relax in, this lends itself admirably to a concentration of scented plants.

Particularly appropriate for terraces and walled back gardens are the abundant scented climbers. The fact that they will cast their fragrance into the house through a nearby open door makes them especially desirable. As the year progresses, honeysuckles, jasmines and *Magnolia grandiflora* open successively. Into winter, the rather tender *Buddleia auriculata* continues to flower. Among rose climbers, those which dispense their perfume most nobly include 'Compassion', 'Clg. Etoile de Hollande' and

'Mme Gregoire Staechelin'. Then there is 'Maigold' with its piquant, hayfield scent.

Other scented plants throughout the year
The year begins with winter sweet (*Chimonanthus praecox*), one of the doyens of the scented brigade. But if your budget is hard pressed, remember that it flowers only in the two months when, generally, little time is spent in enjoying the garden close to. Following soon after is *Acacia dealbata* and other mimosas which you may have seen in wonderful displays when wintering in the Mediterranean. Native to Australia in fact, their rich yellow clusters of flowers pervade the air with a delicious perfume. At the mimosa's foot could be *Daphne odora* which smells like sweetened lemons, and flowers for weeks on end.

Open ground plants without which no fragrant collection is complete include *Mahonia japonica,* offering lily-of-the-valley-scented spikes from autumn through to spring in sun or shade, on lime or acid soils. It's a truly remarkable plant and ideal in a courtyard.

In cold areas virtually the only plants which flower with fragrance in late winter/early spring are *Hamamelis*

More must be said about roses. The sweet briar is the outstanding scented subject, and whether you plant the wild *Rosa eglanteria* or one of its scented hybrids such as 'Lady Penzance', its true scent – a lovely apple fragrance – is clearly noticeable at fifty yards when its leaves have been bruised with rain and the air is fairly still. But like many of the old-fashioned types – including the gallicas, damasks and centifolias – it has the disadvantage that although it is immensely fragrant it has only one short flowering season in early summer. If you choose the sweet briar, put it in an inconspicuous position and trim it to size each year to keep it in its designated area. Then, having forgotten about it, every now and then on a still summer evening you will remember it with gratitude.

For long effect, the rugosas, especially 'Blanc Double de Coubert' and 'Roseraie de l'Hay', are beautifully scented and what they lack in flower form they gain in a rather longer season. Obviously the modern hybrid roses are supreme in this regard. Particularly recommended for scent are the hybrid teas 'Fragrant Cloud' – geranium lake with a musky, fruity perfume; 'Alec's Red' – crimson; 'Prima Ballerina' – pink; 'Wendy Cussons' – rose red. For a wall, even in shade, the old climbing 'Crimson Glory' is not easily bettered. 141

The perfumed garden

Philadelphus coronarius

A scented laburnum walkway.
Viburnum fragrans (syn. *farreri*)

For a cool greenhouse or more accessibly in a conservatory, an even wider range of exquisitely scented plants can be cultivated. The effect of enclosed warmth (noticeable outside) is of course increased under glass, and plants just too tender for growing outside become possible. Experiment with *Buddleia asiatica* in winter, for example, or maddenii rhododendrons in spring, and *Cestrum nocturnum* for summer; the range is endless as are the surprises which you will experience as you begin to observe and discover for yourself chance fragrances in other gardens. A handful of fallen leaves from *Cercidiphyllum japonicum* were shown to the author a month ago; he was surprised to discover that something in nature could smell exactly like treacle pudding!

Scented plants: a select list

Aromatic leaves
(see *Planning a herb garden*)

Fragrant flowering
Trees
Acacia dealbata
Azara microphylla
Drimys winteri (and aromatic leaves)
Laburnum alpinum
Magnolia kobus
   x *loebneri*
   grandiflora
   salicifolia (and aromatic leaves and bark)
   stellata
Myrtus apiculata
Malus (many)
Prunus (many)
Tilia spp

Shrubs
Buddleia spp
Chimonanthus praecox
Choisya ternata (aromatic leaves)
Citrus spp (aromatic leaves)
Clethra spp
Coronilla glauca
Cytisus battandieri
   racemosus
Daphne (most)
Elaeagnus spp
Erica arborea 'Alpina'
Genista aetnensis
Hamamelis mollis
Hoheria glabrata
Magnolia (most)
Mahonia japonica
Osmanthus spp
   x *Osmarea burkwoodii*
Philadelphus (most)
Pittosporum tobira
Rhododendron (many)
Ribes odoratum
Rosa (many)
Sarcococca spp
Spartium junceum
Syringa vulgaris cvs (lilacs)
Viburnum (many)

Cytisus battandieri

Viburnum x *burkwoodii*

Coronilla glauca

Decumaria sinensis

Scented climbers

Clematis cirrhosa
　montana
　rehderana
Decumaria sinensis
Holboellia latifolia
Jasminum officinale
　polyanthum
　x *stephanense*
Lonicera caprifolium
　etrusca
　japonica
　periclymenum
Mandevilla suaveolens
Stauntonia hexaphylla
Trachelospermum spp
Wisteria spp

Scented perennials

Amaryllis belladonna
Aruncus dioicus
Cardiocrinum giganteum
Convallaria majalis
Crinum (all)
Dianthus
Filipendula ulmaria
Gladiolus tristis
Hemerocallis (many)
Hesperis matronalis
Hosta plantaginea
Hymenocallis (many)
Hyacinthus cvs
Iris (most)
Lilium (most)
Lupinus polyphyllus cvs
　arboreus
Narcissus spp and cvs
Paeonia (some)
Phlox paniculata cvs
Smilacina racemosa
Speirantha gardenii
Zantedeschia aethiopica 'Crowborough'

Wisteria sinensis

Scented annuals/biennials

Calendula cvs
Cheiranthus cvs
Dianthus cvs
Iberis cvs
Lathyrus cvs
Matthiola cvs
Nicotiana cvs
Petunia cvs
Primula cvs
Verbena cvs

Nicotiana alata

Dianthus 'Pike's Pink'

Lathyrus odoratus

143

Creating a haven of tranquility

The Japanese garden

In making a Japanese garden a *niwashi*, or traditional garden designer, attempts to create a mood of timelessness and tranquility, and to capture something of the essence of nature. The atmosphere he is seeking is described by the Japanese word *yugen*. There is a hint of the mysterious about it, something almost transcendental.

He may achieve it by an art which in its deceptive simplicity seems quite artless (as in the *chaniwa* or tea-garden), or through highly abstract and symbolic terms as in the *kare-sansui* or dry garden. The *niwashi* works largely intuitively. His art has been passed down from generation to generation, and from an early age he has been steeped in plant, rock and water lore. He makes a life-long study of nature, drawing his inspiration from it, but never merely copying it.

There are few *niwashi* left today. A new class of university-trained landscape gardeners and designers has emerged. And with the greater demand for gardens together with the rise in living standards it is hardly surprising that the elements of mass production have crept in. But those who work within the true tradition of Japanese gardening are still moved by the original spirit of the old *niwashi* and guided by the same basic principles.

The principle of 'in' and 'yo'
This concept, better known by its Chinese names, *Yin* and *Yang*, is central to all oriental thought and art. The idea is that everything is balanced, completed by its opposite. Night balances day; male, female; strong, weak. Following this principle, balance in art is achieved not by dividing space into equally weighted halves, or in a garden by planting the same number of the same tree on either side of a central path, but by balancing opposites – mass with empty space; vertical with horizontal forms; movement with stillness; dark with light; the enduring with the transient. Regularity and the symmetrical layout characteristic of formal Western gardens is alien to a Japanese garden. Ponds are never found round or rectangular but always irregular in shape. Paths tend to wander and, if they do run straight, then the stones they are paved with are laid in an irregular pattern. The focal point in many gardens is a pine tree whose trunk is twisted as if by centuries of winter gales, with one of its branches reaching earthward in a dramatic flowing sweep. There will be straight-limbed trees in the background, but such a tree would never be used as the focal point. To a Japanese eye, it lacks interest.

Vantage point
All Japanese gardens, whatever other purpose they may serve, are designed to be viewed from a ground-floor room in a house or other building. The traditional house made of wood and other natural materials blends harmoniously with the surrounding garden. You sit on the floor, either on the wide, unbalustraded, unpainted wooden verandah or inside the room on *tatami* mats with the *shoji* or sliding screen doors pushed back. The house is raised a metre or so above ground level so you look directly on to trees, rocks and water. Often a tree is planted close to the house so that the garden is seen through its branches. With the *shoji* open, the sounds and scents of the garden reach you. The garden seems to enter the house and the relationship between them is a very intimate one. Formal Western gardens, on the other hand, were designed to be looked down upon from a large first-floor reception room. Only from this height could the beauty and complexity of the intricate geometric design be appreciated.

Mood
The creation of a mood of calm and peace is central. Throughout the turbulent years of civil war – and Japanese history is as bloody, if not bloodier than most – the arts of peace were cultivated as a counterbalance to

the violence. A garden was a place to come back to, where you could restore your *wa* or inner harmony. That need is felt equally today and so the atmosphere of tranquillity is cultivated.

Space, depth and perspective
A Japanese garden is never overcrowded. The aim is to create a place of quiet beauty using the simplest materials. A common design in a Western garden is to have an open central space framed by flowers, shrubs and trees arranged with the smallest in front and the tallest behind. In a Japanese garden quite large trees like pine and maple are often planted in the foreground. Their leaves and branches are thinned and trimmed so that you look through the foliage to the space beyond. A smaller tree planted a little way behind then seems by contrast to be much farther away than it really is and makes the garden seem larger. Large leaved shrubs like *Aucuba japonica* are placed in the foreground with small-leaved azaleas or box behind for the same effect. Winding paths that disappear into woodland create a similar illusion. *Shakkei*, or borrowed scenery – a glimpse beyond the garden of hills, perhaps, or mountains, trees or roofs, – is incorporated into the design and makes the garden seem larger. In

Kyoto, which is surrounded by forested mountains, there are gardens such as the one at Tenryu-ji temple where the use of *shakkei* is quite magical.

In making a garden you work to eliminate, to cut out, to take away. Your concern is not to fill every inch, but to create space where the viewer's imagination can play. This is an essential aspect of all Japanese art. Japanese art is not a consumer item but a participation event where the viewer is always expected to contribute to what is presented and, imaginatively, to complete the work.

Colour

A Westerner accustomed to gardens ablaze with colour and blossom is somewhat taken aback by the sobriety of Japanese gardens. Indeed the Japanese garden has been described as a monochrome garden. The famous Zen garden at Ryoan-ji is reduced to the silvery greys of sand and stone. More typically, the garden is a meditation upon shades of green. However, colour and flowering plants do have a place, especially to mark the changing seasons. Restraint remains the key though, one flower or a single tree being considered more poignant and moving than a mass of colour. So a single plum or delicate mountain cherry will announce spring, an azalea

Above: Japanese principles of gardening bring tranquility to a western site. **Below:** *Shakkei* put into practice.

will glow in early summer, a maple catch fire in autumn. But the predominant colour is green.

Use of indigenous plants

The plum, cherry, Azalea and maple mentioned above all grow wild on the mountains of Japan. It is extremely rare to find any imported or exotic plants in Japanese gardens. As a rule only plants that grow in the area, or that look natural, are used.

Attidude towards and use of the garden

In the West, in fine weather, a garden is often treated as an extra room, an extension of the house. The children play, meals are eaten and guests entertained in it. A Japanese garden is never used by children playing ball or by adults for barbecues or sundowners – though it *is* used for the Japanese style of entertaining. It is rather regarded as an oasis of peace and quiet where you can retreat from the pressures of the world, contemplate nature and restore your inner harmony. As Western-style life encroaches more and more on traditions, people are beginning to have gardens where they can 'live outdoors', but these are Western-style gardens, not Japanese ones.

Making a Japanese garden in the West

It is not possible to have a truly Japanese garden outside Japan for all sorts of reasons. One is that the climate differs and so you cannot have exactly the same plants and, even if you stick strictly to indigenous Japanese plants, they will be subject to different weather and soil conditions which will effect their shape and growth. The rocks and stones are different – the differences may be slight but the whole effect of a Japanese garden is brought about by subtleties of tone and texture. Another thing is the quality of the light. It is strong and bright – much stronger than in England. This light filtering through overhanging foliage reaches the shaded places softened but still bright, whereas the much less intense English light may scarcely penetrate the gloom. Then there is the fine warm rain and the drifting mist which adds so much to the charm of Japanese landscape.

What often happens when foreigners try to make a Japanese garden is that they concentrate on the externals – the stone lanterns, bridges and bamboo fences – rather than on the essence.

Quite apart from the practical difficulty of finding authentic-looking examples of such items, such a garden must fail because all they have done is copy details without understanding the basic concepts of space disposition, asymmetry, distance and perspective.

It is best after all to aim at simplicity. For this, albeit a deceptive simplicity, is the key-note in most Japanese gardens. A Japanese garden is a private space, a retreat of cool shades and scents where an atmosphere of timelessness and tranquility is cultivated. Ornaments (and this cannot be too strongly emphasized) should be used only if they enhance this mood. 145

The Japanese garden

Site for a Japanese garden

The appeal of Japanese gardens, like so much Japanese art, is that they achieve so much with so little, and often in so little space. They can create beauty in a well between buildings or on a strip of damp earth at the side of a house. So, they are well suited to cities. Those long, sunless yards between walls, that impossible stretch behind terrace houses may be suitable for a mossy Japanese garden. In Japan, walls are never white-washed but left

the colour of the natural material, but in these conditions they may need to be painted to reflect light. If so, they should be lightly disguised with an open lattice-work bamboo fence or a planting of light-foliaged shrubs and small trees – bamboo, heavenly bamboo (*Nandina domestica*), maple and willow would be suitable. A tiny garden can even be made in a cramped basement area. A stone basin with bamboo or heavenly bamboo beside it and a maple or weeping cherry to lean over it (they could even be in pots) make a welcome change from the usual basement window view.

If you have a larger garden you may like to turn part of it into a Japanese corner. In deciding whether to site it near the house, take the style of the house into consideration. Wherever you site it, try to mark it off from the rest of the garden with a hedge or fence. Entering the Japanese garden from a Western environment you should feel as if you are entering a different world.

Maintenance

One great advantage of Japanese gardens is that, depending on the design, they need relatively little maintenance work. However, like all things they respond in proportion to the amount you put into them. There is no grass to cut and no annuals to be

Above left: the Japanese achieve so much with so little, often in a small space. **Above:** illustrates the principle of 'in' and 'yo' in a garden seen through drifting mist (a place to restore your 'wa').

planted out, but they do need to be kept tidy, dead branches removed, leaves swept up, the stones sprinkled with water before a guest arrives. Too precise a neatness is to be avoided however. There is a story about the great Tea Master, Sen-no-Rikyu, who after the garden had been meticulously tidied for the reception of guests shook a maple tree so that a few bright leaves floated down to lie on the moss.

Approach

The first thing you must decide is the layout. The most important factor to consider will be the space you have at your disposal and the features which already exist. Begin by deciding on the main feature and focal point. This could be a stone basin with a lantern set nearby, softened by an overhanging maple or willow. In a larger garden it might be a waterfall or pond with an asymmetrically-shaped pine or cedar for height. If you choose a dry garden, it will probably be a group of stones. You must decide whether you want water and in what form – waterfall, pond, stream, stone basin. Your choice will depend on personal preference as

well as on the amount of space at your disposal. Or you may want a dry garden – easier to look after, but more formal. It would suit the clean lines of a modern building but not a period cottage. Having got this far you already know something about the stones you want.

Ask yourself how you want to use the garden. Do you want to walk and sit in it or is it simply to be looked at? If you want to walk in it there will be paths, stepping stones and possibly bridges to think of. Where to put the rocks? It is something you cannot finally decide until you have seen them and tried them out. What about plants? What kind of plants and where should they go? And do you want any ornaments?

The process of reaching a final plan – which of course is not final because you will change it again when you see the rocks and find you cannot obtain all the plants you want – does not go ahead, step-by-step, in a nice orderly fashion like a recipe, but involves constant modification and review. This is true even if you employ a landscape designer. Look at as many photographs and books on Japanese gardens as you can, until you know what you really want and even then be prepared to change. A garden is an act of creation, never pure imitation.

Elements in a Japanese garden

Rock and stone

The earliest garden designers in Japan were priests known as *Ishitate-so*, literally 'priests who arrange stones', which indicates the importance of stones in a garden. In Shinto, the indigenous religion of Japan, the world is seen as peopled by *kami* – spirits or gods – which were thought to inhabit certain trees and rocks as well as mountains and waterfalls. Delight in nature and a sense of closeness to it is one of the strongest characteristics of the Japanese. With such a background it is easy to see why rocks are so important.

Rocks represent endurance and changelessness in a world where everything changes. In gardens they form the framework on which the entire design depends. Other elements in the garden change - plants grow, change their shape, water may alter its course, or even dry up; only stone remains unchanged. It is therefore crucial to choose the right stones and a *niwashi* may spend months searching before he finds one with the quality he is looking for. Having found it, days may then be spent finding exactly the right place and position for it.

In Japan there are connoisseurs of stone as there are connoisseurs of wine and fine furniture elsewhere, and a *niwashi* is judged by his choice and placement of stones. There is no lack of material to choose from, rather the 'embarras de richesses' tests his taste, discrimination and design sense to the utmost. Since every stone is unique, the aim is to perceive its essence, to understand its mood - whether aspiring, powerful, turbulent or tranquil - and to recognise its 'inner spirit'. The following are more practical points to be considered in selecting stones:

Rocks represent endurance in a world where everything changes.

Shape

Five main shapes are recognised:

Tall vertical, or monolithic (sometimes called the 'body stone'); low vertical (the 'soul' stone); horizontal (a long, low, flat-topped stone known as the 'mind and body stone'); arching; reclining (so named because it is roughly the shape of someone lying on their side with their head propped on one arm).

The shape can suggest an island, promontory or mountain range, but should never be over-elaborate or grotesque. Since the bulk of the stone, usually at least two-thirds, is buried in the earth or lies below the surface of the water, it is necessary to discover the 'front' or 'face' of the stone (the part that will remain above the surface) and imagine how the stone will look when in place. This is easy enough with a rock dug out of the earth, less so with a stone cut from a quarry.

Texture

All stones, unless they have been cut or quarried, show the marks of erosion and weathering and these are highly prized. They may be worn smooth by flowing water, pitted by the action of waves, fractured by frost and ice. Moss or lichen may grow on the surface giving the valued quality of *sabi*, the

patina of age. In some stones the strata lines can be clearly seen, ancient paleozoic, metamorphic rocks, like granite and andesite, are the favourites in Japan. Volcanic rock is rarely used.

Colour

Stone should not be brightly coloured and white stones are not used because they stand out too strongly. Greyish-green stones with an aged appearance are the most sought-after. But other colours, provided they are subdued and weathered-looking, are also used. Japanese gardens are most beautiful after rain when everything is fresh and the stones gleam wetly.

Style

Certain traditional styles of rock are used. These are stones whose natural shapes suggest certain poetic ideas, for example a boat setting out on a journey. Other stones or groups of stones may symbolise certain birds or animals. The crane and the tortoise, both associated with longevity, are common subjects. Others are names for the function they suggest or perform – long flat stones are placed at the edge of a pond as 'night mooring stones', and 'wave-dividing stones' are set in the bed of a stream. In a dry stream bed a 'cascade stone' may suggest a waterfall.

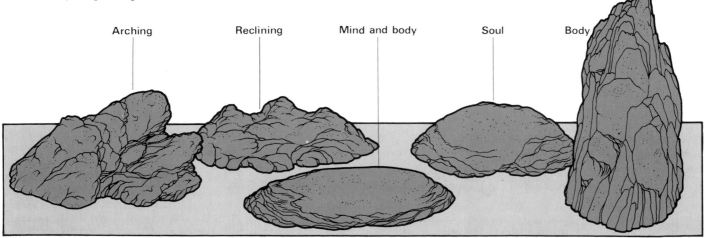

Arching   Reclining   Mind and body   Soul   Body

Creating a haven of tranquility

The Japanese garden

Grouping and placement of stones

Everything else in a Japanese garden depends upon this. There are many rules about the placement and grouping of rocks. They were first stated in the *Sakuteiki*, an eleventh century treatise on gardening and the world's earliest handbook on garden design. Groups of two or more stones are placed at important points in the garden and can represent concepts or things. Stones are always arranged in odd-numbered groups and, except where two stones form a group, there will be an odd number of stones in each group. For example, six stones would be arranged in three groups consisting of three, two and one stone respectively. Fifteen stones would be in groups of seven, five and three.

Within the groups, stones must be of different sizes, yet must harmonize with and relate to one another. Tall, monolithic 'body' stones are used for dramatic effect and usually placed towards the back of a group. The low, vertical 'soul' stone takes a position towards the front. Flat-topped horizontal stones are used as harmonizing elements in a group and help to create a mood of tranquility. If an arching stone is used, it is placed to one side of the group and near the front, while the reclining stone often forms the axis of the whole composition and occupies a position in the foreground.

When placing stone the natural 'grain' or strata of the rock should be taken into consideration. Normally this runs parallel to the earth and when placed upright has a dramatic and dynamic effect which can be disturbing if you are trying to create a peaceful mood. Rounded and horizontal shapes generate an atmosphere of calm.

It is essential that stones be well planted in the earth. They must stand firmly *in* (*tatel*) and not sit *on* (*oku*) the earth. They should look as if they have always been there. Wooden rollers or a sled can be used for moving large stones. Alternatively a strong log or steel bar can be used as a lever. A block and tackle rig may be needed to lift large stones into place. Stones should be wrapped in sacking during moving as a precaution against damage.

Dig a hole deep enough to take the part of the stone to be buried. The stone must be lifted and set in it and then manoeuvred into the right position. When you are satisfied, fill in the hole round the rock and tamp the earth down firmly and leave to settle. Moss, ground cover and other small plants grown around the base of the stone help to make it look as if it belonged there.

Stones are also used in building 'mountains', lakes and islands, in making waterfalls and stream-beds, for paths, stepping-stones and bridges.

Paths and stepping stones

Paths invite you to enter and explore the garden, either imaginatively in expectation, or in person. A path leads you through the garden and turns you at just the right moment to catch a glimpse of a half-hidden lantern, a view of borrowed scenery or tree in bright new leaf against darker foliage. Paths may be of earth or gravel, of cut or natural stone, of old tiles or crosscuts of wood, but the most characteristic and best suited to an informal and natural setting are stepping stones. Like so much else in Japanese gardens they were first used in the *Chaniwa* or Tea Garden – so that guests could keep their feet dry and free from mud.

Paths nearly always wind – a winding path slows you down, makes you change your pace and take time to respond to the atmosphere. They encourage you to linger and, in exploring the garden, re-discover your peace of mind. Stepping stones (*tobi-ishi*) are placed close together with the same aim – to make you take smaller steps and take your time. They are set about 100 mm (4 in) apart and laid well into the earth (between 3/4 and 7/8 of their depth) so that they will be perfectly steady to walk upon. The stones should be at least 350 mm (14 in) in diameter but at key places – where a path divides or turns or comes across a vantage point – larger stones are used, millstones being popular for this purpose. These key-stones are the first to be laid when making a path. When natural stones are used the size and shape is varied, a concave surface being followed by a convex one. Sometimes one or two cut slabs are used for variety. A large flat-topped boulder is often placed at the entrance to the house or tea-house where it serves as a *kutsunigi-ishi* or shoe-receiving stone!

Stepping stones are also a way of crossing water. Here it is even more important that they should be absolutely steady. They should be at least 80 mm (3 in) above the water level.

Water

Water is another essential element in a Japanese garden. Sometimes it is present only symbolically, as in the *kare-sansui* or dry gardens where lines raked on white sand represent the sea, but its presence is always acknowledged.

If stone represents the enduring, unchanging, *yo* element in a garden, then it is balanced by the presence of water which, volatile and constantly changing, is the *in* element. Like stone, water has religious associations, being used for purification both in Shinto rituals and in the *Chaniwa* or Tea Garden.

Summers in Japan are hot and sultry and the sound of water – gurgling over pebbles, splashing into a pool or dripping from a *kakei* (bamboo pipe) into a stone basin – has a welcome cooling effect. Water is also used to reflect and enhance the beauty of overhanging branches or of reeds and irises planted along its edge. Moving water is endlessly fascinating to watch and helps to detach us from our preoccupations.

Water is invaluable in helping to create depth in a garden. A stream is one device. Streams are always winding and naturalistic. Here water runs freely, quietly murmuring or more noisily splashing over a waterfall in its active *yo* form. As water is so abundant in Japan, it was often possible to incorporate a natural stream into a garden. So, when making a stream, try to give the impression that water is passing through your garden, even if it is being re-circulated artificially. Water always runs *out* of a pond as well as into it.

In ponds and lakes water lies quiet in its passive *in* form, reflecting whatever comes near it. Ponds, lakes and islands are always irregular in shape with inlets and promontories which can be walked round or upon, offering different views of the garden and making it seem larger. The gourd-shaped pond is popular.

Pond and stream edgings

As well as being used on the bed of a stream or pond, stones are set into banks edging water. Usually a variety of edgings are used. A natural bank is reinforced with rocks planted to look as if they belonged there. Low clipped bushes of box or azalea are often grown among them. Elsewhere there may be a small beach of pebbles or shingle with one or two night-mooring stones set among them. Low wooden posts are another common method of supporting a bank. The posts, usually charred to discourage

attack by fungus and rot, are sunk directly into the earth (not set in concrete which, being acid, would eat into the wood). They stand about 150 mm (6 ins) above the water, being about level with the earth behind. At each end of a stretch of posts there should be a rock, clump of reeds or other natural feature to link it to the rest of the bank. Plants such as reeds, flags and irises make a natural and attractive edging to water.

Bridges

Many types of bridges may be found, ranging from the highly elaborate and ornamental – mainly confined to large or public gardens – to simple slabs of natural stone. The arched red-lacquer bridges often seen in so-called Japanese gardens abroad are in fact of Chinese origin and rarely used in Japan itself. Hand rails are rare on bridges. The most common types of bridges are:

The arched wooden bridge

This is made by laying logs close together crossways on an arched wooden frame. Earth may be packed between the logs and moss encouraged to grow on it.

The plank bridge

This consists simply of two strong planks laid side by side but with one partly behind the other so that you have to side-step (and pause to look) as you cross. They rest on wooden supports driven into the pond or stream-bed. At Korakuen Park at Okayama there is a famous zigzag version of it.

The stone slab bridge

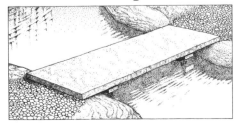

This very popular bridge is often used across a dry stream bed. It consists simply of a large horizontal piece of stone, either natural or cut, supported by rocks on either bank. Two slabs supported in the middle by a boulder or small island may be used to cross a wider stretch of water. When a cut slab is used it is sometimes slightly arched.

Large rocks are usually set into the bank on either side of the bridge and there is often a lantern to illuminate it at night. Stepping-stones are of course another way of crossing water.

Dry gardens or kare-sansui

The materials used in a dry garden are simplicity itself – sand, stone and a few plants. Maintenance too is reduced to a minimum. The sand used should be quite heavy and coarse – fine gravel is suitable, or marble chips can be used.

Pale beige or light grey are better than white which tends to glare, especially in sunlight. Since most people choose this kind of garden because they have little time to spend looking after it, it is best either to lay a concrete screed or alternatively to line the area with a polythene sheet (as when using an impermeable membrane to damp-proof a basement). In either case you will have to allow for drainage. Slope the level slightly and leave an outlet at the lower side. Also remember to leave holes for plants. If you place your rocks in position before laying the screed or polythene sheet, you will be sure to leave holes in the right places since your plantings will be associated with the rocks. The 'sand' should be at least 50 mm (2 in) thick and is likely to need topping up from time to time. You will need a wide-gapped rake if you want to draw lines on the sand which will need to be re-drawn after rain. The most effective are wooden. The sand *must* be kept clean or the effect is lost.

The Japanese garden

Plants

Trees, shrubs and ground-cover plants form the changing element in a garden. They grow, change shape and encroach on empty space. Even though they are trimmed and shaped, when planning, the designer must try to envisage how the plants he includes will look in five, ten or fifteen years' time.

In Japan the business of moving fully grown trees has been brought to a fine art and it is possible to buy from nurseries trees which have taken years to shape or indeed to order a tree to be shaped for use in five or ten years' time.

What plants?

The plants you choose will depend largely on the soil and climatic conditions in your garden, but there are seven plants found in nearly every Japanese garden which you should try to include. They are:

Pine. Either the red pine (*Pinus densiflora*) or the black pine (*Pinus thunbergii*) or the slow-growing *Pinus densiflora* 'Umbraculifera'. This is often shaped and used as a focal point.

Maple. The Japanese greenleaf maple (*Acer palmatum*), used for its spring and autumn foliage.

Azalea. There are many varieties. The dwarf satsuki azalea (*Azalea gumpo*) and the hybrid evergreen azalea (*Azalea kiusianum* 'Kurume') are commonly used.

Plum or cherry. If possible the Yoshino cherry (*Prunus yedoensis*), otherwise the plum blossom (*Prunus mume*) or any delicate cherry, but *never* the massy pink and white double varieties.

Camellia. In at least one of its many varieties.

Bamboo. Bamboo is a giant grass and there are literally hundreds of varieties. It likes a slightly acid, well-drained heavy soil which should never be allowed to dry out completely. The root system spreads horizontally sending up new canes as it grows. The canes should be thinned and dead ones removed. In their natural habitat bamboos grow from 2 to 15 m. There are also dwarf varieties. Kumazasz (*Sasa veitchii*) makes a good ground cover and in autumn the margins of the leaves dry out and turn the colour of straw. Two other dwarf varieties are clamezasa (*Shibataea kumasasa*) and the dwarf fernleaf bamboo (*Sasa disticha*). Consult your nurseryman about which of the larger varieties of bamboo will grow in your district.

Top: an almost bare-branched pine and willow frame the interest created by low-lying features. **Above**: dwarf bamboos make attractive foils for structures. **Top right**: evergreen plants show off autumn colour. **Below right**: a Japanese corner in a large garden. **Far right**: spring interest as the magnolia flowers; see too the azalea in the foreground.

Moss

This is the most characteristic ground cover. Lawns are never found in the older Japanese gardens and are not common even today. In the damp climate of Japan moss grows luxuriantly, but it is not difficult to cultivate in shaded places and – as many gardeners know to their cost – is very resilient and not easy to get rid of once established. Small patches of moss can be planted in shady spots and if kept moist should take root and begin to spread. Milk rubbed on to stone is said to encourage the growth of moss. If allowed to dry out moss turns brown and appears dead but given water it will quickly revive.

Using plants to make the garden seem larger

Some of the techniques used to make a garden seem larger and to give a feeling of depth have already been mentioned.

A tall but carefully shaped and thinned tree may be set near the house – the main vantage point for viewing the garden – so that smaller trees planted beyond appear to be larger trees planted further away. Large-leaved plants are used in fore-ground planting to create the same illusion. A branch is trained to sweep down and half obscure part of the garden, or a grove of Castillon bamboo (*Phyllostachys bambusoides*), thinned out and with the leaves stripped from the lower stems, form a living fence through which the garden is glimpsed. In both cases, by making a part seem a separate space, the whole garden is enlarged in the mind of the viewer. A garden seldom appears as one open space. Hedges, fences and groups of plants divide it, if only in the imagination, into separate but integral parts.

Plants as hedges

If you are concerned with making an enclosed space, then trees and shrubs are excellent material for both boundary and background, shutting out undesirable views and creating a sense of privacy and quiet. Bushy dark-leaved evergreens like *Camellia japonica*, cryptomeria and rhododendrons or azaleas are favoured. They are planted close together, often allowed to grow quite tall (3 or 4 m) and clipped to form a dense wall of green. *Photinia glabra* and, in very mild climates, *Cinnamomum camphorum*, the camphor tree, are also used and box is used for low hedges. Bamboo too can make a beautiful hedge when clipped, though perhaps its bright and delicate foliage might not make such an easy background as plants with darker leaves.

Shakkei

Shakkei or 'borrowed scenery' is another technique for creating the illusion that the garden is larger than it is. The idea is that if you are lucky enough to have an attractive view from your garden of mountains, the sea, trees in a neighbour's garden or perhaps simply a weathered roof, you incorporate this into the design of your garden. First, disguise the boundary of your property with a hedge of shrubs and trees of the right height and mask any discordant elements such as street lights with suitable screens. Then choose plants and trees that will be compatible with those in your bit of *shakkei*.

Colour and seasonal change

As we have noted dark-leaved evergreen trees and shrubs are used as background. They provide a foil for spring foliage and blossom and for autumn colouring. Although the majority of the traditional plants used (pines and conifers, camellia and bamboo), are evergreen, some deciduous plants which colour and lose their leaves as well as one or two flowering trees and shrubs are included to reflect the rhythm of the seasons. These however are used sparingly and green remains the dominant colour throughout the year. Discrimination must be shown in selecting and grouping plants with regard to the different shades of their foliage.

Scent in the garden

Highly-scented flowers are not cultivated but the fragrance of earth after rain, the freshness of rain-washed foliage, the scent of pines are appreciated. Delicate subtle fragrances are enjoyed but nothing heavy or cloying. Japanese apricot (*Prunus mume*) which has a deliciously delicate fragrance is planted in the path of the prevailing wind so that its scent will give most pleasure.

Pattern and foliage

Maple, weeping willow, weeping cherry and pine, among other trees, are loved for their inherent asymmetry, brought out by skilful pruning and shaping. Such trees are often the focal point in a garden. They are never placed centrally but always to one side, either of the garden or of a group within it.

Pruning and shaping

Pruning is done to prevent overcrowding, for the health of the plant, to open up the lower branches to the light and to create space. It is also done to bring out the line of a branch or tree. Trees are thinned so that they do not darken buildings too much, especially when planted close to the house.

A low horizontal branch may be trained to sweep down and overhang a pool or a gate or to veil a roof. In spring when the sap rises and branches are flexible, a stone or other weight is tied to the branch to weigh it down. Stakes may be used to hold it in position. The short side branches and twigs that point downwards are cut away and those pointing upwards are thinned to bring out the line.

The trunk can also be shaped. Plant a pliant young sapling (about 2 m (6ft) tall) diagonally in the ground. Remove the alternate left and right branches, then bend the trunk so that you have an 'S' shape. Tie the tree securely to the stakes with rope, protecting the bark with a pad of cloth or straw. After one or two years, when the tree can hold its shape, the stakes can be removed. This will probably only be done with one tree in a garden. Pine is a favourite subject.

Deciduous trees are pruned in winter for shaping, and thinned in late summer or early autumn. Flowering trees are trimmed immediately after blooming. Bamboos are cut back to the live twigs in winter. Evergreens may be pruned at any time, but preferably in the autumn. 151

The Japanese garden

Accessories

These are considered last because they are the least essential element. You can have a Japanese garden without any of them and the addition of any number of them will not by itself turn a garden into a Japanese one. The thing to remember about stone ornaments is that they should be used sparingly and only when appropriate. All ornaments were originally functional and many had a religious significance. They were never used merely for decoration. A frequent mistake in Japanese-style gardens outside Japan is the mixing of Chinese and Japanese ornaments.

Stone lanterns

Unlike so much else in Japan these are not of Chinese origin but came from Korea. Over the centuries Japanese taste has modified and adapted the design. Lanterns carved from granite were originally used as votive offerings in Shinto shrines and Buddhist temples. They were not used in gardens until around the fifteenth century and then they were first used in tea gardens to light the *roji* or path when an evening tea ceremony was being held.

A lantern should only be placed where it serves to give light – at a bend in the path, near a bridge, beside the *tsukubai*. It should be set obliquely, not straight on, so its light falls where it is needed. It is most moving when sheltering under and half-hidden by an overhanging branch and with grasses and ferns growing around its base.

A lantern is made in several pieces: **1.** the roof or canopy which rests on **2.** the lamp box, usually square or hexagonal. This stands on **3.** the platform which in turn is supported by **4.** the pillar. There is also sometimes a base or pedestal. The most popular types of lantern are:

The Kasuga-doro or pedestal lantern This is tall (from 1 to 3 m – 3¼ft to 10 ft) with a hexagonal lamp-box, rather formal and mainly used in large or public gardens.

The Yukimi-doro or snow viewing lantern This has a wide, gently sloping roof which holds the snow, hence the name, and gracefully balances on three (usually) arched legs. It is often sited near water.

The Rankei-toro or cantilever lantern is suspended on an arched cantilever so that it may ride out over a stretch of water. This elegant form suits a large or more formal garden.

The Ikekomi-doro or buried lantern lacks a pedestal and so has a natural informal feel about it. It is often used near the *tsukubai*.

Genuine old lanterns are practically unobtainable nowadays. In Japan reproductions are widely available. Outside Japan it is less easy to find stone lanterns but some companies do make them. Failing all else an enterprising potter might be persuaded to make one, or you could try your hand at carving one from natural stone. A new lantern, like any new stone ornament, will acquire the desired weathered look more quickly if kept damp. Candle light is the best light to use in a stone lantern. Protect it with oiled-paper screens to soften the light even further. Wooden or iron lanterns can be hung from the eaves of a house or placed on a flat topped boulder.

Japanese lanterns

Yukimi-doro

Kasuga-doro

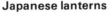

Ikekomi-doro

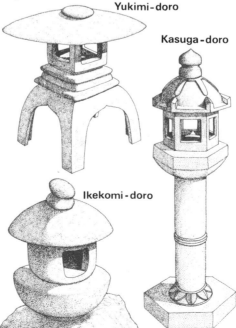

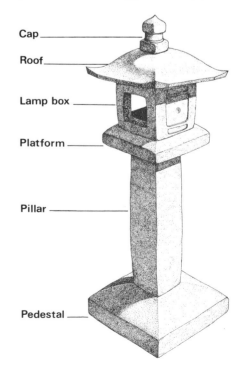

Cap

Roof

Lamp box

Platform

Pillar

Pedestal

Kakine (fences) and Mon (gates)

Fences delineate, divide, screen, shelter and protect. They are nearly always made of bamboo, though wood is used occasionally. There are many kinds of fences, some like the *yotsumi-gakine* being open lattice-work affairs that half-conceal, half-invite. They are so light as to be no more than a gesture towards forming a boundary or keeping anyone out. These are mainly used for decoration, dividing the garden psychologically rather than physically. Others like the *shiba-gaki*, are tall, sturdy and impenetrable. There are also *sode-gaki*, half or sleeve fences, which are used to conceal rubbish bins or some other undesirable sight. All fences are supported on strong wooden posts, often charred as a precaution against rot and insect attack, burnished and then set securely into the ground. These posts are hidden by the bamboo in most fence designs. Bamboo is used for the horizontal framework on to which the uprights or diagonals (depending on the design) are attached.

Chozu-bachi (stone basins)

Like stone lanterns, stone basins were first used in the tea garden. Guests still wash their hands and rinse their mouths at the *Chozu-bachi* using the kakehi or bamboo dipper which rests on it. Originally simply a hollow carved in a natural stone, innumerable variations have developed, some being smooth and round, others tall and cylindrical, square and rugged, simple or elaborately carved. Varying between 45 cm (18 in) and 1½ m (5 ft) in height the *chozu-bachi* is most commonly placed low down so that one has to stoop to use it. A large flat stone for standing on is set beside it and, where the water overflows from the basin, the ground is covered with pebbles to stop it getting muddy. Water runs into the basin through a bamboo pipe or *kakei*. Plants, usually including ferns and *Nandina domestica*, grow round it and a lantern often stands nearby.

A *kakei* is not difficult to make. You will need piping (plastic is easiest), two pieces of bamboo large enough to take the piping which will have to be pushed through them, and a small block of wood. The wood should be stained dark. Measure the height you want upright to be and the length of the spout, allowing for the part that will go into the block of wood. Remove the nodes that divide the bamboo into compartments so that the pipe can be pushed through.

Drill two holes the size of your pieces of bamboo in the block of wood, one going straight into the base for the upright, the other going into the side of the wood at a 15 degrees angle for the spout. The two holes should intersect so that you can first insert the bamboo upright and

push the plastic piping through it and out of the angled hole. Then fix the other piece in place as the spout. The spout end should be cut at an angle. Connect the pipe to the water source. The flow of water should be little more than a trickle.

Shishi-otoshi (deer scarer)

This makes a pleasant clear sound in the garden. It is basically a *kakei* with a bamboo pipe that can pivot on its supports set below it so that the water from the *kakei* runs into it. The internodes in the lower pipe have not been removed and so, as the upper part of the pipe fills with water, it gets heavier and the weight tips it forward. The water runs out and the pipe swings back striking a stone placed behind and making a clear pretty sound. The tone of the note depends on the size of the pipe.

Bamboo deer scarer

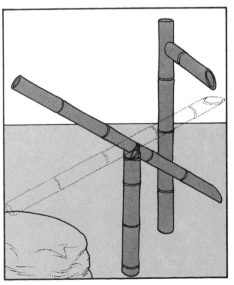

Traditionally, fences were held together by *shuronawa*, strong twine which has been dipped in pitch for protection. Nowadays nails are often used instead, but they are always cunningly concealed by beautifully tied knots. Bamboo is obtainable from specialist bamboo shops. The best, which lasts longest, comes from temperate regions. If you want to try and make your own fence use zinc nails and a rot-proof, firmly twisted black twine. Bamboo fences are now made in Thailand and imported into Japan where the cost of labour has pushed the price of locally made fences out of reach of the average person. Plastic imitation bamboo fences are now being produced. If you do not know they are plastic, they look quite effective and have the advantage of lasting much longer than the real thing.

The Japanese Embassy or Consulate in your country should be able to advise you about local or foreign suppliers of materials for Japanese gardens.

The Alpine garden

There are two good reasons for building a rock garden. One is to provide a suitable setting for alpine plants; the other to enjoy creating a very special garden feature derived from nature – a miniaturised mountain landscape with its own form and shape.

Preferred growing conditions

Alpine plants can of course be grown outside of the traditional rock garden. But like any other group of plants, they need certain fundamental environmental conditions in which to grow successfully.

Site

As one would expect from considering their natural habitat, the majority of alpines like an open, sunny position. In the northern hemisphere, the ideal is a gentle slope falling from north to south or south-west, free from shade-producing trees or buildings. In practice, almost any site open to light and air will serve well enough, as long as it isn't exposed to cold winds or subject to early morning sun when frost is about.

Some outstanding specimens, though a minority, look for cool or partially shaded conditions. Ramondas, haberleas, cassiopes, and forms of *Anemone nemorosa*, all grow well under shade cast by adjacent rocks and shrubs.

Soil and drainage

The one essential condition is good drainage. Alpine plants like a loose soil and copious quantities of water passing rapidly through it, not lingering about their roots. Adding anything to the soil to clog it up is not advised. Of course such a thirsty, hungry soil needs some feeding; compost will be necessary.

Compost

The following formula could be used throughout the rock garden if you have taken the decision to rid it of an unsuitable heavy clay soil. But even if you have a free-draining sand, the formula is advised since the soil is naturally hungry. The vitally important point is that the compost you use serves its purpose as nutrition for plants without in any way hampering the free passage of water through the soil.

The formula

The formula consists of two parts loam (or good top-spit garden soil), one part fine grade moss peat and one part sharp sand or fine grit. Should you have to use clay topsoil, greatly increase the sand or grit component. If peat is unavailable, leaf-mould or well-

Though they can be grown elsewhere alpines look and do best in a rock garden.

rotted garden compost is a good substitute. Never use yellow builder's sand; it will clog the soil rather than provide sharp drainage.

For each ton of rock, use at least one cubic yard of compost. A precise prescription is not possible since it will depend on the method of building – more rock, less compost. But always err on the generous side and never top up with less than well-rotted material.

It is tempting to say that if you have a heavy, water-retentive clay soil you would be better off without it; import or make up your own mix from a drainage agent (coarse sand, for example), peat, and topsoil.

It depends how bad your soil problem is. On a flat clay site, you can dig a deep hole in the centre and fill it with coarse material, such as old bricks, clinkers or gravel. You can even use similar drainage agents to build up the mound and provide a more satisfactory soakaway to help cope with surplus water. But if the clay is really heavy the water could stagnate in the hole, and you're back to square one. If you are committed to a rock garden on clay soil, drastic measures must be taken to keep the soil open.

Lime is sometimes recommended for improving the crumb structure of clay soils so making them easier to work, warmer and better draining, but for

Mixed bed of gazanias

Sedum, lychnis and campanula

There are no rules as to amount of rock or size.

rock gardens this is poor advice. To begin with, one very popular group of alpines, which includes all the autumn flowering Asian gentians and the dwarf ericaceous plants such as gaultherias, vacciniums, cassiopes, ericas and rhododendrons, insists upon a lime-free, acid soil. Furthermore, lime-tolerant and lime-loving alpines will grow satisfactorily in neutral or even acid soil. Consequently a neutral or slightly acid soil gives the widest choice.

Pockets of lime-free soil can be introduced into an alkaline soil rock garden, but if they are, set them at a higher level than the alkaline plantings. Otherwise 'hard' water will infiltrate lower placed lime-free areas.

Preparation

Begin by digging the site over. Take great care to remove all permanent deep-rooting weeds, such as docks, dandelions and thistles, at this stage. If you don't, they are sure to crop up later, probably between rocks where they are very difficult to eradicate.

Now is the time to install a drainage system, unless you are blessed with a sandy or gravelly soil which lies open to air and water.

Always select existing local stone or rock in preference to importing 'foreign' stone. Compatibility of garden materials remains an essential principle here, but practicality and economy is

important too. Conveying heavy rock over long distances is an expensive operation.

Only general guidelines are possible as to amount or size of rock. It is reasonably safe to order one ton for each 100 square feet, using the largest rocks that can be comfortably handled.

If you can obtain it, tufa rock is an attractively unusual planting medium. Tufa, very light and easily manageable, is a limestone-based stone, formed by water deposits in much the same way as stalagmites and stalagtites. It is soft and very porous. By drilling rooting holes you can actually grow alpines in the rock itself. Place rooted cuttings into holes about 10 cm (4 in) deep and secure the plants in a nest of silver sand. They will work their way into the tufa and watering is all they need. Obviously you must avoid lime-hating alpines.

Design

There exist rock gardens which have been so skilfully and artistically constructed that they would stand on their own merits even if left unplanted.

Being faced with a pile of rocks in assorted shapes and sizes is a daunting prospect. But it is at this stage that the creative juices really begin to flow.

The two golden rules are to take your time and the opportunity to observe.

First it is a good idea to observe how other gardeners have succeeded or failed. This could mean a trip or two around public gardens. They will of course be much larger than yours, but the principles of design should hold good. Then look carefully at the rocks you have bought. Lay them out before you. Try a few in position before excavating and remember that they will not, finally, sit on the surface but be embedded in the soil, emerging naturally from the surface. Pick out the largest stones as the foundations for the overall design and consider how the smaller ones can be grouped between them. Gradually, a picture will begin to emerge out of this process of observation and experimentation.

At all times keep an image in your mind of how your rocks would appear in a natural outcrop. Keep the natural stratum lines running in a horizontal direction, and ensure the stones are set at similar angles into the soil.

There is a practical side too to taking time. Rearranging poorly set plants is easy, but digging up and lugging around large poorly positioned rocks is altogether a different matter.

The Alpine garden

Final preparation

Set the rocks in the soil so that they are really stable, and as you do so have to hand plants suitable for growing in rock crevices. Sempervivums, sedums, many saxifragas, dwarf phloxes and gypsophilas, arabis and dwarf campanulas (bell flowers) are appropriate and easy to insert during this rock planting stage, less easy later.

As you position the rocks, make sure that they fit snugly into the soil. Unnecessary gaps between stone and soil provide ideal but unwanted homes for slugs and the like. Ensure also that all the rocks tilt on the same plane. This is an important point in the overall aim to imitate a natural outcrop (arranged in all and opposing directions, the rocks would provide an artificial, higgledy-piggledy effect), but if tilted back towards the ground, the stones will also serve to direct water to plant roots.

When the rock garden has been built and all the plant pockets filled with compost, allow the soil a settlement period before planting. If the weather is dry, liberally soak the area and when the compost settles down, top it up.

Design

As ever when introducing a special feature into a garden plan, thought must be given to integrating it with its surroundings. Imaginative planting can provide the rock garden 'picture' with a 'frame', something to lead the eye into neighbouring features or focus interest on the rock garden itself.

Shrubs are useful surround plantings in this respect. They can provide a link between the specialized interest of the alpine plants and more conventional garden plants. One slow-growing conifer which comes immediately to mind is the dwarf mountain pine, *Pinus mugo*, which develops into a gnarled, low tree, full of character. Cistuses and heathers are found growing naturally on rocky mountain sides. Again, tree heathers such as the tall growing *Erica arborea* and *E. lusitanica* are worth considering though they do prefer acid soils and are not widely successful in North America. The dwarf forms of *E. carnea* and the taller *E. erigena* (*E. mediterranea*) will tolerate alkaline conditions.

Think carefully about linking the rock garden to the whole image of the garden. In nature, rock formations rarely come to an abrupt halt. Perhaps yours could 'peter out' and leave no hint of artificial construction. If you are fortunate in having an open view into fields or wooded landscape, encourage the eye to pass unimpeded and naturally from rock garden to it.

Planting a rock garden

It has been said that the glory of a rock garden is in the spring, and that for the rest of the year it might as well be screened off and forgotten. This need not be true. By choosing well, beauty and interest can be maintained throughout the year – even during the winter months.

When to plant

The conventional planting periods are spring and autumn, but since almost all alpines are raised in pots they can be planted at any season provided the soil is not frozen. One other proviso – if planting in the height of summer ensure regular irrigation and consider providing some form of temporary shade to minimise moisture loss through evaporation. Once the plants have developed root systems capable of seeking moisture at deeper levels, less close attention will be required.

Initial purchasing

The choice is considerable and for the beginner can be bewildering. There are some principles of purchase worth bearing in mind, however.

* You may inevitably start by buying more easily established plants, moving on, as your knowledge increases, to those which demand special treatment. But if you do, be aware of some consequences. Easily grown, quick-spreading aubrietas, alyssums and arabis will need constant cutting back, and if you only plant these spring-flowering subjects, large blank areas will appear later in the year.

* In your selection, aim at sustaining colour throughout the year.

* Be aware of the limits set upon your choice of plants by soil and other environmental conditions. Capitalize on shade provided by rocks and shrubs to grow the very attractive subjects suited to shaded conditions.

* Always be aware of a plant's mature size. Plan so that smaller, less vigorous plants are not overgrown by more robust neighbours.

* Be prepared to replant as your experience widens and special interests develop in particular plant groups.

Year-round colour

Dwarf alpine bulbs provide the earliest colour in the rock garden. A choice of snowdrops *(Galanthus spp)*, tiny narcissi, bulbous irises, crocuses and scillas will reward you well in the otherwise bleak months of late winter.

Remember too the autumn flowering bulbs: the smaller colchicums, *Crocus speciosus* and its forms, *Sternbergia lutea* and the autumn-blossoming snowflake *Leucojum autumnale* – all these lend brightness to the fading months. But be careful. Mark the positions of these bulbs so as not to disturb them when planting other subjects during their dormant season.

One of the best-loved, wild, spring flowers is the dainty wood anemone, *A. nemorosa*, and cultivated forms of this exist which are ideal for the rock garden. They enjoy cool positions and are very useful as under-plantings for dwarf shrubs. Quite similar in their needs, but sufficiently distinct in appearance, are the several forms of *A. blanda* and *A. appennina* – some are vivid blue, others are pink or white.

The genus *Saxifraga* provides plants which will flower according to kind from the earliest days of spring right through into the autumn. There are hundreds of species, hybrids and cultivars from which to choose and this genus is an ideal one to go for if you like the idea of specializing in one particular family. You may find great pleasure in gathering together as many varieties as possible. Here, there is only space to mention the few which can be regarded as indispensible. Among the earliest are the cushion-forming kapschia saxifrages. *S. apiculata* carries clusters of yellow flowers on 3 in (75 mm) stems, and has a pretty, pure white albino. All the various forms of *S. burseriana* are particularly attractive when their tight domes of closely packed grey-green leaves are studded with short-stemmed white flowers. Those of special merit are *S.b.* 'His Majesty' and *S.b.* 'Gloria'; one, 'Lutea', probably of hybrid origin, is soft yellow. The almost stemless lilac flowers of *S. irvingii* and the similar *S. jenkinsae* rest on neat hummocks of grey-green leaves.

Following these early gems will come the silver saxifragas, such as *S. callosa* *(lingulata)*, whose narrow, ensilvered leaves form tidy rosettes out of which erupt plumes of abundant white flowers. All the many forms of *S. aizoon* are worthwhile, especially the pink *S.a.* 'Rosea' and the yellow *S.a.* 'Lutea'. The glory of the summer-flowering saxifragas is *S. longifolia* 'Tumbling Waters', which will make massive rosettes of strap-shaped, silver leaves in symmetrical array and eventually produce a vast spike, often 60 cm (2 ft) long, bearing hundreds of white flowers. Like the forms of *S. callosa*, it is seen at its best when planted in nooks and crannies between rocks.

Into such chinks you might also like to tuck some of the fleshy-leaved rosettes of lewisias, of which there are several colourful hybrid strains. They don't like growing on the flat, nor do they like soil with much lime, but they are sun-lovers. You could also go for cushion phloxes, mostly forms of *P. subulata* or *P. douglasii*, in these postions since they are easy and tolerant, and show vivid pads of colour. But beware of acaenas and cotulas. These make wide mats of attractive foliage and crimson, burr-like flower heads, but they are very invasive. If you don't want them to usurp too much space, use them in cracks between paving stones or areas which you need to cover quickly.

After spring

To follow on after the major spring display try campanulas and dianthuses, both large groups containing a great many beautiful plants. Choose the dianthuses with care; there are a lot of hybrid pinks which, though undoubtedly very handsome, are really out of context in the rock garden. Adhere to the species, forms and hybrids of species, but remember that whatever kind you use (with one or two exceptions such as *D. neglectus*) they are avid sun and lime lovers. The basis of a good collection of campanulas would be *Campanula carpatica*, both blue and white flowered, *C. portenschlagiana*, *C. barbata* with its bearded blue or white bells on 22 cm (9 in) stems and planted away from smaller plants, the gorgeously rampageous *C. poscharskyana*. The latter, if planted in a mixture with the hairy grey leaves and chartreuse flowers of *Alchemilla mollis*, will provide a summer-long scene of beauty.

Gentians are a important family and no rock garden can be complete without some samples. *G. verna* flowers in early spring, with vividly blue, star-shaped flowers borne over neat tufts of dark green leaves. A little later will come the great trumpet gentian, *G. acaulis*, while for mid-summer there is 'everyman's gentian', *G. septemfida*, which will grow anywhere and in almost any soil, faithfully producing, in increasing abundance, heads of blue flowers on 22–30 cm (9–12) stems year after year.

Autumn and winter

For late summer through autumn and even on into winter, turn to the Asian gentians, but remember that they will not tolerate lime under any circumstances. If you have the right soil, you'll have carpets of narrow, lush-green leaves turning to azure from midsummer onwards. The most characteristic is *G. sino ornata*, but there are several others of equal merit, such as *G.* 'Macaulayi', *G.* 'Inverleith', *G.* 'Midnight' and *G. farreri*. All of these come in shades of blue from soft Cambridge to deepest Oxford; if you think this might become a little monotonous, there is a pure white form of *G. sino ornata* which can be used to break up the groups.

A good companion plant for these late gentians, where winter is not too severe, is *Polygonum vaccinifolium*. The larger kinds of polygonum can be highly invasive and difficult to eradicate when firmly established. For this reason they have become unpopular with many gardeners. You should have no problems with this smaller species, however, as it is very well behaved and produces dense mats of trailing, woody stems set with tiny, pointed, thickish leaves which in autumn take on rich tints of red and bronze. At the time when the gentians are blossoming, it produces copious slender spires of heather-pink flowers. It will remain attractive well into the early days of winter.

Autumn is the time when *Cyclamen hederifolium* (better known as *C. neapolitanum*) comes into its own. The leaves are preceded by innumerable rich pink flowers with the typical reflexed petals that one expects from a cyclamen. The leaves themselves are ivy-shaped, handsomely patterned with white marbling on a deep green base. There is an albino version which can be grown very successfully with it. If you plant *C. hederifolium*, *C. coum*, *C. purpuracens (E. europeum)* and *C. repandum* together, you stand a good chance of having a cyclamen in flower at any time during the year. They are all hardy and they like a cool position and soil that is rich in humus.

The Alpine garden

It is inevitable that there will be a scarcity of flowers in winter, although the 'dead' period can be surprisingly short. For this time of year, in lime-free soils, the several dwarf callunas with their richly coloured foliage will be as effective as any blossom. For alkaline soil, *Erica carnea* has good leaf colour.

The winter will not have loosened its grip when the winter aconite *Eranthis hyemalis* makes its appearance, with its golden flowers resting on a tiny saucer of green bracts. Like the slightly larger and more richly coloured *E. cilicica*, it should be in flower come soon after mid-winter. Usually planted as a dry bulb it is actually more likely to establish well if planted 'in the green' (after it has flowered but before the leaves have died away).

In hedgebanks or by the roadside you may notice the lesser celandine, *Ranunculus ficaria*, one of the first flowers to appear each year. However tempting it may seem, don't under any circumstances bring this lovely little fiend into your garden. It spreads far and wide and is extremely difficult to eradicate. Choose instead the several forms of this plant which are well-behaved and trustworthy, the best of which is *R.f.* 'Aurantiaca' with its glowing coppery-orange flowers. There

Helleborus niger

are also double-flowering forms and an albino. All these variants have been discovered growing in the wild, in Britain, where you can gain a lot of pleasure by looking at native colonies and discovering an aberrant form.

If the rock garden is large enough to accept a few fairly tall-growing plants, one or two of the winter-flowering hellebores can make a welcome contribution. *Helleborus foetidus*, the witches' hellbore, makes a hummocked bush of erect, leafy stems which terminate in heads of drooping, cup-shaped flowers with a rich brown edging to each petal. The Christmas rose, *H. niger*, is equally appropriate and can offer large white flowers in the middle of winter.

If you can secure a position which is either north-facing, or is cool and moist – but not boggy – it is worth tucking a few plants of *Primula edgeworthii (P. winteri)* in humus-rich soil at the base of a rock. A Himalayan primrose, it makes neat rosettes of farina-covered leaves in the centre of which sit, in the depths of winter, clusters of clear, pale blue primrose flowers.

Rock garden shrubs

Besides being an important means by which a rock garden can be linked to neighbouring garden features, dwarf shrubs with their characteristic shapes and often colourful foliage and flowers, add materially to the effect produced by alpine plants. No other shrub could do this, for though these are larger than alpines, they are never overpoweringly so.

Numerous dwarfs could be used, but beware of specimens masquerading as dwarfs. There are many so-called which will all too quickly outgrow their welcome and become embarrassingly large. Moreover, removing a well-established, large conifer is a major operation.

One of the best true dwarf shrubs of columnar shape is *Juniperus communis* 'Compressa'. This delightful pygmy forms a tiny tree shaped like a candle flame in sombre green. Very slow growing, even twenty-year-old specimens will be no more than 45 cm (18 in) high.

A useful planning principle: Set columnar conifers or shrubs anywhere other than at the highest point in the rock garden. As in nature, such positions are best reserved for flat-growing spreading types. Of the latter, the slow-growing, bun-shaped pygmy forms of *Chamaecyparis obtusa* are useful. There are also several prostrate junipers, mostly forms of *Juniperus sabina*, *J. media* and *J. horizontalis*, which should be remembered. One position filled admirably by these is over a pool, their branches spreading horizontally over the water.

Not everyone likes dwarf conifers. A well-known Scottish horticulturist once disparagingly described an English acquaintance as 'a Sassenach, untruthful; and I strongly suspect him of being fond of dwarf conifers!' It is certainly a good idea to observe mature specimens before making a selection. If, like the Scot, you like none of them, there are other pygmy shrubs which can take their place. The holly (*Ilex crenata* 'Mariesii') for example, forms a very evergreen shrub, its rigid branches clothed in small, glossy, dark green leaves. Its inconspicuous flowers

Shrubs in the rock garden
They can provide the necessary link between the specialized interest of alpine plants and more conventional garden plants. Within the rock garden itself, they can represent a pleasing contrast of form and colour which will continue through the seasons.

Top left: Early summer at the rock garden at Wisley, England. **Above:** *Daphne collina*, an ideal evergreen for the small rock garden. **Above right:** *Chamaecyparis obtusa* 'Nana Lutea', a slow-growing, bun-shaped pygmy conifer. **Right:** colour strips of heaths and in the foreground, *Juniperus horizontalis* 'Glauca'. **Below:** 'Nana Gracilis', a chamaecyparis with shell-shaped sprays of foliage.

are often followed by glistening black berries.

Daphnes are popular, and there are a few dwarf enough for the smallest rock garden. *D. collina* grows as a rounded evergreen hummock and in early summer is smothered with heads of intensely fragrant, rose-purple flowers. In late summer, it will nearly always offer a second flush of blossom. *D. cneorum* is a more loose specimen, spreading in habit, its leafy, woody stems ending in heads of rich rose-red flowers which are scented.

Betula nana is a sprawling miniature birch. It will never achieve a great height but its branches are capable of

spreading over a wide area. It has tiny rounded leaves in summer and equally diminutive catkins in spring. The absolutely prostrate broom *Cytisus pilosa* ('Procumbens') is invaluable when placed so that its woody stems can spread out over the surface of a rock. In early summer it becomes a sheet of golden flowers.

There is a compact, shrubby rowan, *Sorbus reducta*, which has rigid, erect stems ending in clusters of cream flowers followed by red berries. It is deciduous and seldom grows higher than 45 cm (18 in). Another dwarf broom, *Cytisus scoparius* 'Prostratus' is attractive even when not in flower, but in early summer its rich yellow flowers and woody, downswept stems will cascade out of a sunny crevice.

Some of the most attractive dwarf shrubs are found among the willows. *Salix boydii*, a natural hybrid once found on a Scottish mountainside, is very slow growing indeed and makes a small, gnarled bush of erect, woody stems clothed in round, leathery grey-green leaves and, in spring, large silver and cream catkins. *S. reticulata* is completely prostrate. Its slow-spreading stems are dressed with rounded, rather leathery leaves which are strikingly marked. It, too, displays catkins in spring.

159

The water garden

Water in the garden

One of Frances Perry's earliest recollections is that of digging holes in the garden for ponds in which to rear tadpoles. The pools invariably leaked, but with misplaced optimism she and her brother planted forget-me-nots and marsh marigolds and kept adding water, until the message got home: *you can't make a pool just by digging a hole and filling it with water!*

All this, of course, was long before the days of fibreglass and plastic sheeting, either of which can be used by today's children to make watertight receptacles with every prospect of success. Today anyone can have a water garden, whether they live in a cool climate or a hot one, and garden on clay, sand or chalk.

Water features open up a wide range of fascinating possibilities for gardens. They can be teamed with many other types of gardening: rock gardens or patios, for example, wet boggy areas or flat formal expanses of grass surrounded by flower borders. They can form key features to liven up dull places or be the source of delight at the end of a winding path. They can provide a means of converting a natural stream into a flowery dell, or be the beautification of an old farm pond or a damp, derelict piece of land.

Water has unique properties. It reflects nearby trees and plants like a mirror; it attracts birds, butterflies and a variety of other creatures; and if stocked with brightly coloured fish it brings life and movement to the garden. There is peace and serenity in the neighbourhood of still water, and musical effects can be achieved in various ways – the laughter of a rippling stream, the rushing of a waterfall or the gentle splash of a fountain. In hot countries the sight and sound of moving water conveys an effect of coolness. And in addition to all these attributes, water in the garden provides an opportunity for gardeners to grow plants which would not live anywhere else.

Planning principles: What sort of pool do you want?

Before starting to build a water garden, first consider its surroundings. There are formal, unashamedly man-made pools, as well as the informal, natural-looking variety. Which kind would best fit in with your own garden and its surrounds?

If the terrain is flat with stylized or geometrically arranged paths and borders, a formal pool with raised edges and possibly a fountain will probably be the most suitable. The enclosed gardens of warm countries

Following excavation to the required depth and shape, Leslie Godfrey lines his informal pool using bricks to hold the lining in place as it is filled with water.

like Spain, Morocco or tropical South America always have at least one pool, often with fountains and elaborate pieces of statuary; their walls and paths are patterned with tiles or mosaics of brickwork. For irrigation purposes, and so that they can receive stray droplets from the fountains, flower beds are often made slightly lower than the pathways. Frequently, they are enclosed with hedges to protect them from the hot dry air, a significant evaporating agent. Scented clumps of myrtle, verbena, rosemary and mignonette are favourite choices, and caged birds are hung in the trees to bring music as well as fragrance to these enchanted spots.

Formal pools

Wherever they are sited, these should be solidly constructed and have either raised coping edges or broad, paved borders so that one can walk right up to the pool. Round, rectangular, square, hexagonal and other geometrical shapes are contained within raised borders made of solid material, brick faced with concrete for example, or solid concrete.

Informal pools

These are perfect partners for rock gardens, especially if a pump is installed so that a trickle of water can spill down from the highest point to

collect in pockets at various levels, and then pour out in waterfalls before finishing up in a pool at the lowest level. This is what happens naturally in springtime in mountain gorges when the snows start to melt. In the garden, pumps will enable you to use the same water over and over again so that the effect is continuous but not wasteful. But remember not to let hard water infiltrate a specially prepared bed for lime-hating alpines.

Pool making
Excavation
Pools which have to be frequently emptied or, like public pools, are subjected to hard wear need to be made of concrete. First the soil must be excavated to the depth required, plus 150 mm (6 in) for the thickness of concrete normally required to ensure a watertight basin. Tamp the base and make it level and spread a 25 mm (1 in) layer of course sand or ashes over it if the soil is stony.

Foundations
Now lay 150mm (6in) of wet concrete right across the base and with a trowel score the edges to a width of 150mm (6in) to leave a rough surface for the sides to adhere to later. There are various ways of constructing the sides. They can be built of brick and then faced with concrete, or a frame can be constructed of stout timber which will temporarily stand 150 mm (6 in) inside the excavation. Pour concrete in the space between soil and frame to make the sides. Leave the concrete several days to harden. If the boards are oiled they will be easier to remove.

Ready-mixed concrete is available in most areas today and will save you a lot of hard work in mixing your own ingredients, but do tell the contractor what it is for so that the proportions of cement, sand and aggregate are right. Bear in mind the fact that concrete starts to set in twenty minutes so speed is essential. Don't skimp on thickness either – a leaky container is not a pool! Finally paint over the sides and bottom with a water-proofing compound.

Pool liners and shells
For home gardeners a simpler method of pool-making is to install a water-proof liner. Besides being quick and easy to install, a pool fitted with a liner is cheaper to make and, if you decide that you want to remove it at a later stage, more readily disposable than concrete. After excavating the soil to the required depth, firm the base and add a layer of sand to leave it flat and even. Spread a sheet of strong reinforced PVC or butyl rubber sheeting (obtainable from aquatic dealers) over the hole and weight it at the edges with house bricks or chunks of paving stones. Run water into the sheeting, which will then stretch and sink under the weight of the liquid, so effectively lining the excavation. When the pool is full cut off any surplus material with scissors, except for a 150mm (6in) margin all round the sides. Tuck the latter out of sight beneath soil, turf, rocks or paving stones, according to preference and the type of pool being built. In informal water gardens, canals and streams can also be dug out and similarly lined.

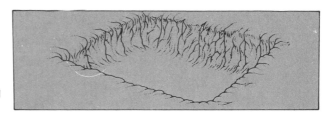

Excavate to the required depth, but allow an extra 150 mm (6 in) for the depth of the concrete base. Ensure a level base in the same way that you level a lawn seed bed (page 75).

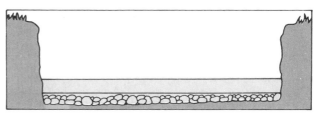

Add a 25 mm (1 in) layer of sand or ashes to the subsoil base and spray it with water to discourage it from absorbing water from the concrete. Pour concrete to a depth of 150 mm (6 in).

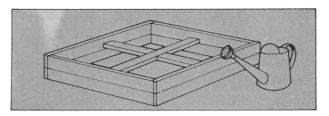

As it hardens score the edges to give a good key for the pool walls. Make a rigid frame 50 mm (6 in) smaller all round than the hole. Oil the frame to facilitate removing it later.

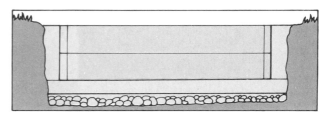

Place the frame on the pool floor one day after laying it and pour concrete between frame and earth walls. Tap the frame's inner face to ensure compaction of the concrete walls.

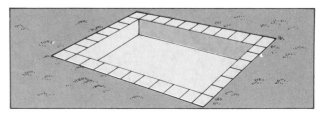

Smooth off the top surface. Cover the pool with polythene for a day and remove the frame two days later. Paint over the sides and bottom with a water-proofing compound.

Section of an excavated pool lined with PVC or Butyl rubber sheeting.

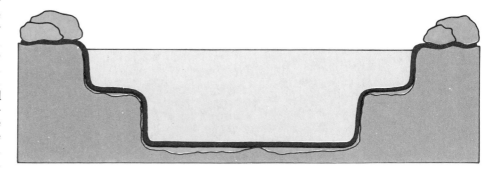

To calculate the amount of stretchable liner required, measure the pool's length and width and to each measurement add twice the maximum depth. Thus for a pool 2.4 m (8 ft) by 1.8 m (6 ft) and 45 cm (18 in) deep you will need a liner 3.3 m (11 ft) by 2.7 m (9 ft). The 150 mm (6 in) marginal wrap-over flap or edging is ignored as the elasticity of the material allows for this.

A third method of installing a pool is to sink a prefabricated, resin-bonded, glass fibre shell into a previously excavated hole. Prefabricated pools come in various shapes and sizes and there are even sections fashioned like narrow streams which can be fitted to link one pool with another. Such pools are strong, light to handle, easy to install and quickly removed when

The water garden

necessary. For cool climates, though, they are often rather shallow, and unless you protect it the water can freeze in a really hard winter. If you instal a prefabricated pool check and double check the foundation with a spirit level – nothing is more irritating than a badly balanced pool with the water forever tipping out at one side.

Planting time

The most favourable time for transplanting water lilies and other aquatics is soon after their dormant season has passed and new growth is emerging. In cool countries, this is normally in spring, while in the tropics it comes after a drought when falling rain restarts root and shoot growth. True water plants do not need rich soil – their growth would become lush, with an abundance of foliage but few flowers.

Water lilies and nelumbos, which produce much annual growth, are exceptions. They need a fair amount of nourishment. Today they are usually planted in baskets which can then be lifted and replanted from time to time when the plants deteriorate through the soil becoming exhausted. Cane or wicker baskets can be used for this purpose – or even pots will do – but since water lilies benefit from having water all round their roots, baskets with openwork sides are better than solid containers.

Most aquatic dealers sell plastic aquatic baskets with holes punched out round their sides. These are stronger than those made of natural material. For planting purposes use loam which has been stacked for several months so that all organic matter has rotted away. If this isn't available, use heavy garden soil instead, taking care to pick out plant roots and weeds. To six parts of this add one part of rotted cow-manure, or fairly coarse bonemeal, at the rate of two cupfulls per basket of loam. (A word of warning: always wear gloves when dealing with bonemeal, which can be infected with anthrax, better still buy sterilized bonemeal.)

Use the mixture when it's fairly damp and line the basket with a layer of thin polythene to prevent soil escaping before the roots take hold. Spread the roots and plant the lilies very firmly, with their crowns just exposed. Finally topdress the soil with a layer of washed shingle or clean sand so that the soil does not come into direct contact with the water when the basket goes into the pool. This also prevents fish from burrowing into the mud and disturbing plant roots. Place the basket gently in the pool. If the lilies are small or the

Formal and informal pools
Above: a formal pool in keeping with the geometric shapes of its surroundings. The circular blocks offset the severe horizontal and vertical lines elsewhere.
Right: the less formal, irregular shaped pool echoes the forms of its 'natural' setting. Appropriately accommodated, the variety of aquatic plant life adds interest and tranquility to any garden.

Planting positions
Cross-section of pool to show different planting positions for aquatics, oxygenators, marginal plants and those suitable for the bog garden.

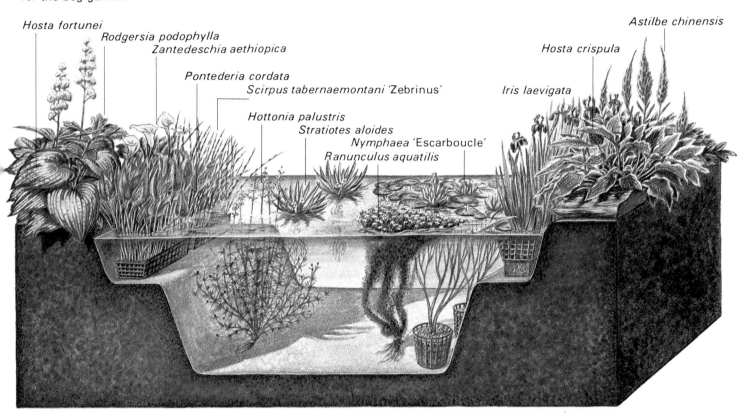

Hosta fortunei
Rodgersia podophylla
Zantedeschia aethiopica
Pontederia cordata
Scirpus tabernaemontani 'Zebrinus'
Hottonia palustris
Stratiotes aloides
Nymphaea 'Escarboucle'
Ranunculus aquatilis
Astilbe chinensis
Hosta crispula
Iris laevigata

water rather deep, raise them on bricks for a week or two – so that they are just beneath the surface – until they recover from the move and start to throw out new leaves.

Ordinary aquatics, like water irises and flowering rushes, only need to have their roots submerged – everything else grows above water. They require nothing more elaborate than loam in which to grow, though it is advisable to topdress the containers or pockets (if you are planting a prefabricated pool) with shingle. Submerged oxygenators, so necessary for clear water (see page 168), should be thrown into the pool in small bunches after several stem ends have been bunched together and weighted with narrow strips of lead. Floaters are simply placed on the water surface.

Making the most of what you have
Every garden site has its problems and peculiarities and when considering water features it is best to make use of existing levels. Excavating and moving soil is not only a heavy and laborious undertaking, it can also be expensive if the work must be put out to contract. Unless time is no object, it is as inadvisable to plan a level, formal type of water garden on sloping ground as it would be to plan a large rock garden where the terrain is flat.

Another item to be taken into account is the availability of services, especially water and electricity. Sadly, natural springs and streams are available to only a few. Where they do exist they open up the possibilities of rills, cascades or slow moving streamlets. If dammed, they can create a wide surface of water which will make a miniature lake or pond.

If you have a natural spring or stream, first check whether it is permanent. Springs come from underground sources fed from water higher up, so a little knowledge of the topography together with local observations will determine whether or not this source of supply will survive the summer. If it does not, it may be possible to make the supply constant with tap water, provided that this is allowed by the local authority. Otherwise, instal PVC liners to trap some of the spring water and move it on by means of a submersible or surface pump.

Gardening consultants are often asked to advise on gardens which are always wet and soggy in winter, yet look dry and hard in summer – quite the wrong way round for plants! Frances Perry, in one typical instance, discovered that bad drainage and hidden springs accounted for most of the moisture, while thirsty crops plus warm weather were responsible for its disappearance later. She found that by turning a ditch and installing a lining of plastic sheeting 30 cm (12 in deep), then returning the soil mixed with sand and compost, some of the water was trapped and conserved for summer use. Making slits and holes in the plastic sides, 75 mm (3 in) down, prevented it from turning into a pond, and instead it became a bog garden in which astilbes, kingcups, rodgersias and primulas not only thrived but set seed and colonized. In time of drought the water level could be augmented from a hose.

If natural rock is present and you use it as the foundation of a rock garden, a charming additional feature can be created with the aid of a pump and the use of prefabricated cascades, rock streams and waterfall basins (all obtainable from specialist nurseries).

Fine views and vistas which lead the eye to a water garden should be retained. Never mask these with tall trees, high hedges or walls. If shelter is needed to protect the pools at certain times of the year, think carefully about what plants or materials to use and where to place them.

The water garden

Planting ideas
Planting a formal pool

If a flat formal pool is suitable, avoid over-planting it. Keep vegetation low, with perhaps one or two water lilies and a few groups of irises to interrupt the flatness. Enhance its character with tailored lines of plants like *butomus*, *scirpus* and *pontederias*, rather than fussy or soft-leaved plants like *Caltha polypetala* or tall rushes which are liable to flop about after heavy rains or a thunderstorm.

Wild and wet –
planting a natural scene

A garden that is large and normally rather damp can feature a wild area that requires little maintenance. Make it serviceable in all weathers by constructing a few paths of grass, with stepping stones set in turf, or gravel. Beyond an annual clearance of weeds and the cutting down of rampant perennials and overgrown bushes, damp wild gardens need little upkeep and properly planted will prove of interest right through the year. Suitable plants for such features include dwarf willows, naturalized narcissi, prim green and white snow-flakes, golden calthas, autumn flowering colchicums, bright-berried pernettyas, the large arum-like lysichitums, feathery astilbes, late summer ligularias and even wild geraniums, commonly called cranesbills, which come in a variety of colours.

Water in a small garden

Even small town gardens can have water features. A sawn-down cask sunk into the ground, or an old bath or water tank will provide the foundation, and if kept low and flooded over from time to time will create a damp area where mimulus, water forget-me-nots, bog primulas and other small, moisture-loving plants will grow. A brick-edged pond of formal design adjacent to a wall, with a wall fountain behind – lion's heads are particularly popular – brings life and movement to a quiet corner and if a few fish are introduced these soon become tame enough to feed from the hand.

In general, it is best to choose colourful fish which swim near the surface. For warm climate pools or heated indoor pools there is a marvellous choice of tropical fish – guppies, sword-tails, gouramis and many more. In mild climates you might choose the golden orfe or golden tench; probably the only sufficiently hardy goldfish will be the comet. Wherever you garden, consult your local supplier before ordering.

Water and statuary go well together, providing peaceful effects and doubling their charm through reflection in still

water. The French have long been masters of the mechanics of moving water – Vaux le Vicomte and Versailles being perfect examples of the changes which can be effected by means of different types of fountains. Water staircases and other features can be seen at Chatsworth and Stourhead in Britain, or Longwood and Longvue in the United States, and in various places in Italy and Austria.

Some of these effects, though on a smaller scale, can be reproduced in our own gardens, including illumination from underwater sources or top lighting to highlight key features.

Planning for interest through the year

There are, of course, countless plants that will grow in or near water. Though ultimate choice depends to a great extent on personal taste, it is always a good idea to group together plants which complement each other and are 'in character' at approximately the same time of the year.

Marginal aquatics can be planted in pots placed upon a pool shelf which allows only their roots to be submerged. Obviously they will also flourish in flooded 'bog' gardens. In spring, bog and water gardens come to life with glimpses of the marginal king-

cups or marigolds (*Caltha spp*), 'shining like fire in swamps and hollows grey', as Tennyson wrote. There are single and double calthas, gold-flowered and white ones, most of them under 30 cm (12 in) high, although *C. polypetala* will reach 90cm (3ft) in a wet situation. Plant kingcups in wet ground or shallow water, within nudging distance of blue water forget-me-nots (*Myosotis palustris*), so that their colours blend. The large yellow and white spathes of *Lysichitum americanum* and *L. camtschatense* respectively are out with nearby pussy willows (*Salix spp*) and the green-tipped snowflakes (*Leucojum vernum*) and fritillaries (*Fritillaria meleagris*), whose chequered purple-red and white bells (pure white in some cases) hang modestly from the tips of their 15-20 cm (6-8 in) stems.

Creating a bridge between land and water

Later on come bog primulas – the candelabra types like *Primula japonica* and *P. pulverulenta*, with their flowers arranged in whorls at intervals along 45-60 cm (1½ ft-2 ft) stems. The colours of these are arresting, even fairy-like: buffs, oranges, yellows, soft pinks, rosy salmons and even crimson reds will very likely all be present in mixed collections. Primulas are plants which like to feel the influence of water without being overwhelmed by it, so grow them in damp, marshy soil rather than in the pool. If they are happy they will seed and increase bountifully, whereas if the roots are drowned they soon sicken and die. Ferns make ideal partners for primulas, as do various irises like the clematis-flowered *Iris kaempferi*, whose richly coloured flowers with their flat, horizontal falls look like flocks of brightly coloured butterflies perched on 60 cm (2 ft) stems at the water's edge. They flower in mid-summer, needing plenty of moisture at that time but less in winter.

The better known Siberian irises, often grown in herbaceous borders, also do well under damp conditions. They have neat, grassy leaves and several dainty flowers poised on each 60 cm (2 ft) wiry stem. Although there are white and cream forms, most *Iris sibericas* come in shades of blue – from light to dark tending towards a reddish purple. There is also a variegated form with cream-suffused foliage. Among the true acquatic irises two species reign supreme. They are the European *I. pseudacorus*, often known as the yellow flag or 'fleur de lis' of France, and the Japanese *I. laevigata*. The latter species should be grown in shallow water and carry their flowers on 60 cm (2 ft) stems. *Iris pseudacorus*, which can be grown in any moist situation, bears its flowers on 1.2 to 1.5 m (4 to 5 ft) stems.. There is a pale yellow form of this, but the deep blue *I. laevigata* has a number of forms with pink, white, or bicoloured blue and white flowers. There are also variegated leaf forms of both these species, which add splashes of cream and gold to the surrounding greenery.

Further interest from marginal aquatics

Further variegations are available in other aquatics, notably *Acorus calamus* 'Variegatus', which has cream and green iris-like leaves, pungent aromatic rootstocks and short brown heads of flowers, which protrude from the stems like curved cattle horns.

There are also two rushes, both of which are aberrations of the well known bullrush *Scirpus palustris*, frequently used in Europe and Asia in the making of rush mats, rope, chair bottoms and for thatching. They are 'Zebrinus', the Zebra rush, which has fat green rushy stems alternately barred with sections of cream and green, and 'Pictus', often known as *Scirpus albescens*, which has the stems striped lengthwise in white and green.

As summer advances, flowering rushes (*Butomus umbellatus*) carry umbels of three-petalled, pink flowers on smooth 60–90 cm (2-3 ft) stems, contrasting happily with the white spikes and arrow shaped leaves of the arrowheads (*Sagittaria sagittifolia*) and its forms, particularly the double 'Flore Pleno' and also the blue inflorescences of the pickerel weeds (*Pontederia cordata*). The latter is one of the best marginal aquatics for ornamental pools, growing 60–90 cm (2-3 ft) high with smooth, heart-shaped leaves on long stems and spikes of soft blue and white flowers.

All of these should be planted in shallow water, while in the deeper areas water lilies with white, yellow, pink or red flowers will open flat like dahlia blossoms on the water surface.

Deep water aquatics

In tropical regions, or if you have a warm greenhouse pool, you can grow tender water lilies, both the night and day flowering species and cultivars. Unlike the hardies these carry their blooms 15–30 cm (6–12 in) above the water and have narrow petals with countless petal-like staminoids, some of which hold pollen and all of which are gold tipped with the same shade of blue, mauve, white, pink or red as the flower petals. They are usually very sweetly scented and die down in winter to a small, nut-like tuber.

Night-flowering water lilies open at dusk and have broader petals than the day kinds. There are only red or white forms – never blue.

Plants for drier parts of the bog garden

There is a rich miscellany of flowers in summer, and provided the roots are kept damp these will bloom for long periods. They include the feathery flowered astilbes, with deeply cut leaves and plumes of white, pink or red flowers of leafy 60–90 cm (2-3 ft) stems; brilliant musks (*Mimulus spp*) with plain or spotted antirrhinum-like flowers of gold or scarlet, all of them excellent for edging purposes; several members of the daisy family, like the black stemmed *Ligularia przewalskii* which has thin, palmately-lobed leaves and 120-180 cm (4-6 ft) spires of small yellow flowers; and the giant Chinese groundsels *L. veitchiana* and *L. wilsoniana*, both of which reach 180 cm (6 ft) in height. Group these with clumps of *Lobelia fulgens*, which has 90 cm (3 ft) stems, well clothed with narrow crimson leaves and masses of scarlet, sage-like flowers. Alternatively, where it is more readily available, as in North America, use *Lobelia cardinalis* as a companion.

Late summer brings the loosestrifes, particularly *Lythrum salicaria* and its forms, many of which glow like fire when the sun illuminates their petals in later afternoon. Especially effective is the rosy purple 'Firecandle', the deep rosy red 'Lady Sackville' and 'Mordens Pink', a good pink form. All grow about 1.2m (4ft) high and have narrow, oblong leaves. Another late bloomer is the obedient plant, *Physostegia virginiana*, so called because the rosy-pink, sage-like flowers can be moved around the 60–120 cm (2-4 ft) stems and stay where placed. The white flowered 'Alba' should be grouped alongside for contrast, and if there is shade, back the group with a clump of yellow waxbells (*Kirengeshoma palmata*), an outstanding plant blooming in early autumn and growing 60–120 cm (2-4 ft) high with purplish stems supporting large, thin, jagged-edged leaves like vine leaves and loose sprays of pendent, 50 mm (2 in) waxy, bright yellow, tubular flowers.

Variety and continuity in the water garden

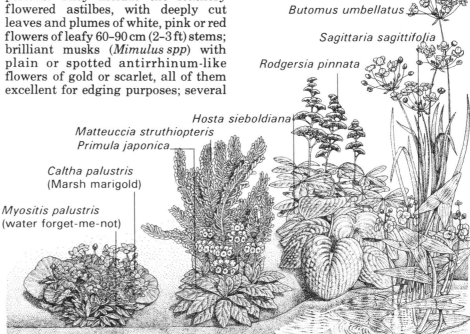

Butomus umbellatus

Sagittaria sagittifolia

Rodgersia pinnata

Hosta sieboldiana

Matteuccia struthiopteris

Primula japonica

Caltha palustris (Marsh marigold)

Myositis palustris (water forget-me-not)

The water garden

Fine foliage round the water garden

Fine foliaged plants always set off a garden feature and the water garden is no exception. In milder areas, where there is room, the giant rhubarb-leaved *Gunnera manicata* presents an impressive picture with its huge, rough, prickly-backed and stemmed leaves 180–240 cm (6–8 ft) across and 1.5–3 m (5–10 ft) high. In early summer the large, brownish-green 90–120 cm (3–4 ft) flower spikes resemble giant bottle brushes.

Other good foliage plants of more modest proportions (but winter hardy everywhere) are the hostas, all of which favour damp soil and make good edging subjects with their green, glaucous-blue or golden leaves, both plain or variegated, and spikes of white on purplish flowers. The New Zealand phormiums are also useful in mild climates, and are best kept on the dryish side in winter. So too are many of the rodgersias: *Rodgersia aesculifolia* from China grows 1.2 m (4 ft) tall with many branched sprays of tightly packed white or pink flowers and bronzed leaves, deeply cut like those of the horse-chestnut. *R. tabularis* has round, parasol-like leaves 30–90 cm (1–3 ft) across and creamy flowers. *R. sambucifolia*, 60–90 cm (2–3 ft) tall, has bright green pinnate leaves and creamy white flowers. There are many others, including a number normally grown in herbaceous borders like the aconitums: *Gentiana asclepiadea*, the blue willow gentian and its white counterpart, *Euphorbia palustris*, a tall 90 cm (3 ft) spurge with yellow flowers, *Eupatorium purpureua*, the 'Joe Pye' weed, with 1.8–2.4 m (6–8 ft) stems terminating in flattish heads of purplish rose florets; and the splendid false goats-beard, *Aruncus dioicus*, a noble plant which reaches a height of 1.8m (6ft) when well sited, and has heavy plumes of creamy, hay-scented flowers and large, deeply cut leaves. Keep all these plants moist but not saturated at the roots.

Framing the water garden picture

As with any focal point in the garden, water relies for its impact partly upon its surrounding structures and plants. Fine foliage associates well with water, often resembling the rise and fall of a fountain. In turn, this is well set off by the broader, more rounded form of *Gunnera manicata*, hostas and water lilies.

Plant grouping for the water garden

Attractive plant associations add immeasurably to the general effect of any garden feature. Many combinations occur by accident but here are a few that Frances Perry has admired in the water gardens of others, or made herself through the years.

Spring
Pool margins:
Blue water forget-me-nots with golden marsh marigolds (*Caltha palustris*) and pink and white scrambling bogbeans (*Menyanthes trifoliata*).

Lysichitum americanum & *Primula rosea*

Bold *Lysichitum americanum* with 60 cm (2 ft) yellow, arum-type flowers and double, golden marsh marigolds (*Caltha palustris* 'Plena').

Boggy surrounds
White snowflakes (*Leucojum vernum*) with pussy willows, marsh orchids in grass, and white narcissi.

Gold and yellow trollius with purple and black chequered *Fritillaria meleagris* and blue camassias.

Summer
Pool:
Red water lilies with blue *Pontederia cordata* and pink flowering rushes (*Butomus umbellatus*), *Acorus calamus* 'Variagatus', blue *Iris laevigata* at margins, with yellow or white water lilies in the water, and the yellow water fringe, *Hydrocleys nymphoides*.

Pool surrounds:
Pink and white astilbes, blue *Iris sibirica* and feathery white, bold leaved rodgersias.

Iris sibirica, pink and red *Primula pulverulenta*, ferns and blue meconopsis.

Day lilies (*Hemerocallis spp*) with scarlet *Lobelia fulgens* and red and yellow mimulus.

Hostas and astilbes.

White astilbe amongst other marginals.

Autumn
Pool:
Blue *Pontederia cordata* with white arrowheads (*Sagittaria spp.*), variegated rushes and red water lilies.

Pool surrounds:
Red berried actaeas, pink lythrums and yellow ligularias.

Blue aconitums with blue *Gentiana asclepiadea* and purple-leaved phormiums.

Winter
Pool surrounds:
Scarlet and pink-berried pernettyias and pink and white heathers.

Tropical pool plantings
Blue water lilies, pink nelumbo, *Cyperus papyrus*, *Thalia dealbata*, floating water hyacinths and *Myriophyllum proserpinacoides* over the sides of the pool.

Nelumbium nucifera

Water lilies
Deep water: 75 cm (2½ ft): 'Gladstoniana', white; 'Colonel Welsh', yellow; *N. tuberosa rosea*, pink.

Nymphaea 'Gladstoniana'

Medium depths: 45–75 cm (1½ – 2½ ft): 'James Brydon', red; 'Rose Arey', pink; 'Escarboucle', deep crimson; 'Gonnêre', white; 'Gloriosa', rosy-red; 'Sunrise', yellow.

Nymphaea 'Escarboucle'
Nymphaea 'Rose Arey'

Shallow water: under 30 cm (1 ft):

Nymphaea 'Pygmaea Helvola'

'Pygmaea Helvola', yellow; 'Pygmaea Alba', white; 'Ellisiana', red; 'Paul Hariot', pinkish, ageing to yellow. 167

The water garden

Like all other garden features, pools and streams need periodic attention. Dead leaves and flowers should be regularly removed or they will rot and foul the water. Over-exuberant plants require dividing occasionally and seed heads are best cut down before they discharge their contents and produce unwanted seedlings.

Autumn is a trying time, for then falling leaves from nearby trees find their way into ponds. Before they begin to decay they should either be dredged out with a rake or prevented from entering the water in the first place by placing wire mesh over the pool. Tack strips of netting to thin wooden slats the length and width of the pool. The frame can be put on or removed when required. Such frames are also useful to prevent herons, kingfishers and even cats from taking ornamental fish; in a cold winter they can be left in place and covered to prevent excessive freezing.

Artificial pools should not be allowed to freeze over in winter. Frost may damage the fabric and injure plants and fish. In extremely cold climates it may be necessary to drain shallow pools and cover them with boards and a tarpaulin, keeping the plants and fish under cover elsewhere. Under cool, temperate conditions, however, it is sufficient to keep an opening in the ice. This is best achieved by floating a block of wood in the unfrozen pond. When the ice is 12 mm (½ in) thick, remove the block by pouring boiling water over it and siphon out an inch of water. Then cover the opening with a plank of wood or piece of thick material. The remaining ice then acts like a light frame preventing further freezing. When a thaw sets in top up the water to its old level and repeat the process as necessary.

Keeping the water clean

Keeping the water transparent and clean is an essential part of water gardening, as important as eliminating weeds in the surrounding features. The cause of discolouration is basically due to pollution in the form of mineral salts released to the water from rotting vegetation or too much organic material in the pond. This encourages the rapid spread of algae which feed upon the salts, using natural light as a source of energy. It is also important not to let fertilizers come into direct contact with water; the chemicals they discharge will adulterate the water and encourage disfiguring algae growth.

Prevention is better than cure so check all composts before planting water lilies and other aquatics (as already recommended) and, as above, either protect water from tree leaves and other organic debris or remove them as soon as they arrive.

Oxygenators

To help in the battle of eliminating algae, another group of water plants is required; the submerged oxygenators. These are rarely seen, since they spend most of their lives underwater, although some come to the surface to flower. Nevertheless their effects are considerable and they have various functions, all highly important to the gardener.

Firstly they provide the fish with three essentials - protection from their enemies, shade in hot weather and a nursery where eggs can be laid and the young fry may hide and develop in comparative safety. In addition, a variety of small creatures lurk in underwater vegetation, providing food for fish, which will themselves also eat bits of plants from time to time.

Underwater plants, with their filmy, fern-like appearance, are pretty to look down upon, especially the flowering types, but their greatest use comes from their ability to use soluble salts to promote growth (thus competing with and taking precedence over the algae), and the fact that this function involves the discharge of oxygen into the water.

This process, which is known as photosynthesis, is of course shared by land plants. Their green leaves take in carbon dioxide through myriads of pores, use the carbon and combine it with water from the roots to make sugars, and then return the unwanted oxygen to the atmosphere. In garden pools the oxygen goes into the water, helping fish and other creatures - even plants - to breathe. During this particular function, which is called respiration, oxygen is taken into the plant or animal and carbon dioxide exhaled. Each process therefore complements the other. Moreover,

The natural life-support cycle

dead insects and other material liable to pollute the water are used as fertilizer by oxygenating plants and thus rendered harmless.

You cannot have too much submerged vegetation in the early life of a pool when everything - water, plant compost and even the fabric itself - is new. Even the ornamental aquatics are not sufficiently established for the roots to function to full capacity. Later, surplus vegetation can easily be removed with a rake, but at the outset allow a dozen plants to approximately each square metre (3ft) of pond surface.

Naturally some kinds are better oxygenators than others. Arguably the best for maintaining water clarity are the elodeas - *Elodea canadensis* and, in mild areas, *E. callitrichoides* and their near relative *Lagarosiphon major* (*Elodea crispa*), a robust, many branched, curly leaved species. Then there are the milfoils, species of *Myriophyllum*, all of them efficient oxygenators and pretty to look at.

Hottonia palustris

Other useful plants include the starworts - *Callitriche hermaphroditica* (*C. autumnalis*) and *C. palustris* (*C. verna*). Their green leaves bunch at the surface like pale stars in both autumn and spring. The water crowfoot, *Ranunculus aquatilis*, which has small floating white flowers in spring, is well worth considering, as is the water violet, *Hottonia palustris* (so called because of its spikes of mauve flowers which are thrust well above the water surface in early summer).

Finally, by suppressing strong sunlight, algae growth can be greatly depressed. The floating leaves of water lilies are ideal for this purpose but while they are becoming established, introduce a few plants which float naturally on or near the surface: the frogbit (*Hydrocharis morsus-ranae*), for example, or water soldier (*Stratiotes aloides*), which looks like the top leafy rosette of a pineapple plant. Both have white flowers and are simple to plant - simply throw them into the pool.

Warm indoor pools

In predominantly cold climates, it is becoming fashionable to instal a water lily and fish pond in a sun room or conservatory, which will be light but frost-free. Since many water plants die down in winter, the pond could be emptied then, leaving you free to display the remaining plants in pots inside the house or in the greenhouse.

Polyanthus with *Aucuba japonica* in foreground, a Lawson cypress 'Pembury Blue', left, backed by *Hedera canariensis*.

You could cover the pool with a sheet of wood and use it as a table. If you do decide to build a pool under cover, it is advisable to use concrete and build raised sides. Besides providing support for the winter 'table', the sides will prevent toddlers, pets and mobile household objects of any kind falling into the water in other seasons.

The value of pools in warm climates

In areas of the world which receive plenty of sunshine and where winter is not excessively harsh – such as southern Europe, Florida, California, parts of Australia and southern Africa – pools are particularly popular as they suggest coolness.

Tropical pools can be constructed by any of the methods already suggested. Use plant composts advised for hardy aquatics, covering the soil with shingle as before. Elaborate effects can be achieved by introducing fountains and growing bog plants near the edges.

If the pool edges are raised you can mask their stark finish by growing the Brazilian parrot's feather, *Myriophyllum proserpinacoides*, near the edges and letting their soft green, feathery fronds drape over the sides. The tips of the leaves go red in autumn, which adds to their attraction.

Planting a tropical pool

Tropical water lilies should be planted in early summer, after they have been started in shallow pans of water in a warm, brightly lit place. Their tubers are small, scarcely larger than a walnut, and the shoots are brittle, so handle them with care. Aquatic dealers sell both day and night blooming varieties. Some of the most popular day-bloomers are *Nymphaea caerulea* and *N. capensis*, both blue; 'American Beauty' – fuchsia red; 'African Gold' – deep yellow; 'General Pershing' – pink; and 'Mrs George Pring' – white. 'O'Marana' – glowing red, 'James Gurney' – deep rose, 'Frank Trelease' – deep crimsom and 'Missouri' – white, are night-flowering sorts. Most of these need about 30 cm (12 in) of water over their crowns at flowering time, but there are miniatures for very shallow pools if required. Ask your dealer about these but remember they are a little more difficult to rear than hardy lilies.

Nelumbos are strong and vigorous when grown in warm sheltered places; their huge parasol-like leaves poised on central stalks stand several feet above the water, while the large peony-like flowers of rose, white, red or yellow are frequently fragrant. Nelumbos have long, banana-shaped tubers which need planting horizontally – not upright – in deep soil.

Several spectacular marginal aquatics are suitable for pot culture, especially the Egyptian paper reed, *Cyperus papyrus*. This is thought to be the plant

Lillies with *Rhododendron luteum, Yucca gloriosa* and *Smilacina racemosa*.

which sheltered the infant Moses. It grows 2–3 m (6–9 ft) high in cultivation (more in nature) with thick triangular stems topped by huge grassy inflorescences which resemble greenish-brown household mops. The crushed stems provided early man with paper – the papyri of the ancients.

Thalia dealbata is another noble aquatic, producing glaucous lance or heart-shaped leaves on 90 cm–1.2 m (3–4 ft) stems and spikes of purplish-red, pendent flowers. Giant elephant's ears, a species of *Xanthosoma* – so called on account of their leaf shape – is another worth growing. These have purple stems and veins and yellow arum-like flowers. There are also several floaters for warm pools like the water hyacinth, *Eichhornea crassipes*, which has heart-shaped leaves arranged in rosettes, 30 cm (12 in) or so across, each leaf poised on a swollen, sausage-shaped leafstalk. The latter is full of

spongy tissue which makes the plant buoyant. They bob about like corks in the water, flaunting showy spikes of lavender-blue and gold flowers in summer. The water lettuce, *Pistia stratiotes*, resembles a floating green rose with its rosettes of crinkled, petal-like leaves 75–100 mm (3–4 in) across.

Finally there is the scrambling water poppy, *Hydrocleys nymphoides*, which wends its way across the pool, producing masses of floating, small ovate leaves and bright golden, three-petalled flowers.

Maintenance

A few underwater oxygenators are necessary to keep the water fresh, as are a few fish – either goldfish varieties like shubunkins, fantails and comets, or tropical fish, which are normally smaller. Your pet dealer will tell you which kinds will live together without fighting.

Tropical water lilies die down in autumn and can be lifted and stored in a damp medium if you wish to empty the pool during winter. The other plants should be kept growing elsewhere under cover.

Creating a haven of tranquility

The tropical garden

Gardening in a warm climate

When people get older they often change their way of life and seek the sun, either for retirement purposes or to find a holiday home. Others may find their jobs take them to a milder climate where they have a house and garden. Much is written about gardening in cool countries but less literature exists on the subject of gardening in a warm climate. Although there are basic similarities, the choice of plants offers different planning possibilities.

Tropical and subtropical gardens

In the tropics and subtropics the climate is all-important. There are no frosts, weeds rampage and you know precisely when it will get dark, that whatever the season, there will be a definite number of daylight hours. Some plants which thrive in Europe or North America will not do well in such a climate simply because they miss the cold, which induces a period of rest, when growth is arrested. Typical examples are rose bushes, which never stop growing and so have a shorter life expectancy. In a warm climate they will get weaker and weaker and ultimately fade out. Similarly with daffodils and other hardy bulbs. Don't expect them to spread and naturalize in the manner in which they do in temperate zones. They won't do so. Warm soil, lack of moisture and overmuch sun soon sap their vitality and they rapidly disappear. But rest assured that if a plant you enjoy refuses to do well, there are plenty of others that will.

There will also be periods of intense heat in the tropics, followed by cool nights and a sharp temperature drop which again all plants do not relish. But the big problem in any warm climate is water, or the lack of it. If you can control this you can have a gorgeous garden, lush and full of colour all through the year. But a source of supply is imperative and if this can be arranged in a 'ring' system all round the garden, you are home and wet. Even when you go away on business or holiday, a capable friend or neighbour can turn on a tap and adjust the watering to those areas which need it. Other ideas are explained on pages 36 to 39.

Water suggests coolness and attracts birds so that water features embodying fountains or streams are invaluable. And since most of these can be regulated by pumps (which use the same water over and over again) there is little waste of this precious fluid and only moderate expense.

Shade also is highly important in

tropical and subtropical gardens, so use trees to provide natural shade and take every advantage of that cast by nearby buildings. Organic materials like bark fibre, dried buckwheat or corn husks, peat and similar substances should be worked into the ground or used as a mulch over the soil and between plants in order to conserve moisture. This will also rot down eventually and make plant food.

Of the tall, shade casting trees consider the brilliant scarlet corals (*Erythrina coralloides*), the pink floss silk trees (*Chorisia speciosa*), red lagerstroemias, mauve jacarandas, the exquisite royal poinciana *(Delonix regia)* whose scarlet, yellow and white patterned flowers look like orchids or brightly coloured birds poised atop the umbrella shaped branches, and the sausage tree *(Kigelia pinnata)*, which has pinnate leaves, dark red, bellshaped flowers and huge grey hanging fruits like giant cucumbers.

Evergreens for extremes of heat

Eucalyptus are trees capable of withstanding extreme heat. The species produces a variety of heights and sizes and have variously coloured flowers. They grow quickly, have the power of regeneration when cut to the ground and their tough, wax-covered leaves hang downwards rather than spread horizontally like those of most

It is in the tropical or sub-tropical garden that cool greens and the sound of moving water are seen to exert a modifying effect on extreme heat. But see too how plant forms are arranged in groups to show off an accent plant.

deciduous trees, so that transpiration losses are reduced. Eucalyptus are planted all over the world's tropics and in various extremes of heat and climate, from the high Andes and the Highlands of Kenya to the Caribbean and flat Mediterranean gardens; also occasionally in cool climates. Other useful evergreens are *Podocarpus spp.* with their tough, narrow, deep green leaves and rather upright growth. Useful for coastal planting are the graceful, slender stemmed she-oaks or casuarinas, so named, because of their feathery appearance, after the casuary bird.

Grass - real or artificial
The smooth green lawns of English gardens - the envy of gardeners throughout the world - will prove impossible to reproduce in warm climates since the fine fescues, so characteristic of these lawns, will not tolerate heat and drought. Instead one must use coarser grasses like zoysia or Bermuda grasses to make a green carpet and perhaps cover areas subjected to hard wear with paving stones or concrete.

Although unthinkable for temperate climates, artificial grass can be used to great effect in tropical gardens. It already is in places like Brazil, Colombia and even on some Greek islands. Made of tough plastic artificial

lawns seem to retain their green colouring in spite of hot sun and can be hosed down to keep them clean and free from dust. They are most effective where they can be seen from above, as in well gardens between tower blocks.

Decorative planting
When it comes to planting remember that the exotic house and greenhouse plants of frost-prone countries thrive outdoors in the tropics. Bromeliads, cacti and even orchids can be planted on branches or between rock stones, while zebrinas, *Lochnera (Vinca) rosea*, impatiens and tradescantias provide ground cover for taller plants and tropical trees. Green colouring is highly important as it suggests coolness, so put in plenty of leafy shrubs as background for prominent, highly coloured plants.

Vegetables and fruit
You won't be able to grow apples and pears or even plums to a state of perfection, but recompense derives from the successful culture of exciting alternatives - like various kinds of citrus, bananas, figs, passion fruits, loquats, guavas, even mangoes, avocados and pineapples. These will crop much better than cold climate fruits, although peaches should do well. Similarly with vegetables. Tomatoes, Jerusalem artichokes, various kinds of beans, cucumbers, sweet corn and onions remain a possibility - even cabbages and lettuces in lowland areas; but there are new kinds to try like Chinese cabbage, okra, sweet potatoes and in some places yams.

Colour planning
When it comes to the general planning of ornamental features bear in mind how hot and bright are the colours of tropical flora. Interplant them with something more subdued so as to mute these strident and sometimes conflicting shades. Foliage plants of a silvery nature or with soft green leaves, or pastel hued flowers, are ideal for the purpose. As always study neighbouring gardens; we can all learn from others and the juxtaposition of certain plants.

Cover fences, trellis, walls and garden buildings with flowering climbers. There are so many of these with large showy flowers that there is no need to mix them for extra effect. If you want something really brilliant in a sunny position use vivid, orange red, tubular flowered *Pyrostegia venusta* as a background climber, fronting this with scarlet and gold flowered cannas and planting between them here and there a bush of the yellow *Cassia multijuga* or a golden, trumpet shaped allamanda - all are long flowering. For a quieter

effect blend mauves and pinks; perhaps the morning glory (*Ipomoea learii*) clambering up trellis or wrapping itself around supports up a tree trunk. Put pink oleanders around, and front the display with low-growing, red-leaved *Iresine herbstii*, pink and white *Lochnera rosea* or even pink, ivy-leaved pelargoniums, which riot in the sub-tropics.

Climbing bouganvilleas are characterized by vivid long-lasting bracts; purple-red in the type species but white, pink, orange or yellow in various cultivars. They climb high over any bush or building or can be pegged down to make an unusual ground cover. When clipped, mixed bouganvilleas also make an unusual hedge, as does the variegated leaved, scarlet flowered *Hibiscus rosa-sinensis*. Hibiscus are of course among the commonest flowers thriving in warm conditions: their huge, saucer-shaped flowers with protruding staminal columns come in a wide range of colours and colour combinations. Scarlet and pink ixoras, euphorbias - including large specimens of the well known Christmas poinsettia - are commonplace, as are lantanas with small round flower heads which change colour from white to orange or pink to rose as they age.

Deep moist shade affords the opportunity to grow some exotic South Americans like the banana-leaved, vivid scarlet and gold, rather rigid-flowered lobster claws (*Heliconia spp*) Then there are the delicate 60-90 cm (2-3 ft) caladiums, with leaves shaped like elephant ears in a variety of shades such as green suffused with rose pink or red, as well as cool green with white patternings.

Scent for day and night
Highly fragrant shrubs are a joy in the tropics and among the most outstanding are the frangipanis and jasmines.

The former, *Plumeria rubra*, often known as the temple tree, makes a large shrub or small tree with thick oval leaves on rather ugly branches which are full of white sap. But the flowers are magnificient, gathering in large clusters at the end of the branches, tubular and pure white with golden centres and so richly scented as to be almost overpowering. Pink, red and even yellow forms are available.

Most tropical jasmines are fragrant but always have a plant of the night blooming jessamine, (*Cestrum nocturnum*) near the house. This near relative is a shrub with narrow greenish tubular flowers which open at dusk emitting an exquisite fragrance which beggars description. 171

The spring and summer garden

Trees for Flower

Many of the trees discussed elsewhere have good flowers, but they have usually been suggested for their other features. Most of the trees which are most spectacular in flower in temperate climates have little else to recommend them and it is unlikely that they would otherwise be grown at all. The great majority of the outstanding flowering trees are cherries and crabs and few of them, as indeed is the case with laburnums, have other redeeming features. Nevertheless there are places where some of these can be an asset and many are such a superb sight in flower that they cry out to be grown somewhere!

Sargent's cherry, *Prunus sargentii*, makes a cloud of soft-pink single flowers early in the season and in time will become quite a big tree. It earns a place also for its very early bright red autumn colours. An earlier flowering hybrid of this, 'Accolade', is a spreading, thinly crowned tree up to 6 m (20 ft) high which is a glorious rosy pink, becoming more opulently flowered every year.

Prunus 'Hally Jolivette' is later and looks supremely elegant with its bright and pale pink, long-tubed semi-double flowers. Of the big-flowered Japanese cherries, the first in flower is *P. serrulata* 'Shirotae'. This has bright glossy green leaves above hanging bunches of pure white single and semi-double flowers. The ubiquitous, suburban street cherry, 'Kanzan', is medium late and fulsome, though its uniform pink may not be to everyone's taste once the red early buds are open. There is, however, a very stylish hybrid of it with 'Shimidsu Sakura' which is called 'Pink Perfection', and has bronzed green leaves and flowers which fade all the way from red to white. 'Shimidsu Sakura' itself positively exudes class. Leaves and long pendant buds of misty violet pink open to green leaves and big, double, pure white flowers late in the season. At the same time – sometimes even later – the other aristocrat of cherries, 'Shirofugen', opens pink, hanging buds beneath dark red leaves to big, ice-white flowers in long rows of bunches. After some two weeks they turn pink again. The top class example of these cherries is 'Tai-Haku', which was lost to Japan around 1700 to be rediscovered in a Sussex garden in 1923. It has huge, single, white flowers beneath deep red leaves.

Crab apples proliferate, but too many of the purple-flowered ones are impossibly shapeless and dull for fifty weeks of the calendar. Every year, though, the Japanese crab, *Malus floribunda*, is a reliable, foaming mass

Malus floribunda, the Japanese crab

of red buds and white flowers. 'Van Eseltine' is similar but narrowly upright, which makes it ideal for small spaces. The Hupeh crab, *M. hupehensis*, soon grows 1 m (3 ft) a year from seed, and then bushes out to a sturdy tree. It is quite superbly covered in long sprays of pale pink buds, which open to a mass of large, pure white, single flowers. 'John Downie' is upright at first and has starry white flowers in late spring, with the added bonus of branches wreathed with conic fruit of bright, shiny yellow and scarlet (which also make the most delicious and pellucid pink jam). 'Siebold's Crab' is a dense bushy tree crowded with small starry white flowers and very spectacular, while 'Sargent's Crab' is a smaller bush of the same kind.

Many magnolias are fine flowering trees. A choice selection would always include *Magnolia sprengeri diva*, because its huge flowers are so fine a pink and it grows fast and flowers when younger than most. At Westonbirt, after sixteen years growth, one was 15 m (60 ft) tall and bore 550 flowers. The snowdrop tree, *Halesia monticola*, makes a rather coarse tree, but it flowers when young in late spring and the rows of hanging white flowers are showy, especially in the hairy-leafed form, var *vestita* and its pinkish form 'Rosea'. The related

Styrax obassia and *S. hemsleyana* are handsome in foliage and fine in flower with spikes of white, yellow-stamened bells from every shoot.

The mimosa, *Acacia dealbata*, dies back to the ground in severe winters, but this is of no great consequence for it seeds itself, and within three years the plants are roof-high again, covered in blue-grey, ferny leaves and quantities of yellow, puffy flowers. It is best against a sunny wall, except in warm, generally sunny regions where it grows freely. The Chilean firebush, *Embothrium coccineum*, best in the form var *lanceolatum* or 'Norquinco', is a striking sight when its long, erect shoots are wreathed in slender, tubular, brilliant scarlet flowers, but it is a lank, dull-leafed tree. The snowy mespilus, *Amelanchier lamarckii*, spreads on to sandy commons as a tall bush but can be trained into a tree and is covered in white flowers in mid-spring unless bullfinches have been active. The foliage turns a good deep red in autumn.

Of the laburnums there is really only a place for the hybrid *Laburnum* x *watereri* 'Vossii', as its long, densely flowered racemes are so markedly superior to the others. You might like, though, to consider the curious Adam's laburnum (see page 184).

Choice trees with strong colour interest

Although one would not normally plant them purely for their flower, there are a number of other very desirable trees which have not been mentioned earlier and which exhibit a strong colour interest.

Three horse chestnuts are in this category. The yellow buckeye is an exceptionally valuable, very hardy tree. *Aesculus flava*, previously known as *A. octandra*, grows to 40 m (130 ft) in the Great Smoky Mountains of Tennessee, but is generally nearer 10 m (30 ft). Its leaves have elegant, slender lanceolata leaflets on slender stalks.

Prunus sargentii, soft-pink flowers

These leaflets are bright, glossy green and often cupped, while in autumn they turn orange, scarlet and crimson. The flowers are yellow – an unusual distinction in a horse chestnut – and the tree is a tall dome, an asset in any landscape. The Japanese horse chestnut, *A. turbinata*, is of interest because its foliage is twice the normal size, the leaves on young trees being up to 60 m (2 ft) across on 45 cm (18 in) stalks. They turn orange in the autumn. The flower heads are similar to those of the common horse chestnut, 30 cm (12 in) long but narrower. The Indian horse chestnut, *A. indica*, has three unusual features of some worth. Its leaves unfold orange-brown; it flowers in early summer and its conkers are often coal-black. The leaves have pink stalks (the leaflets are stalked too) while the flowers are often rosy pink from a distance.

Euodia hupehensis has no recognised English name unless it be 'the euodia'. It grows fast and exceptionally well in cities. It has smooth grey bark and opposite pairs of pinnate leaves with pink stalks and glossy, cupped leathery leaflets. It has white flowers, unusual because they are sorted according to sex, with male and female heads appearing at random in late summer. They still have time to form orange-red berries by mid-autumn.

The Turkish hazel, *Corylus colurna*, is a remarkably vigorous, sturdy tree which can grow up to 25 m (80 ft) tall with a shapely conic crown of luxuriant foliage. It has been adopted by town and city planters, especially in the USA, and has been a great success. It has substantial catkins very early in spring and big, glossy, wonderfully spined fruit husks.

The red maple, *Acer rubrum*, is a particularly good flowering tree for siting by water, as it grows wild in every swampy bottom from Cuba to Texas. It has slender, whip-like shoots wreathed in rich red, bunched flowers before the leaves unfold. The leaves are silvered beneath and some become red in autumn; in the tree's native setting they are ablaze with colour from scarlet to purple.

Creating seasonal interest with shrubs

Shrubs are important in the all-year-round garden because their four main elements – flowers, fruit, bark and foliage – make unique contributions to the scene at different times of the year. Not all, of course, exhibit characteristics of interest in every season and the onus is on the plant planner to site shrubs so that their best aspects are noticeable when they appear, and to make a varied selection so that there is always something of interest to see.

Some spectacular spring or summer flowering shrubs lapse into a dull starkness for the rest of the year. In a large garden, the bare or uninteresting patch which they leave may be tolerable, but in a small one it isn't. The secret is to site such shrubs as these near other plants which, though they may have only a modest early display, come into their own in the colder months and draw the eye away from their bare, dormant partners.

Forsythia is one shrub whose year-round value is dubious. In full flower it contributes an unmistakable yellow splash to the landscape. But once it is finished, it sinks into a green obscurity. In fact most forsythia take up so much space – up to 2.75 m (9 ft) – that their use in the small garden should be very carefully considered, although the small, slow-growing *F.* 'Arnold Dwarf' might be suitable in a small, well-planned site.

The same criticism could be levelled at *Magnolia stellata*, the deciduous shrub, in that once it has flowered there is nothing else to look forward to. But it is less urbane than the forsythia in appearance; its snow-white clouds of star-like petals are special and it does display charming silky-grey buds.

In larger gardens the fuller growing *M. liliiflora* is a first-class variety with glossy leaves and purple flushed tulip-shaped flowers sustained over a long period. 'Nigra' has flowers of a rich vinous purple on the outside with white inside. You need a big garden to accommodate the broad spreading nature of most *M.* x *soulangiana* varieties or that of its parent *M. denudata*, but they make a superb feature wherever they are established and the white, pink or purple stained flowers are breathtaking when spared by late frosts.

At one time the camellia was considered something sent by the gods to try the patience and skill of the experienced cultivator. Now this myth has finally been dispelled and these beautiful evergreens are available to all in mild climates who care to grow them. Protection will be needed if you want to grow them in more demanding conditions. From the thousands of varieties in existence, several hundred are generally available. They encompass a wide range of sizes

Magnolia stellata

and shapes with flowers in various combinations of white, pink and red. The slower-growing varieties are suitable for growing in containers while others are useful either as free standing specimens or as wall shrubs, but a hot, dry situation is unsuitable.

One of the most exotic for general cultivation is *Camellia williamsii* 'Donation' which has large, double, orchid-pink flowers in profusion. Over the years it has received numerous major horticultural awards and there are few other shrubs to equal it. Its habit is tall and vigorous and it lends itself to being trained against a wall or to a stout frame in a bed or border.

The spring and summer garden

Those who garden on an acid soil might consider another evergreen in the shape of *Pieris* 'Forest Flame'. Its springtime showers of small, white, pitcher-shaped flowers are accompanied by new growths which gradually change from brilliant crimson to pink, then to cream and finally in summer to a bright glossy green. It really is a shrub for special effects and needs careful placing so that it can display them to best advantage. If you covet a pieris but have a chalk soil there is a fair substitute in the shape of *Photinia* x *fraseri* 'Robusta' and 'Red Robin'. These are evergreens of the *Rosaceae* family. The flat heads on tiny flowers are not carried on young plants, but the young growths are a brilliant coppery red. Successive pruning during the summer replaces these colourful growths, although they never quite match that first exciting flush. It is a large shrub, ultimately, but can be kept within manageable size by careful pruning. It makes a successful hedge and is commonly used for this purpose in parts of Australia and New Zealand. 'Birmingham' is the principal American cultivar. It is widely planted in the South for its brilliant foliage and is hardy – in a sheltered spot – as far north as New York City. It is often sold simply as *Photinia* x *fraseri*.

Paeonies are amongst the aristocrats of the plant world. The magnificent wild moutan or tree paeony *Paeonia suf. fruticosa*, with its huge, white, maroon-centred blossoms is a summer treat, but for spring-flowering the smaller but nonetheless colourful cup-shaped, yellow flowers of *P. lutea ludlowii* are something to be enjoyed for several weeks. It is a tall robust shrub with magnificent foliage and as such is surely one of the best dual-purpose shrubs in the garden spectrum.

Two other shrubs which you might like to include if space permits are *Cytisus* x *praecox* and *C.* x *kewensis*. The former reaches 1.2 m (4 ft) and lines its slender shoots with rich cream pea flowers to create a colourful splash. The flowers are deep yellow in the variety 'Allgold', and white in 'Albus'. *C.* x *kewensis* is a low-growing shrub with spreading branches flooded in spring with cream coloured flowers.

Climbing plants
If there is space on a fence or wall one or other of the small flowered clematis should be planted. The European *C. alpina* with blue and white lantern flowers (which are substantially larger in the variety 'Frances Rivis') is a slender stemmed climber and is just as happy scrambling over a rock or through a low deciduous shrub.

Pieris 'Forest Flame', which prefers an acid soil.

Paeonia lutea ludlowii

Cytisus x praecox
Hebe speciosa 'Alicia Amhurst', summer flowering.

Equally attractive is the Chinese *C. macropetala* with violet-blue flowers – rose-pink in 'Markham's Pink' – which flowers later than *C. alpina* and continues its flowering into summer to form a colourful and satisfying link between the two seasons.

Summer interest
Summer is the season of plenty as far as flowering shrubs are concerned. Once the initial rush of spring is finished summer's flowers seem to come and go at a more leisurely pace.

Two important groups of deciduous shrubs for early summer are *Deutzia spp* and *Philadelphus spp*, each having many varieties from which to choose for both large and small gardens. The gardening world owes a great deal to the French nursery firm of Lemoine for the many attractive hybrids of deutzia.

Among the white-flowered varieties for which they are responsible are a handful possessing rose or purple-tinted flowers. 'Mont Rose' is one of the best; it is erect and robust in habit, growing 2 m (7 ft) tall and bearing its rose-pink flowers in large clusters. Those of 'Perle Rose' are more softly coloured whilst 'Magician' has larger flowers of mauve-pink, edged with white and tinted purple on the reverse. All should be given a position in full sun. The choice of philadelphus is, for large gardens, just as difficult, although strong contenders are the compact 1.8 m (6 ft) 'Belle Etoile' with large, deliciously scented white flowers, which are stained maroon at the centre, and the equally delightful but taller 'Beauclerc', whose flowers bear a light cerise stain.

Those with small gardens are well served with lovely philadelphus from the charming, small-leaved and flowered *P. microphyllus* to the large, white, purple-stained and almost square flowers of 'Sybille'. Both of these are richly scented. A choice deutzia for the small garden is *D. elegantissima* 'Rosalind', which is graceful and slender branched and very free with its deep carmine flowers.

Kolkwitzia amablis is another excellent flowering shrub. Known as the beauty bush, it is deciduous, reaching up to 2 m (7 ft), and has many soft pink, bell-shaped flowers in early summer.

One of the most free-flowering of all shrubs is *Abelia x grandiflora*, whose small pink and white tubular flowers with conspicuous dark red calyces crowd the branches and are carried over a long period through summer into autumn. Another group of shrubs which give good value are the hebes. 175

The spring and summer garden

The hebes

The most colourful unfortunately tend to be the least hardy, but in mild climates it is worth growing one or more for the amount of flower spikes they produce over a long period. Among the more spectacular can be recommended 'Alicia Amhurst' (deep purple), 'Gloriosa' (bright pink), 'La Seduisante' (bright crimson) and 'Simon Delaux' (rich crimson). Their habit is low and either rounded or dome shaped, and they are evergreen. Be sure to site them in a warm and sunny position.

Carpets of colour

For colour in the heather garden at this time several varieties of *Erica cinerea* and *E. vagans* can be planted. Both are well represented by numerous colour forms but the bright purple *E. cinerea* 'P. S. Patrick' and *E. vagans* 'Pyrenees Pink' are most representative of their kind. To add to these one might choose a few varieties of the true heather *Calluna vulgaris*, of which the satiny pink, double-flowered 'H. E. Beale' is outstanding. If ever a visit to a nursery is both rewarding and frustrating it would be to a well-stocked heather nursery in late summer. To gaze upon the carpets of different colours and hues is like witnessing a scene from the Arabian Nights; one needs great self-discipline to avoid choosing the whole mass!

Making colour reflect the shifting seasons

Perhaps nothing would be less attractive than a bright plant in flower for twelve months. One needs changes in the garden – changes of seasons, changes of colours, changes of emphasis. The snowdrops of early spring, for instance, are all the more welcome for their long absence from the garden scene. It is quite unnecessary to have drifts and beds of them, because there is pleasure in looking for them in their own private nook.

Choosing roses not just for colour of flower or scent

In temperate regions, roses begin to contribute to the colour of the garden in spring when their young leaves appear. For all our love of yellow, red and blue, we must not forget that the most important and most peaceful colour in the garden is green; and that the leaves of plants, although green through the presence of chlorophyll, are as changeable as the sky, and encompass a huge variety of shades and hints.

In the days of old garden roses, the leaves were as a rule rather coarse in appearance, light in colour, and not very handsome in the autumn. The

Calluna vulgaris 'H. E. Beale'

Adonis vernalis (see page 177). *Rosa* 'Canary Bird'

fashion was to segregate the roses, because although their flowers were greatly enjoyed in summer, the plants were dull during the rest of the year. This situation was entirely changed in the nineteenth century by the arrival of tea-scented China roses. They brought into our garden roses with shiny leaves of deeper green than before, and some varieties had young foliage with delightful red, purple or copper tints. These tints disappear when the leaves become mature, but for a few weeks in spring the leaves of many roses have a fresh and glittering polish upon them.

Modern hybrids with good foliage

Hybrid teas and floribundas are planted largely for their flowers, but their handsome leaves are an asset too, especially if they are healthy. Some of the hybrid tea varieties that bear them are 'Alexander', 'Cheshire Life', 'Chicago Peace', 'Lady Sylvia', 'National Trust', 'Peace', 'Pink Favourite', 'Pot o' Gold', 'Pristine', 'Red Planet', 'Silver Jubilee' and 'Wendy Cussons'. Of the floribundas, 'Allgold', 'Anna Ford', 'Congratulations', 'Dame of Sark', 'Glenfiddich', 'Letchworth Garden City', 'Matangi', 'Queen Elizabeth' and 'Southampton' all have good foliage.

These are all modern hybrids and should be listed in any catalogue.

Among other roses, the rugosas are notable for their handsome, light green leaves: 'The Fairy' for its small green ones, brightly burnished; *R. rubrifolia* for its reddish purple ones, all through the summer, and *R. beggeriana* and *R. fedtschenkoana* for their pale ghostly leaves. There are, of course, many more fascinating variations of rose foliage, but the point is that rose leaves are an important and integral part of the garden scene when flowers are generally reckoned to claim all the attention.

Roses that bloom before the hybrid teas and floribundas

As spring changes into summer, some of the earliest roses bloom. There are three main categories of these early roses, each beckoning the eye to a different level, and each deserving to be represented. First, a climbing hybrid tea or 'Banksian Yellow' on a warm wall; secondly, a soft yellow wild rose, or variety thereof, to grow as a shrub (such as 'Canary Bird', 'Golden Chersonese', or *R. primula*); thirdly, a low-growing Scotch rose, which may, if necessary, be trimmed after flowering to keep it low, such as 'Williams' Double Yellow', 'William III' or 'Mrs Colville'. The purple and plum shades of the latter two varieties amaze people who have never seen them before.

Between those early birds and the main rose season, a great many wild (or near-wild) and old garden roses are at their best, as are some of the earlier climbers. Some of the best investments among the more or less wild roses are the white shrub 'Nevada', or its pink sport 'Marguerite Hilling'; and forms of *R. moyesii* or *R. macrophylla*, especially 'Geranium', 'Fred Streeter' or 'Doncasteri' whose hips will be valuable later. Among the old garden roses, the beautiful albas are easily the most handsome plants, especially 'Celestial'. And among the climbers 'Mme Grégoire Staechelin' (a deep rose pink) is the greatest, the most beautiful, the most colourful and fragrant of early summer, after which it shuts up shop for the rest of the year. 'Maigold', amber yellow, is also very beautiful and later more generous.

The summer roses
After these, the summer roses bloom in their usual profusion, and there is no problem about continuity of flower for some time. Note, however, two factors: hard-pruned plants bloom later than those which were pruned more lightly, and where quantities of one variety are grown, the bed, so spectacular in bloom, is liable to be out of bloom with equal unanimity. There is a profound difference in the speed with which different varieties flower again. Outstanding for promptness are 'Allgold', 'Iceberg' and 'Pink Parfait', which are widely catalogued.

Continuity with perennials
In early spring, the dominant colour among perennials is yellow, but some subjects have a tinge of green and a very characteristic sheen. This occurs in two members of the Adonis genus which follow *A. amurensis* 'Fukujukai', one of the earliest plants to flower each year. One is the smaller *A. amurensis* 'Plena', with near-double flowers 50 mm (2 in) across; the other is *A. vernalis* with very appealing, shiny, single yellow flowers at the tips of bushy, fern-like stems, 38 cm (15 in) high. *A. volgensis*, which is of similar habit, is a week or two earlier.

The glistening yellow flowers of calthas – the marsh marigolds – make a brave show. The double form, *Caltha palustris* 'Plena', though a moisture lover, is much easier to grow in ordinary soil than the wild type. Then there is the *Euphorbia* genus, some of which will grow best in poor, dry soils. *E. polychroma* (syn. *E. epithymoides*) is a must in any good collection, as it does quite well in poor conditions and is long lived. The tall *E. wulfenii* (syn. *E. venata*) and the blue-grey leaves and sulphur-coloured flowers on short trailing stems of *E. myrsinites*, are

Trillium sessile

equally outstanding. The doronicums are tolerant of some shade; their yellow daisies, double and single, 15-45 cm (6-18 in) high, are early in flower and good value.

Complementing spring yellows
These yellow spring flowers all harmonize perfectly with the bright blue of *Brunnera macrophylla*, the lowly but lovely *Omphalodes spp*, the white, pink and orange *Epimedium spp* and even the magenta of *Anemone x lesseri* or the various shades of the hellebores, all of which are in flower at the same time. White trilliums and the deep maroon of *Trillium sessile* are another telling combination. Almost every colour but scarlet is seen in the welter of hybrid primulas allied to the primrose, polyanthus and *Primula denticulata sieboldii*, and *P. rosea* 'Delight'. A spring display for cool positions could also include some of the less common bulbous subjects such as the fritillaries and erythroniums (trout lilies, U.S.A.) and, where sunny and well drained, the perennial *Cheiranthus cheiri*.

Summer plants to hide gaps left by dormancy
As spring merges into summer so there is less and less bare soil to be seen. Where, as in the mertensias, erythroniums, and the two earliest adonis, *A.* 'Fukujukai' and *A. amurensis*, dormancy follows quickly after flowering, it is possible to juxtapose plants which will hide or cover the fading foliage of these early spring beauties. The June-flowering hardy geraniums, such as 'Johnson's Blue', the later *G. wallichianum* and *G.* 'Russell Prichard', have just the right outward

Euphorbia polychroma

spread for such a purpose. Their long display ends in winter dormancy, and as they have a modest root system they will cause no conflict with other plants in close proximity. Most euphorbias, the trilliums, omphalodes, brunnera, *Primula rosea* and *denticulata* and epimediums have a more expansive leafage after flowering. These too can be used to hide up gaps caused by dormancy, which of course also applies where early bulbs are planted.

The flowers of *Papaver orientale* (the oriental poppy) are huge and gorgeous, and come in many colours, but they do not last for very long. They tend to fall over, and when their untidiness becomes intolerable they will have to be cut back to ground level. There is little we can do to mask this gaping void with neighbouring plants, while waiting for the base leaves to reappear. Consequently these poppies are best confined to small groups, particularly in a restricted space. Early summer irises likewise have a fleeting display, but at least the foliage remains after flowering is finished.

Rectifying planning errors
It is a good idea, as the summer advances towards the peak flowering month (July in Britain), to make a note of any discrepancies, faults or ways of improving harmony so that you can rectify these in later months when the plants concerned are out of season. Perhaps an old clump of a member of the *Compositae* (daisy) family, such as *Pyrethrum spp*, *Chrysanthemum spp*, *Helenium spp* or *Solidago spp*, has withering leaves and will soon need dividing or replanting. Or the way you have set out 177

The spring and summer garden

Phlox maculata 'Omega'

Anemone japonica 'Louise Uhink'

Geranium armenum

your collection may seem to be unbalanced now that you have seen it in flower. If a new planting does not appear to be in keeping, be patient at first and give it the benefit of time. Maybe, when it has become established it will harmonize more effectively. If, however, an obvious mistake or misplacement has been made, the sooner this is safely remedied the better. It is generally safe to plant out of season provided environmental factors do not obviously prohibit your doing so.

You may find that you have too many plants flowering in the ten weeks from mid-June onwards, and that some look too much alike. A good balance involves one kind complementing rather than duplicating another, not only in height and colour, but also in habit and foliage.

Colour and flowering times

By opting for plants which spread over the longest possible period, it is possible to place together kinds which, if they flowered together, would clash. In Britain the most troublesome period for discord in the garden is likely to be July and August, when, for example, the more violent red and magenta shades are far more in evidence than earlier in the year.

Decisions about colour should always be made with blooming times in mind. It is best to restrict the variety of kinds which will flower in high summer in order to leave sufficient room for those flowering before and after this peak period. To place the fierce magenta *Geranium armenum* next to the scarlet *Lychnis chalcedonica*, which also flowers in June and July, would be offensive to most people's tastes. But if planted alongside a similarly coloured phlox, which flowers in August and September, the clash is avoided and continuity of colour is thus maintained. Incidentally, beware of heavy, limy soils where phlox is concerned. They are liable to sulk, as well as being susceptible to eelworm.

Using foliage to neutralize colour contrasts

The strategic use of good foliage plants is one way to avoid such conflicts. White-flowered plants too come into their own here. There are white phlox and astilbes, or you could use a combination of these and other white flowers such as the achillea 'W. B. Child', the white delphinium or *Anemone japonica* interspersed with light blue-flowering plants like *Scabiosa caucasica* or *Campanula lactiflora* to tone down any possible clash between red and magenta.

Using different shapes for variety

The value of placing spiky-flowered plants next to ones with a more level or rounded shape is most obvious in the peak-flowering period when so many of the *Compositae* family (as well as most phlox) make their display. One such combination is to place *Salvia* x *superba* with its violet-purple tapering spikes next to the deep yellow, flat-headed *Achillea filipendulina* 'Gold Plate' or 'Coronation Gold'. The same combination can be most effective with the silver-leafed, lemon-yellow *Achillea 'Moonshine'*, which is of similar height to the dwarfer salvia *S. x. superba* 'May Night'.

The spiky sidalceas are also effective for interspersing. All are in shades of pink from 75 cm (2½ ft) to 1.2 m (4 ft) or so tall, and though they would clash with the fuller reds such as the scarlet and crimson seen in some phlox and in the tall *Lychnis chalcedonica*, they look well set in between brownish and yellow helenuims or the blues of the *Agapanthus* genus or the blue delphinium belladonna hybrids. The latter are, of course, uniquely spectacular in early summer, but they are far from trouble-free and the taller they grow the more essential it is to stake them carefully. Such heavy spikes simply cannot withstand strong winds

Swathes of instant colour from summer bedding plants.

Hosta 'Royal Standard'

Rudbeckia sullivantii 'Goldsturm'.

and nothing looks more forlorn than these when staking is neglected. Even the new breed of dwarf hybrids *D.* 'Blue Heaven', welcome as they are for being more manageable than those twice their height, are unlikely to be self-supporting in all weathers. The aconitums are indispensible to intersperse delphiniums and their relations, because few other blue subjects exist with this spiky habit.

Delphiniums are often dubbed 'Queen of the border' but there are many other varieties which can claim to be equally indispensible. In this context the *Hemerocallis spp* must rank highly. They are hardy and long-lived, have a good overall appearance with complementary foliage, are adaptable for sun or partial shade and come, nowadays, in a vast range of colour. Thanks to a proliferation of the genus in America there is a welter of varieties to choose from.

Hostas also are gaining in popularity. Already over one hundred species, variations and hybrids exist, whereas fifty years ago you would be luckly to find ten in a nursery. Hostas have less spectacular flowers then hemerocallis and fewer colour variations, but they have gained their popularity mainly as foliage plants. Given reasonably moist

soil and some shade for those with variegated leaves, they can be left alone for years. They make excellent weed smotherers and, like hemerocallis, come in very useful for hiding the lower, sparse parts of tall plants such as delphiniums or lupins.

Most hostas flower during the peak summer period, with purplish, mauve and white on spikes of varying length. Though few would be worth growing for the flowers alone, any selection should certainly include the tall *H. rectifolia* with handsome spikes of light violet, *H. ventricosa* and the white 'Royal Standard'. All three are very adaptable, and have an abundance of greenery. Being sun tolerant, they harmonize well with ligularias such as 'The Rocket', 'Sungold' and *L. przewalskii*, which have stately spikes of yellow and golden-orange. With care in spacing – always necessary where plants have a wide spread of foliage or a very branching habit – *Heliopsis spp* also can be used for contrast, as can the newer crocosmias, especially the fiery 'Lucifer'.

Heliopsis spp have few rivals among the yellow sunflowers/Daisy members of the *Compositae* family, with the possible exception of rudbeckias, *R. laciniata* 'Goldquelle' and *R. sulli-*

vantii 'Goldsturm'. They are way ahead of most helianthus, solidagos and many heleniums in terms of flowering continuity and their ability to flourish for several years without having to be divided and replanted. Like helianthus and solidagos, though, they have little variation in their shades of yellow and orange, whereas heleniums include tawny browns.

In conlusion it is worth repeating the principle that in planting the average garden it is wise to overcome the temptation to stock varieties which only flower in high summer. Leave room in your plan for subjects which flower both before and after the peak period.

Annuals and biennials for instant colour

Annuals and biennals are at their peak in early summer when they can provide a good deal of the colour interest in a garden. The speed with which they grow can be very useful; they can cover bare patches around young plantings; they can grow over the unsightly leaves of bulbs now over; they can provide instantaneous colour in a garden which you are still in the process of planning out. And as we have seen they are also invaluable for use in pots and other containers. 179

The spring and summer garden

Summer bedding plants

Not all of these are annuals, but they are all tender plants and will be killed by frosts. They may be perennial in habit such as pelargoniums (geraniums) or annuals like the marigolds. In cold climates tender perennials are generally treated as if they were annuals and discarded at the end of the flowering season. They can of course be lifted and overwintered in frost-free conditions.

The function of summer bedding plants is to provide something like four or five months of continuous bright colour. In order to achieve eye-catching displays the plants are often mass planted (several kinds together) ensuring that they either contrast effectively or blend harmoniously. That is why it is necessary to raise reasonably large quantities of these plants. There is a tremendous range from which to choose. Among the most popular are antirrhinums, ageratums, asters, alyssums, begonias, gazanias, annual carnations, heliotropes, lobelias, matricarias, marigolds, nemesias, petunias, salvias, tagetes, verbenas and zinnias. Should you decide to incorporate them into a shrub border, choose carefully. Those which associate well with shrubs include heliotrope, fuchsias, nicotiana and fibrous-rooted begonias. Summer bedding plants are more usually grown in their own special beds, or in window boxes and other containers, including hanging baskets. But there is no reason why bedding subjects should not be included in mixed borders along with shrubs, hardy perennials and roses.

Maintaining continuity of flower

Flowering can be prolonged by snipping off the flowers once they have begun to wither. Left alone, a plant concentrates its energies on producing seed pods but if they are prevented from forming, the plant reverts to producing flowers.

A place in the rock garden?

Open, sunny positions suit annuals and such conditions prevail in a rock garden. While it is not a place where one would normally think of growing annuals, there are a number of kinds which can be used, in season, to mask temporary bare spots, where perhaps some cherished alpine has perished or a putative dwarf conifer has proved too vigorous and has had to be moved elsewhere.

One splendid annual for the rock garden is the large Mediterranean pimpernel *Anagallis linifolia* in either its red or azure blue form. In its natural habitat it may prove perennial but in a

Site mass-clumps of marigolds carefully so they don't overawe their neighbours.

more temperate climate this is unlikely. From South Africa come two delightful dwarf annuals with blue, daisy-like flowers. One is the well-known kingfisher daisy, *Felicia bergeriana*, the other is correctly termed *Charieis heterophylla* but is listed in most catalogues as *Kaulfussia amelloides*. Another daisy which comes in blue, amongst other colours, is the swan river daisy from Australia – *Brachycome iberidifolia*. Yet another vivid blue annual, this time with bell-shaped flowers and emanating from western U.S.A., is *Phacelia campanularia*. Finally, a very dwarf form of the poppy *Eschscholzia caespitosa*, which produces a variety of brilliant colours, is also suitable.

Flowers for beds and borders

The China asters and the zinnias are ideal subjects for massing in clumps, particularly those varieties which grow no higher than 30 to 38cm (12 to 15in) tall. Dwarf China asters include the deep-rose, chrysanthemum flowered *Callistephus chinensis* 'Chater's Erfurt', the double-flowered *C.c.* 'Dwarf Queen Mixed', and the variously coloured, tightly flowering 'Lilliput'. Zinnias hate being moved. Once you can get hold of them prick them out of their greenhouse seeding boxes and transfer the seedlings into peat pots so that when you plant them

out in early summer there will be minimum disturbance to their roots. The dwarf forms of these come in a wide variety of colours with single or double flowers.

All these half-hardy annuals flower quite late but will last into autumn when their colour will be much appreciated. Before they bloom you might consider the species of *Nemesia* which come in heights ranging from 15 to 60 cm (6 to 12 in) and a wide range of colours. Then there is *Phlox drummondii* of similar height and available in fragrant crimson, scarlet, pink flowers, some with white markings. Both of these can be removed to make way for later flowering plants.

The African and French marigolds bloom early too and continue flowering for the whole summer provided they are not allowed to set seed. The French (*Tagetes patula*) are small, the tallest being about 60cm (12in). The African (*T. erecta*) is a branching plant 30 to 60cm (1 to 3ft) high. Their orange and red flowers tend towards the garish, so site them carefully lest they overawe their neighbours. Petunias, 20 to 45 cm (9 to 18 in) tall, in shades of blue, crimson, scarlet, pink, violet, yellow and cream, also flower all summer long but are, perhaps, less suited to the border than to a window box, tub or

180

some other container (see page 128). They do not like shade, so an open sunny position is a must.

Hardy annuals of intermediate size – say 30 to 90 cm (1 to 3 ft) – include the cornflower (*Centaurea cyanus*) and the larkspur (*Delphinium ajacis*) with their blue and pink flowers. They are excellent for cutting. The three half-hardy chrysanthemums – *C. carinatum* (syn. *C. tricolor*), *C. coronarium*, and *C. segetum* – are also worthy of consideration mid-bed or border.

Because of their short lifespan there are only a few annuals that are so tall they need staking. *Helianthus annuus*, the sunflower, is one obvious exception. Indeed most gardeners prefer to seek an extended flowering season from their annuals rather than great height. Perhaps it is more rewarding to look to the biennials for an impressive backbone in a summer display of annuals.

Canterbury bells (*Campanula medium*) and hollyhocks (*Althaea rosea*) have the additional advantage of bringing with them a sense of the old-style cottage garden. The former is about 90cm (3ft) tall (though the genus includes all sorts of dwarf varieties). *C. medium* blooms in white and many shades of pink, mauve and blue. There are pink, crimson, yellow and white hollyhocks and some will grow up to 1.5m (5ft) tall. Then there is the similarly lofty hardy biennial foxglove, *Digitalis purpurea*, to add height and yet more colour to the summer garden.

Flowers for colour and scent
Plant planning a scented garden is discussed elsewhere, but there are a number of annuals and biennials which popularly form a part of colour gardens, which are also noteworthy for their fragrance. *Matthiola spp* (stocks) are a must. Varieties come in a range of colours.

But for really exquisite scent, plant *Matthiola bicornis* beneath a window and leave it open on warm summer evenings. *Lathyrus odoratus* (sweet pea) is another firm favourite, fragrant and available in many varieties and colours. The nicotianas have been mentioned on page 141, as has the wallflower which associates well with many bulbs. Among the cultivars are shades of red, orange and yellow.

Flowers that climb
There are some good climbing annuals for growing up walls or fences. The various morning glories, species of *Pharbitis*, but often listed as *Ipomoea* or *Convolvulus*, will give a splendid display of sky blue flowers with yellow throats in warm summers, but may be disappointing if the summer is cool and wet. The red or yellow-flowered *Eccremocarpus scaber* is usually listed as half-hardy and certainly looks as though it should be, but once in the garden it tends to seed itself around. *Adlumia cirrhosa*, a kind of biennial climbing dicentra, is hard to obtain, but is worth getting for its ferny foliage and heads of pink 'bleeding hearts', while the cup and saucer vine (*Cobaea scandens*) will soon cover a large expanse with its violet and green bell-shaped flowers from mid-summer to mid-autumn.

Positioning bulbs to best advantage
There are few gardens which cannot make use of a considerable number of bulbs in one way or another. But where and how the early-flowering subjects are planted presents some difficulties.

Very often they are planted in a mixed border where their distinctive display can get lost in an otherwise fairly deserted side. And when you come to cultivate the soil in the autumn, over-enthusiastic spading can damage them just at the point when they are in full root-growth. Moreover many bulbs become somewhat unsightly after they have flowered, when their leaves elongate and spread over the ground. It is not enough to cut the leaves down as soon as the bulb has finished flowering, because as we have seen bulbs are fed by their foliage and the leaves must be allowed to ripen naturally.

There are various ways of overcoming this problem. If it is an otherwise deserted border at this time of year, you might consider planting the bulbs at the back so that later flowering plants take over at the point that the bulbs become unsightly. Alternatively you could interplant the bulbs with flowers such as forget-me-nots (*Myosotis spp*) which will hide the lengthening leaves to some extent. If your bulbs are positioned on a cool bank, hardy ferns suitably placed in groups will allow the bulbs space during their flowering time, and then develop to cover their remains. Indeed any young shrub planting will perform as efficiently.

It is the grassy leaves of the true bulbs which are particularly unattractive. The leaves of anemones are actually quite pleasing and those of the hardy cyclamen are nearly as attractive as the flowers, particularly *Cyclamen hederifolium* (*neapolitanum*). Perhaps the very difficult cases, such as the autumn flowering colchicums, whose leaves appear in spring and persist until summer, are best planted in front of a shrubbery where their leaves will pass almost unnoticed.

Spring bedding bulbs
If you use bulbs as spring bedding you can remove them before they have had a chance to complete their growth cycle. This is particularly useful in a small garden where replacing them with other plants such as annuals and biennials is an effective way to promote colour continuity. Provided that you take care not to damage their roots when lifting the bulbs, they could be replanted in a more convenient situation, say a row in the kitchen garden. There they can ripen off without seriously weakening them for ensuing seasons.

In this respect daffodils are more reliable than tulips, which in any case do not persist for long in many gardens as they prefer a rather light soil and very quick drainage.

If you do lift tulips, do so when the foliage starts to turn yellow. Then hang them up in an airy, dry situation until early winter when you can replant them.

Bulbs in outdoor containers – window boxes, tubs, vases, etc. – can also be lifted and planted elsewhere in the garden once they have completed their growth. But be sure whenever lifting bulbs that you keep them out of the soil for as little time as possible. Most bulbs and corms spend the summer without leaves or roots, just a store of food for the next season. However, chemical changes are taking place inside during these resting stages. Snowdrops provide an exception to this general rule. They move best while still in active growth.

Summer bedding bulbs
Spring bedding bulbs can be mix planted with wallflowers or forget-me-nots to be replaced at the end of the season with the summer bedders, such as cannas (impressive foliage and brilliant, if untidy, flowers), dahlias and gladioli. These are all planted out when there is no risk of frost and may be lifted after the first frost of autumn and kept in airy, dry, frost-free conditions until the next spring.

However, the dwarf dahlias such as 'Coltness Gem' are best treated as half-hardy annuals. In fact as far as all the dahlia tubers are concerned it is reckoned that they will flower more freely if you start them in heat in the spring and take the shoots as cuttings when they appear, growing them on in gentle heat until such time as they can be hardened off.

181

The spring and summer garden

Bringing indoor bulbs out into the garden

If you have successfully anticipated spring by forcing bulbs for the home, don't neglect them once they have flowered. If they are kept watered and protected for at least six weeks after flowering, and then water witheld so that the leaves dry off and the bulbs ripen, they can be planted out in the garden where they will continue to give pleasure for many years. The tazetta narcissi 'Paperwhite' and 'Soleil d'Or' are slightly tender in temperate climates but they will usually survive if the bulbs are planted extra deeply. The Tangier iris (*I. tingitana*), on the other hand, rarely survives for long outside. Tulips, daffodils and hyacinths will do well, and even if they are not too brilliant in the first year after forcing they will soon make up the lost ground.

Early spring bulbs

If crocus and snowdrop see winter out, the narcissus and scillas must be the first sign of spring. The daffodils range from the dwarf *N. cyclamineus,* with bright yellow flowers, and the exquisite ivory *N. triandrus,* to great hybrids up to 30cm (1ft) tall such as 'Golden Harvest'. Most of these are either yellow or white, but there are some daffodils with pinkish trumpets. The most popular scilla is the dwarf, bright blue *S. sibirica,* and with them come the related chionodoxas, with larger, flatter flowers, usually with a white centre, though *C. sardensis* is all blue and much resembles *S. bifolia.* It is still a little early for tulips, but in the rock garden *Tulipa pulchella* with pink or violet flowers will be out and so will the pale yellow *T. turkestanica,* which has a head of flowers, unlike most tulips. The dog's tooth violet, *Erythronium dens-canis* will open its pink or white flowers close to the ground at about the same time. Its taller North American relatives, *E. tuolumense,* with yellow flowers, and 'White Beauty' with attractive mottled leaves and white flowers wait until well into spring. The 'Crown Imperial' will reach a height of 60 cm (2 ft) and its copper or yellow flowers open. It is not particularly easy, but like the Madonna lily, it has been known to grow well in cottage gardens.

Mid-spring bulbs

Fortunately *Fritillaria meleagris*, which comes out in April in Britain, is not very difficult to grow and will seed around. Its chequered flowers are either purple or white and are one of the great charms of April, reaching a height of 22 cm (8–9 in). Many of the narcissus continue into April, which is also the flowering month for many tulips, including the various hybrids of the water-lily tulip *T. kaufmanniana,* and the enormous

scarlet flowers of *T. fosteriana* and its hybrids of which 'Madame Lefeber' is the best known. These are not tall compared with the later-flowering darwins, reaching only to about 20 cm (8 in). The taller florist's tulips start a little later and may reach 60 cm (2 ft) in height. Bluebells, *Endymion non-scripta* and the larger flowered *E. hispanicus,* both occasionally reaching 30 cm (1 ft), can be found in blue,

Above: *Fritillaria meleagris* 'Alba' and *F. m.* 'Purple King' love riverside meadows (as in Christ Church meadow, Oxford). **Right:** shown off by a striking pocket of a *Primula polyanthus* hybrid is a 'natural' planting of *Endymion non-scripta.*

Top: *Erythronium revolutum* 'White Beauty', a real beauty which does well in damp conditions. **Above**: the dwarf *Scilla sibirica*, the most popular of the genus. **Left**: the summer-flowering *Galtonia candicans*, reminiscent of the hyacinth.

white and pink.

Late spring, early summer

The tulips continue into May and the easy – but expensive – *T. sprengeri* with orange-red flowers may even persist into June in Britain. Both the poppy anemones and the starry St Bravo anemones flower from mid to late spring. The Asiatic ranunculus start to flower in late spring and their great buttercups of red,

white, copper and yellow go on into early summer. They need a warm situation but are magnificent when established. The last and largest of the diminutive hardy cyclamen, *C. repandum,* with carmine flowers, is out in late spring and so too, at the other end of the scale, is the yellow Foxtail lily *Eremurus bungei (stenophyllus),* which may reach a metre (3 ft) in height. The narcissus season ends with the intoxicating fragrance of the pheasant's eye, *N. recurvus,* of which both single and double forms exist. The first of the paeonies probably open in late spring; but in Britain June is their main month. May is also the prime month for the ornamental garlics – from the dwarf *Allium karataviense,* with very attractive leaves, to the large *A. christophii (albo-pilosum)* with its great head of violet stars on a 15 cm (6 in) stem. The blue and white camassias from western North America grow to 45 cm (18 in) tall and are inexpensive and reliable.

Summer bulbs

Early summer sees the huge spikes and pink flowers of *Eremurus robustus* and *E. himalaicus,* which may reach to 2.7 m (9 ft) in height. The hybrids between these giants and the dwarfer *E. bungei* are in pastel shades and reach around 1.3 m (4 ft 6 in). Dutch and Spanish irises with stems up to 30 cm (1 ft) are inexpensive and the dwarf nanus gladioli, around 30 cm (1 ft), also flower now. So too does the magenta, hardy *G. byzantinus,* which reaches 60 cm (2 ft). From western North America come the brodiaeas with heads of starry flowers in violet and yellow, reaching around 20 cm (8 in), in height and usually nice and cheap.

July is when the florist's gladioli come into their own in Britain and another bulb is the hyacinth-like *Galtonia candicans* with stems up to a metre high. Lilies are the glory of summer. They range in height from 60 cm to 160 cm (2 ft-5 ft) according to variety. A smaller flowerer is the English iris, which is rarely more than 20 cm (8 in) tall. Among dwarf subjects is the fragrant *Cyclamen europaeum* which comes out now, but is not so easy as *C. hederifolium (neapolitanum),* which has the bonus of attractive leaves – a rarity among bulbs. It may open some of its flowers quite early in summer, but its main display spreads over the summer period. This also applies to the dahlias. Bulbs of the tigridias are cheap. They have brilliant flowers, which only last for a day but come in such numbers in mid-summer that a clump of them will always be showing some flowers. Soon afterwards the pink lilies of *Amaryllis belladonna* start to appear.

The autumn and winter garden

Continuity of display

If a garden has been stocked with spring and summer displays solely in mind, it is inevitable that a period of drabness and monotony will follow. But by careful planning this can be avoided and there is no need to wait until spring for beauty to be restored. In autumn and winter a different but no less fascinating world comes to light, a world which reveals the underlying shape and form of leafless trees, the colours of newly exposed bark, the brightness of winter berries, the texture and subtle colour shifts of evergreens and conifers – even a brave display of winter blossom and flowers. Indeed these features evoke a richness and subtlety of colour, form, texture and scent which is evident at no other time of the year.

Often, at this time of year, the impact of seasonal characteristics and qualities of plants are emphasized by their isolation from the now dormant, lusher aspects of the plant life of other months. Some plants are actually at their best in autumn and winter; others have aspects which may earlier have been hidden from view, but which now gain a particular significance. As the year draws to a close it is never more clearly true that it is best to choose plants which display a pleasing aspect, in one form or another, at most times of the year, rather than those which offer a brief, if intense, interest during spring and summer. A case in point is the marvellous spectacle of Adam's laburnum (x *Laburnocytisus adamii*). This freak result of grafting the little rock garden purple broom, *Cytisus purpurea*, onto a laburnum produces a splendid and quite irresistible display of pinkish-purple laburnum flowers, some ordinary yellow ones and also bunches of *C. purpurea's* purple flowers and leaves. But the plant dazzles for barely a month. For the rest of the year, this scrawny little tree can lay claim to being quite the ugliest in the garden, and it is therefore hardly one to choose if space and resources are limited. Part of the fascination of the garden is to watch the way the changing seasons bring about an ever interesting metamorphosis in specific plants and, indeed, whole areas of the garden.

Once autumn is past, you will probably not be spending a great deal of time in your garden for relaxation. It is important, then, that any plants you have chosen for their winter aspect should be visible from the house. On the other hand, avoid placing them so that they get in the way of any seasonal maintenance work such as composting or other soil improvements. If you have to leave a bed com-

Salix alba 'Chermesina' has striking, orange-scarlet shoots.

pletely empty over the winter, lead the eye away from it by planting an adjacent display.

Trees for autumn and winter

With sufficient foresight, the trees in your garden can provide colour and interest all the year round. Evergreen trees may well, by virtue of their sheer size and proportion, form the backbone and hence the design framework of the garden through the whole twelve months of the year. While their green, gold, silver, and variegated foliage is invaluable when other plants appear distinctly bare and drab, winter is also a time when the underlying structure of plants becomes apparent and in this respect deciduous trees also have an important role to play. Once denuded of their leaves attention becomes focused on their variously coloured bark and their crown patterns. We tend to think of the wood of trees as being basically brown, but in fact it runs the whole gamut of colour from a delicate silvery grey to a rich chestnut hue. We have already seen, in **Planning ideas for the small garden,** how many of them have important characteristics for the autumn and winter garden. Whether it is the distinctive appeal of the Japanese pillar apple with its leaves turning from orange and scarlet to rich red, or the fruiting of this or the hornbeams, or the hues of the

maples and the rowans which attract you, autumn is unquestionably a vibrant season of colour. And in form alone, the winter aspect of trees such as the pyramidal hornbeam is outstanding, with its straight slender branches, and the Dawyck beech (page 101) can be very rewarding. Bark colours, like autumnal leaves, can be just as bright as many flowers, and may be found on young shoots alone or on mature boles. Witness the white vertical streaks on an enamel-smooth grey or green background which characterize the snake-bark maples. The tree equivalent to the shrubby dogwood with young red stems is the little coral-bark maple, *Acer palmatum* 'Senkaki', while the violet willow and the similar *Salix irrorata* are valubale alternatives. The Tibetan cherry, *Prunus serrulata*, and some birches are, from a distance, even more striking than the snakebarks. This cherry has a rich mahogany bark which peels in lateral rolls to leave glossy smooth areas with a satin-like quality. Planted near a path it is assured of regular stroking, as few can resist it, and this keeps it bright and stops dull blackish scales forming.

The best birch for winter is undoubtedly the form of Chinese red-barked birch, *Betula albo-sinensis* var *septentrionalis*. This can be seen in Branklyn Garden, Perth, but is hard to

Peeling bark of *Prunus serrula*.

Acer palmatum 'Senkaki', the coral bark maple.

obtain commercially. The soft pink-purple bark is clearly visible in summer too, because the slender elliptic, dark, grey-green leaves are held out in open hanging sprays. The Szechuan birch, *B. mandshurica* var *szechuanica*, has chalky white bark and solid dark leathery rounded leaves, but its crown lacks shape. The Himalayan birch, *B. utilis*, is shapely and vigorous with good shiny leaves on red stalks while its bark can be mottled in browns or a good white. The purest white form is usually called Jacquemont's birch, even when it has the leaf of the true species.

Persian ironwood, *Parrotia persica*, provides good bark and winter flowers. In neither is it outstanding, although it does add good autumn colour to the garden. The bark develops well only where this tree of bushy tendencies has been made to stand on a single clear trunk. Then it is broadly mottled in brown and yellow and resembles a London plane. The flowers are bright, deep red tufts, which are usually out by midwinter.

The classic winter flowering tree, however, is the winter cherry, *Prunus subhirtella* 'Autumnalis', a quite remarkable specimen. It has an untidy mop of a crown often poorly matched to the bole of wild white cherry upon

which it is grafted, but its ability to flower is highly commendable. It starts flowering even before it has shed its leaves, but this is not an attractive aspect to everyone because the leaves are by then pale yellow and partly mask the small, nearly white flowers. Once the leaves are away, the flowering picks up. On longer stalks, a part of each bunch of buds opens pale pink. Every time there is a sharp frost, the open flowers brown off but are replaced almost at once. In the absence of frost, the number of flowers open is sufficient for it to make quite a splash as a flowering tree. Flowering continues unabated until the new leaves are almost due, when the last buds, mostly near the tips of the shoots, all open together in a final burst.

Two trees with marginal winter flowers merit inclusion for other reasons too. The strawberry tree (page 103) flowers early in winter (about November in Britain) probably followed by bunches of scarlet fruit. The young bark has some red in it, constrasting with good evergreen foliage. The Chinese privet (page 104) has splendid year-round foliage and its creamy, fragrant flowers open from autumn to midwinter. A fine tree which tends to carry some bunches of bright orange red fruit into the winter is the alderleaf whitebeam (*Sorbus alnifolia*).

The white or pink fruit, usually in generous bunches on the Hupeh rowan, *S. hupehensis*, fools the birds in some areas into thinking they are not yet ripe and so remain quite well into the winter.

Autumn colour shrubs and roses

The arrival of autumn signals a change of colour emphasis. Some shrubs will still be in flower, but more often than not, flower colours are outshone by the tints of dying leaves and the rich colours of fruit. There are few shrubs better fitted to the autumnal garden than the native English guelder rose, *Viburnum opulus*. It is a large shrub with maple-shaped leaves which, in autumn, colour brilliantly at the same time as large bunches of glistening red berries begin to weigh down its branches. A true all-rounder, in spring it bears lovely white lace-caps. Similar in effect is the snowy mespilus, *Amelanchier lamarckii*. In spring, the flood of white flowers on naked branches gives the illusion of snow when seen from a distance, but in autumn its leaves of red or orange hues glow like a bonfire. If unavailable, *A. canadensis* is a good substitute.

The berberis clan contains a large number of subjects which will provide autumn colour. There are several

185

The autumn and winter garden

hybrids with names like 'Buccaneer', 'Bountiful' and 'Pirate King', but none has ever entirely replaced the shrub which E. H. Wilson introduced from China early this century and christened *Berberis wilsoniae* after his wife. Its small, compact habit and brilliant display of autumn leaves and berries is still the most reliable and pleasing species for the garden – large or small.

If you have a large border to fill, you could do no better than plant a selection of the large cotoneasters; even a single specimen can be very attractive. Their reliability in fruit is beyond question and they will usually last into winter. Many are hybrids of the Himalayan *C. frigidus*, which is worth growing for its large heavy bunches of red berries. 'St Monica' and 'Cornubia' are two excellent red-berried seedlings, while for contrast the yellow-berried 'Rothschildianus' could be included.

Climbing plants

When it comes to covering a house wall, there is little to compete with ivy. A close runner is the so-called Boston ivy, *Parthenocissus tricuspidata*, a deciduous self-clinging creeper whose maple-shaped leaves turn the most incredible shades of orange, red and sometimes bronze-purple in autumn. This Chinese vine has largely replaced the true Virginia creeper, *P. quinquefolia*, in our gardens but both are unbeatable for decorating large areas of brick. They can also be planted at the foot or stump of a large tree, up which they will climb just as they do in the wild. To see the brilliant curtains of their hanging stems and their tall columns of fire-coloured foliage is one of autumn's finest memories.

Dual purpose roses

When thinking about dual purpose shrubs which will provide different kinds of interest at various times of the year, don't forget the rose species. In temperate climes, roses continue to flower until the days become too dark and the nights too cold. Jack Harkness recalls one long mild spell when there was no time without them for a period of about twenty-one months. In warmer countries this happens more regularly. Again, some varieties come consistently later into bloom than others. Choose 'Alexander' or 'Anne Harkness' or 'The Fairy' for late blooming bushes and definitely 'Crimson Shower' as a climber. Sometimes they earn condemnation for being late – most unjust since, like runners in a relay race, they take the field fresh and vigorous as others fade.

Two other gifts await us in the autumn: those hips so red against the sky – held

Berberis thunbergii 'Atropurpurea' turning colour in autumn.

Autumn berries of *Cotoneaster* x *rothschildianus* (yellow) and *C.* x *watereri* (scarlet)

up by *Rosa moyesii* (best planted, as so often in the wild, amongst other shrubs where their heads are clear and bare stems hidden), *R. macrophylla* and *R. rubrifolia* (or usually by the selected forms of the first two). The other gift is autumn foliage colour, for which the great roses are the wild ones from North America – particularly the beautiful *R. virginiana*. This graceful shrub has pink flowers in summer, red hips in autumn, and leaves which turn to red and yellow. It is an ideal hedge rose wherever it can be allowed the space to grow to about 1.5 m (5 ft) wide and high. Another beauty is *R. nitida*, which takes up only a small space. Its leaves are brilliantly polished in

summer, and like the sun, glow with colour before they fall. Finally, if you choose the vigorous suckering roses such as *R. pimpinellifolia*, *R. rugosa*, and their hybrids, site them carefully, for although they are splendid in both flower and fruit they will overtake more delicate neighbours.

Flowering shrubs

Flowering shrubs are still an important part of autumn and although the choice is smaller than for spring and summer there are several which, if space permits, should be included. The slightly tender evergreen *Mahonia* x *media* in any of its named forms (such as 'Charity', 'Buckland' and 'Winter

Top: *Rosa moyesii*, a very valuable dual-purpose plant which grows up to 3 m (10 ft) tall and produces deep, crimson-red flowers with cream stamens in summer and bright red hips in autumn. **Top right:** *Potentilla fruticosa* is a deciduous shrub valuable for its long flowering season from mid-spring through to early autumn. Illustrated here, the variety 'Goldfinger'. **Below** the fruticosa is *Ceratostigma willmottianum*, another valuable late-flowering shrub frequently grown against a wall. Its foliage tints red in autumn. **Far right:** *Mahonia* x *media* 'Charity' is later flowering still, slightly tender, but a good feature plant as is *Mahonia* 'Buckland' (**near right**). All mahonias are useful evergreens.

Sun') is a splendid addition to the garden in suitable climates. In America it is successful mainly in California and the Pacific Northwest. Its full stems clothed with large handsome leaves are crowned in autumn with long yellow flower spikes borne in clusters from the shoot tips. They are perhaps best grown as an isolated specimen, carefully sited in a lawn or in a bed surrounded by smaller plants. One of the best all-purpose shrubs is the nutmeg, *Leycesteria formosa*. Its summer white flowers give way to autumnal clusters of almost black fruit on bright green stems.

A quartet of shrubs which carry their

flowers from summer into autumn are *Potentilla fruticosa* (and hybrids), *Ceratostigma willmottianum*, *Fuchsia spp* (many hybrids) and *Phygelius capensis* 'Coccineus'. Between them, these small shrubs bring a rich variety of colour and interest to the autumn garden and help fool the unwary that summer never really ended. For colder regions you might substitute *Hibiscus syriacus* 'Diane', *Clerodendrum trichotomum*, and *Elsholtzia stantonii* for the three last-named shrubs.

Shrubs which flower in winter are all the more precious for their scarcity and the best use should be made of them. *Jasminum nudiflorum* provides a

wealth of yellow blooms and is reliable whatever the weather. It needs to be trained against a wall or fence, or even a tree perhaps, and have its old flowering shoots pruned each spring. Otherwise it can quickly get out of hand and become a tangled mass choked with dead shoots. If you can tolerate the slowness of the winter sweet, *Chimonanthus praecox*, to reach flowering size, your patience will be well-rewarded with its yellow flowers with crimson-purple centres and exquisite fragrance. But scent can be far more easily and quickly obtained with *Viburnum* x *bodnantense* 'Dawn' which gives autumn tints of red and purple into the bargain.

The autumn and winter garden

Like most other winter-flowering shrubs the viburnum can be cut for indoor display where it quickly fills the room with scent. *V. glauca* has blue-green berries, while *V. betulifolium* (up to 4m (12 ft) tall) has dense clusters of shiny red berries. Another favourite shrub for cutting is the witch hazel, *Hamamelis mollis*. There is a touch of humour in its curious deep yellow spider-like flowers crowding the twigs and it is really a must for the large garden. 'Pallida' is a hybrid with even larger flowers of an exquisite sulphur yellow. Both are sweetly scented. To associate with the yellow-flowered witch hazels one might plant *Rhododendron dauricum* or *R. mucronulatum* whose bright, rose-purple flowers offer a wonderful contrast. In unsheltered, colder regions, for example the mid-Atlantic states of North America, you might prefer to opt for *Corylopsis pauciflora* (a relative of the witch hazel) and *R. mucronulatum*. However, March and April is about as early as you could expect their blooming times to coincide.

Low-level plantings

To form a carpet beneath the hamamelis and rhododendrons, or to have on their own, there are a considerable number of winter-flowering heathers. These hardy evergreen shrubs can go a long way towards livening up the dullness of the garden scene throughout autumn and winter as well as making a good contrast with other plants that flower then. The classic winter heather is *Erica carnea*, which may be listed as *E. herbacea*. This compact plant rarely grows taller than 15–30 cm (6–12 ins) and has the additional merit of growing quite happily in a fairly alkaline soil (though, as most heathers, it *prefers* acid conditions). There are many forms which enjoy a very long season of flower through winter and spring; none do well in shade. 'Loughrigg' (a purplish crimson) and 'Winter Beauty' (rose-pink) are recommended. In mid-winter 'Ruby Gem' and 'C. M. Beale' have white flowers, while in late winter 'James Backhouse' (deep pink), the prostrate and vigorously spreading 'Springwood Pink' and 'Springwood White', or the carmine red 'Vivellii' (with its bronze foliage) come into their own.

A little taller than *E. carnea* is *E. x darleyensis* ('Darley Dale' is the original hybrid of *E. carnea* with *E. Mediterreanea*). It has pale mauve flowers, while the varieties 'Arthur Johnson', 'Furzey' and 'J. W. Porter' have deep pink blossom which will last through winter and spring. *E. x. darleyensis* 'Silberschmelze' is silvery-white, fragrant and will be in flower between mid-winter and early spring.

A carpet of winter heather, *Erica carnea*.

Foliage, bark and berries in the winter shrub garden

Winter is a good time to admire and appreciate the foliage and bark of shrubs. One of the most striking of evergreen shrubs for mild climate gardens is *Elaeagnus pungens* 'Maculata'. It is big and bold – growing up to 2.5 m (8ft) by as much across, and needs controlling where space is at a premium. But it does have the most colourful leaves which bear a large golden central blotch or stripe. Sometimes the entire centre of the leaf is gold and there could be no better evergreen to brighten up a winter, especially in the shade of a building or beneath trees.

By the same token, the ivy *Hedera helix* 'Goldheart' can be put to use in scaling a wall or tree trunk. The three-lobed leaves are splashed with gold and the effect is both striking and satisfying. Another ivy to consider for this purpose is *H. colchica* 'Dentata Variegata' with its bold, creamy-white variegated leaves. For a low wall, stump or the wall of a new house, especially one built of red brick, there is no more spectacular climbing evergreen. In colder regions you might wisely substitute variegated cultivars of *Euonymus fortunei*.

At least one conifer should find its way into the winter garden and here the choice is daunting. A favourite is the juniper *J. communis depressa* 'Aurea'. Its low spreading habit is ideal for the edge of a path or bed and it has beautiful, butter-yellow young growth in spring. It remains yellow throughout summer, turning an unusual bronze in winter. A possible

challenger for inclusion would be *Thuja occidentalis* 'Rheingold' and if both could be accommodated, all the better. The erect, conical habit and rich coppery-gold winter foliage make 'Rheingold' one of the most conspicuous items in the winter garden.

The hollies are some of the noblest evergreens for the garden. There are several with coloured or variegated foliage, but if space allowed for the inclusion of only one, it would surely be *Ilex aquifolium* 'Madame Briot' which, in addition to its rich gold-margined leaves, floods its branches with conspicuous red berries. Apart from hollies, berries in winter are few and far between, but there are notable exceptions. One is *C. serotinus*, a member of the *Cotoneaster* genus typically good for autumn fruiting. Another evergreen, this makes a sizeable shrub up to 3 m (10 ft) tall. In mid-summer it floods its arching branches with white flowers and its small but freely produced orange-red berries will see the winter through and are normally ignored by birds.

If there is enough room, consider establishing a colony of the Himalayan raspberry – *Rubus biflorus*, principally for its shoots in winter which look as if they have been whitewashed. Only the shoots of the current year bear this feature and old shoots should be cut away like those of the common raspberry after fruiting. The ghostly white shoots of this shrub stand out starkly against the darkness of an evergreen tree or a wall, and low perennials or bulbs can be planted at its feet to make the best use of space.

Fine foliage and grasses classified as perennial

It is, inevitably, in the colder months of the year that full appreciation is accorded to plants with fine foliage. The majority of these are less spectacular in spring, if only because it takes time for their leaves to develop. Hostas are outstanding, provided the garden is free from severe autumn and early winter frosts. Ornamental grasses are very valuable particularly for the drama they lend both autumn and winter gardens. The varieties of *Miscanthus spp* are effective until mid-winter. The striped variegated forms of *M. sinensis* stand out more than the green, with wide grassy leaves up to 1.5 m (5 ft) in height. Not all miscanthus flower, but they are still well worth planting. *M.*'Silver Feather' is one that does flower and makes a good display through autumn until mid-winter with its lofty 1.8m (6 ft) plumes. The ubiquitous but still noble Pampas grass (*Cortaderia spp*) is a firm favourite for a position of some isolation. Indeed any of the taller grasses are best placed thus, or in front of a dark background of evergreens or an unsightly building. Consider too *C. selloana* with its silky cream plumes and narrow glaucous leaves extending 2.75 m (9 ft) in length.

Dwarfer grasses also have their uses, but those with variegated blades are still the most effective. *Carex morrowii* 'Evergold' is outstanding for year-round effect. Best placed where it can readily be seen on a cold winter day, it makes a wide clump only 30 cm (12 ins) high. The very easy-to-grow *Festuca ovina* 'Glauca' keeps its bluish silver sheen throughout the year and is an excellent edging plant.

Taller grasses are sometimes not suitable in a closely-planted mixed border, because they have such an individual appearance and need sufficient space to enable their 'architectural' qualities to be shown off to best advantage. This is also true of the red hot poker (*Kniphofia spp*), of which there are several late autumn flowering varieties, such as *K. galpinii, K. caulescens* and *K.* 'C. M. Prichard'.

The large, handsome foliage of the genus *Acanthus* will survive well into winter, while the giant reed *Arundo donax* has red summer plumes which fade in autumn to white and will see the winter through. Space these larger plants carefully among tall shrubs, with which they can play a complementary role. Alternatively, interplant them with *Nerine bowdenii*, one of the most valuable of tall autumn-flowering bulbs, which can be safely left undisturbed for years and will produce deep

Top: *Miscanthus sinensis* 'Zebrinus'. **Right**: *Arundo donax.* **Below**: the Pampas grass *Cortaderia selloana* 'Sunningdale Silver'. **Beneath**: *M. sinensis* 'Silver Feather'.

pink trumpet flowers during autumn. The *Schizostylis* genus, whose pinks and reds may continue up to mid-winter is a good alternative to *N. bowdenii*, but as it is surface rooting, it should be replanted every other year.

Finally, from the vast range of evergreen ferns (including the recommended *Blechnum spicant* and *Polystichum acrostichoides*) comes *Polypodium vulgare*, whose long narrow fronds remain and are at their best in mid-winter at a time when many others die down. One of the best of cool wall plants, the polypody will feel its way along wall joints furnishing them with its lacy fronds.

The autumn and winter garden

Perennials
Among perennials, the change from a bright summer display is usually gradual, but once the peak is passed, focus falls on the relatively few autumn glories. These are by no means confined to Michaelmas daisies and chrysanthemums. If you have taken the trouble to make some sacrifices when allocating space to summer-flowering plants, you will now be rewarded.

Autumn companions for Michaelmas daisies
The time has passed since people relied solely upon Michaelmas daisies and consequently breeders have tended to stop producing 'novelties'. This has encouraged gardeners to look to the many less frequently used but very worthy subjects which can, in imaginative groupings, enhance the whole range of Michaelmas daisies. What is needed to set off the lavender, violet, purple, mauve, pink and crimson reds of these flowers are yellow and white subjects, especially those displaying spikes. Stately *Cimicifuga spp* and *Artemisia lactiflora* (with its creamy plumes) are outstanding for this purpose, so are the yellow rudbeckias (cone flowers). But avoid the tallest growing specimens, such as *Cimicifuga racemosa* and *Rudbeckia laciniata* which can grow 2m (7 ft) tall. The variety *R. laciniata* ' Goldquelle' grows only to a shapely 90 cm-1.05 m (3-3½ ft) with full double flowers of chrome yellow, whilst *R. deamii* (syn. *R. fulgida*) makes a splendid show along with the long-flowering *R. sullivantii* 'Goldsturm'.

There are also singles, with a dark centre, such as the warm, deep pink *R. purpurea* (syn. *Echinacea*), 'Robert Bloom'. None of these need supporting. The *Aster novae-angliae* 'Elma Potschke' does, but it is worth the trouble.

Colourful beds without stakes
Among the range of *Aster amellus*, the section of mere dwarfs (45 cm-90 cm 1½ ft-3 ft) should be given serious consideration. Like the even smaller *A. thomsonii* 'Nana' and *A. spectabilis* (a dwarf aster, particularly useful for front positions in a border), these asters rid us of the problem which characterizes the taller perennials - namely that of keeling over at the slightest breath of breeze. Using taller spiky subjects such as the already mentioned cimicifuga and rudbeckia as a background (possibly mixed with the late flowering agapanthus (African lily) and aconitums such as *A. arendsii, A. fischeri* and *A. wilsonii* to provide the necessary blue shades), a really colourful autumn bed or border can be planned. You might also choose some hardy chrysanthemums for additional tones of yellow, pink, copper and red.

Aster novae-angliae 'Elma Potschke'

Winter colours
By the end of the first months of winter Michaelmas daisies are looking somewhat bedraggled and it is left largely to the hardy chrysanthemums to provide warm shades of colour. There are so many of these, both double and single, that you may find it helpful to limit your choice to bright and cheerful yellows, coppery and red tones. Very valuable too are the single-flowered rubellum types such as the old 'Clara Curtis' for pink, though most other colours are also represented. Single chrysanthemums are less prone to weather damage than doubles and, on the whole, hardier. So too is the little button-flowered type, which makes shapely bushes 60 cm-90 cm (2 ft-3 ft) high, studded with small double flowers in several colours.

Late winter
Adonis amurensis 'Fukujukai' is always the first true perennial to raise its greenish gold buds above the cold soil. It emerges at roughly the same time as the winter aconites, but with flowers five times the size. Some hellebores appear even before the Christmas rose, *H. niger*, which in Britain seldom shows until late January. *H. colchicus* in deep pink and *H. atrorubens*, maroon, are true harbingers of spring. Even though the frost-bound soil may make them droop their cups, hiding the golden anthers within, they will always recover. In a mild winter, then, there is a good number of different flowers to anticipate spring, which are further increased as spring arrives with the pulmonarias and hepaticas in pink and blue, and the wealth of variations (white, cream, pink and purple) on *Helleborus orientalis*, the Lenten rose.

Alpines in late winter
Remember that alpines are also hardy perennials. They can be very useful in the interest-through-the-year garden because in nature many come from high altitudes and their peak period for flower is several weeks ahead of taller subjects. This is invaluable for the late winter/early spring period. Planning alpines with an eye for year-round colour is dealt with on page 157. In an area of say 4.5m (15 ft) by 3m (10 ft) over one hundred different kinds of plants can be grown, with something of interest from late winter to early winter the same year. To satisfy the various needs of these plants, it is advised that you prepare three pockets of specially prepared soil. A scree mix containing 50% grit (chippings, crushed stone and sand) to make a depth of at least 30 cm (12 in) will accommodate the choice 'high' alpines, mainly liking lime. A sandy or gravelly loam will do for the easy, adaptable kinds. A pocket of peat-based, humus-rich soil (up to 80% peat with lime-free sand and loam) should be created for the rest. Try to arrange these so that there is a measure of shade over the peaty area for those kinds which do not like full sun. There is no need for barriers between the plots, but if desired, a stepping-stone walkabout would serve well. Gentle slopes which maintain an average soil depth of 30 cm (12 in) could be incorporated; if they are, use a sheltered slope for the peat mix.

The easy adaptable aubrietas.

Colchicum speciosum 'Atrorubens'

Nerine bowdenii

Cyclamen coum, Gallanthus nivalis

Bulbs, corms and tubers

Autumn sees the *Colchicum* family come into its own. *C. speciosum* is probably the finest specimen with large globose flowers coloured from deep mauve (*C.s.* 'Disraeli') to pinkish lilac (*C.s.* 'Lilac Wonder') to white (*C.s.* 'Album'). Still earlier in flower comes *C. autumnale* with its lilac-pink, crocus-like flowers (a subject eminently suitable for lawn planting). The deep yellow flowers of *Sternbergia lutea* will also be out as the season begins as will the autumn snowdrops, *Galanthus corcyrensis* and *G. nivalis reginae-olgae*. Remember too the last of the hardy cyclamen, *C. cilicium*, a scented pale pink flower with a red marking at its base.

Colchicum autumnale is often known as the autumn crocus because of the shape of its flowers. Beware the confusion with the true varieties such as *Crocus pulchellus*, with its pale lavender flowers, and the even earlier flowering *Crocus speciosus*. This last-named crocus is most highly recommended not just for the bluish mauve colouring of its bloom but for its free-flowering habit prior to leaf development and its free-spreading nature (both by seed and small corms).

For taller subjects, look to the deep pink headed *Nerine bowdenii*, which appear in early autumn on 45 cm (18 in) stems. They insist upon a sunny position but are

particularly valuable as cut flowers for display indoors at a time when little else is suitable. *Crinum* x *powellii* is another tall growing bulb for early autumn when it produces heads of lily-like pink ('Krelagei') or white ('Album') flowers on 1m (3 ft) long stems.

Early flowering bulbs

The earliest bulbs in the New Year are, strictly speaking, winter-flowering, though many people welcome them as the very first signs of spring. Very severe or unreasonably mild weather may in turn delay or advance flowering but on the average one may expect a number to flower in winter. Among these are *Cyclamen coum* in its many forms, which come under a number of aliases such as *atkinsii, hiemalis* and *orbiculatum*. They will usually be among the first of the New Year's flowers. They are very dwarf with rounded leaves, either plain or marbled, and the flowers will usually be in a carmine shade. There is an early form of the giant snowdrop, *Galanthus elwesii*, but otherwise the earliest snowdrop is *G. caucasicus*, of which the double form increases prodigiously and continues to flower even when the clumps are left for years. The earliest crocus is *C. imperati*, which is also one of the loveliest. It is large for a crocus, with a rosy-mauve flower which is invisible until there is sufficient warmth for it to open. The Winter Aconites (*Eranthis hyemalis*) are often in flower at about the same

time. They are very dwarf when in flower, although the stems later elongate. The fairly large blue flowers of the exotic-looking *Iris histrioides* will come up through snow and frost and give what seems an unseasonable brilliance to the end-of-winter garden.

This is followed by the taller *Iris reticulata*, usually with purple flowers and with a delicious scent of violets; there are also pale blue and reddish-purple forms. This is one of the finest late winter flowers, although the best known must be the snowdrop, *Galanthus nivalis*. There is also an early-flowering form of the gentian-blue *Scilla bifolia*. Another scilla which usually opens is the pale porcelain-blue *S. tubergeniana*. In a mild year the various blues of *Anemone blanda* make a welcome appearance, while a little later many crocuses open their flowers, including the old favourite 'Dutch Yellow', the various forms of *C. chrysanthus*, the prolific *C. tommasinianus* and many others in shades of mauve, yellow and white.

Indeed, in Britain, most crocus species open in February and it is only the larger Dutch hybrids which wait until March. All these February flowers are 15 cm (6 in) or less in height. The daffodil 'February Gold', which is slightly taller, is somewhat optimistically named and in fact you will rarely find it out before spring.

191

Indoor plant planning

Using plants indoors

In many homes, use of potted plants has advanced some way beyond placing the odd few examples in individual pots along window ledges. If we can think of the humble tradescantia as the forerunner of the modern houseplant, then it is not difficult to see how far planning possibilities have stretched. From the solitary plant of a few years ago we now have a trend where plants are being used as decorative alternatives to conventional pieces of furniture. Containerized plants are invariably more attractive and interesting than a piece of furniture, and in most instances less expensive. So, besides their aesthetic appeal plants can, in most instances, be a more economical proposition when it comes to filling space indoors. Increasingly we now see plants as specially designed features that serve as an important part of the general decor.

They may be selected for their sculptural presence in which case lighting and the colour of a background wall become significant factors. They could simply be chosen for their ability to disguise unpleasant features or, more ambitiously, to create visual illusions. Tall, thin plants, such as the elegantly trunked, palm-like *Dracaena marginata*, might be selected to heighten a low ceiling, for example. But whatever function they are chosen to fulfil, never lose sight of *their* needs and avoid the temptation to move them around the house. They need a settled environment.

Developing a sense of colour, growth rate and habit

There are people who have a natural ability when it comes to displaying things. 'Things' can be almost anything from soft furnishing, to plants, to decorating materials. It is in integrating plant life into the overall design concept of a room that success lies. This demands a sound sense of colour scheming – how one colour blends and contrasts successfully with another.

Plants for a purpose

Indoor plants can be used as focal points in a room or to highlight other parts of the decor. Just as in the garden, a feature or focal point needs to be framed (frequently with foliage plants that direct the eye and evoke background interest with subtle colour variations, textures and contrasting growth habits) so indoor plants can fulfil the same purpose to show off favourite items.

When introducing colour into arrangements, as **below right**, you can choose tones that will highlight colours in the room, perhaps drawing attention to a painting or some feature other than the display itself.

The elegant *Dracaena marginata,* **above right**, gives a height to a low-ceilinged room in effective conjunction with a grandfather clock.

With the possible exception of multi and brightly coloured plants of the croton tribe, the majority of purely foliage plants are not difficult to match with interiors. Some flair is needed when brightly coloured flowering plants are brought into play. But by incorporating plants with soft, cool green foliage, (ferns for example) you can tone down most strong colours and introduce subtlety into an arrangement.

Unlike conventional flower arranging, when creating an indoor plant display in a container, you should avoid the temptation to pack in too many plants to provide an immediate effect. The plant collection should grow and evolve into a natural and pleasing shape over a period of many months. Try to imagine the eventual rather than immediate effect when placing plants in position. This will entail allowing them reasonable growth space, and it may also mean placing more spreading and trailing plants such as ivies, tradescantias and *Ficus pumila* around the *outer* edge of the container. More upright plants such as fatshedera, sansevieria and heptapleurum (sometimes sold as *Schefflera venulora erystastachys*) should be placed in the centre of the arrangement.

Inclusion of flowering plants in permanent arrangements can present problems as at some point they leave the collection bereft of colour. That may suit you, but consider leaving plants such as African violets, cyclamen and begonias in their original growing pots within the arrangement. This will mean watering them independently of the rest, but you can then easily remove the flowering plant as soon as it has passed its best so that something else colourful can be introduced. Arrangements that consist entirely of flowering plants can be very effective and though they will test your skill, you shouldn't be afraid to experiment. One of the principal benefits of the purely foliage selection is that a good light location is not so essential.

Creating a display
Make growth habit work for you in a display. Look for an overall shape appropriate to its position and introduce incidental features within it.

Environment

In a book about outdoor gardening it is perhaps unusual to find a section on growing and using plants in the home, but in fact there are very few true gardeners who do not take their hobby indoors. With houseplants, as in the garden, it is important to select the right sort of plants for the conditions the house has to offer and to have clear reasons for your choice.

Plants of quality
Shopping around for quality plants will prove to be a rewarding exercise – even though the chosen plants may be a little more expensive.

Even the best indoor plants require some help if they are to survive an indoor environment, so there is little hope for a poor and weedy specimen clinging desperately to life as a result of poor culture or indifferent handling.

Growing conditions
In recent years, the range of quality plants available has increased phenomenally, but one should still choose with care as many of the more tender plants are only suitable for the experienced grower and require very sympathetic conditions if they are to thrive. Most plants offered for sale will have tags attached giving brief directions on how the particular plant should be cared for – information on temperature, room position, feeding, watering and such like.

Creating a favourable environment
The plants that you buy will have been grown in a greenhouse environment for many months, perhaps years, while they are reaching maturity.

Smaller plants such as *Ficus pumila* will have occupied greenhouse space for around nine months, while specimen plants of *Monstera deliciosa* will have had careful professional attention for three to four years. Very few, if any, of the millions of plants that change hands annually will have any sort of conditioning treatment to help

them to adjust to the very different conditions that prevail within the home or office after the moist, warm and humid air that prevails in the glasshouses. Consequently, during the settling-in period it is not unusual for many plants to suffer some form of setback. Shedding of some leaves in the case of *Ficus benjamina* is a possibility, also the loss of flower buds in the case of hibiscus. But, provided adequate light and reasonable warmth are made available, the majority of plants will settle down remarkably well.

Surprisingly, the constitution of many plants appears to have changed in that previously difficult plants, such as *Scindapsus aureus*, are now much easier to manage, both indoors and in the greenhouse, than they were a decade or so ago. One wonders why this should be. Clearly cultural conditions and knowledge of plant needs have improved, but mainly the careful selection of the best material when propagating new plants has made it possible to achieve hardier, more tolerant strains.

When creating displays in the home it is important to ensure that the chosen location is free from harmful draughts, and that plants are not placed too close to fires or radiators as these will dehydrate the foliage, and certainly scorch any leaves that come into direct contact. In rooms that become excessively hot and dry, the introduction of a humidifier will have a marked improvement on their performance and be well worth the extra cost. Excessively dry conditions will cause havoc with the majority of houseplants which require a reasonable amount of moisture in the atmosphere in order to do well. In order to provide localized moisture around plants, a fine hand-sprayer – used once or twice each day when temperatures are high – is quite effective, though generally the installation of a humidifier or utilization of the pebble-and-water technique mentioned on page 195 is preferable.

Light and temperature
Environmental conditions sympathetic to plant growth are not difficult to establish indoors. Temperatures can be lowered or increased and if there is insufficient natural light, an artificial lighting system is a good practical substitute. A temperature in the region of 16° to 21°C to (61° to 70°F) suits the majority of plants.

Artificial light
Indoor plants like permanent darkness no more than outdoor plants. There is no reason why indoor plants should suffer from a lack of light, even in the most dingy environment. Flourescent tube units have been designed specifically to alleviate the problem, and are readily available. Even ordinary domestic tubes can be used, but select the 'daylight' variety rather than 'cool white'. Reflectors will help concentrate the growing properties of light where it is needed.

The proximity of light source to plants is an important consideration and a distance of 30 to 45 cm (12 to 18 in) is generally recommended. Placed too far away from the light source, a plant will grow a long, weak stem as it struggles to reach it. Placed too near, there is a real danger of bleaching or shrivelling.

Lighting for plants with colourful or variegated leaves
Plants with colourful or variegated leaves such as crotons, tradescantias, or ivies will do better and retain their colouring in good light; whereas those with green leaves such as monstera, philodendron and rhoicissus will be better suited to light shade. Indeed, some of the latter can survive dark areas that might seem quite alien.

Of all the purely foliage plants that are at present offered for sale *Scindapsus aureus*, with its attractive yellow and green variegation, is one of the finest. These plants can be encouraged either to climb or trail depending on what is wanted, and it is one of the very few variegated plants which will do extremely well in conditions that offer relatively poor light.

Lighting for flowering plants
In order to give of their best, all flowering plants such as cyclamen, begonias, poinsettias and saintpaulias (African violets), must be placed in the lightest possible location. The exception is in very hot countries where plants will need to be taken down or protected with a sheet of newspaper while the sun is at its hottest.

Water
The good gardener knows that water can be life or death to many plants.

Providing a sympathetic environment

* Keep the room free from draughts.

* Avoid rooms with fluctuating temperatures.

* Keep plants away from radiators that will dehydrate their foliage.

* Discover what conditions your plants like. Not all plants prefer sun, though adequate light and

reasonable warmth must be provided. All flowering plants need maximum light.

* Use a humidifier if a room is excessively hot and dry. Alternatively, regular hand-spraying can be effective.

* Regulate water supply seasonally and to suit individual subjects.

Care and maintenance
Make sure that water reaches roots in the lower part of the pot. Check for obvious signs of pests and fungal diseases. Ensure the container is the right size, and feed regularly during the plant's active period.

Check for pests and diseases.

Ensure an easy passage of air and water.

Some neglected plants need to be submerged in water.

A layer of pebbles in an outer container reduces root rot problems and ensures adequate moisture.

Ironically, the majority of pot plants die from too much, rather than too little watering. Whatever method of watering one adopts it is most important to ensure that the soil in the pot is thoroughly soaked each time the plant is watered. When watering from the top of the pot, surplus water should be seen to drain from the holes in the bottom of the container. Surplus water that has accumulated in the container or dish in which the plant is standing should be tipped away. Thereafter, it is extremely important that the soil in the pot should be allowed to dry appreciably, before watering again. Less water is generally needed in winter, and some plants (azaleas and hibiscus being examples) require much more frequent watering than others (plant care cards are usually reliable).

It is worth noting that some of the plants mentioned here and above, such as cyclamen, poinsettias, azaleas and hibiscus are regarded in America as 'gift' or 'holiday' plants and not bought as houseplants as they are in Europe. It is also interesting that American homes are generally kept very warm and dry in winter. Wherever they are grown, such conditions do not suit these so-called gift plants in the long term.

Watering
An important point to remember when watering, is that the majority of roots in almost all potted plants are in the lower part of the pot. It is essential,

therefore, that water should reach this area and not simply moisten the surface of the soil. Potted azaleas should be watered by submerging the plant pot in a bucketful of water. This is the best way of watering any plant that has become excessively dry for one reason or another. When older plants form a hard crust of surface soil, use a pointed stick or pencil to break up the hard soil thereby improving aeration and allowing water to penetrate more readily.

Maintaining a healthy environment
Pests and diseases
It is important to ensure that new plants are free of pests. Of course, a healthy and vigorous plant will always be less susceptible to pest and disease attack. It is seldom possible to inspect minutely every leaf of a plant, but do check for more obvious signs of unwanted visitors in the shape of greenfly, whitefly, mealy bug and scale insects – all of which can be clearly seen by the naked eye. Remember that pests on recently acquired plants will quite quickly move to and infect other plants.

Besides the more mobile insects, plants may also suffer from fungal problems such as mildew and botytis – the latter produces rotting foliage, while the former shows as a white powdery deposit on the upper surfaces. Begonias are particularly susceptible to mildew

and should always be carefully inspected. Dank and airless conditions in the greenhouse or in the home favour all forms of fungus that may attack prime plants. So, maintaining a buoyant atmosphere should be a prime consideration through, fortunately, only a small percentage of houseplants are affected by fungus and there are numerous proprietary fungicides available to treat it. However, in the event that a plant becomes badly affected it is best to remove the worst leaves, and in extreme instances, it will be wise to destroy the plant.

Potting and feeding
As soon as a plant is brought indoors, it should be fed with one of the many commercially available proprietary fertilizers. Regular feeding should continue while plants are most active; but avoid feeding for several months after re-potting into larger containers. Re-potting should be undertaken from spring to early summer to ensure that plants have settled down in their new pots before the winter, when their growth naturally tends to be less active. For preference, a properly prepared potting mixture should be used – there are many different kinds available. But do ensure that it is reasonably fresh and has not been lying around for months with the retailer. Potting should be done with firmness but the soil should not be packed too hard as many indoor plants have very fine root systems that cannot easily penetrate compacted soil. The re-potting sequence should be a gradual process, with each new pot being only a little larger than the one from which the plant is transferred. To improve drainage in a clay pot it is essential to place a few pieces of broken flower pot in the bottom, but this is not necessary when using plastic pots as they are provided with many more drainage holes.

Decorative outer pots will considerably enhance the general appearance of almost all plants. To obtain the best effect, it is important that the outer pot should be a good fit, and it is extremely important that the growing pot should periodically be removed to ensure that water draining from the inner growing pot has not accumulated in the decorative outer one. Indoor plants which have been allowed to stand in water for long periods will inevitably develop root rot troubles as a result of roots being badly aerated. When standing plant pots in a saucer or in a decorative outer pot it is advisable to place them on a layer of small pebbles. Not only is there less possibility of damaging their roots but they will benefit from the additional moisture in the surrounding atmosphere.

195

Planning ideas

While it is true that houseplant growers will always be concerned with plant care, there is an increasing awareness of how effective multi-plant containers and hydroponic systems are as display media. Indeed, Rochfords – England's foremost indoor plant specialists – receives more and more questions about how plants should be *displayed* rather than how much water or feeding they require.

There are many types of planters, which can accommodate a selection of plants. These can be filled with soil and planted conventionally, or they can be utilized as hydroponic units that use water, clay granules and special fertilizer to maintain plants in good condition. If soil is incorporated great

care must be exercised when watering, as few of these containers have drainage holes in their base.

To obviate the possibility of overwatering these units, consider inserting a plastic tube filled with soil. The tube should protrude above the soil surface so that a cane of suitable length can be used as a 'dipstick' to ascertain whether or not water is accumulating in the bottom of the container and likely to become a hazard.

There are many hydroponic systems that one can employ to good effect and comprehensive directions are usually available when units are acquired. Possibly the greatest benefit of growing by this method is that the

watering problem can be eliminated. In hydroponic systems, water levels are clearly defined. There is no possibility of over or under watering provided that simple rules are obeyed.

When purchasing plants, remember that it is a general rule that a few mature, bolder types of plant prove much more satisfactory in the long run than a motley collection of small plants. Smaller plants are usually more difficult to care for, and it really is wishful thinking that all small plants will, in time, develop into mature specimens. Ordinary indoor conditions are only very occasionally conducive to lush plant growth of the sort that one would expect in the greenhouse of a professional grower.

Today, plants are seen as part of the decor, but sometimes one or two bold feature plants (such as *Monstera deliciosa*, **far right**, or one of the range of the popular *Ficus* species, **below**) can, in the long run, be more successful than a motley collection of smaller plants. Of course, if you decide to give space to a plant room (**left**), the opportunities are enormous provided you remember the plants' needs as well as yours. **Right:** shows the skilful use of a climber to frame and focus a view.

197

Bringing the garden indoors

Planning ideas

Suspended units

Plants can be put to many uses indoors but one of the most attractive ways of setting them off, and giving them a very good chance of doing well, is to place them in a hanging container of some kind. Decorative pots filled with plants and suspended in macrame hangers can be important and colourful features. When locating hanging plants, the same rules still apply in respect of light, warmth and fresh air. Suspending plants at too high a level will present problems when it comes to watering and general maintenance, and the majority of plants are more attractive when placed a little above head height. It certainly makes it much easier to check their needs and attend to them. Plants placed in wall brackets seldom do as well as hanging ones, as the brackets made for this purpose are invariably intended for small pots which, in turn, are extremely difficult to maintain when pinned to the wall as they dry out more rapidly there than in almost any other position.

Although mixed collections of plants suspended in containers can be attractive, it is generally much better to place plants of one variety in each basket or pot. Probably the best plant for this purpose is the *Scindapsus aureus* mentioned earlier. Besides this there are tradescantias in wide variety, and closely allied to these is the very fine *Zebrina pendula*. The nephrolepis (Boston) fern (in its many varieties) can also be spectacular, and for differing shades of green there are *Rhoicissus rhomboidea, Philodendron scandens* and *Ficus pumila*. These are only a few examples of suitable plants and many other interesting and colourful ones can be found.

Of the flowering plants for use as hangers, a popular choice is busy Lizzy, or *Impatiens spp.*, of which there are now many very interesting variations. Like all flowering plants in the home, these require good light if they are to flower as well as they are able to.

Above: a suspended unit can double as a room divider. **Below left:** *Scindapsus aureus* is a trailer liking warm shade. This variety is 'Marble Queen'.

The ivies make easy-to-manage hanging plants, seen **below** arranged with *Neanthe bella, Ficus benjamina, Rhoicissus rhomboidea* and *Dieffenbachia picta.*

Room dividers

Indoor plants can be functional as well as decorative, and this is probably best illustrated in the modern open plan office interior. By definition, few solid dividing walls exist, and to segregate one section from its neighbour, containers filled with potted plants may be put to very good use. In using plants, the entire floor plan is suddenly more flexible. The various sections of the office can be enlarged or reduced with little effort. In fact, many of the plant containers are designed with just this sort of flexibility and movement in mind; they are fitted with castors that make re-positioning a very simple task.

Above left: *Rhoicissus rhomboidea*, one of the toughest house plants can be used as a feature plant or as a trailer, as can *Philodendron scandens* (**above right**).

Below: the art of screening is, as outside, not to obliterate the view altogether, but to distract the eye. **Below right:** the vigorous *Tetrastigma voinerianum*.

In larger rooms in the home, plants can also be used to section off one part of the room from another, and plants used for this purpose are frequently referred to in the trade as room dividers. They are available in various shapes and sizes, perhaps the most popular being *Rhoicissus rhomboidea*. This has fresh green colouring, tri-lobe leaves and is a very durable climbing plant if given some form of support (a patterned trellis is ideal). The same plant could also be used as a natural trailer. Other plants that can be encouraged to climb in similar fashion are *Philodendron scandens*, which has green heart-shaped leaves, *Cissus antarctica*, which is also green but somewhat coarser in appearance, and possibly the most vigorous of them all, *Tetrastigma voinierianum*. The latter is a natural climbing plant, not so attractive alone, but ideal as a backing plant. It will tolerate very severe pruning should it get out of hand.

Room dividing plants may be left in their pots or alternatively a trough type of container can be used. Smaller plants can then be placed around the taller ones to achieve a more complete effect. However, remember that the lower plants will usually be in shade, so choose only more durable plants. Do not plant so densely that the divider obliterates a view.

Integrating house and garden

Bringing the garden indoors

Creating a natural link between the garden and the house is something that can be done either simply and at little cost, or on a grand scale which may involve a considerable outlay. For the simple approach there can be no better choice than that made for the old fashioned English cottage with its honeysuckle and clematis growing in profusion on walls and even across windows. (One wonders why they never seem to grow as well on modern buildings!) The link here was invariably a galaxy of geraniums and other flowering pot plants placed on the window ledge inside the house. The view from outside the cottage was a perfect example of the unification of home and garden by the simple use of collections of quite ordinary plants.

Another way of providing this link is with window boxes – ensure that they are a snug and secure fit. The box can then be filled with all sorts of interesting plants and for little more than the effort of watering and feeding will provide a colourful and interesting display for much of the year. You may decide to change the planting according to the season, but there is no reason why the container should not be filled with a collection of dwarf conifers and trailing ivies that in mild areas will survive throughout the year. See also page 130.

The dedicated houseplant grower may prefer to fit the box on an inside ledge and fill it with a collection of foliage and flowering houseplants. For the real enthusiast, the happiest match of all would be to have a window box on the inside *and* outside ledges so that maximum benefit may be obtained. As ever, when planting these boxes, avoid the temptation to overfill at the beginning, for plants put into boxes with fresh potting mixture will very soon grow to their allotted space. Overplanted, a box may become congested to the point at which few plants will do very well. Selection of plants is a matter of personal choice, but it is important not to use plants that are likely to become too tall in the centre of a window box. These should be kept to the sides, if they are used at all, in order to preserve the purpose of the window to let light into the room.

For an attractive home and garden link, there can be few better investments than a pair of wide and handsome french windows. When open they will let all the smell and feeling of the garden into the home. If space and finances permit, the ideal is for the french windows to lead into a conservatory or garden room, which in turn would lead into the garden. With a little

thought and effort, even without heating, the garden room can provide colour and interest right through the gardening year.

But it is important when contemplating a garden room to ensure that the leisure aspect is not forgotten. It may be very tempting to fill the place with plants, but it will be more appealing if a reasonable area can be earmarked for chairs and tables so that one may better enjoy the surroundings.

As with all indoor plants, a clutter of smaller plants will seldom have as much appeal as fewer and bolder plants, and the latter will need less care and attention. The floor should be attractively tiled or slabbed over and the only permanent fixtures a few climbing plants against the solid wall of the house. Otherwise everything should be in containers so that they may be moved to form new arrangements. Having a portable display also gives one the advantage of placing many of the container out on the patio or in the garden during the summer months when space in the garden room is more in demand. Plants can then be returned to the glassed area for protection during the winter.

You should consider the area immediately inside the french windows. This

would provide a natural link between both areas, even before one considers the introduction of plants. A continuation of the tiled area could become a garden of exotic plants within the living room itself. (Arrange the plants in a crescendo of height and interest to meet the doors.) There is the added benefit that water spillage presents fewer problems on tiles. If starting the house design from scratch there would be every reason for fitting the tiled plant area with proper drainage, even a water supply if the area was large enough to justify it.

Plants placed on cool, moist paving within the house will be infinitely happier and grow very much better than similar plants standing around on carpets or pinned to the wall in generally arid surroundings.

Framing a door

For a tall and graceful plant there are few that compare with the ever popular *Ficus benjamina*, its glossy green leaves are borne on branches with a natural weeping appearance. Very similar, but with finer leaves and a more pronounced weeping habit is *F. benjamina nuda*. (In poor light both of these plants have a tendency to shed leaves. However, direct sunlight streaming through a window pane should be avoided.) Another tall

growing plant with attractive cut-out leaves and an erect habit is *Philodendron pertusum*. In appearance it is very similar to the popular monstera but does not have the same spread of leaves which makes it more suitable for indoor life. There are many other taller plants which can be employed for framing the door out to the garden – a wide selection can be found at any good plant shop.

When considering a major plant purchase, seek the advice of the supplier. This service will almost invariably be free and it may save a lot of costly disappointment if the right plants are chosen at the beginning.

With each indoor display a balanced assortment of heights is best and one should endeavour to select plants that will be compatible and likely to prosper in the conditions that are being provided. Besides the taller plants there will be intermediate sizes, or plants raised on pedestals if they should be lacking in stature. To complete the arrangement you will need a collection of compact or spreading plants for filling in the front, and there is no shortage of these. There are masses of different ivies and tradescantias, small leaved ficus, dieffenbachias, aglaonemas, marantas, with anthuriums and spathiphyllums to provide additional colour when their striking flowers are produced.

French windows provide an ideal means to integrate house and garden. A 'wall' of glass (**above left**) ensures glimpses of garden foliage through skilfully placed hanging baskets. **Below:** a balcony garden brings brighter cheer to a city skyline.

If the room is to open directly on to a paved patio, as many do, there could be a good argument for using patio plant containers that are complementary to the indoor ones, so that there is a further link between the two areas.

Patios that are provided with a timber overhang can give another dimension to the garden when viewed from inside and out, particularly when suitably filled hanging baskets are suspended from the timber support.

201

Putting the garden to use

Home growers rarely raise fruit and vegetables for reasons of poverty or frugality, although if the gardener's time is not at a premium, money can be saved. They do so because a well-planned vegetable or fruit garden will yield harvests of a quality far beyond that available in most retail outlets, and because a 'productive' plot is the source of a very special satisfaction – its harvest is appreciated collectively; it is almost always a shared enjoyment.

The original English cottage gardeners – workers living largely off the land – would marvel at the formality of the plans detailed here. They used to scatter their vegetables in amongst flowers and shrubs. Some more modern gardeners might actually welcome formality for its own sake. But the *raison d'etre* of the plans and the 'greenhouse as powerhouse' section, is a drive for efficiency, effectiveness and utility, and is grounded in sound common sense. The experienced grower may have other interests in the plants themselves – their origin and development, their relationship to each other and to wild and garden flowers. But he will, above all, appreciate their different cultural needs and welcome a straightforward plan that is designed to produce a healthy, tasty crop, year after year, without using chemical poisons and insecticides.

The plans for the herb and flower arranger's garden, on the other hand, recommend more of a balance between aesthetics and utility. The reader is encouraged to be aware of the historical associations of herbs, their colour and form, as well as to plan according to their medicinal, culinary and other uses. Again, the principles behind the flower arranger's garden arise out of a respect for the whole garden's appearance as much as the arranger's art.

The vegetable garden

There is a great sense of achievement in growing your own vegetables, particularly if they look as good as the pictures on the seed packets and taste a little better than most of those in the shops. It is not always possible for the commercial grower to put taste at the top of his list of priorities as his crops must travel well, look good value for money and make a show on display. Taste will be somewhere on his list but not in the first three places. With the amateur gardener it is right there at the top. He grows varieties that you just cannot buy - such as Little Gem lettuce or Tom Thumb, Gardener's Delight tomatoes or Tiny Tim, and those small, full-of-flavour Marvel peas. It is not just that *you* have grown them, home-grown vegetables really can taste better if you take sufficient care. To say nothing of the pleasure of walking round the garden, selecting what you want, picking them there and then, and eating them within the hour.

If you want to throw flavour to the wind and grow the biggest carrot in the world to impress the neighbours, you can do so. The choice is yours.

Most amateur vegetable gardeners like to feel that growing their own can save a bit of money. It doesn't come out that way if cost of labour is included but as most of us need the exercise anyway we are generally happy to give our labour free of charge.

A real advantage is being able to grow crops completely free from artificial insecticides, fungicides and herbicides.

Of course, great care is taken by manufacturers to make these products foolproof but mother nature, with a little help and encouragement, can do very well without them. Again, there is a choice.

But vegetable growing is not all free choices. To grow really top quality produce year after year in the same plot means that there are some essential rules to follow and some planning which has to be done.

Without these rules the soil will become thin and starved and almost certainly diseased. You may know what it is like to inherit gardens like that. Fortunately matters can usually be put right.

Why our plants have different needs

If you have a vegetable garden big enough to keep a family of four supplied with a variety of produce for most of the year - perhaps freezing some - you may want to grow over thirty varieties or types of vegetable. Even if you have just one modest plot of 6 m by

3 m (20 ft by 10 ft) you might still want to grow ten different things.

This is quite a tall order considering that our vegetables have originated from many different parts of the world. In some cases their origins are lost in the mists of time, but it seems that beet came from the Mediterranean countries, cucumber from the north of India, carrots and parsnips were native to Britain and Europe, tomatoes and potatoes grew in America and were 'discovered' by the European explorers, runner beans came from South America, and in the bronze age the lake dwellers of Switzerland were eating a type of broad bean. Right back through history the onion has been much prized. The ancient Egyptians were sensible enough to award it divine honours - a vegetable fit for the gods.

As vegetables come from all these varied parts of the world, do they not need quite different growing conditions? Fortunately, over the centuries, Man with his ingenuity has been breeding and selecting varieties of these plants so that they will grow side by side, and flourish, in most of the temperate zones of the world and in large areas of the tropical zones too, if they can be supplied with enough water. But plants do have different needs in spite of the selecting and reselecting that

has gone on. And, in addition to this, gardeners make differing demands upon the plants.

Carrots and parsnips must have good straight roots because that is the part which is eaten. What the leaves are like is unimportant, whereas with cabbage, spinach and lettuce it is very important that the leaves develop the way we want them to. With potatoes it is the tubers that are sought after, with peas the seeds and with runner beans the seed cases. With marrows, zucchini or tomatoes, it is the total 'fruit'.

How they are all treated depends on the part of the plant to be eaten. Runner beans and zucchini courgettes need plenty of compost or manure at their roots to produce a good crop, but if carrots are reared on new manure they grow all forked and tangled. And it is no good going to the other extreme and growing them on poor soil or they will be weak, unlovely things. Give them a deeply dug soil that was manured for a previous crop and then they will grow long and straight and true.

On the other hand brassicas - the cabbage family - thrive on newly manured ground. They are a large family with the botanical name *Cruciferae* which includes Brussels sprouts, broccoli, cauliflower, kale,

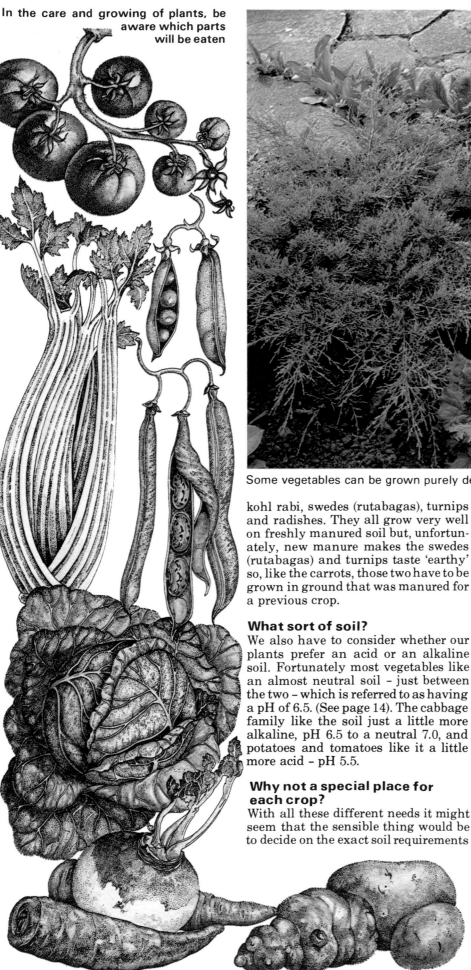

In the care and growing of plants, be aware which parts will be eaten

Some vegetables can be grown purely decoratively.

kohl rabi, swedes (rutabagas), turnips and radishes. They all grow very well on freshly manured soil but, unfortunately, new manure makes the swedes (rutabagas) and turnips taste 'earthy' so, like the carrots, those two have to be grown in ground that was manured for a previous crop.

What sort of soil?
We also have to consider whether our plants prefer an acid or an alkaline soil. Fortunately most vegetables like an almost neutral soil – just between the two – which is referred to as having a pH of 6.5. (See page 14). The cabbage family like the soil just a little more alkaline, pH 6.5 to a neutral 7.0, and potatoes and tomatoes like it a little more acid – pH 5.5.

Why not a special place for each crop?
With all these different needs it might seem that the sensible thing would be to decide on the exact soil requirements of each type of plant, give it its own special place in the garden and grow it there each year. In fact perennial crops like asparagus and globe artichokes do very well raised in their own beds.

But for most vegetables it just won't do. Like the rest of the plant and animal kingdoms, vegetables suffer from pests and diseases. Some are air borne and will get at your plants anyway, but many of the serious ones are soil borne. They stay in the soil ready to infect plants of the same family in successive years. You may have had it happen or seen it happen in someone else's garden – marvellous crops the first two or three years and then deterioration as diseases got a hold. And because the same kind of plants were being grown in the same spot there would probably also be a deficiency of certain necessary plant nutrients.

Our ancestors used to call it 'soil sickness' and let a part of their land lie fallow each year with no crops on it at all. It helped to cure the soil sickness but meant they grew less crops. Today's gardener doesn't want land lying fallow, but does want to avoid nutrient deficiency and the survival from year to year of soil borne pests and diseases. This can be achieved by crop rotation.

205

The vegetable garden

Crop rotation

This means growing different crops in a specific order to avoid exhausting or contaminating the soil.

Plants belong to families and a disease of one plant can affect other plants in the same family. Club-root, a well known disease of cabbages, can be passed on *through the soil* to another member of the cabbage family, broccoli or turnips, say, but will have no effect on potatoes. Potato blight, which can affect tomatoes (a close relative), has no effect on runner beans. So if you know the botanical family to which each plant belongs, you can work out a system of rotation to ensure that no member of a particular plant family is grown in the same place more than once in three years, or preferably four.

This rotation system will give plant diseases a chance to die out or decline in severity before the same type of crop is grown in the same place again. It will prevent many pests and diseases getting a hold in the first place and produce healthier plants to withstand attacks from the air borne nuisances.

The rotation system based on four plant groups

A three-year rotation system is commonly recommended, based on (a) peas and beans (b) brassicas and (c) roots. Although it is better than no rotation system at all, it is not good enough. It doesn't classify plants according to their families and consequently you may get close relatives following each other too soon in the same bed. This is not a good plan. You could, for instance, have sprouting broccoli following swedes (rutabagas)

and as some types of sprouting broccoli spend a year in the soil from planting to final harvesting this might mean a real build-up of club-root.

For a good rotation system you need to classify plants in such a way that:

* The plants in each group have the same cultivation needs as regards manuring and lime.

* Any pests or diseases left in the soil will not affect plants grown in that place next year. You can help them to die out by depriving them for a while of the species upon which they live.

* The classifications reflect the fact that some plants can improve the soil for others. For instance, peas and beans have nodules on their roots containing bacteria that can stabilise nitrogen extracted from the air. If their roots are left in the soil after they are harvested this can help leaf crops subsequently planted in that spot.

Bearing all these points in mind, over forty types of vegetables have been classified into four main groups. It is assumed they will all be grown outdoors; if your locality doesn't suit every one substitution is easy.

In most cases all members of a plant family are in the same group but there are a few exceptions. Turnips, swedes and radishes are brassicas but have different manuring needs, so are listed in the roots group. Be careful when drawing up sowing plans that they never follow in exactly the same soil as leaf brassicas, otherwise diseases may be passed on.

The botanical families to which vegetables belong

Chenopodiaceae	Beetroot. Spinach Beet. Seakale beet. Spinach.
Compositae	Lettuce. Chicory, Endive. Globe artichoke. Jerusalem artichoke. Salsify. Scorzonera.
Cruciferae	Cabbage. Kohl rabi. Broccoli. Cauliflower. Kale. Brussels sprouts Radish. Turnip. Swede. Chinese cabbage.
Cucurbitaceae	Marrow. Courgette. Cucumber. Melon.
Gramineae	Sweet corn.
Leguminosae	Peas. Runner beans. French beans. Haricot beans. Broad beans.
Liliaceae	Onions. Leeks. Shallots. Garlic.
Solanaceae	Potato. Tomato. Capsicum.
Umbelliferae	Parsley. Celery, Celeriac. Parsnip. Carrot.
Valerianaceae	Corn salad.

Fitting the jig-saw together

In deciding on an overall plan, you need to take the following into account:

* To avoid the build-up of diseases in the soil you need to follow a four-year rotation system.

POTATOES GROUP	LEGUMES GROUP	ONIONS AND BRASSICAS	ROOT GROUPS
Capsicum	Legumes: Broad beans	Brassicas: Broccoli	Beetroot (beet)
Courgette (summer squash)	French beans	Brussels sprouts	Carrot
Cucumber	Haricot beans	Cabbage	Chicory (sugar loaf)
Lettuce (late)	(snap beans)	Cauliflower	Endive
Marrow (zucchini)	Peas	Chinese cabbage	Parsnip
Melon	Runner beans	Kale	Radish (early)
Potato	Celeriac	Kohl rabi	Salsify
Seakale beet (Swiss chard)	Celery	Radishes	Schorzonera
Spinach beet	Jerusalem artichokes	Garlic	Spinach
Sweet corn	Lettuce	Leek	Swede (rutagaba)
Tomato	Parsley	Onion	Turnip
		Shallot	
		Salad onion	

* Compost or manure must be present for those plants that need it but not where it would be specifically harmful.

* If tests demand it use a controlled liming programme to ensure the right amount is present for each group each year. Bear in mind the needs of next year's crops as well.

* Remember that one crop may improve the soil for another.

* Some crops are in the ground for a long time, such as leeks and sprouting broccoli. Keep them together in the same part of the garden convenient for winter digging, in a place where they won't be in the way of next year's seed sowing or manuring programme.

* The layout should be such that tall plants like runner beans don't overshadow shorter ones.

* You need a continuous supply of crops of different kinds throughout the year without experiencing a glut one month and scarcity the next.

* Each row of plants must have ample room to grow and mature.

* No ground should be wasted during the growing season.

By putting these pieces of the jig-saw together a picture of your vegetable garden plan will emerge. You will find in later pages a set of detailed cropping and sowing schemes for different sized plots called **The Master Plans**. But first you should consider where your vegetables will be grown in your garden – and how they will fit into your total plan.

A place for vegetables
A well tended kitchen garden is a handsome sight but not everyone would want it as the focal point of the landscape. However don't be tempted to tuck it away in a shady corner of the garden where nothing else will grow. Failure will be your reward. Hide it with flower borders and shrubs if you wish, but do make sure the vegetable garden is sited right out in the open where it will get the greatest amount of light. This may not be easy as almost all gardens are surrounded by hedges, fences, walls or perhaps trees.

Trees. They are beautiful, of course, but if you try to grow vegetables under them or near them you will be disappointed. The roots of most trees extend at least as far as their branches and take plant nutrients and copious amounts of water from the soil. Admire their magnificence but keep your vegetables away from them.

Planning the structural elements
A vegetable garden should be
- open to light
- away from thirsty roots
- sheltered from draughts and turbulence
- demarcated by loosely laid, solid paths
- arranged in rows to attract maximum sun

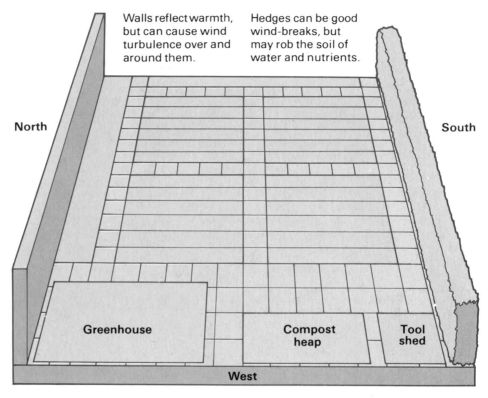

Walls reflect warmth, but can cause wind turbulence over and around them.

Hedges can be good wind-breaks, but may rob the soil of water and nutrients.

North

South

Greenhouse

Compost heap

Tool shed

West

Hedges. They are usually very good to look at and often better than walls as they filter the wind. But like trees, they rob the soil of plant foods and water. Put a path between any hedge and the vegetable plot. Then, in early spring and summer, take a sharp spade and cut right through any hedge roots that protrude into the vegetable plot from under the path.

Fences and walls. These are mixed blessings. The sunny side is ideal for growing tomatoes and capsicums but the shady side will produce thin leggy plants as they struggle to the light. Both walls and fences reflect warmth, all to the good, but they also produce air turbulence instead of filtering the wind as a hedge does. Fences can cause nasty draughts through the space underneath them so block this up with planks of wood, bricks or tiles. Remove these during the winter so that they don't cause the fence to rot.

Paths. These are an important consideration in a vegetable garden. Soil tends to get dumped, spilt or trodden on them in the natural course of events, so grass, gravel and ash paths are not recommended. You may have to put up with what already exists but if you have a choice, paving slabs are the best solution. They are easy to clean and are ideal for a 'planned garden' as they act as a permanent ruler round your plots, making it easy to get each row of crops in just the right place. They are not difficult to lay and can be taken up and relaid without too much trouble if you want to change the plan. So don't cement them in but put them on a sound foundation of ash or sharp sand. Without this foundation the wanderings of worms underneath will soon tilt the slabs and make the path uneven.

North, south, east or west
Wherever you live the same basic rules apply: if your garden is on the level, run the rows of plants from north to south. They will then get the sunshine on one side in the morning and on the other side in the afternoon. If you run the rows from east to west, then each row will shade the one behind it.

This rule doesn't apply if your garden is on a slope of one in five or more. If the slope is away from the sun you won't get the best possible crops, but if it is towards the sun they will enjoy extra warmth and will tend not to shade each other. In this case forget the north/south rule and run your rows the easiest way to work them which will be across the slope and not up and downhill. The gradient can easily be checked with a spirit level, a length of wood and a rule.

The vegetable garden

The plots

Ignoring the size of your garden for a moment, look at basic principles. You will need to divide your vegetable garden into four plots. These will probably be in the same part of the garden. They may even be adjoining with no paths in between. On the other hand they could be in quite different places – even in separate gardens.

One group of vegetables is grown in each plot. In subsequent years the groups move into different plots until by year five they are back where they started. This gives time for soil borne pests and diseases to die out, or severely diminish, before any group of plants is back in the same soil.

Label your plots A, B, C, D (or however you wish). The key point is that the plots *stay* as A, B, C, D, for it is only the plant groups which move.

You will find this sequence very easy to follow if your four plots are laid out in a row, but more difficult if they are in different places or in a square pattern.

For instance, if labelled as below left,

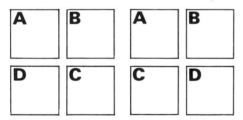

it is easy to remember that the plant groups rotate in an anti-clockwise direction. What is in Plot B one year goes into Plot A the next.

If you label them as above (right) you will need a computer to recall what went where in previous years, even though it looks logical at first sight.

So label square layouts in a clockwise or anti-clockwise way. If they are labelled in a clockwise sequence, the plant groups move anti-clockwise.

What size plots?

This depends on the size of your garden and your family's needs.

The three master plans are based on the following sizes:

The large master plan. 4 plots each 6 m × 6 m (20 ft × 20 ft).

The medium master plan. 4 plots each 4.5 m × 4.5 m (15 ft × 15 ft).

The small master plan. 4 plots each 3 m × 3 m (10 ft × 10 ft).

208

Divide the garden into four plots

A Potato group

B Legumes group

D Roots group

C Onions and brassicas

The whole principle of crop rotation is to keep the soil healthy. Sufficient time passes before a group uses the soil again.

However the plots are laid out, label them and make sure that no group reaches its original position until the 5th year.

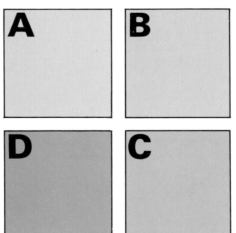

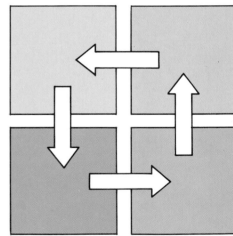

Organise plots in a sequence
Crop plan suitable for any garden. The clockwise plot layout and the annual anti-clockwise rotation translates into the following schedule suitable for any vegetable garden.

	Plot A	Plot B	Plot C	Plot D
Year 1:	Potato group	Legumes	Onions & Brassicas	Roots group
Year 2:	Legumes	Onions & Brassicas	Roots group	Potato group
Year 3:	Onions & Brassicas	Roots group	Potato group	Legumes
Year 4:	Roots group	Potato group	Legumes	Onions & Brassicas
Year 5:	Back to year 1			

The Large Master Plan   Year 1
Four plots, each 6m (20ft) square

PLOT A.   Potato Group

```
1'0"                                              1'0"
        ——————Outdoor Tomatoes——————
2'6"                                              2'0"
      Marrows
         •   •   •   •   •   •   •   •   •
3'0"                      Sweet                   2'0"
  or Courgettes
                          Corn                    2'0"
         •   •   •   •   •   •   •   •   •
2'6"        2'0"              1'6"                 2'0"
                                                  2'0"
        ——————Seakale Beet——————
1'9"
              Early Potatoes
           Followed by Lettuce
1'9"
             ——Early Potatoes——
2'0"
           ——————Maincrop Potatoes——————
2'0"
           ——————Maincrop Potatoes——————
2'0"
           ——————Maincrop Potatoes——————
1'6"
```

PLOT B.   Legumes Group.

```
1'0"
9"        ——————————Lettuce——————————
9"        ——————————Lettuce——————————
1'6"      ——————————Lettuce——————————
9"        ————Tall Broad Beans————
          ————Tall Broad Beans————
2'3"
9" 40 Celery-        ————French Beans————        1'6"
9"  —plants -        ————French Beans————        1'6"
9"                   ————French Beans————
          5'6"
2'0"
1'0"      ——————Dwarf Broad Beans——————
          ——————Dwarf Broad Beans——————
2'0"
6"        ——————Dwarf Peas——————
1'9"
          ————Runner Beans————
1'3"
          ————Runner Beans————
1'0"   ——Parsley——————————Early Lettuce——
6"
```

PLOT D.   Roots Group.

```
1'0"
9"        ——————Swede——————
9"        ——————Early Radish——————
          ——————Swede——————
1'6"          Turnips
1'0"      Followed by Spinach or Lettuce
1'6"          Turnips
          ——————Spinach Beet——————
1'6"      ————Parsnips————
1'0"      ————Parsnips————
1'0"      ————Parsnips————
1'0"      ————Carrots————
1'0"      ————Carrots————
1'0"      ————Carrots————
1'0"      ————Carrots————
1'0"      ————Beetroot————
1'0"      ————Beetroot————
1'0"      ————Beetroot————
1'0"      ————Beetroot————
1'0"      ——Sugar Loaf Chicory——
1'0"
```

PLOT C.   Onions and Brassicas.

```
1'0"
1'0"      ——————Leeks——————
1'0"      ——————Leeks——————
1'0"      ——————Leeks——————
1'0"      ——————Onions——————
6" 6"     ——————Onions——————
6"  6"    ——————Onions——————
1'0"      ——————Shallots——————
1'0"      ——————Kohl Rabi——————
1'0"      ——————Savoy Cabbage——————
1'0"      ——————Radish——————
1'0"      ——————Spring Onions——————
2'0"      Followed by Savoy Cabbage
          ——Broccoli – 'Calabrese'——
1'3"      ——————Kohl Rabi——————
1'3"      ——————Brussel Sprouts——————
1'6"      ——————Summer Cabbage——————
2'0"      Followed by Winter Radish
          ——Broccoli – 'Purple Sprouting'——
1'0"
```

Plot preparation – Action hints

* The lines on the plans show exactly where the drills for the seeds should be taken out and the distances given are those between one drill and the next. Keep to the plans if you want the best results – things are placed where they are for a reason. For instance, the tomatoes have been kept away from the potatoes – the latter could stand a mild attack of potato blight but it would put paid to the tomatoes if it spread to them. The two sets of broad beans are kept apart to minimize the spread of black fly. Sweet corn is grown in a block to assist pollination,

and self-blanching celery is also in a block so that it will blanch better. The distances between the celery plants are critical. Any closer and you'll get poor plants, any further apart and they won't blanch properly. Kohl rabi and summer cabbage are so placed in order that they will be out of the way for the broccoli and sprouts to develop. Parsley is where it is because it can stand the partial shade caused by the runner beans – most other plants couldn't. The early radish will be out of the way for the swedes (rutabagas).

* When you plant out the savoys just

pull enough spring onions (if they are still in the ground) to make way for each savoy plant and then pull the rest as the savoys need the room.

* Take up that row of potatoes by the seakale nice and early so that the seakale will have room to develop.

* Seed sowing
Sow at the correct depth and distance apart as the seed packets say. This is important with all plants, but particularly with celery, corn, swedes and brassicas. It is better to have ten good cabbages than fifteen poor ones.

The vegetable garden

All three master plans
Year 1

Plot A. Potato group. Dig and manure in autumn/winter. Put no manure where tomatoes are to be grown or they will be all leaf. Put plenty under marrows (zucchini). No lime on this plot this year – it makes the potatoes scabby.

Plot B. Legumes group. Dig and manure in autumn/winter. Apply plenty of manure under the soil where the runner beans or celery will be. Lime in late winter to achieve pH 6.5. Sow lettuce half a row at a time for continuity of supply.

Plot C. Onions and brassicas. Dig and manure in autumn/winter. Add plenty of manure under leeks. Leave the bean and pea roots from previous year in the soil. Lime in the winter to achieve pH 6.5 to 7.0.

Plot D. Roots group. Dig the plot in stages as it becomes clear of crops from the previous year. No manure at all for this plot. Lime only if pH has fallen below 6.0.

Years 2 and 3

Follow these same action hints for each group as they move round in rotation into different plots each year. Plot C, for instance, which has been manured in year 1 for the onions and brassicas, will not be manured in year 2 when it is growing roots. Plot D, which has not been manured in the first year, will be manured in year 2 ready for the potato group. This principle will apply in each successive year.

The long garden

Even if the shape of your garden forces you to lay out your four plots in a straight line, you should still follow the same rotation system. Remember the importance of aspect - the rows of plants should run north to south, unless you have a steeply sloped site.

The little plot

If you only have room for one little vegetable plot don't risk diseased soil by growing the same thing each year. Use the four-year rotation system and grow a different plant group each year to keep your soil healthy. It is better to have different crops each year that are healthy than to have a sickly crop of the same thing.

If you have a single plot of 4.5 m × 4.5 m (15 ft × 15 ft) use the **medium master plan** and if it is 10 ft × 10 ft or under use the **small master plan.**

In the fifth year go back to year one and keep on the 4-year rotation system.

The long garden

Should you choose to lay the plots in a row, run the crop lines from north to south so that they enjoy the sun on one side in the morning and on the other in the afternoon. Running lines east to west results in each row obscuring the sun from the next. If gardening on a slope, this is not the case. In fact lines are easier to work if laid out across a slope rather than up and downhill.

The Medium Master Plan Year 1 Four plots, each 4.5m (15ft) square

A
- Outdoor Tomatoes
- Bush Marrows or Courgettes
- Sweet Corn
- Seakale Beet
- Early Potatoes Followed by Lettuce
- Early Potatoes
- Early Potatoes or Maincrop

B
- Parsley   Early Lettuce
- Runner Beans
- Dwarf Peas
- Dwarf Broad Beans
- 24 Celery Plants   French Beans
- Lettuce
- Lettuce

C
- Swede
- Early Radish
- Swede
- Turnips Followed by Spinach or Lettuce
- Turnips
- Spinach Beet
- Parsnips
- Parsnips
- Carrots
- Carrots
- Beetroot
- Beetroot
- Sugar Loaf Chicory

D
- Leeks
- Leeks
- Onions
- Onions
- Onions
- Shallots
- Kohl Rabi
- Spring Onions Followed by Savoy Cabbage
- Kohl Rabi
- Broccoli 'Calabrese'
- Summer Cabbage Followed by Winter Radish
- Summer Cabbage
- Broccoli 'Purple Sprouting'
- Radish

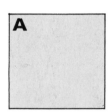

The Small Master Plan Four plots, 3m (10ft) square

A
- Outdoor Tomatoes
- Early Radish
- Marrows or Courgettes
- Early Radish
- Seakale Beet
- Early Potatoes Followed by Late Lettuce
- Early Potatoes

B
- Dwarf French Beans
- Dwarf French Beans
- Lettuce
- Lettuce
- Dwarf Broad Beans
- Dwarf Broad Beans
- Runner Beans
- Runner Beans

D
- Turnips Followed by Spinach or Lettuce
- Turnips
- Parsnips
- Parsnips
- Carrots
- Carrots
- Early Beetroot
- Main Beetroot
- Early Lettuce Followed by Sugar Loaf Chicory

C
- Leeks
- Leeks
- Onions
- Onions
- Kohl Rabi
- Kohl Rabi
- Summer Cabbage Followed by Winter Radish
- Spring Onions Followed by Savoy Cabbage

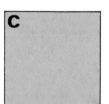

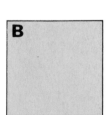

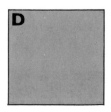

Alternatives

If you decide to grow the alternatives suggested, one small packet of any will suffice. If you grow garlic, one small 'clove' is used for each plant and there are about eight garlic cloves to the ounce Jerusalem artichokes are grown from tubers. They are planted one foot apart and twenty tubers will weigh about 2 lb depending on size.

If there are some vegetables in the **Master plans** you don't care for, substitute one of the following alternatives - chosen so as not to upset the rotation system.

Suggested alternative	To replace
Artichoke – Jerusalem	Maincrop potatoes
Cucumber – outdoor	Marrows (zucchini)
Celeriac	Celery – self-blanching
Celery – American green	Celery – self-blanching
Cauliflower – summer heading	Calabrese or summer cabbage
Cauliflower – autumn or winter heading	Brussels sprouts or broccoli or savoy cabbage
Chinese cabbage	Kohl rabi
Corn salad (lambs lettuce)	Anything in Onion and Brassicas Group
Endive	Sugar loaf chicory
Garlic	Shallots, onions or leeks
Haricot beans (snap beans)	Any beans or peas
Kale – curly	Sprouts, Savoy or sprouting broccoli
Salsify or Scorzonera	Any crop in the Roots Group
Spinach	Seakale beet
And two others that require the protection of a frame of cloches unless you live in a warm climate:	
Capsicum (sweet peppers)	Tomatoes
Cantaloupe melons	Marrows (zucchini) or sweet corn

More preparation action hints
* Digging

Here are just a few guidelines for the vegetable garden. If you have a very light sandy soil, don't dig deeply. Keep the manure or compost near the surface, or even use it as a mulch, and let the worms take it down.

Dig medium and heavy soils in autumn/winter, incorporating manure or compost within the top spit of soil but leaving the plot rough for the winter frosts to break down the clods. Every four years, double dig: Mark out the plots for trenches two-spades wide; dig the first trench to spade depth, stacking the soil on the path; break up the subsoil base of the trench with a fork and work in manure or compost; dig the next trench along, again to spade depth, but this time fill the first trench with the soil that you remove; work manure or compost into the subsoil base, and so on.

Decide on your sowing plan before you start work. Put marking sticks in your plots to show where the hungry feeders like runner beans, peas and marrows are to go, and give those places an extra ration of manure as you dig. And, of course, don't mix the soil of one plot with that of another.

* Lime

If you garden on chalk you probably won't need to add any lime but most soils are too acid and need lime to correct this. The right pH level will make a big difference to your vegetable crops. Too much lime is just as bad as too little, so use a simple soil testing kit to check your pH levels each year. Don't mix lime and manure together. Sprinkle the lime on the surface of the soil in late winter or early spring, several weeks after you have finished the digging and manuring.

Consult local or national societies for which varieties to choose. Much will depend on whether yield, flavour or looks are important.

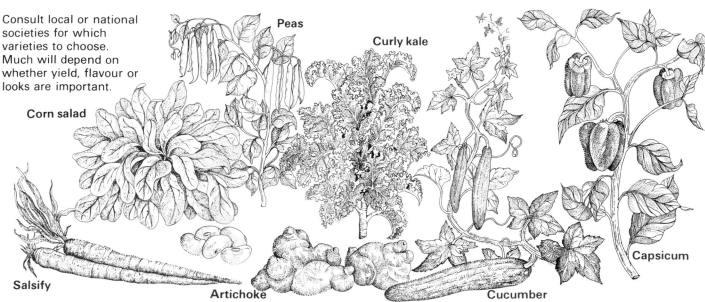

Corn salad

Peas

Curly kale

Salsify

Artichoke

Cucumber

Capsicum

The vegetable garden

Storing your crops

The master plans are designed to give a continuous supply of vegetables – most can be used straight from the ground but others are kept by drying, storing in sand or freezing. If you use all these methods the large master plan can keep a family of four in vegetables for most of the year.

These stay in the ground

Broccoli, brussels sprouts, curly kale, leeks, parsnips, savoy cabbage, swede (rutabaga), winter radish.

Or you can store parsnips or swedes in a clamp near the kitchen door. Put a layer of parsnips straight on the earth, then cover with a 50 mm (2 in) layer of soil, another layer of parsnips, another layer of soil, and so on.

Many vegetables can be grown in raised beds – a great benefit to the elderly, handicapped or those with paved gardens. Make sure that spacing between rows allows sufficient light and air to reach the smaller subjects.

Seeds to order

The amount of seed you get in a packet varies depending on its cost of production and its size – from very small seeds like celery to large ones like peas and beans. You will find helpful advice in catalogues and on some seed packets but generally speaking a small packet of each variety will be sufficient whatever size plan you use.

Sets and tubers

You will need the following quantities of sets (for onions and shallots) and tubers (for potatoes). The weights are approximate as the sizes of each will vary.

Store dry: Garlic, onions, shallots.

Lift when the tops have died down, leave in the warm sun to dry for a few days, then put in slatted grape or peach boxes and store in an airy frost-proof place. Or pickle shallots or small onions straight away.

Marrows. Pick marrows (zucchini) when fully ripe, hang them up in nets or store them on a shelf in a cool, dry, frost-proof place.

Potatoes. Start digging the earlies when they are in flower and use straight away. Dig the maincrop when the tops have died down. Dry in the sun for a few hours then store in hessian sacks or wooden storage bins in an airy frost-proof place, away from light.

Tomatoes. Pick any remaining green ones before the frosts come, put in grape boxes in a cool, dry, frost-proof place and bring into room temperatures as soon as they start to turn colour to complete their ripening.

Store in sand, peat or dry earth (if your winters are severe). Beetroot, carrot, celeriac, parsnip, salsify, scorzonera, swede, winter radish. Use plastic dustbins, buckets or wooden boxes. Cut off the leaves (twist for carrots) down to an inch of stem. Put a 50 mm (2 in) layer of sand in the container, then a layer of roots, another layer of sand, another layer of roots etc. Store in a cool, dry, frost-free place.

If your winters are mild these crops may be left in the ground.

	Large Master Plan	Medium Master Plan	Small Master Plan
Onions	900g (2 lb)	450g (1 lb)	225g (½ lb)
Shallots	1125g (2½ lb)	900g (2 lb)	—
Early potatoes	3000g (7 lb)	3000g (7 lb)	1500g (3½ lb)
Maincrop potatoes	3000g (7 lb)	—	—

Freezing

Most of your vegetables can be frozen. Pick them young and tender and freeze within the hour. Wash, prepare and blanch them before freezing. Blanching halts enzyme activity and helps to preserve colour, flavour and some vitamin C. The process involves scalding them with boiling water for a strict period of time and then immediately chilling them in very cold water for the same period.

Method. Have enough water boiling in a large pan to accomodate a wire basket containing the cut up vegetables so they can move freely in the water. The water must return to the boil within one minute of putting in the vegetables – or they may go mushy. So do not put in too many at one go. Start timing the very second that the water reboils.Take them out at once when the time is up and plunge into cold water for the same length of time. Keep the water cold with ice cubes and by letting the tap run. Drain thoroughly, pack into polythene bags and suck out as much air (with a straw) as possible. Then label them and put them into the freezer straight away. Use the same 'boiling' water for several loads to preserve vitamin C but always change the 'chilling' water to keep it cold. Pack your vegetables in 'meal-sized' helpings but blanch no more than a pound at any one time.

Freezing chart
Vegetable blanching: preparation and cooling. (The time is given in minutes and is of the same duration for both processes.)

Beans		
Broad	2	Use young ones no larger than a man's thumb nail
French	2	Use whole tender ones that snap easily
Runner	2	Cut into pieces
Runner	1	Sliced
Broccoli		
Sprouting	3	Tender shoots. Cut off tough stalks
Calabrese	4	Tender shoots. Cut off tough stalks
Brussels sprouts	3	Small firm sprouts with loose leaves taken off
Carrots	3	Sliced large ones or whole young ones
Cauliflower	3	Cut into small florets
Celeriac	4	Peel them and cut into 1-inch cubes
Celery	3	For use in cooking. Cut into 2-inch pieces
Chives	nil	Just chop up and freeze with no water
Courgettes (Summer squash)	1	Small ones cut into 2-inch slices or in half lengthways
Cucumber		Make into cucumber soup and freeze
Curly kale	3	Use young leaves and shoots. Trim off stalks
Kohl rabi	2	Peel young ones and cut into quarters

Leeks	2	Wash all soil out. Cut into 2-inch length pieces
Mint	nil	Chop up young mint, add a little water and freeze as ice cubes
Parsley	nil	Just chop up and freeze with no water
Peas	1	They must be young ones. Blanch in muslin bag
Rhubarb	nil	Cut young rhubarb into 1-inch pieces and freeze raw
Salsify	2	Cut young roots into 2-inch pieces. Cool in the air, not in water
Seakale beet: (Green leaf part)	2	Strip leaf from ribs. After chilling press out excess water before freezing
(Middle rib)	3	Cut into 2-inch pieces
Spinach and **spinach beet**	2	Strip leaves off stalk. After chilling press out excess water
Sweet corn (Medium cobs)	6	Take off husks and silk from tender young cobs. Blanch and freeze whole or cut off kernels and freeze them
(Small cobs)	4	
(Kernels only)	3	
Tomato	nil	Freeze tomato purée
Turnip	3	Peel and cut young ones into quarters

213

The fruit garden

What can be grown and where

If you have a large garden it is worth allocating a part of it especially for growing fruit. With a medium-sized garden you will probably want to incorporate your fruit into the total plan by making specific decorative features of it. Fruit trees add grace and colour to a garden both during the spring when they are in flower, and in autumn when they are heavy with fruit. If you have a small garden you may like to grow just soft fruit such as raspberries and strawberries.

There is one essential rule: unless you have a very large garden, avoid planting 'standard' trees. They will take up too much space (also you will need a ladder to pick the fruit). A standard Bramley or Delicious apple tree can be 8 m (25 ft) across. Keep to trees grown on dwarfing root-stocks as cordons, pyramids, spindle-bushes, bush trees or trained forms.

Forms of trees

Most fruit trees are grafted on to different root-stocks which are classified according to their effect on the growth habit of the fruit tree. So when you buy a tree, do make it clear to the supplier which type you wish to grow.

A bush apple will be about 3 m (10 ft) across and 2 m (7 ft) high. A bush is certainly the most easily managed form of fruit tree. Other trained trees must be carefully pruned and managed to achieve the ultimate shape you require, but as they can become very handsome features in the garden it is well worth the trouble. The most common forms are illustrated here.

The birds, the bees and the weather

Don't be tempted to buy one apple or pear tree and plant it on its own. It probably won't bear fruit. The transfer of pollen from one flower to another is essential for fertilization and is mainly done by bees and other insects.

With apples, pears, plums and cherries there is the added complication that only a few varieties will set fruit with their own pollen. More than one variety has to be planted and chosen to flower at the same time. Even then some are incompatible – the technical reasons are complicated and depend on whether their chromosomes are diploid, triploid, tetraploid or hexaploid.

For instance, sometimes tree A will pollinate tree B, but B will not pollinate A in return, so C has to be grown to pollinate A. With apples alone there are over one hundred and fifty different sorts so it can be a complex question to get the right trees mated.

Training fruit trees

You can buy a tree ready-trained (two or three years old) or as a 'maiden' (a one-year-old whip). Be absolutely sure that the nurseryman knows what growth habit you want and that the tree is grafted onto the appropriate root stock.

If you buy a 'maiden' plant, more skill is required to train it, but there are prescribed techniques for training fruit trees at whatever stage of growth. These are based upon the principle that terminal buds, when left unpruned, actively inhibit the development of side or lateral shoots.

If planting a cordon, espalier or fan, remember that wall footings are sheltered and probably dry. Avoid planting right up against the wall, therefore, and as with all tree planting, thoroughly cultivate and prepare the soil.

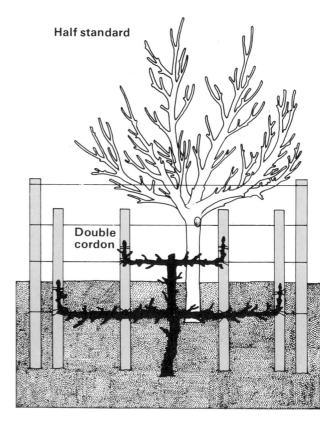

Half standard

Double cordon

Soils and their preparation

Apart from figs and grapes, most types of fruit like a fairly deep, well-drained, medium loam, so it is worth rototilling or double digging in order to encourage good root systems. If your soil is on gravel or sand, plenty of manure or composted material should be incorporated. After all, the trees are likely to be there for your lifetime. Once a fruit bush or tree is planted never subsequently dig deeply near its roots for many of these grow near the surface and so could be damaged.

Most fruits prefer a slightly acid soil or at least one with very little free lime in it. A pH of 6.0 is a fairly safe average going up to pH 6.5 for stone fruits like plums, cherries and peaches. You won't, therefore, get very good results on a chalk soil unless you add quite large amounts of peat, compost or manure.

How to grow different kinds of fruit

The following pages examine some of the more popularly grown fruits and the conditions in which they prefer to grow. With careful selection and planning, a wide variety of types and forms can be grown within a small area to provide you with a long season of supply.

The varieties chosen for the plans on pages 220 and 221 are those known to pollinate each other satisfactorily. If you swap one variety for another, do check with your nurseryman that fertilization is still possible.

Another reason for a poor set of fruit can be bird damage. In Britain bull finches in particular will peck out the buds of many top (i.e. tree) fruits, and later other birds will help themselves to what fruit does form. If you experience this problem in your garden, you may have to put cages over your fruit bushes and throw nets over the trees. (Another advantage in growing only smaller forms is that it is very difficult to get nets over a large tree.) In America the problem of birds tends to be small unless you grow cherries and blueberries.

Frost can also be a problem. Don't try to grow fruit in frost hollows. The danger period is when the flowers are open; the buds and small set fruit are not quite as much at risk. High wind and even rain at pollination time can also cut down on fruit set.

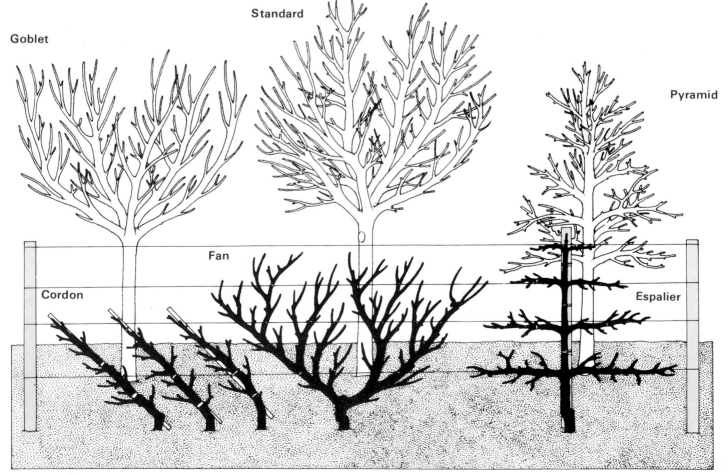

Goblet

Standard

Pyramid

Fan

Cordon

Espalier

The fruit garden

Top (i.e. tree) fruit

Apples

This is the most widely grown top fruit and there are varieties to suit all tastes. They are usually grown as bush trees, spindle-bushes, pyramids, dwarf pyramids, cordons and lastly espaliers, which is the most popular form in America. A single cordon can yield from 2.5 to 5 k (4 to 8 lbs) of fruit. Cross pollination is essential as most varieties will not set from their own pollen.

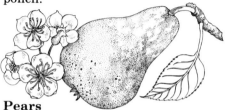

Pears

They are another very easy to grow popular fruit, as long as there are no late frosts. They flower earlier in the season than apples so need the protection of a warm position. They can be grown in the same forms as apples. Cross pollination is essential. Even so-called self-fertile varieties do much better with a mate.

Plums, gages and damsons

They are very early flowering and so may suffer from spring frosts in low lying areas. They are happiest against a warm wall and don't like very acid soils. The latter should be improved by adding moderate quantities of old mortar rubble or modest amounts of lime (just a few ounces to the square yard). They don't do well as cordons or espaliers and are best grown in bush, pyramid or fan-trained forms.

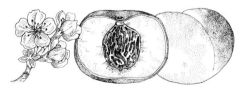

Peaches and nectarines

If you have no problem with spring frosts they will succeed well as bushes. In less warm climates they should be grown against a sunny wall, the aim being to cover the wall with slim branches spread out like the ribs of a fan and tied to a system of wires spaced horizontally, two brick courses apart. Very acid soils should be treated in the same way as for plums, but remember that too much lime is as bad as too little. Peaches will set with their own pollen.

Sweet cherries

This is a delightful fruit but, sadly, no dwarfing stocks are available. They take a long time to bear a crop; they need a pollinator; and they flower early, so the birds will very probably benefit before you do. Sweet cherries are just not suitable for small gardens. If you have a really large warm wall you could try training one as a very large fan on a semi-vigorous rootstock called Colt. But it will need protection from the birds.

Acid (i.e. sour) cherries

These are much easier, for they can be grown as bush trees or fan-trained against a wall. Varieties will set full crops with their own pollen, so they can be planted singly.

Figs

They need a warm situation and are best grown as fans on a sunny wall or, better still, on a corner formed by two walls. Figs are grown on their own roots as no root-stocks are available. The rooting area must be restricted or the tree will be all growth and very little fruit. Plant in a brick or concrete trough, sunk or built in the soil, with no bottom to it, with the base surface tightly packed with rubble or broken bricks a foot deep. The trough should then be filled with good loam mixed with a couple of bucketfuls of old mortar rubble. No pollinator is needed.

Soft fruit

There are no cross-pollination problems in growing soft fruit, but unless your local birds don't like fruit, you should consider growing it in a cage.

Strawberries

This is the fruit that gives the quickest crop, those planted half-way through one year will fruit the next. Some can be planted as late as the autumn. The rows should be 76 cm (2 ft 6 in) apart and the plants 46 cm (1 ft 6 in) apart in the rows. They need rich soil with plenty of humus. Your stock of plants can be increased in future years by selecting runners from healthy plants with plenty of flowers. Remove their flowers as this will stop them fruiting and encourage them to put strength in their runners.

Everbearing strawberries – today increasingly popular – need a highly fertile soil and copious watering. The late summer and autumn crop can be improved by picking off the very early flowers.

Raspberries

Grow these in single rows tied to horizontal wires that are stretched between stout posts buried 60 cm (2 ft) in the soil and up to 1.8 m (6 ft) high above. Have the wires at 60 cm (2 ft), 1.07 m (3½ ft) and 1.5 m (5 ft) – 1.8 m (6 ft) if the variety is vigorous. Space the canes 46 cm (1 ft 6 in) apart in the rows and the rows 1.8 m (6 ft) apart. Each year cut the old canes right down to the ground and tie in the strongest of the new canes.

Fig planting

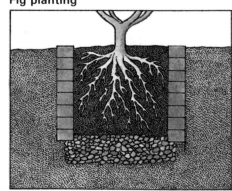

Black, red and white currants, gooseberries and Worcesterberries

These are all related and, in general, like an open sunny position but will tolerate partial shade if they have to. They will accept a wide range of soils as long as they are properly drained and have had compost or manure added – especially to lighter soils. They are all normally grown as bushes 1.5 m (5 ft) to 1.8 m (6 ft) apart, although gooseberries can be fan-trained or grown as cordons on wire supports.

Note that these fruits serve as alternative hosts for white pine blister and consequently cannot be grown in many parts of America. Consult your local nurseryman.

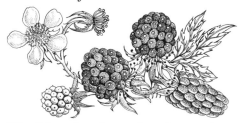

Blackberries, loganberries and other hybrid berries

They will tolerate a variety of soils and even partial shade, but will do best in good soil under full sun. They can be trained against walls, over arches or along boundary fences, but as they nearly all fruit on the previous year's growth (which can be 3.6 m (12 ft) or more in length), it is best to train them on wire supports stretched between posts. You will find that job much less painful if you grow the thornless varieties.

Easy-to-manage training system

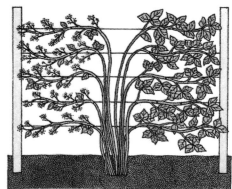

One simple system of training is to tie in the fruiting growth to one side, and the new shoots to the other, to make an easily managed decorative feature as in the illustration.

Blueberries

Very popular amongst American home fruit growers, the blueberry, a relative of the British bilberry, comes in a wide variety of forms from 30 cm to 6 m (1 ft to 20 ft) high to provide an attractive garden feature throughout the year.

In late spring the bushes have pinkish white flowers which develop into the blue fruits with their characteristic bloom. One variety is evergreen and the foliage of many of the others turns red in autumn. Later the red and green twigs and red buds give an attractive contrast to the winter scene. In the right conditions blueberry bushes will survive for many years. They need very acid conditions (pH 4.0 to 4.8) but grow in a variety of soils from the loose sands of the drylands to bogs and swamps but there must be no standing water on their roots in summer.

Most cultivated varieties have a height and spread of 1.5 to 2.5 m (5 to 8 ft). They should be planted this same distance apart and are usually kept pruned back to encourage new growth and allow the sun to ripen the fruit. In cooler regions they can be left unpruned to give some protection from the cold but the fruit will be smaller and of poorer quality.

Grapes

Grapes need a rather complex system of pruning to get the best results. The old wood is cut back each year and the new growth regulated so that a limited number of bunches result. Generally, grapes prefer warm climates, but in many colder parts of America there is a thriving grape industry. A number of selections of hybrid grapes (European *Vitus vinifera* x American species) as well as some cold-resistant selections of *V. vinifera* are popular there. You will find them trained on walls, growing at random to clothe some eyesore, gracefully softening the contours of an archway or growing in formal rows. The leaves are handsome in themselves, and in a good year you may get a respectable crop as well.

The fruit garden

Pruning

It is not this book's purpose to cover in detail the intricacies of pruning fruit-bearing plants. But before consulting a bibliography, it may be helpful to be aware of some general principles.

General principles

The main reasons for pruning, which is normally carried out in the dormant season, are:

1. To train the tree or bush into the desired shape.

2. To encourage the formation of fruit buds – those that contain the embryo blossom. They are usually fatter and rounder than the pointed growth buds.

3. To allow sunlight and air to reach as much of the plant as possible by removing overcrowded growth.

Trees

This includes all forms including those on dwarfing root-stocks.

Initial pruning

One year old trees, with single straight stems, called maidens, need to be cut back to produce side growths to build up the framework for the tree's eventual shape (although the beginner may well prefer to purchase trees up to three years old where the basic shaping has been done by the nurseryman). This will partly depend on the ultimate form of tree required.

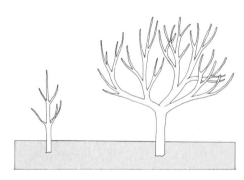

Subsequent pruning

The type of root-stock, the desired shape of the tree and the fruit-bearing habit of the particular variety need to be taken into account. Soil, climate, situation and manuring also affect growth and therefore the pruning required.

Apples and pears bear their fruit on wood which is more than one year old, whereas peaches bear theirs on just the previous season's growth. So with peaches, old wood has to be continually cut out to encourage new replacement growths. These new growths must be limited to ensure the tree does not have too much fruit-bearing wood in one season. This could cause a shortage of growth and fruit in subsequent years.

The three reasons for pruning

To train into shape

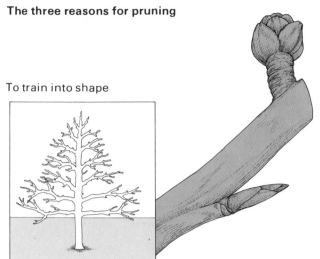

To encourage fruit buds

To facilitate the passage of sun and air

Apples and pears do not require their fruit bearing branches to be renewed in this way. They produce fruit buds on short spurs which develop on wood over one year old. Some apples, and just one or two pears, are also tip bearers. They have fruit buds at or near the ends of two year old shoots as well as on older spurs, so if the new shoots are continually cut back there will be a shortage of fruit buds in future years. Generally speaking, therefore, spur-bearing trees can have their new growth shortened but with tip bearers it is a question of some cutting back and some judicious thinning.

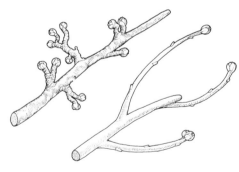

Unpruned apples and pears may come into cropping a little earlier than pruned ones but on the other hand they may lose vigour as the years pass and perhaps become biennial bearing (fruit only every second year).

Pruning to produce new growth is thus advantageous, but on the other hand giving a tree a 'close hair cut' every year is much worse than doing no pruning at all. If in doubt just thin out – to remove overcrowded and crossing growth.

This is especially true of plums. Once plum trees have been established all that is necessary is to remove rubbing and crossing branches and dead wood. Because of the risk of infection by silver leaf disease in autumn and

winter this is best done in early spring just as growth is starting. Paint over all cuts with special pruning paint.

Otherwise, pruning is normally done in the dormant season, with some summer pruning to remove or shorten thin, overcrowded growths.

Cane fruits

These include raspberries, blackberries, loganberries and hybrid berries.

Autumn-fruiting raspberries should have all canes cut down at the very beginning of the season. Otherwise cane fruit should have their old canes cut right to the ground as soon as fruiting has ceased in the summer and the new canes should be tied in straight away to get the full benefit of the sunlight and to prevent them being damaged. They will often need to be thinned in number; be sure to preserve the best.

Gooseberries and currants

They normally only start to come into full bearing after two or three years. When pruning, it is important to consider the following:

Blackcurrants produce their best fruit on one year old wood. White currants and red currants fruit on short spurs on old wood and in clusters at the base of one year old growths with a little fruit further along this new wood.

Gooseberries will fruit on old and new wood and every few years vigorous young growths should be allowed to take the place of old main branches which have been removed. The same applies to established Worcesterberries.

Pruning and thinning out is normally done in the dormant season with some shortening of laterals in the summer.

Grape vines

There are numerous methods of pruning and training vines depending on variety, climate, soil and the whims of the grower. The basic essentials to bear in mind are:

1. Grapes are only produced on the current season's growth and not on old wood, so each season's growth is cut back to the basic framework of the vine unless it is required to build up this framework.

2. The number of branches should be limited, depending on variety and climate, to avoid small, low quality fruit. This is done by rubbing off unwanted buds at the start of the growing season and then pinching off new growths when they have produced the number of bunches required. Look for these tiny new bunches and pinch off the shoot two leaves past them. Or you can merely remove the bunches themselves.

Decorating a pergola

Plant a variety that fruits well on spurs and cut back as in a simple training system. Train the strongest growths up the support and remove all others. At the end of the season, tip back to the strong part of the cane. In year 2, allow the main stem to grow beyond the top of the structure, and at the end of the season, tip back to about 30 cm (12 in) above the structure.

In year 3, train in the laterals across the top of the pergola. At the season's end, cut back 3 to 5 strongest canes to spurs of 2 to 3 buds to provide new laterals for the next season; remove others. The number of spurs can be allowed to build up in subsequent years. The bunches of grapes will hang down under the pergola roof. This system is often known as 'head pruning' and is not just limited to ornamental training. The main stem may be as small as 60 cm (2 ft).

Pests and diseases

Synthetic pesticides, insecticides and fungicides have revolutionized pest control for the commercial grower who needs to use them under controlled conditions, but time is the only true test of their safety and they should be used with caution and only as a last resort.

Some of them can upset the balance of nature by destroying predators as well as pests and in a garden environment those intended for one group of plants can drift on to another with perhaps unfortunate results.

So, in general, try to do without them. Pick off caterpillars, hose off greenfly, pick off and burn infected shoots, keep

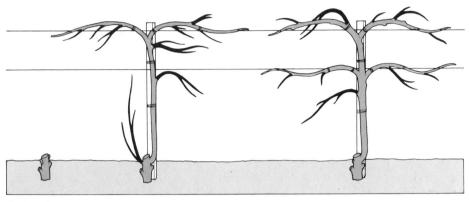

A simple training system
Tie wires to posts at 1.2 m (4 ft) and 90 cm (3 ft) from the ground. Cut back to one or two buds on planting. Allow to grow, just rubbing off any shoots low down. At the end of the first season, select the best two branches and tie in. Cut off the others. In year 2, simply rub off buds low down on the main stem. At season's end, select two canes and tie in, ending up with four laterals. Subsequently, save one strong lateral and tie it along each wire each season. Remove all other laterals but leave a few short spurs near the main stem to provide buds for further canes for the next season.

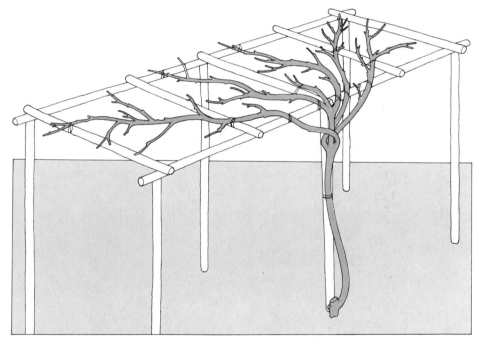

the garden clean and tidy, paint over all tree wounds or cuts with pruning paint and gather up all leaves in the autumn for leaf-mould or compost.

If you do use pesticides follow some basic guidelines:

1. Follow the directions on the container taking careful note of any comments about weather conditions, how long should elapse before it is safe to harvest, and the possible effect on other plants.

2. Proper coverage is essential but never over-spray. As with fertilizers, the principle that if a little does good a lot does more good is not true. Dwarf varieties of trees are naturally easier to spray than large ones.

3. Don't spray in windy conditions.

4. Don't spray near ponds.

5. Don't spray during blossom time.

6. Don't spray during extremes of temperature.

7. Wear rubber gloves and wash your hands and all utensils afterwards.

8. Store all pesticides and poisons in their original containers, never in drink bottles, and keep them out of the reach of children and pets.

The fruit garden

The large fruit garden

This should be planted so that the strawberries face towards the sun, thus minimizing the problem of one crop shading another. Such a garden will give you fruit in abundance for eating either just as it is, or for jams, jellies, tarts, puddings, ice-creams and anything else that takes your fancy.

The damsons and plums must be on the correct root-stocks for bush trees, and the apples and pears for cordons. Those apples marked * must be on M9 root stock or they will be too vigorous for cordons.

Plant cordons at an angle of 45 degrees, sloping away from the sun.

Cordon training

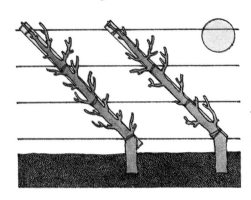

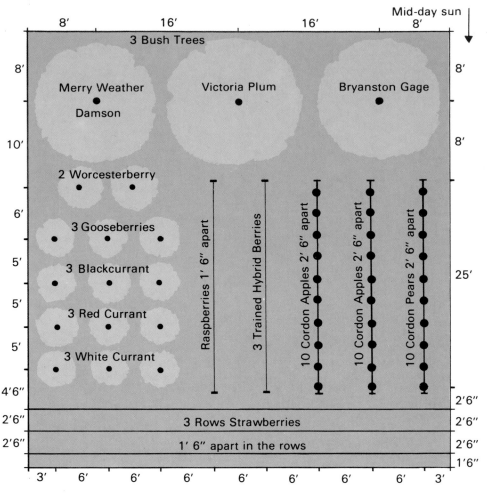

Suggested varieties to give a long season of supply: (U.S. in colour)

Apples (Dessert)

(Early)

Owen Thomas	Early McIntosh*
Epicure	Wealthy
Fortune	Yellow Transparent

(Mid Season)

Lord Lambourne	Baldwin
American Mother	Cartland
Egremont Russet	Fall Pippin
Ribston Pippin	Macoun
Kidd's Orange Red	Milton
Cox's Orange Pippin	Stayman Winesap

(Late)

Laxton's Superb	Empire
Claygate Pearmain	Golden Delicious
Sturmer Pippin	Melrose
Pixie	Mutsu

Apples (Cooking)

(Early)

George Neal

(Mid-Season)

Golden Noble	Idared
Blenheim Orange*	Red Jonathan
Bramley Seedling*	Wagener

(Late)

	Rhode Island
Newton Wonder*	Greening*
Lane's Prince Albert	Rome Beauty
Annie Elizabeth	Spigold*

Pears

(Early)

Williams Bon	Amora
Chrétien	Bartlett
Merton Pride	Moon-Glow
Onward	

(Mid-Season)

Beurré Hardy	Gosham
Beurré Superfin	Seckel
Conference	
Marie Louise	

(Late)

Doyenné du Comice	Beurré Bosc
Beurré Dumont	Beurré d'Anjou
Winter Nelis	Beurré Dumont
	Doyenné du Comice

Raspberries

Lloyd George	Heritage (everbearing)
Glen Cova	Latham
Malling Jewel	Sunrise
Malling Admiral	Taylor

Trained hybrid berries

Oregon thornless blackberry	Oregon thornless blackberry
Thornless loganberry	Thornless loganberry
Boysenberry	Boysenberry

Strawberry

(Early)

Cambridge Rival	Fairfax
Royal Sovereign	Premier

(Mid/late)

Red Gauntlet	New Empire
Talisman	Jerseybelle

Gooseberries

Keepsake	Downing
Lord Derby	Pixwell
Careless	Poorman

Black currants

Boskoop Giant	– (none); white pine
Blackdown	blister rust prohibits
Malvern Cross	them.

Red currants

Laxton's No. 1	Perfection
Red Lake	Red Lake
Rondom	Wilder

White currants

White Grape	White Dutch
White Dutch	White Grape
White Versailles	White Imperial

(Whitecurrants don't give a big crop so you might like to grow more blackcurrants instead.)

The small fruit garden

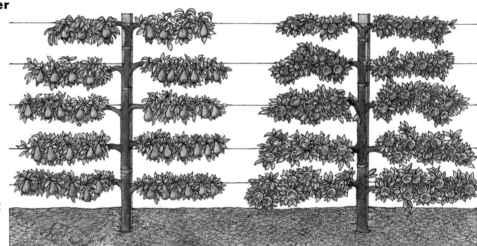

Mid-day sun

3 Trained Hybrid Berries

2 Gooseberry

2 Blackcurrant

2 Red currant

Raspberries 1'6" apart

6 Cordon Apples

6 Cordon Pears

1 Row Strawberries 1'6" apart

30'

Suggested cross-pollinating varieties to give a long season of supply

Choose from the lists in **the large fruit garden** for gooseberries, currants, raspberries, strawberries and hybrid berries.

Apples

Epicure	Empire
Merton Beauty	Idared
American Mother	Macoun
Cox's Orange Pippin	Milton
Pixie	Stayman Winesap
Lane's Prince Albert (cooking)	Wealthy

Pears

Williams' Bon Chrétien	Aurora
Onward	Bartlett
Conference	Beurré Dumont
Doyenné du Comice	Doyenné du Comice
Beurré Dumont	Gorham
Winter Nelis	

Espalier trees as a garden divider

A rustic screen with espalier trees on wires makes a handsome divider between say the flower and vegetable garden. The trees suggested are compatible, flower in the same period, and give a long season of supply. Alternatively, carry out the same idea using cordons to give more variety. Make your selection from the large or small fruit garden plans.

For a small screen consider:
2 pears or 2 apples

Conference and Beurré Dumont	Bartlett and Beurré Dumont
Epicure and Cox's Orange Pippin	Empire and Macoun

Suggestions for wide screen:

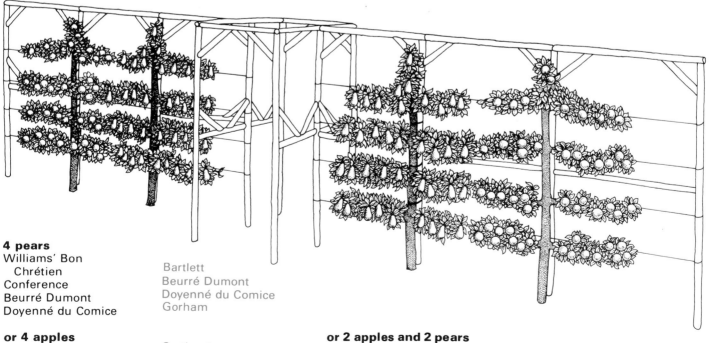

4 pears

Williams' Bon Chrétien	Bartlett
Conference	Beurré Dumont
Beurré Dumont	Doyenné du Comice
Doyenné du Comice	Gorham

or 4 apples

St Edmunds Pippin	Cartland
Epicure	Empire
Cox's Orange Pippin	Macoun
Egremont Russet	Yellow Transparent

or 2 apples and 2 pears

Epicure and Cox's Orange Pippin	Empire and Macoun
Conference and Beurré Dumont	Bartlett and Beurré Dumont

Propagation

The principles of propagation
It is, of course, much cheaper to multiply one's own plants than to buy them from a nursery or garden centre.

Home propagation is also particularly recommended if plants are needed in quantity.

Many permanent occupants of the garden can be propogated in the greenhouse if you require more specimens. For instance, a wide range of trees, shrubs, hardy perennials, alpines and so on can be increased from cuttings, and many of them root very easily even in an unheated greenhouse. One great advantage of a home-raised tree is that it can be planted out at the right age and size.

Home propagation is a good way of obtaining plants which are not otherwise easily available. Remember that many nurseries and garden centres carry only a limited selection of plants – those which are the most popular with amateur gardeners. Somehow, home-raised plants – cuttings from a friend perhaps – are always more special.

Another good reason for home propagation is to replace short-lived garden plants so that you do not lose particular subjects. Typical examples include carnations, pinks, delphiniums, aquilegias, lupins and strawberries. All of these are easily propagated by the amateur gardener.

Methods of propagation
There is space only to outline the various methods. But, as cost is one of the most important considerations in planning a garden, you may find it useful to study the more demanding methods in greater depth. There are many technical books available.

Propagation by division
Not all methods rely upon the controlled conditions of the greenhouse.

Both bulbs and perennial clumps can be propagated by division. With bulbs, it is easy – no cutting or forcing should be necessary. They increase by producing sideshoots or 'offsets'. When their foliage has died back, these can be removed and planted out to grow into full-sized bulbs.

A corm dies after its flowering period, but new cormlets are then evident and should be removed to a potting compost where, within a couple of years, they will grow into full-size flowering corms.

Most tuberous plants (such as the dahlia and tuberous rooted begonia) increase in number too, and these, like rhizomes, are best increased by division.

When dividing a perennial clump, gently tease its roots apart (two forks can be handy), discard the old, woody, central part and replant the outside shoots separately. This should be done in early spring, when growth begins, or during the dormant period.

Propagation by seed
Successful germination depends upon the presence of moisture, free-flow of air and a degree of warmth. The latter condition depends entirely on the type of plant. Hardy annuals and the seed of spring bulbs can be sown outside, as can seed from some trees and shrubs (though the latter are probably best grown from cuttings). Tree and shrub seeds, like the seeds of spring bulbs, may need some assistance – frosting or actual abrasion of the seed coating – to stimulate their ability to take in moisture.

Out-crossing and hybrid plants
Nearly all trees need pollen from another of their kind in order to produce strong, healthy seedlings. A single tree isolated from its own kind will often fertilize a number of seeds with its own pollen, but these selfed plants are often deformed in some way and usually grow slowly.

Any plant with distinctly different parents can only be duplicated by repeating the original cross (or by vegetative means).

Germination in the greenhouse or in a propagating case
It is safe to say that more plants are raised from seeds than by any other method of propagation – most

vegetables, pot plants and bedding subjects are seed raised. For these, the main sowing season under glass is late winter through spring. Many beginners feel that seed sowing is difficult and if one or two failures are experienced there is a tendency to give up. Actually, provided the right conditions are given, raising plants

Ensure warmth, moisture and a free-flow of air.

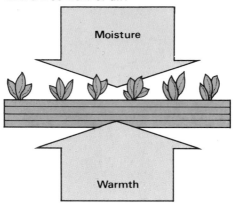

Moisture

Warmth

from seed is straightforward. It is essential to provide the optimum germination temperature which is recommended on the seed packet or in the catalogue. Usually this is in the region of 18–21°C (65–70°F). It is, of course, way beyond the means of most people to heat the whole greenhouse to this temperature and so the gardener generally buys an electrically heated propagating case for the greenhouse – it normally sits on the bench. In such a case the heat is generally provided (very cheaply) by soil-warming cables. The rest of the greenhouse can then be kept at a

Electrically heated propagator

temperature of around 10°C (50°F), which is an acceptable level for a wide range of subjects.

Success is even more easily achieved by the use of modern seed-sowing composts. Many of these are soil-less or all-peat types, but for those gardeners who prefer something more traditional, it is still possible to buy the soil-based John Innes seed compost. Whatever you buy, make sure that it has been produced by a reliable manufacturer.

Cuttings

The next most important method of propagating plants is by means of cuttings. Basically a cutting is a portion of a plant which is severed and rooted in suitable conditions. Fortunately for the gardener, cuttings of many plants are very easy to root either with or without heat, but it is worth mentioning that rooting is generally quicker if heat is provided, as in an electrically heated propagating case.

There are now many modern aids to assist in the successful rooting of cuttings. For instance, it is worth dipping the bases of all cuttings in a hormone rooting powder. This speeds rooting and results in a stronger root system. There are many mediums in which cuttings can be inserted – the traditional one is a mixture of equal parts sphagnum peat and coarse sand. More modern materials include Perlite and Vermiculite. These can be used alone or mixed with sphagnum peat in place of the traditional sand.

There are various types of cutting that the home propagator can make use of but the most usual is the stem cutting which, as the term implies, is a piece of plant stem – generally a new or young shoot. Young side shoots of plants are often used as cuttings. Plants that can be increased easily from stem cuttings include the greenhouse plants pelargonium (geranium), coleus, fuchsia, chrysanthemum and carnation. A wide range of garden plants can also be increased by this method – trees, shrubs, hardy perennials and alpines.

Then there are leaf cuttings, whereby a whole leaf or a portion of leaf is encouraged to root, after which a new plant will be produced. Several greenhouse plants are commonly increased by this method, like streptocarpus, peperomias, saintpaulias, *Begonia rex* and similar begonias, sansevieria, crassula and echeveria.

Finally, some plants can be increased by pieces of root – known as root cuttings. This is an extremely easy method of propagation and it is used for a wide range of shrubs,

Vegetative propagation by cuttings
This method enables you to clone perennials and is particularly useful for duplicating hybrids that do not come true

Non-woody stem cuttings
From early spring to end summer, take young shoots (no more than 75 mm–3 in-long). Cut immediately below a node (bud or leaf joint) and remove the leaves from that node.

Woody stem cuttings
In late autumn, take vigorous stem (about 200 mm–8 in-long) from current year's growth. Remove all leaves from lower half of the stem.

Leaf cuttings
Long-leaved plants, like streptocarpus, can be cut across the leaf. With African violets (saintpaulias), take the leaf stem too. Part of a begonia leaf can be planted so long as you pot a leaf-point that carries a vein.

Root cuttings
Cut up roots or rhizomes and pot the pieces.

trees, hardy perennials and some alpines. cuttings of most of these can be rooted without artificial heat. Take them in late autumn or winter when the parent plants are dormant.

Layering
This is where a shoot is encouraged to form roots while it is still attached to the parent plant, and when rooted it is cut away and planted elsewhere. Many garden plants, like trees and shrubs, can be layered. The runners of strawberry plants are layered to secure new plants. Normal layering involves rooting the shoot or stem in the soil around the parent plant, but there is an adaptation known as air layering where the stem is rooted above ground level. In this case the stem is encouraged to root in a wad of sphagnum moss held in place with a polythene sleeve. Many greenhouse plants, such as rubber plants, can be air layered but weaving into soil afterwards is not always easy.

Grafting
This is where parts of two separate plants are joined together permanently to form a new plant. Grafting is used to produce fruit trees and various ornamentals. A shoot of the plant to be

from seed. Ensure an airy, well-drained medium, and a moist atmosphere for non-woody cuttings where transpiration is rapid.

propagated (known as the scion) is joined to a root system of another plant (known as the rootstock). The idea is that the rootstock controls the growth of the subsequent plant. Grafting calls for highly skilled knifework and a lot of practice to become proficient.

Budding
This is a form of grafting but instead of joining a piece of stem on to a rootstock, a single growth bud is used instead. When this bud has united with the rootstock it produces stems, leaves and eventually flowers. Budding is often used to propagate roses and again is a very skilled operation, needing plenty of practice.

Fern propagation
You can obtain spores from the surface of a fern frond in late summer and sprinkle them on a sterilized seedling mixture. Cover the tray or pot with glass and place it in a shady position in the greenhouse. Avoid disturbing the container (water from below if necessary). Prick out the seddlings when they appear, after about one year, and grow them on in shade. Only when new fronds appear should a gradual hardening off process begin, in preparation for their planting out in the garden.

Production

Greenhouse production

A heated greenhouse should be able to supply all parts of your garden with a wide range of useful and ornamental plants.

It has a special role in planning for decorative interest through the year, not just by providing suitable conditions for raising summer bedding plants, but for shrubs, hardy perennials, alpines and bulbs too. It can also be responsible for providing many cut flowers and pot plants for year-round interest in the home. Alternatively for greenhouse production alone, or for setting out later in the garden, it is an extremely useful instrument for the vegetable and fruit grower.

The greenhouse is, therefore, the garden powerhouse. With imaginative planning, seasonal colour and a timely supply of utility crops can be assured.

Decorative plant production
Half-hardy annuals

See Germination in the greenhouse, page 222. Early spring is the time to sow summer bedders. They will survive outdoor planting in warm climates, but are not frost hardy.

Hardening off

Half-hardy annuals can be planted out in early summer when they will just be coming into flower, but being soft and tender they need to be gradually inured to the effect of transplantation. This process is called hardening off. In a particularly mind spring you may be tempted to risk planting out early, but even if the weather holds, slugs will travel long distances to attack such succulent specimens.

When the seedlings are big enough to handle, prick them out and give them sufficient room to develop (say 50 mm (2 in) apart). When they are making strong growth (and about two to three weeks before they are due to be planted out) transfer them to cold frames. Over this period gradually increase the ventilation during the day, but keep them covered at night. Should unseasonable frosts appear, put covers on the frames. In fact covers are never a bad idea when first removing the plants from the greenhouse.

Biennials

If you sow biennials in the greenhouse in late spring, they will be strong enough to be planted out in late autumn, to flower the following year. Be careful to disturb their roots as little as possible.

Hardy perennials

Many hardy perennials or border plants can be raised from seeds in the greenhouse. If they are sown during late winter (January or February in Britain) then sizable plants will be available for planting in the border at the end of spring to flower in the summer. However, if the seeds are sown later than recommended (say in the period March to May) then flowering will not commence until the summer of the second year.

Border plants which are often raised in the greenhouse include delphiniums, rudbeckias, gaillardias, lupins and lychnis.

Chrysanthemums

Many gardeners with a greenhouse like to grow a few chrysanthemums. There are the early-flowering kinds which bloom out of doors in the autumn (they make excellent border subjects) and the late-flowering chrysanths which are flowered under glass – although they can be grown outside all summer, in large pots.

Both types are raised from cuttings in the greenhouse in late winter and we are especially recommended for flower arrangements.

Pot plants

The greenhouse should, of course, also be used for producing pot plants for the house and if it is heated there should be a succession of subjects right the way through the year. Sowing should take place at various times of the year to ensure a succession of blooms.

For instance, various subjects can be sown in late winter/early spring for summer flowering: impatiens, streptocarpus, gloxinia, pelargonium, schizanthus and celosia. Coleus, grown for its highly colourful foliage, can also be sown during this period.

In late spring/early summer, sow the following to provide plants for winter/spring flowering: cineraria, primula, calceolaria; and, for fruits, ornamental peppers and solanum.

In mid-summer, sow the popular cyclamen, which will flower in the autumn/winter of the second year.

Forcing bulbs to anticipate the flowering season

Pots of early flowering bulbs can be extraordinarily attractive and are not difficult to manage. The important principle here is that all bulbs enjoy a period of cool before they flower. Without it, they will grow with great vigour but may well lose their flowers.

As a rule of thumb, bring your bulbs into the house when the flower buds are visible or palpable. Excessive heat at this stage makes tham think that they have already reached summer, so encouraging them to elongate their leaves, build up a good store of food for their resting period, and sometimes dispense with flowering altogether.

Some bulbs, such as hyacinths and some narcissi, are treated so that they will form flower buds more rapidly. These so-called 'prepared' bulbs should be planted as soon as purchased in a cool, dark place. When their shoots are well advanced, move them into the warmth and light of the greenhouse and, once the flower buds are visible, bring them indoors.

Early, forced bulbs can be grown on in the garden. See page 182.

Vegetables for outdoor cropping

In the spring one can raise from seeds a wide range of vegetables for planting out later. For all of the subjects mentioned below, slightly heated conditions are recommended for raising the plants, although all could be raised at a later date in an unheated greenhouse. A germination temperature of 18°C (65°F) is recommended.

Broad beans can be sown in late winter and the young plants set out in mid-spring, for cropping during early summer. They are perfectly hardy but will produce earlier crops if sown under glass. Plants can be raised either in seed trays or in individual small pots.

French beans are tender and easily damaged by frost – therefore one cannot sow these early out of doors. By making a sowing in a heated greenhouse in spring and planting out at the end of the season when all danger of frost is over, early summer pickings are assured. Again raise plants either in seed trays or, preferably, in individual small pots.

Although hardy, several brassicas can be raised in the greenhouse to ensure earlier maturity. For instance, Brussels sprouts can be sown in late winter and planted out in mid-spring, to achieve pickings by late summer. Cauliflowers may be sown in February or March in Britain and the young plants set out in April/May. Heads will then be produced during the summer. Brassicas should, ideally, be grown in individual small pots such as compressed peat pots.

Celery is raised in a heated greenhouse in the spring. As it is frost-tender do not set the plants out until the end of spring or early summer. One should be able to start pulling sticks of celery in late summer/autumn.

Celeriac, which is a root vegetable known as the turnip-rooted celery (it has a celery flavour) is raised in exactly the same way. Both can be grown in seed trays to start with.

Ridge cucumbers make a useful crop for the cold frame and can be raised in a heated greenhouse. Sow the seeds in mid-spring in individual small pots; plant out in the frame in the first month of summer. They can even be successfully grown out of doors in a warm sheltered spot. Fruiting will commence towards late summer.

Sweet corn should be sown under glass in mid-spring, one seed to a small peat pot, and the young plants can be set out in the open garden during late spring or very early summer. Cropping takes place in the summer – there are early, mid-season and late varieties.

To obtain young tomato plants for setting out of doors in late spring, sow seeds in a heated greenhouse during the first spring months. Always grow the plants in small pots. Successful cropping out of doors does depend on the summer weather – if you experience a warm summer then a good crop of ripe fruits will be produced, but in a poor summer you may end up with a load of green tomatoes.

Vegetable marrows (squash) will start to fruit earlier if plants are raised in a heated greenhouse. Make the sowing mid-spring, one seed to a small peat pot, and plant out at the end of the season to crop during the summer.

Finally you can sow onion seeds in seed trays in mid-winter (say January in Britain) and plant out the young plants late spring. They will be ready for pulling in late summer.

Vegetables for the greenhouse

Aubergines (egg-plants) are rapidly gaining in popularity as they become better known. Sow in heat in early spring and plant out when 15 cm (6 in) tall. Provide some heat until the season ends to protect from frost. Cropping will commence in late summer and continue into autumn.

Cucumbers for the heated greenhouse are sown in late winter or early spring and are planted out when 15 cm long. They will crop freely throughout the summer, given good treatment.

Capsicums or sweet peppers, like aubergines, have gained popularity in recent years as gardeners have found that they are as easy to grow as tomatoes – indeed, they require the same conditions. Sow the seeds in early spring and plant out when 15 mm tall. Fruits will be produced in the summer and autumn.

Tomatoes are considered by many gardeners to be the major greenhouse crop. If borders are used as tomato beds, it is very important to sterilize them annually. Sowing time depends on whether the greenhouse is heated:

To produce plants for a heated structure, sow the seeds in late winter and prick out the young plants when they are about 15 cm in height. The plants should start cropping in late spring and continue throughout the summer and into the autumn. If you have an unheated greenhouse then delay sowing until early spring. Fruits will be produced from about mid-summer onwards.

There are several salad crops that can be grown under glass, the main one being lettuce. Most gardeners produce lettuces under glass from winter through the following spring by making sowings of suitable varieties from late summer to autumn. Radishes are easily grown under glass and sowings can be made in succession during late summer and autumn – the roots can be pulled three to four weeks after sowing.

If you want some really early young carrots then make a sowing of an early variety very late in the winter. Given gentle heat you will be able to start pulling young roots from the end of spring onwards.

Forcing vegetables

The greenhouse can also be used for gently forcing certain vegetables which are grown to maturity in the open garden.

Chicory is sown outdoors in the spring but in the autumn the roots can be lifted, potted and taken into the greenhouse to be forced in gentle heat (10°C) and darkness. The resulting shoots (or chicons) are then harvested for salads.

Rhubarb crowns can be dug up in mid-winter and boxed in old potting compost. Then take them into the greenhouse and keep them dark and warm. You will then have winter supplies of rhubarb (especially if crowns are forced in succession) every two weeks during the first couple of months of winter.

Fruit

The greenhouse can be used to produce various fruits, the most popular being strawberries and melons.

Young strawberry plants can be potted in mid-summer and kept outdoors till mid-winter when they are taken into the greenhouse and given a temperature of 10°C (50°F). This is gradually stepped up to 16°C (60°F). Fruiting will commence around the middle of spring, many weeks ahead of outdoor plants. Most gardeners divide off part of the greenhouse to maintain a higher temperature specially for their strawberry plants.

Greenhouse melons need plenty of heat and should not be grown unless a temperature of at least 16°C can be provided at all times. Sow seeds in early to mid-spring and plant in late spring. Fruits will be ready for picking in the summer. If you have an unheated greenhouse then you could grow cantaloupe melons which are much hardier and can, in fact, be grown in cold frames.

225

The greenhouse

Siting the greenhouse

A greenhouse should be sited in an open but sheltered situation – in other words, not shaded by trees or tall buildings but protected from strong cold winds (otherwise heat loss will be considerable and heating bills extremely high). In a very exposed situation, wind damage may also occur – in a glazed house, panes may be broken and in a polythene structure the covering material may be torn to shreds.

Ideally, a greenhouse should be built on level ground, never in a hollow or at the foot of a slope where cold air may collect into a frost pocket and make the greenhouse extremely expensive to heat. If there is no alternative to siting the greenhouse on a slope then the best position would be half-way down.

Most people would prefer to have the greenhouse near to the house so that it is more convenient to manage. Also, services like electricity and water will be cheaper to run to the greenhouse if it is situated nearby.

Having chosen a site, the orientation of the house needs to be considered – in other words, which way should it face?

If possible, ensure that the ridge runs from east to west as this allows maximum light to enter the house. This is very important for winter crops, which will get the best of the low winter sun. If you opt for a lean-to greenhouse, then a south or west-facing aspect is best for the majority of plants. Of course if you intend growing mainly shade-loving plants then position the lean-to in a north or east aspect. This advice is applicable to gardens situated in the northern hemisphere and should be adapted to the sun's path when siting a greenhouse in the southern hemisphere.

Solar houses for hot and mild climates

Solar greenhouses are the coming thing, and you don't have to live in a very hot climate to benefit from their money-saving purpose.

Orientation is even more important when planning a solar house. Observe both winter and summer paths of the sun across your garden, and if possible remove any obstacles to them. Make sure that the intended site will, at the very least, enjoy the benefit of the mid-morning to mid-afternoon sun in winter. Obviously these houses are most efficient where the sun is in evidence most of the time, but in mild climates a well-constructed, imaginatively designed house can prove successful. There, it is an overcast sky (more than the relatively low temperature of the sun's rays) that is the biggest problem.

Above: a sloping-sided cedar greenhouse suitable for an 'ornamental' situation and well-designed to make the most of the low-angled winter sun.
Right: well-suited for a small garden, the curved aluminium house maxi-mizes space inside.
Below left: a similarly designed conservatory.
Below right: this hexagonal all-cedar house makes a spacious unusual alternative.

Orientate the house to make the most of the sun through the seasons.

A well-orientated, lean-to structure is the best choice in a mild climate. Design the house to be as *long* as possible so that it makes the most of the sun's daily arc across the sky. You could also angle or tilt its exterior wall (say 60 degrees) to make the most of the low arc which the sun traverses in winter.

The question of how much glazing you will need is also dependent upon the volume of interior space you want. Solar performance drops off as the volume of interior space increases. This principle would seem, therefore, to favour a long, *thin*, lean-to solar house.

Insulation
This is important in all greenhouses and too many can justifiably be criticized as 'thermal sieves'. But it is vital in the case of the solar house that is poorly served by sun in winter. The converse of the principle: 'more glazing, more heat and light', is: 'the more glazing the greater the heat loss'. Lean-to structures have a built-in advantage in this respect over free-standing structures (the dwelling house wall not only reduces heat loss, but actually contains it). The type of glazing you choose is also important. Plastic glazing materials, common glass, fibreglass, all have widely varying resistances to the outflow of heat, and advice should be sought about their R-value. Fibreglass is much better than common glass; styrene and urethane plastics are particularly efficient.

Double glazing is recommended for mild climate solar houses, and there are insulating curtains, panels, shutters, etc. variously effective at retaining heat during the night or prolonged periods of overcast weather. Their efficacy depends partly upon their ability to seal off a 'dead' air space between 'curtain' and glazing.

Solar storage
Drums of water, painted matt (flat) black to maximize solar energy absorption, are, pound for pound, more effective than bricks, rocks or concrete, but a combination of materials may be preferred and advice should be sought. The important point is to allow sufficient space for the system at design stage and place it, as far as possible, in line with the sun's rays.

A solar house for a mild climate garden

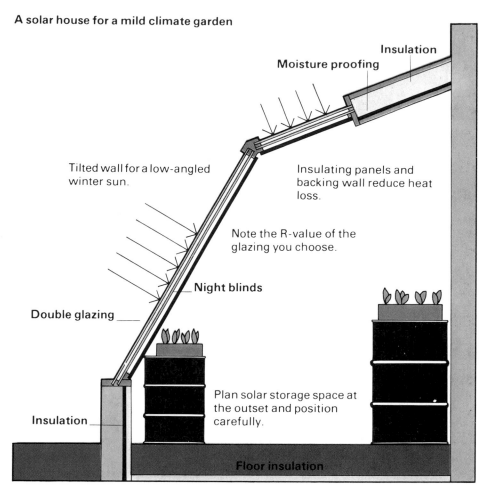

Above: a cross-sectional view of a solar lean-to house. **Below**: similarly economic, this greenhouse could share its colour, scent and warmth with an adjacent room.

Other types of greenhouse
How big should the greenhouse be? Bear in mind that it must be in proportion to the garden and should not dominate the site. Having said that, choose the largest that you can afford, or the garden can comfortably take, for a greenhouse is very quickly filled. It is probably best to go for a house which is one size larger than you think is necessary at the present time. Of course, many modern gardens are very tiny – pocket handkerchief plots – and for these there are many mini-greenhouses and lean-to structures to choose from.

To be more specific, the average-size garden will comfortably take a 1.8 m by 2.4 m (6 ft by 8 ft) greenhouse, or a 2.4 m by 3 m (8 ft by 10 ft) model. Both of these are very popular sizes, particularly the former.

These days greenhouses are constructed of wood or aluminium alloy. Wood, of course, blends in well with most gardens and may be the best choice if the greenhouse is to be set in an ornamental part of the garden as opposed to a vegetable plot. Western red cedar is ideal for an ornamental situation, but if you have to economize (or if the house is for the utility part of the garden) then there is softwood, which has to be painted or treated with a timber preservative (a horticultural type).

Aluminium alloy houses are very popular today; they require far less maintenance than wooden houses and admit more light. However, except for those with an anodized bronze finish, such houses do not blend in very well with the ornamental garden.

227

The greenhouse

There are various shapes to choose from. The traditional design has a pitched roof and is the same basic shape as the ordinary dwelling house. Timber and aluminium models are available, either glass to ground or with solid (e.g. timber) sides to a height of 60–90 cm (2–3 ft). The glass to ground house admits maximum light and allows crops such as tomatoes and lettuces, to be grown at ground level in a soil border or in grow-bags. Solid sides to bench height ensure better heat retention than all-glass, and such a house is particularly recommended for pot plants, which are grown on benches, or for home propagation.

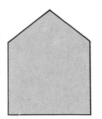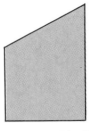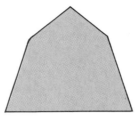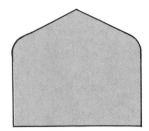

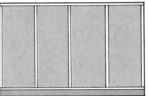

Left to right: traditional pitched roof, tilted sides model, an economical lean-to, an aluminium space-saver. **Right:** glass to ground for light; solid sides for heat retention.

The traditional span-roof house has been slightly updated recently, and there are now models available with curved eaves – a very pleasing design and particularly recommended for an ornamental setting. Only glass to ground is available in this design, with an aluminium framework (anodised in some models). There is also a model available which can be double-glazed.

Ideal for small gardens, or even for setting in a lawn or on a patio, is the octagonal greenhouse. Most models are glass to ground and the framework may be timber or aluminium. This is a very pleasing design (and remarkably spacious inside) and looks good in an ornamental setting.

Appropriate to the space age is the dome-shaped greenhouse which is constructed of triangular panes of glass in an aluminium framework. Not only is it decorative, but it lets in plenty of light.

A much older design is the uneven-span greenhouse – the side and roof sections are of different sizes and they slope at different angles to ensure good light transmission (and thus good plant growth). Available in timber or aluminium, some models are clad in clear, rigid, corrugated plastic.

Many mini-greenhouses (too small to get inside) are available today. Most are in aluminium, generally with a sliding door for access. In spite of their size they are useful for raising bedding plants, vegetables, etc., and for growing a summer crop of tomatoes, for instance.

Flexible-polythene houses have been introduced in recent years and are most appropriate to the utility part of the garden. Indeed they are especially suitable for growing vegetables. Generally they are tunnel-shaped, and the plastic sheet (clear or white) is stretched over a tubular-steel or aluminium framework. The polythene

Above: list what is important to you; is easy access one consideration?

will need replacing every two or three years.

Timber or aluminium lean-to greenhouses are available, either glass-to-ground or half-timbered. There are also models with curved eaves. Their advantages in terms of containing heat and insulation have been noted above.

Mini-lean-to's are available for use where space is limited, and could be erected on a balcony or patio. The framework is aluminium.

Finally we come to the conservatory. This is generally built to the customer's requirements (size and design) and is considered an integral part of the house. It is used for plant display and very often as a living area too. A conservatory can be very expensive,

228

but of course it adds value to the house. One can have a traditional or a modern design. In the former style, conservatories are built of timber with brick sides to bench height; modern designs might have an aluminium frame. Generally, there is direct access from the house. Sun rooms come in this category and many are light enough for plants, especially if a clear, rigid plastic roof is provided.

Growing under artificial light
In America, propagating and growing plants under artificial lights inside the home is extremely popular and this form of gardening is now catching on in Europe too. The beauty of it is that plants can be grown in very dark places – gloomy corners, dark passageways or even in cellars – and there is no need to go to the expense of building a greenhouse.

The equipment
Fluorescent tubes are normally used but they must be of a type which produces suitable light for plant growth. The following are recommended:

1. Warm white.

2. Daylight types.

3. Grolux – this is the brand name of a fluorescent tube specially developed for plants. The first two are normal domestic tubes and are generally cheaper than Grolux.

Most convenient are 1.5 m (5 ft) long tubes with a rating of 65 to 80 watts.

Installing the lights
A typical lighting system consists of six 1.5 m tubes mounted 10-15 cm (4-6 in) apart on a board with reflective foil behind them. The board is suspended no more than 60 cm (2 ft) above the growing area (bench, shelf, etc.). If you are a DIY enthusiast then you may consider building a special open-fronted cabinet for your plants with the lights built into the top. But it should be stressed that the wiring of a lighting system must be undertaken by an experienced electrician. For the majority of plants, the lights should be turned on for a period of twelve hours per day.

Uses of indoor lighting
Much can be done indoors under artificial lights. Propagation immediately comes to mind – all kinds of plants can be raised from seeds, including vegetables, pot plants and bedding plants, either for the greenhouse or for planting outdoors. Cuttings of all kinds of plants can be rooted under lights. Though not essential, rooting time is often reduced.

Above left: curved roof conservatories, a versatile design. **Above and below**: an ideal link between house and garden that can also be another room.

Various kinds of vegetables can be grown to maturity in these artificial conditions but remember that you could be restricted by the space beween bench and lights in some small ready-made systems. There, lettuces are a good choice provided you keep them really cool, together with other salad crops like radishes. Tomatoes grow really well under lights in warm conditions but you will probably need to choose a dwarf bush variety (one which attains only 30–45 cm (12-18 in) in height).

229

The greenhouse

Organising the greenhouse

Layout should be planned to maximize space. First of all a path is needed and generally this runs down the centre. You can use concrete slabs, 30–60 cm (1–2 ft) wide according to the width of the greenhouse, or 12 mm (½ in) shingle to a depth of 50 mm (2 in) and retained with side boards. On one side of the path you could have a soil border in which to grow plants such as tomatoes in summer and lettuces in winter. Borders should be sterilized annually, especially if tomatoes are grown. But if you don't want a border then you could cover the area with shingle and grow these crops in grow-bags or pots instead.

On the other side of the path it is usual to have staging on which to grow pot plants, raise seeds and so on.

Bench-type staging is often built with aluminium or timber and the maximum width should be 90 cm (3 ft) for comfortable working. It should be about waist height. With tiered staging you can make maximum use of space. The width of each tier will depend upon its height from the ground – it is easier to stretch to the back of a 90 cm (3 ft) shelf if it is at waist level than if it is the bottom tier of a three-level staging. Staging is ideal for the back wall of a lean-to or conservatory but can also be used in free-standing houses.

To make use of the space above bench height it is usual to have shelves. These can either be permanent or temporary, and might take trays of seedlings in the spring when the house tends to become overcrowded. Remember that shelves cut down the amount of light reaching the plants below, so it is usual to have fairly narrow ones. They can be slung below the eaves under the ridge or on the back wall of a greenhouse.

Equipment
Heating

Heating the greenhouse greatly widens its scope and is virtually essential if one is considering raising a wide range of ornamental plants and vegetables for the garden. Today there is a wide choice of heating methods and these are discussed below.

Gas

There are many portable gas heaters available and some are fully automatic. Modern heaters have all kinds of safety devices so it is quite safe to leave them if, for instance, you wish to have a few days away. Some run off natural gas which means that a gas supply must be run to the greenhouse. Others run off bottled propane gas but this works out more expensive than natural gas. Gas heaters are thoroughly

recommended for greenhouse heating and they give off carbon dioxide which is essential for healthy plant growth.

Paraffin

Portable heaters which burn paraffin are extremely popular today and are considered the cheapest method of heating a greenhouse, even though this fuel has rocketed in price in recent years. They are particularly useful if you want to heat the greenhouse in the spring only to raise seedlings, but they do create condensation.

Electricity

This is considered the most expensive form of heating but it is very reliable, clean and the heaters can be left for long periods by gardeners who spend a lot of time away from home. There are various kinds of electric heater for greenhouses and these are as follows:

1. Tubular heaters are banks of pipes which have internal heating elements. They are fixed to the greenhouse walls, generally under the staging just above ground level so that the warmed air rises among the plants. Like all electric heaters they are thermostatically controlled.

2. Portable fan heaters are generally placed on the greenhouse path. The fan sucks in cold air which is warmed as it

passes through a heating element and it is then blown out.

3. Warming cables are low-voltage electric cables which are far cheaper to run than tubular or fan heaters. In fact, they are really meant to heat only comparatively small areas. There are air-warming cables which are useful for heating small spaces, such as a mini-greenhouse of a frame. They are secured around the walls of the structure. Then there are soil-warming cables which are buried in soil or compost to provide bottom heat. These can be used, for instance, in a propagating case, or in a soil border in which it is intended to grow subjects like tomatoes, peppers and lettuces. Such cables are run from a transformer and are thermostatically controlled.

Solid-fuel boilers

The boiler heats water which then flows around the greenhouse in pipes which are generally positioned around the sides of the structure. One can certainly achieve plenty of heat with such a system and modern boilers will burn any type of fuel, including the cheapest. They need stoking twice a day and the ash is removed once a day. The system can be thoroughly recommended if fairly high temperatures are required for only a moderate fuel bill. Boilers can also be gas or oil-fired.

Lighting

It is useful to have some form of lighting in the greenhouse so that one can work or inspect plants during the short days of winter. Generally a fluorescent tube fixed immediately under the ridge will do.

Insulation

If the greenhouse is heated it is sensible to insulate it to reduce heat loss. This will in turn reduce heating bills. Basically the method of insulating a house is to line it internally with either polythene sheeting or netting, leaving a gap of about 25 mm (1 in) or so between the glass and the liner. A popular type of polythene is known as bubble polythene which consists of thousands of air bubbles sandwiched between two layers of the material. There are many brands of this on the market today. It can result in up to 50% reduction in heat loss. Such a lining is best taken down for the spring and summer as it does reduce light a little. It should also be noted that greenhouses lined with polythene usually drip; ventilation can help to reduce excess moisture which must be avoided in winter. A material which can be left in place all the year round is a special type of netting which provides insulation in the cold weather and shading for the plants in the summer.

Shading

We have already touched on shading but let us now consider some of the many products available. There are liquid shading materials which are mixed with water and applied by brush or sprayer to the outside of the glass. Such shading should be applied mid-spring and removed in the autumn. The modern materials cannot be washed off by rain but are easily removed with a rag at the end of the season.

For more accurate control of shading one needs to install roller blinds. There are external types made of plastic strips, wooden laths or canes. Of course, one has to be on hand to raise and lower them according to whether the sun is in or out. If you have money to spare you could have automatic blinds – but these really are expensive. You may prefer to have internal blinds which may be in white translucent plastic or linen. These do a very good job and are generally quite reasonably priced.

Ventilation

Invest in one or two automatic ventilation arms which raise and lower ventilators according to prevailing weather conditions. They are solar operated and can be used on ridge or side vents.

Greenhouse equipment to regulate heat, light, water and humidity – the significant elements in a greenhouse environment – will reflect outside climatic conditions and what you intend growing. But always remember your needs too, particularly when planning work surfaces.

Watering

There are several ways of watering plants in greenhouses – overhead misty sprays, individual 'drip tubes' for pot plants, and sub-irrigation. For the general run a sub-irrigation bench is probably the most practical. One can make up a bench, line it with polythene sheeting and cover this with a 50 mm (2 in) layer of sharp, coarse sand, perlite or special thick plastic foam sheeting. The pot plants are stood on this base which is kept wet by turning on the trickle lines as often and for as long as is necessary. If the plants are in plastic pots it is sufficient to give them a firm twist to ensure that the base is really in contact with the wet base. If ordinary clay pots are used the normal piece of 'crock' or broken pot over the drainage hole is replaced by a tuft of glass wool such as one buys for insulating lofts. This ensures contact between the soil in the pot and the wet bench. The plants will draw up as much moisture as they need and no more. Even easier to install are plastic trays which come in various shapes and sizes up to two feet square. These may be stood on a slatted or solid based bench and filled with the same or other material.

Overhead watering is less effective because it is not always desirable to wet the foliage. In hard water areas unsightly lime deposits will appear on the leaves; moreover, keeping the foliage or flowers wet can encourage disease in many plants.

There are sub-irrigation systems where a constant level of water on the bench is maintained automatically by the use of a cistern and ball valve connected to the main water supply. This kind of installation is excellent when the owner of the greenhouse is likely to be away from home for any length of time.

At one time it was normal to have a rain water tank in the greenhouse. The idea was that the water would be at the same temperature as the house and this would be more acceptable to the plants than cold water straight from the tap. The trouble with a tank is that if a watering can brushes against a diseased leaf and is then dipped into the tank the water soon becomes contaminated ('disease soup' as it is cynically termed). Research has shown that it is better to give plants clean water from the mains. After all, a can or two could always be filled with water and left to warm up overnight for plants that need special cossetting.

Another very useful piece of equipment is a trigger-operated, two-foot long lance which can be plugged into the end of a short length of lightweight plastic hose attached to a mains tap inside the house. With this one can reach easily across a wide bench, and watering is much less arduous than holding up a can weighing 5 Kg (1 stone) or so.

The flower arranger's garden

Plant planning for the flower arranger

Interest in flower arrangement has grown to the point where it has made gardeners out of flower arrangers. Sheila Macqueen started her garden by growing plants to cut, and wasn't interested in the garden as anything other than a storehouse of materials for her art. In those days it was not possible to buy good background plants from florists and there was no alternative but to cram her garden full of everything she would need.

This approach certainly kept the weeds down, but plants do not appreciate being grown cheek-by-jowl. If you want good delphiniums, for example, you have to give them space to grow.

In developing an interest in plants in the garden, she became something of a plant collector. New and sometimes exotic plants added range to her flower arrangements. She began to appreciate plants in different ways, which benefited both indoor and garden displays. She became conscious of the constant flow of new varieties which, in some cases, reduce garden maintenance as well as enhancing her arrangements. For example, tall plants need staking and are unattractive for so long in the gardening year. But now there are new shorter subjects which are extremely attractive and far less labour intensive.

In thinking about the look of her garden she decided to concentrate her energies upon decorative shrubs (amelanchier and a few shrub roses are a good start), rather than concentrating on the more time-consuming annuals. Not only did this decision break up her border displays, it provided a far richer source for picking right through the seasons.

Preserving the garden scene

Indiscriminate picking can damage plants and spoil the garden by leaving gaping holes.

If you want a row of gladioli solely for picking there is no need to place them in full view; tuck them behind something else. Think carefully, too, about what to cut and where to take from a plant. It takes a long time for young shrubs to mature before they can be cut without damaging them. Think about the effect your 'pruning' will have on any shrub or tree. A good rule of thumb is to walk around a bush six times before cutting. Irreparable damage can sometimes be done for future seasons. If you have lots of old trees there is less need to worry, but be strict with yourself when tempted to apply your secateurs to a new Cox's

orange pippin or hack away at an azalea bush. Again, the autumn reds and browns are nature's way of saying that a plant is almost over. You can have two days of unequalled brilliance inside the house, but it is a criminal shame to denude a tree or shrub of numerous branches when you know in advance that they will not last.

Beginning a flower arranger's garden

Initially, go for plants which are good *basically*. Alpines are lovely in spring, but you soon exhaust the supply. Bulbs, particularly the little delicate fritillaries, are special, but mostly used for miniature arrangments. First and foremost choose plants with big bold leaves and those which stand well. Viburnums, jasmin, yellow mahonias are a good investment because they will provide you with interest throughout the year. Then, treat yourself to a few lines purely for picking and be sure to position them so that the garden doesn't suffer when they are gone.

'The only things I grow purely for cutting,' says Sheila Macqueen, 'are a row of paeonies, a row of gladioli and perhaps some tulips (though the pheasants eat most of these). Gladioli never look really good in a border, but they're super to cut and last a long time in water, so I keep these at the back. I usually have a few dahlias most of which I tuck away, allowing just a few pride of place.'

The arranger's needs can direct a garden plan towards unusual plants and decorative shrubs for interest across the seasons. Roses are good focal points.

There is no one plan suitable for everyone, as displays depend so much on the occasions that they are for, the environments they are to highlight, and the personality of the arranger. But here is a list of ten plants you shouldn't be without:

Alchemilla mollis
Cynara scolymus (the artichoke)
Arum italicum 'Pictum'
Bergenia spp
Euphorbia spp
Hedera spp
Helleborus spp
Hosta spp
Phytolacca americana
Sedum spp

The list provides an essential range of plants from winter to summer. Golden privet might be added. It is not unlike the privet hedge, but instead of clipping it close, let it go so as to encourage a rich gold foliage. Later you can cut it in abundance.

Other suggestions for round-the-year cutting

In late winter, go for a background of branches. Look in the garden for interesting forms and make it special with a bunch of early daffodils which you can buy at this time from the florist. Perhaps you might even

consider using a houseplant in the centre of a group of green to give the arrangement that bit more body.

Even in the coldest month you can pick a branch of hazel catkins and enjoy watching them come out in water. There's a plant called *Garrya elliptica* which is particularly recommended for its huge long catkins. Then there are the big variegated ivies and many different hellebores. In fact there should never be a time when you cannot make an arrangement with some sort of green.

A tip for the hellebores, hosta leaves, young beech branches or the very young growth of almost anything – condition the stems before arranging them in the vase. Put their stems in boiling water and leave them for several hours, or overnight. This will expand the stems, dispelling any air bubbles present, and allow them to drink more freely. The Dutch cut everything under water for the same reason; they never allow air into stems right from the start.

Winter form
The vase will dictate the form of the branches you pick. If you have a cylindrical container than pick something tall and slim to put into it. It is generally easier to create a successful arrangement in a vase with a pedestal or foot rather than a container which is solid from top to bottom. Pick naturally curving stems and leaves to hang down over the pedestal.

Always pick for one arrangement at a time, and if you want a branch running out to the left of the vase pick one that runs out from a shrub in a similar direction. Make the arrangement in your hand as you walk round the garden. Then, and only then, buy. Because then you will know what you are looking for.

The colour and scent of spring and summer
As winter gives over to spring make use of some early bulbs in a miniature moss garden. Collect the moss during the previous autumn and store it in a plastic bag. Crocuses, snowdrops, scilla, irises and polyanthus all have comparatively short stems, so arange them in bunches in little tucks in the bed of moss. You can create a lively tapestry of spring colour in this way.

It is quite a good idea to dig your snowdrops up altogether and plant them in bowls for indoor display. Then, when they have finished flowering, take them out of their bowls and split them up, returning them to different parts of the garden. Not only is this the best way to display snowdrops in the home, but it ensures that you split up your bulbs.

Scent becomes much more important as the flowering season gets going. Hyacinths are lovely in the spring. And soon there will be sweet peas (*Lathyrus odoratus*), tobacco plants (*Nicotiana spp.*) and of course roses

too. Roses are frequently the focal point in an arrangement. Concentrate on the hybrid teas for cutting. The great thing about a rose bed is that different subjects can be selected to flower for much of the year and in a decent sized bed it is very difficult to spoil the effect by over-picking.

Many annuals make ideal cut flowers. The cosmos last very well in water and the rudbeckias and marigolds are especially recommended for the yellow and orange you may need. Midsummer is the best time of the year for reds. The gladioli, antirrhinums (and of course the roses again) help here.

Of the summer grasses *Stipa calamagrostis* and *S. pennata*, both with slender, erect stems are most useful for floral arrangements. But now is also the time to think about dried plants for winter. The plume-like heads of *Lagurus ovatus* make extremely decorative features when cut and dried, as indeed do the elegant seed heads of *Briza maxima*, known as quaking grass. There are many annuals: the tiny white flowers and green, cup-shaped calyces of bells of Ireland (*Molucella laevis*) make very successful winter decorations, dried; the pink or yellow strawflower, *Helichrysum bracteatum*, and the statice, *Limonium sinuatum*, particularly the colourful mixture of 'Pacific Giants', are also useful. Other everlastings such as the purple, pink or yellow flowering heads of *Gomphrena globosa*, the bright rose pink *Helipterum manglesii*, and the double-flowering poppy annuals can lend vital tones to an appropriate winter arrangement.

Bracken and ferns press well as do branches of autumnal coloured beech. Any good seed head of delphinium, hollyhock, foxglove or lupin, if hung up to dry, makes good background material for winter chrysanthemums. Drying in water is, oddly enough, an excellent method of preserving delphiniums, larkspur and the heads of hydrangeas. Remove any leaves, stand them in a small amount of water and keep them over the boiler or in the linen cupboard.

Silica gel is wonderful for preserving small pieces of hellebores, dahlias and zinnias. Place in boxes and scatter the powder over the flowers until they are completely covered. Keep them in a very warm place for several days. Bells of Ireland goes green if you hang it upside down to dry, but if you put it in one part glycerine and two parts water, and allow it to soak up the mixture, it will turn cream. Beech, *Mahonia bealei*, and sweet chestnut leaves go brown and shiny and last for ever if treated in this way.

233

The flower arranger's garden

Arranging colour in the garden and for display

There are various schools of thought ranging from the symbolic ideas of Ikebana to the very modern Western preoccupation with apparently haphazard abstract arrangements. But when it comes down to it, form, colour and scent is what it is all about.

Summer is the time for colour in the garden, and it is important then to choose subjects which highlight the colours in the room in which they will be placed. This will naturally influence your plans.

Garish colours are not necessarily out. A vital red might be just the thing to pick out the colour of a cushion, the page boys' costumes at a wedding . . . Your choice will depend on the environment in which the display will sit, and if it is to be a public display, make sure that you leave time to research that fully.

Sheila Macqueen recalls one particular party when she chose an arrangement of grays, greens and blues to place beneath a painting. The next day she was thanked by the hostess who said that the picture had never before been so admired, even by people who had been in the house many times before. It is a question of leading the eye, choosing colours which will enhance an environment.

Looking for colour with a flower arranger's eye takes experience. But if you aim for harmony in the garden you will find it easier to exploit such harmonies in display. Arrange beds tonally as they might appear in a vase.

If you have a coral-pink maple (*Acer pseudoplatanus* 'Brilliantissimum'), plant it in a bed with apricot or cream azaleas. Don't be afraid of rooting out poor colour combinations and capitalize on successful chance associations as you wander round the garden creating your displays.

Green is a very important colour and one with which mistakes are commonly made. Look for lime greens rather than dark heavy greens. Somehow a mass of pine, spruce, laurel or rhododendron leaves deaden an arrangement. They sap all the colour in the display and make it look heavy. This is one occasion when what looks sparkling and beautiful outside becomes dull indoors where there is no natural light behind it.

Bold foliage is also very important. Even in a very flowery vase, bold leaves tucked in at its base give the arrangement an undershadow and

Left: spring display of narcissus. forsythia, hyacinths, cherry blossom, viburnum foliage. **Above left**: thalictrum, poppy head, *Eryngium giganteum*, hosta, *Helichrysum petiolatum*. **Above right**: near-black and white arrangement of phytolacca, elderberries, blackberries and roses. **Below left to right**: lilac, paeony and *Anthriscus sylvestris*; seedheads and preserved foliage; bunches of spring flowers tucked into a bed of moss.

bring the weight of the display down to the bottom of the vase. But use light or variegated foliage to create the background effect.

Autumn planning

In the autumn, when they are mature, hardy ferns come into their own. Use them to create a tracery effect for the outer edges of displays. In simple terms, what you are trying to do is to get some spiky shapes round the side of the vase. Then, thin the display towards its centre, making 'a flower with a face' (a dahlia, chrysanthemum or rose) the focal point.

We have said that the reds and browns of autumn do not last long indoors, but if you're prepared to sacrifice a little bit of *Parrotia persica*, conspicuous for its brilliant orange-red and scarlet autumn colouring, place it with some dahlias and the last of the orange roses. It will give tremendous value. Then there is the *Viburnum opulus* 'Sterile' which has big rounded clusters of white flowers in early summer but in autumn produces very striking scarlet leaves and bright red berries. The leaves stand on their stems; they may shrivel a little, but do not fall off. So this is certainly worth having in the garden.

Of course it is not always possible to re-create the glinting effect of the sun's light on autumn foliage. But autumn arrangments succeed, like those at other times of the year, when they characterize nature's seasons. Autumn foliage merges perfectly with hips and hawes, and berries. As you gain experience you get a feeling for the rightness of things, a feeling which is so often first experienced among the plants in your garden.

235

The herb garden

Why herbs?

There is little doubt that in recent years, there has been a remarkable resurgence of interest in herbs and herb gardens. Yet while it is safe enough to make such an assertion the reason for it is less clear. Perhaps it is that herbs can satisfy the diverse needs and enthusiasms of all gardeners whether they are owners of historic gardens or simply window boxes.

From a garden design point of view a well-conceived herb garden can epitomize Vita Sackville West's dictum which she applied to the making of Sissinghurst – it can display 'the maximum formality of design with the maximum *in*formality of planting'. Hence the essential naturalness of herbs (almost all are true species or near-species; the art of the hybridist has hardly affected how they look at all) associates admirably with paving and other hard surfaces, terrace plantings and containers. There is a danger that many plants in herb gardens can appear rather weedy, but the range is so wide that there is no need to fall into this trap.

What is a herb?

Botanically, a herb is any plant which does not develop overwintering woody tissue: thus any annual, biennial or *herb*aceous perennial deserves the epithet. In the popular context of herb gardening, a herb may be of any perennation type from a tree (*Laurus nobilis* – sweet bay) to ephemeral annuals (*Portulaca oleracea* – purslane). What is certain is that all are plants of use to man, not just as food (though some, the pot-herbs, are) but also as life-enhancers. Herbs do not as a rule support life but make it more agreeable. This indistinct aspect of luxury in essentially common plants adds a further attraction.

Herbs may be culinary, medicinal, dye plants or producers of several of the essential oils used in commercial perfumery. Some plants can legitimately take their place in more than one category. Thus rosemary has culinary, perfumery and even medicinal roles in addition to its obvious visual attraction in the garden scene. (Such a plant is bound to be of particular value in the context of herb garden planning.)

Again, different herbs produce their virtues through different parts of the plant; seeds of coriander and caraway, leaves of parsley and savory, roots of liquorice, flowers of chamomile.

Different herbs for different needs

A herb garden concerned even marginally with educating its viewers is

bound to display a more or less representative collection of species and their forms from each category. Another may strive to be markedly formal and hence require a far more visual approach. A third may be directly planned to provide herbs for constant culinary use and perhaps be sited near a kitchen door. A fourth may be concerned with recreating a part of the garden of a historic house or a small cottage garden. Fortunately the diverity of herbs is sufficient to make each possible.

Much of the interest and attraction of herb gardens can be seen in cultural (as distinct from horticultural) terms. While to some people the allusions may not be immediately obvious, relevant literary associations throughout our Western civilisation are frequent. Biblical references ("Purge me with hyssop and I shall be clean." "Oh, that's hyssop, is it!" – a common reaction on meeting this plant) are legion as are those from Chaucer, Shakespeare and many other writers up to our own day.

Planning according to use

If this is the guiding principle of your herb garden plan, the arrangement should indicate the general category of each herb. Except in purely private, personally supervised herb garden collections, it is wise to separate the obviously culinary from the indelible dye-plants and those of medicinal importance. In the latter group there are several of the most poisonous plants which can, culturally, be grown outdoors in temperate zones. A conscious choice must be made whether, in the interests of comprehensiveness, one should grow them. *Atropa belladonna*, for example, is the one British native of which great care should be taken. The berries are shining black, luscious and blandly pleasant to taste: **half a dozen will kill a child.** Thus it fully deserves its vernacular name, deadly nightshade. (Its generic name too is a nice Linnaean choice, commemorating Atropos, the third of the Greek Fates; this old crone is invariably shown holding the pair of scissors with which she cuts a man's lifeline.) In the specialist's garden, atropa might be grown in order to demonstrate the clear difference between the related, but relatively innocuous woody and black night-shades which are frequently accredited with the more exciting name. Other equally poisonous plants are given in the lists at the end of this section. While they should all be treated with respect, only those with parts likely to be eaten, such as juicy fruits, are of great concern. If they are to be grown careful labelling is essential. A colour-coding method indicating use as well as danger is recommended. Neither precaution is fool-proof.

Planning as to historical association

It is simple to create a medicinal collection into groups which separate the relatively few species used today in orthodox medicine from the many used by homeopaths and the even greater number used (with whatever degree of efficacy) in times past. But if the aim of the herb garden is mainly historical the edges of all these groups become very blurred. In the first place, it is desirable to choose a definite period to illustrate. The site and its associated house or buildings should guide the choice, efforts being made to research contemporary styles of garden and to ensure that incongruous modern cultivars do not spoil the effect.

Plotting history

If no local association of period or date presents itself, your choice could light upon the publication date of an important early text book. For example, if the first edition of John Gerard's *Herbel* is taken, there, conveniently listed with their uses, are virtually all the plants one is likely to want. If not described, presumably they were not in cultivation in 1597. National interest might well govern the choice of authority. Leonhard Fuch's *De Historia Stirpium* of 1542 might be a German choice. In Britain John Parkinson (The *Theatrum Botanicum* of 1640) or an early edition of Culpeper might be an alternative to Gerard.

Origins and growing conditions

Whatever your motivation, it will, naturally, be reflected in your herb garden's design. But before making a

definite choice, consider the range of plants eligible for inclusion from an ecological point of view. This reflects so much upon their effective cultivation. Virtually all peoples have, from prehistoric times, developed a knowledge of those indigenous plants fit for food or other needs. Of these, herbs have a lineage as long as any and most of them have been used in the form in which they are found in the wild for hundreds or even thousands of years. And as our present civilization is built so clearly upon the classical cultures of Greece and Rome it is not surprising that very many herbs known to the ancients have come down to us with a very clear pedigree.

Thus almost all the aromatic-leaved shrubs and sub-shrubs – lavender, rosemary, savory and so on – are plants of dry Mediterranean hillsides where they eke out a thin living from poor alkaline soil with spiny brooms, scrub oak and other members of the maquis.

The essential oils which man finds so attractive are, presumably, produced as a defence system designed to discourage browsing herbivores. Observation of the progress of a herd of goats scrabbling through the maquis, however, shows that the mechanism is not always successful!

In addition to these woody plants many annual and biennial herbs have a similar habitat. Their cultivational needs therefore are obvious: full sun and perfect drainage are the most desirable. This is particularly important in northern Europe (which must include the British Isles) where many Mediterraneans are bound to be close to the borderline of frost-hardiness. Even when winter temperatures are not a problem these plants grown soft lack much of their aromatic qualities.

Not all herbs are obligate sun-lovers or denizens of dry soils. The wide range of mints, statuesque angelica, even the essential parsley need moist soil and all accept shade as one way of maintaining it. Thus, fortunately, it is possible to plan and plant a formal herb garden in which all aspects are furnished.

'Furnishing' is a vital word here if a herb garden is going to maintain the billowing profusion expected of it in summer and strong bones even in winter. While these bones, where possible, should be actual herbs, it is reasonable to use what might be called 'herb garden associates'. It is also feasible to add any plants that offer colour or further scents if they have an aura of the old-fashioned, or an accepted cottage-garden connection.

Thus internal hedges of santolina and helichrysum maintain the Mediterranean grey-leaved, aromatic theme; while pinks, candytuft, love in mist (*Dianthus, Iberis* and *Nigella spp.*) nasturtiums and scented-leaved pelargoniums add summer interest. The latter are, of course, tender sub-shrubs normally surviving winter outdoors only in very mild climates. They have thus to be treated like any of the bedding geraniums, cuttings or the old plants which prefer to spend winter under glass. They are especially valuable as container plants, placed where the foliage is brushed by the passer-by when they will emit their varied fragrances upon the air.

Fortunately, there are few herbs in general use which insist upon greenhouse help (although many annuals can be brought on earlier, as half hardy annuals, and planted out from pots). One, however, in the British climate, is apt to be a very difficult plant. This is basil, *Ocimum basilicum*. This and allied species, all with utterly distinct peppery scents are truly tropical plants for whom the open garden before summertime is anathema.

Herb garden design

Although many of the best known herbs are perfectly good and indeed invaluable in their own right in the general garden, a herb garden needs to be seen as an independent entity. It may be a single bed or no more than a chequer pattern in an open site with alternate flag-stones and gaps for planting. Yet even here some form of enclosure is desirable to concentrate not only the viewing eye and questing nose, but the contemplating mind as well. The designer has the opportunity not only to produce a garden picture, but also to *encapsulate* an ideal that is connected quite overtly with times past.

237

The herb garden

On a bigger scale a herb garden is definitely *entered*. It should be enclosed from outside view; it is consciously 'apart', almost other-worldly. It is formal in outline with, as has already been emphasized, its informality coming from a profusion of plant material. While simple designs of balanced beds are easily built up, it is possible, if some historical verisimilitude is required, to refer to woodcuts of early gardens and adapt sixteenth and seventeenth century knots or simple parterres to modern needs. Such designs had themselves developed from the more simply cultivated pleasure-garden of monastic times. These enclosed cloister gardens retained the form of classical patterns known from excavations at Pompeii and Herculaneum. Thus, tradition is maintained, not only in the plants grown but in the way they are arranged.

Enclosure could be of hard materials, with walls creating a courtyard effect. In open sites the most formal hedging plants might be preferred: yew, beech and holly (either separate or mixed: a 4:1 ratio makes a good pattern). In mild areas hedges of sweet bay (*Laurus nobilis*) continues the herbal theme successfully.

Paths, raised beds and land sculpting with herbs

If scale is sufficient to permit main paths of 2 m (6 ft) in width grass could be used. But hard access is generally desirable as it permits entry in all weathers (and just after summer rain, is often the most pleasant). Grass edged with some 40 cm (16 in) width paving or bricks permits plants to spill forwards: this softens the basic formality of the beds and permits the plants their typical habit.

Hard materials must be chosen to blend with the 'cottage-garden miscellany' of plants. Natural stone is a natural choice, but many modern reconstructed stone or concrete flags are admirable alternatives. Choice should be restricted to one or at the most two colours and textures that relate to any associated building. Local gravel, hand rolled, is often cheap and a highly satisfactory alternative. Brick sets or cobble insets or borders may be considered, the aim being to provide safe, easy access and a frame which enhances the plant picture.

The use of raised beds as a part of the general design has much to commend it. An architectural effect is immediately produced, and plants are brought closer to eye and nose. On heavy and badly drained soil, raised beds specially prepared provide the conditions demanded by the grey-leaved Mediter-

With herbs, there are many planting possibilities. Hard surfaces are useful as they permit access for picking in all weathers; they are also an attractive foil for the plants. But as is shown by the angelica, sorrel, chives and mint (**below left**), a herb garden can be planned in a less formal style, making the most of their ornamental characteristics.

raneans and others impatient of winter wet. Retaining walls and coping must be in accord with the path material and may well repeat it.

A sloping site, with inevitable steps and retaining walls, offers splendid opportunities for the contrast of hard materials and billowing plant growth. Even a simple pair of borders following the contour conventionally cut and filled provides the desirable variation in aspect and position to suit a wide diversity of herbs.

Colour and form
In the arrangement of the planting, emphasis (if the visual effect is at all important) will be on those species which look well for much of the year. Hence the evergreen, ever-grey 'herb-shrubs' will provide the main focus. Internal hedges, compartment-forming edgings to the beds and solid blocks within them give the strength of form which so many herb gardens lack, especially in winter. One rather difficult decision has to be made. *Salvia officinalis* 'Purpurascens' and *Santolina pectinata*, for example, are splendid flowering shrubs. But if these are permitted it may be at the expense of form and foliage, so plan matching blocks in the parterre which could perhaps be clipped in alternate years.

There are not many tall plants suitable for shaping, though sweet bay is one obvious example. Ultimately a dense and robust evergreen shrub, it is nevertheless amenable to clipping, and any simple architectural form – dome, obelisk, cone or lollipop-standard – can be produced for use as a centre piece. But, though fine examples flourish outdoors as far north as Dundee, it is doubtfully frost-hardy. Alternatives are box or yew, both acceptable through their old-world associations. Form and height can also be provided by timber tripods for climbing plants such as honeysuckle, madder (*Rubia tinctoria*, producer of the famous rose-madder dye) or hops, both green and golden. The two latter are herbaceous but the tripods themselves remain.

Generally, aim to build up a balanced planting of mainly shrubby material in the dominant central beds, leaving the surrounding borders, themselves given form by their hedges, to contain most of the herbaceous plants. In this way, provided you have chosen an open site, the central area is fully exposed while every aspect, shaded and sunny is available in the borders.

Planting times
Many herbs are available from nurseries in containers and, in theory at least, they can be planted at any time of the year. The most satisfactory planting time, however, is in the autumn. The present climatic pattern in North West Europe seems to provide a long, open and relatively mild autumn and a spring (traditionally warm and moist) both cold and dry. Planting left till spring often results in heavy losses. It should also be remembered that many of the herb-garden annuals are of Mediterranean origin, adapted for autumn germination. Thus these can be sown 'in situ' at the same time. If you do, they are often in ripe fruit (desirable in coriander, caraway, anise etc.) by early summer. The chervil can squeeze three seed-to-seed generations into twelve months.

The really tender tropicals and sub-tropicals, basils, castor oil, rose-geraniums, agave, aloes and citruses cannot be planted or stood outside until late spring – and only then in sheltered herb gardens (the traditional enclosure helps here). Moreover, they will require frost-free housing in autumn in most temperate climates.

Care and maintenance
Subsequent maintenance is no different to the catering for other mixed plantings of shrubs and herbaceous subjects. Care is necessary to ensure that the naturally vigorous do not overpower the less rampant: mints, for example, especially in a moist soil, need to be separated by vertical sunken slates to restrict underground stolons. Where several mints are grown together, this is particularly important.

Few herbs are subject to killing pests or diseases, though both mints and mallows (and hence hollyhocks) have their own host specific rusts. The roses are susceptible to mildew but not much to black spot.

Thus care is remarkably simple, only re-propagation to keep stock young and healthy is necessary to maintain a feature of absorbing interest, pleasure and use for very many years.

239

The herb garden

Selected lists of plants suitable for herb garden cultivation

While the lists have been classified by use it is safe to assert that all culinary herbs also have folk or alternative medicinal uses claimed for them. The reverse is emphatically not so. Plants are listed alphabetically by the most common vernacular name. The final cultivation columns are only general guides: D and M indicate preferences; most of the plants do not like extremes of either. Where both D and M appear, there is no particular preference.

List A Culinary Herbs

Herb	Family & Botanical Name	Height & Spread in ft	Type & Brief Description	Flower Colour & Seasons	AS = Accept Shade AS	Soil Dry	Soil Moist
Alexander	Umbelliferae *Smyrnium olusatrum*	2½ x 2	Evergreen perennial. Good glossy leaves	Greenish white. Spring	AS		M
Angelica	Umbelliferae *Angelica archangelica*	5-6 x 3	Statuesque biennial. Seeds itself around	Spherical heads. Lime-green	AS		M
Aniseed, Anise	Umbelliferae *Pimpinella anisum*	2 x 1	Thin annual, cow parsley like	White. Early summer		D	
Alecost	Compositae *Chrysanthemum balsamita*	4 x 2	Glaucous perennial. Scented spearmint	White & yellow daisies. Summer		D	M
Basil / Bush Basil	Labiatae *Ocimum basilicum* / *O. minimum*	1 x 1	Tender annual. Pepper-scented purple-leaved forms available	Purple. Insignificant			M
Borage	Boraginceae *Borago officinalis*	2 x 1	Annual or biennial. Bristly leaves	Blue or white. Summer		D	
Balm	Labiatae *Melissa officinalis*	3 x 2	Robust perennial with lemon scented leaves. Golden variegated form useful and less vigorous	Insignificant	AS		M
Caraway	Umbelliferae *Carum carvi*	2 x ½	Conventional umbelliferous biennial. Feathery leaves in year 1.	White. Summer		D	M
Chervil	Umbelliferae *Anthriscus cerefolium*	2 x ½	Annual. Useful for autumn sowing to give winter greenness	White, Spring summer	AS	D	M
Chives	Liliaceae *Allium schoenoprasum*	½-¾ x ½	Perennial, tuft forming onion. Good for edging. Evergreen.	Purple. Late Spring	AS		M
Coriander	Umbelliferae *Coriandrum sativum*	1½ x ½	Another small annual umbellifer. Distinctive, orange-scented fruits.	Whitish pink. Summer		D	
Dill	Umbelliferae *Anethum graveolens*	2-3 x 1	Delicate annual. Like small fennel	Yellowish. Summer		D	M
Fennel	Umbelliferae *Foeniculum vulgare*	4-6 x 2	Perennial with clouds of delicate leaves. Green or bronze.	Yellowish Summer			
Fenugreek	Leguminosae *Trigonella foenum-graecum*	1½ x 1	Clover like annual plant with long seed pods.	Pale yellow. Summer		D	M
Garlic	Liliaceae *Allium sativum*	2 x ½	Perennial. Bulb offsets (cloves) planted in mid-winter			D	M
Horseradish*	See below						
Juniper	Cupressaceae *Juniperus communis*	5 x 5	Evergreen conifer: various forms available			D	
Lovage	Umbelliferae *Levisticum officinale*	5 x 3	Robust perennial	Greenish heads. Early summer	AS		M

240

Herb	Family & Botanical Name	Height & Spread in ft	Type & Brief Description	Flower Colour & Seasons	AS = Accept Shade AS	Soil Dry	Moist
Mints	Labiate *Mentha spp*	1½ x 1	All robust spreading perennials (separate with vertical slates)	Purple flowers in summer	AS		M
Peppermint	x *pipetita*	1½ x 1			AS		M
Eau de Cologne mint	*piperita* var *citrata*	1½ x 1			AS		M
Pennyroyal	*pulegium*	1 x ½	Low creeping habit		AS		M
Applemint	*rotundifolium*	2½ x 1	Soft round leaves. Variegated form exists.		AS		M
Spearmint	*spicata*	1½ x 1			AS		M
Gingermint	x *gentilis*	1½ x 1	Fine golden variegation		AS		M
Marjorams Pot marjoram	Labiatae *Origanum onites*	1½ x 1	Greyish perennial: doubtfully hardy in Britain.	White or pink		D	
Sweet marjoram	*O. marjorana*	1½ x 1	Perennial sub-shrub lacking hardiness. Hence often grown as annual.	White in small gobular heads		D	
Wild oregano	*O. vulgare*	1½-2 x 1	The hardiest marjoram. A fine golden leaved form exists which does not flower. This needs ½ shade.	Pink-purple heads		D	M
Nasturtium	Tropaeolaceae *Tropaeolum majus (climbing)*	1 x 1 6-8	Tender annuals. Leaves used in salads. Useful for quick height.	Orange, red, yellow. Summer	AS	D	M
Parsley	Umbelliferae *Petroselinum crispum*	1½ x 1	Bright green biennial. Smooth (French) and curled forms. Good as edgings.	Green-yellow. Summer	AS		M
Onions	Liliaccae *Allium cepa* cvs	1 x 1 2 x 1	Welsh onion makes usually non-flowering clumps of leafy growth. Egyptian or Tree onion produces bulblets at the top of flowering shoots.		AS AS	 D	M M
Rosemary	See below						
Salad burnet	Rosaceae *Poterium sanguis-orba*	1-2 x 1	Elegant divided foliage. Flowers insignificant & best removed to encourage leaf and longevity.			D	
Savory summer winter	Labiatae *Satureja hortensis* *Satureja Montana*	1 x ½ 1½ x 1-1½	Thin aromatic annual. Evergreen sub-shrub thus available for winter use.	Summer, purple Summer, pinkish		D D	
Sorrel Sorrel French	Polygonaccae *Rumex acetosa* *Rumex scutatus*	2 x 1-2	Profuse shining leaves beginning in very early spring. Perennials	Reddish spikes. Early summer	AS		M
Saffron	Iridaceae *Crocus sativus*	½ x ½	A true crocus, flowering in autumn. Leaves follow	Purple & bright orange stigmata		D	
Sweet Cecily	Umbelliferae *Myrrhis odorata*	2 x 2	Robust perennial. Distinctive long fruits.	White. Early summer	AS		M

241

The herb garden

Herb	Family & Botanical Name	Height & Spread in ft	Type & Brief Description	Flower Colour & Seasons	AS	Dry	Moist
Sage	Labiatae	2 x 2	Grey-leaved downy shrub	Purple spikes		D	
	Salvia officinalis		May be clipped into shape	Early summer		D	
	S. o. 'Purpurascens'		Fine purple leaved form	Early summer		D	
	S. o. 'Icterina'		Gold-variegated form	non-flowering		D	
	S. o. 'Tricolor'		Less robust: white, pink & green leaves (All like heavier soil than most Mediterranean shrubs)	non-flowering		D	
Rosemary	Labiatae *Rosmarinus officin-allis* *Various* cvs: 'Miss Jessop' (upright) 'Severn Sea' (clear blue)	3-5 x 4	Dark green shrub with narrow leaves. Prostrate forms less hardy.	Pale blue Early summer		D	
Tarragon	Compositae *Artemisia dracunculus*	2 x 1	Rather tender perennial Needs sheltered site and full sun.	Insignificant		D	
Thymes Garden thymes Lemon	Labiatae *Thymus vulgaris* x *citriodorus*	1 x 1 1 x 1	Small leaved sub shrub Good as clipped edging Golden and white varie-gated forms	Pink-purple Summer Summer		D D	
Wild	*serpyllum*	¼ x 1	One of many creeping thymes for ground cover	Summer		D	
Horseradish	Cruciferae *Armoracia rusticana*	3 x 3	Rampant coarse-leaved perennial. Only the white variegated form suitable for small gardens.	White. Summer	AS		M

List B Herbs from History
Herbs of historical interest still used in folk or alternative medicine. The number could easily be doubled; those chosen are the more visually distinctive.

Herb	Family & Botanical Name	Height & Spread in ft	Type & Brief Description	Flower Colour & Seasons	AS	Dry	Moist
Aconite (Monkshood)	Ranunculaceae *Aconitum spp*	4 x 1½	Strong perennial. Fine spikes. **Poisonous.**	Clear Blue. Late summer	AS		M
Asparagus	Liliaceae *Asparagus officinalis*	4 x 4	Clouds of feathery foliage. Long-lived perennial.	Flowers insig. Red berries		D	M
Artichoke	Compositae *Cynara scolymus*	5 x 4	Statuesque grey-leaved perennial.	Blue 'thistles'. Summer			
Asarabacca	Aristolochiaceae *Asarum europaeum* *Asarum canadensis* (wild ginger)	½ x 1	Heart-shaped leaves at ground level. Good ground cover for shade	Insignificant			
Asafoetida	Umbelliferae *Ferula asafoetida*	4 x 2	Robust fennel-like umbellifer. Perennial	Yellow heads. Summer		D	

AS ˢ: Accept Shade

Herb	Family & Botanical Name	Height & Spread in ft	Type & Brief Description	Flower Colour & Seasons	AS = Accepts shade AS	Soil Dry	Moist
Bearsbreech	Acanthaceae *Acanthus mollis*	4 x 3	Fine, broad leaves and tall spikes of flowers. Perennial.	White and purple. Summer	AS	D	
Burdock	Compositae *Arctium lappa*	5 x 3	Bristly rhubarb-like plant. Biennial or short-lived perennial	Purple. Summer	AS		M
Birthwort	Aristolochiaccae *Aristolochia clematitis*	3 x 2	Invasive perennial. Good heart-shaped leaves	Pale yellow. Summer		D	
Butchers broom	Liliaccae *Ruscus aculeatus*	2 x 2	Spiny evergreen sub shrub	Flowers insig. Fine red berries			
Bistort	Polygonaceae *Polygonum bistorta*	2 x 1	Sorrel-like leaves, white on reverse. Clump forming.	Pink spikes. Early summer			
Bugle	Labiatae *Ajuga reptans*	½ x 1	Creeping plant for ground cover. Several colour forms.	Purple. Spring	AS		M
Bergamot	Labiatae *Monarda didyma*	3 x 1	Aromatic perennial. Several cvs available	Pink, summer whorls of flowers	AS		M
Bogbean	Menyanthaceae *Menyanthes trifoliata*	1 x 3	Aquatic perennial	White flowers. Fringed petals. Summer			M
Cowslip	Primulaceae *Primula veris*	1 x ½	Rosette-forming perennial	Yellow. Spring		D	
Chamomile	Compositae *Chamaemelum nobile*	½ – 1	Creeping perennial, aromatic leaves. Treneague is a non-flowering form for lawns	White. Summer		D	M
Columbine	Ranunculaceae *Aquilegia vulgaris*	2 x ½	Elegant short-lived perennial	White/purple. Early summer	AS		M
Cornflower	Compositae *Centaurea cyanus*	2 x ½	Thin annual. Range cvs available.	Blue. Early summer		D	
Elecampane	Compositae *Inula elecampane*	4-6 x 4	Robust perennial. Good for late effect.	Yellow daisies. Early autumn	AS		M
Flax	Linaceae *Linum usitatissimum*	1½ x ½	Delicate annual	Blue. Early summer		D	
Feverfew	Compositae *Chrysanthemum parthenium*	1½ x 1	Feathery, short-lived perennials. Seeds itself around. A good golden form exists.	White and yellow. Spring – autumn	AS	D	M
Gentian	Gentianaceae *Gentiana lutea*	3 x 1	Tall perennial. Needs cool soil.	Yellow. Early summer	AS		M
Goats Rue	Leguminosae *Galega officinalis*	4 x 3	Branched perennial. Delicate pinnate leaves	Purple/white. Summer		D	M
Hyssop	Labiatae *Hyssopus officinalis*	1½ x 1	Lovaromatic sub-shrub	White/purple/ pink. Summer		D	
Hemlock	Umbelliferae *Conium maculatum*	5-7 x 2	Tall biennial like big cowparsley with purple spotted stems.	White. Early summer		D	

The herb garden

Herb	Family & Botanical Name	Height & Spread in ft	Type & Brief Description	Flower Colour & Seasons	AS	Soil Dry	Soil Moist
					AS = Accept Shade		
Lady's smock	Cruciferae *Cardamine pratensis*	1 x ½	Delicate perennial. A double-flowered form is less fleeting	Pale lavender. Spring	AS		M
Larkspur	Ranunculaceae *Delphinium consolida*	2-3 x 1	Branching annual	White/blue/ purple. Early summer		D	
Liquorice	Leguminosae *Glycyrrhiza glabra*	3-5 x 3	Strong perennial with elegant foliage	Pink insig. Summer			M
Lungwort	Boraginaceae *Pulmonaria saccharata* & other species	1 x 2	Valuable early flowering perennial. Good ground cover.	Blue/Pink. Early spring	AS		M
Male fern	Polypodiaceae *Dryopteris filix-mas*	2 x 2	Beautiful fern: typical dissected leaves		AS		M
Marsh mallow	*Malvaceae Althaea officinalis*	4 x 2	Elegant grey-leaved perennial	Pale lavender. summer.			M
Marigold	Compositae *Calendula officinalis*	1 x 1	Bright annual daises in a range of colours	Yellow/orange. Early summer onwards		D	
Meadowsweet	Rosaceae *Filipendula ulmaria*	2-3 x 2	Elegant perennial: also gold variegated form.	White fluffy heads. Early summer	AS		M
Mezereon	Thymeliaceae *Daphne mezereum*	3-4 x 3	Scented flowered shrub. white form more robust. This has **poisonous** fruit.	Purple. Early spring. Red berries.	AS		M
Lady's Mantle	Rosaceae *Alchemilla mollis*	1½ x 1½	Downy, grey-green leaves. Excellent for ground cover	Lime green. Summer	AS		M
Primrose	Primulaceae *Primula vulgaris*	½ x ½	Common primrose and colour forms. Polyanthus could be substituted for non-purist garden.	Pale yellow. Early spring	AS		M
Poppy	Papaveraceae *Papaver rhoeas*	1½ x 1	The derivative Shirley poppies could be used to obtain a range of colours. Annual.	Scarlet in typical form		D	
Peony	Ranunculaceae *Paeonia officinalis*	2 x 2	Long-lived perennial. Good foliage. Old double red form acceptable.	Red. Late spring			
Pokeweed	Phytolaccaceae *Phytolacca americana*	6 x 4	Enormous perennial. Seeds about	Pink spikes followed by purple berries	AS	D	M
Purple loose-strife	Lythraceae *Lythrum salicaria*	5 x 2	Spectacular perennial. Dead seed heads good	Magenta. Summer	AS		M
Pleurisy root	Asclepiadaceae *Asclepias tuberosa*	3 x 2	Distinctive greyish-leaved perennial	Pink. Summer		D	
Rose	Rosaceae *R. rubiginosa*	6-8 x 5	Sweet briar. Scented leaves	Small pink. Early summer			
	R. gallica officinalis	3-4 x 3	Apothecaries' Rose Shrubs	Fine, double, dark pink. Early summer			

Herb	Family & Botanical Name	Height & Spread in ft	Type & Brief Description	Flower Colour & Seasons	AS = Accept Shade AS	Soil Dry	Moist
Rhubarb	Polygonaceae *Rheum palmatum*	Lvs 3 x 4 Fls 7 x 1	The most ornamental rhubarb with divided leaves. Perennial	Pink in tall spikes. Summer			
Rue	Rutaceae *Ruta graveolens*	2-3 x 2	Fine glaucous foliage (esp. 'Jackman's Blue'). Sub-shrub	Horn-yellow. Summer		D	
Stinking Iris	Iridaceae *Iris foetidissima*	2 x 2	Evergreen perennial. A good variegated form exists but does not flower.	Dull purple but brilliant scarlet seeds in late autumn.	AS		M
Southernwood	Compositae *Artemisia abrotanum*	3 x 3	Grey-green sub-shrub. Highly aromatic	Insig.			M
Thrift	Plumbaginaceae *Armeria maritima*	½-3/4 x ½	Tussock forming perennial. Can be used as an edging.	Pink. Early summer		D	
White Water Lily	Nymphaceae *Nymphaea alba*		Aquatic perennial	White. Summer			
Wormwood	Compositae *Artemisia absinthium*	3-4 x 3	Elegant grey leaved (especially in 'Lambrook Silver') perennial.	Insig.		D	
Sweet Flay	Araceae *Acorus calamus*	2-3 x 1	Aquatic perennial, highly aromatic iris-like growth.	Insig.			M
Yarrow	Compositae *Achillea millefolia*	1½ x 1	Tight divided foliage. Pink forms available. Perennial.	Flat white plates of flowers. Summer			

List C Dyeplants

While many plants produce dyes, especially if accompanied by a suitable mordant (a chemical that fixes a dye on a substance), a few are particularly renowned for this attribute.

Herb	Family & Botanical Name	Height & Spread in ft	Type & Brief Description	Flower Colour & Seasons	AS	Dry	Moist
Dyers' alkanet	Boraginaceae *Alkanna tinctoria*	2-3 x 2	Bristly perennial	Attractive blue flowers. Summer		D	
Dyers' greenweed	Leguminosae *Genista tinctoria*	4-5 x 4	Elegant shrub	Yellow. Early summer.		D	
Lady's Bedstraw	Rubiaceae *Galium verum*	1 x 2	Tussocks of tiny leaves Perennial.	Yellow. Summer		D	
Madder	Rubiaceae *Rubia tinctoria*	6 x 3	Scrambling bristly perennial best grown on tripod.	Yellowish insig.		D	
Woad	Cruciferae *Isatis tinctoria*	3-4 x 2	Glaucous-leaved biennial Fls. followed by heads of black seed-capsules.	Yellow. Summer		D	

245

The herb garden

List D Aromatic Herbs
Plants particularly associated with perfumed preparations.

Herb	Family & Botanical Name	Height & Spread in ft	Type & Brief Description	Flower Colour & Seasons	AS	Soil Dry	Soil Moist
Clary	Labiatae *Salvia sclarea*	3 x 2	Fine hairy-leaved biennial	Blue flowers & pink bracts. Summer		D	
Gum tree	Myrtaceae *Eucalyptus globulus*		Blue-leaved gum, highly aromatic foliage. Not very frost hardy. Best stooled annually.			D	M
Lavender	Labiatae *Lavandula augustifolia cvs*	1½-3 x 2-3	Grey-leaved shrub. Range of cvs e.g. 'Munstead' (dwarf) 'Old English' (robust).	Purple/pink/ white. Summer		D	
Lemon verbena	Verbenaceae *Lippia citriodora*	4-8 x 5	Deciduous aromatic shrub. Rather tender and needs wall protection in most areas.	Insignificant		D	
Jasmine	Oleaceae *Jasminum officinale*	6-15	Vigorous twiner. Best on S or SW wall.	White, highly scented. Summer		D	
Rose	Rosaceae *Rosa damascena trigintipetala*	5-6 x 5	Shrub rose. Source of Attar of Roses. Needs warm position.	Flat pale pink double flowers. Summer		D	
Rose Geranium	Geraniaceae *Pelargonium toment-osum. quercifolium etc.*	2 x 2	Range of aromatic sub-shrubs. None reliably frost hardy in Britain. Best as pot plants.	Pink. Summer		D	
Orris root	Iridaceae *Iris florentina*	2 x 1	Rhizomatous perennial flag iris	White. Early summer		D	
Sweet woodruff	Rubiaceae *Asperula odorata*	1 x 2	Elegant ground cover	White. Summer	AS		M

List E Herb Garden Associates
Some of these have herbal uses but are best considered as ornamentals.

Herb	Family & Botanical Name	Height & Spread in ft	Type & Brief Description	Flower Colour & Seasons	AS	Soil Dry	Soil Moist
Curry plant	Compositae *Helichrysum italicum*	2 x 3	Vivid white aromatic shrub	Hardy yellow, best clipped to prevent flowering		D	
Hollyhock	Malvaceae *Althaea rosea*	6-8 x 2	Spine like biennial or short-lived perennial	Pinks/purples. Summer		D	
Myrtle	Myrtaccae *Myrtus communis*	6-10 x 5	Aromatic evergreen shrub. Needs south wall protection in most areas	White. Autumn		D	

Herb	Family & Botanical Name	Height & Spread in ft	Type & Brief Description	Flower Colour & Seasons	AS = Accepts shade AS	Soil Dry	Moist
Lavender cotton	Compositae *Santolina chamaecyparissus*	2 x 3	Grey-white aromatic shrub	Hardy yellow flowers. Midsummer		D	
	Santolina pectinata	2 x 3	Grey-green aromatic shrub	Cream flowers the best flowering form		D	
Soapwort	*Caryophyllaceae Saponaria officinalis*	2 x 2	Invasive perennial: double flowered form available	Pink. Summer		D	M

List F Tender Herbs
Tender herbs or associates as tub or pot plants which, in mild climates, can be brought out in summer.

Herb	Family & Botanical Name	Height & Spread in ft	Type & Brief Description	Flower Colour & Seasons	AS	Dry	Moist
Aloe	Liliaceae *Aloe vera*	2 x 2	S. African succulent	Scarlet spikes		D	
Agave	Agavaceae *Agave spp.*	5 x 5	Robust monocarpic succulent: good variegated form available	Huge (15 ft) flower spike only after many years.		D	
Citrus	Rutaceae *Citrus spp.*	5-16 x 5	Orange/lemon trees. Size determined only by size of winter space.	White. Spring			M

List G Poisonous Herbs
Plants, extracts of which are used in orthodox medicine. **All are poisonous.** No precautions can be fool-proof. For precautions, see pages 236 and 237.

Herb	Family & Botanical Name	Height & Spread in ft	Type & Brief Description	Flower Colour & Seasons	AS	Dry	Moist
Autumn crocus	Liliaceae *Colchicum autumnale*	1 x 1½	Bulbous perennial. Fine spring foliage	Purple. Autumn	AS	D	M
American mandrake	Berberidaccae *Podophyllum peltatum*	1½ x 1½	Perennial with elegant foliage	Pink. Fleeting. Summer	AS		M
Castor oil	Euphorbiaceae *Ricinus communis*	4-5 x 3	Tender sub-shrub. Distinctive foliage. Red leaved forms exist.	Pink/white spikes. Summer.		D	
Deadly night-shade	Solanaceae *Atropa belladonna*	4-5 x 3	Robust perennial: shining black berries follow flowers.	Purple, bell-shaped. Summer	AS		M
Foxglove	Scrophulariaceae *Digitalis purpurea*	4-6 x 2	Ornamental biennial	Pink etc. Summer	AS	D	M
Henbane	Solanaceae *Hyoscyamus niger*	2 x 1	Annual. Striking seed capsules	Pale yellow			
Lily of the valley	Liliaceae *Convallaria majalis*	½ x	Rhizamatous perennial	White. Late spring.	AS		M
Madagascar Periwinkle	Apocynaceae *Catharanthus roseus*	1½ x 1½	Tender sub-shrub	Pink/white. All year.	AS		M
Opium poppy	Papaveraceae *Papaver somniferum*	3 x 1	Glaucous foliage. Range of colours. Simple and double fowers annual	White/Purple/ Red		D	
Thorn-apple	Solanaceae *Datura strumonium*	2½ x 2	Annual. Prickly seed capsules follow flower	White. Summer	AS		

Index of decorative plants

For vegetables, see pages 171, 225, 203 to 213.
For fruit, see pages 171, 225, 214 to 221.

Index of decorative plants

Index of decorative plants

General index

General index

Picture credits

Michael Warren
Harry Smith Horticultural Photographic Collection
Anthony Huxley
Roy Lancaster
Takashi Sawano
Leslie Godfrey
Alf Shead
Paul Miles
Neville Chesshyre
Rod Shone/Ashley Cartwright
Neil Holmes/Macdonald Educational Ltd
Ministry of Agriculture of the State of Israel
Hozelock Ltd
Rod Shone/ONLP
Susan Griggs Agency
The Mansell Collection
Marshall Cavendish
Alton Greenhouses Ltd
Florada Garden Products Ltd
C. H. Whitehouse Ltd
Simplex of Cambridge Ltd
Florapic Photographic Library
Camera Press

Photographs taken especially for *The Garden Planner* are by Neil Holmes

Picture research by Janice Croot and Anne Usborne

The vegetable and fruit master plans in Section V and the designs of the compost bin on page 31 are the copyright of Leslie Godfrey.

The dry and damp profiles and plans of pages 22–27 were based on original material supplied by Beth Chatto.

The photographs of flower arrangements on pages 232–235 came from *Flower Arranging From Your Garden* and *Complete Flower Arranging* by Sheila Macqueen and published by Ward Lock Limited